A Treasure
of
Promises Kept

A CENTENARY HISTORY

OF

QUEEN OF THE MOST HOLY ROSARY

PRIORY AND PARISH

PORTLAND, OREGON

1894-1994

JOSEPH FRANCIS FOYE

Joseph F. Foye

11-28-99

To Honora and Curt
with love and prayers.

TURNER PUBLISHING COMPANY
Publishers of America's History
412 Broadway•P.O. Box 3101
Paducah, Kentucky 42002-3101
(502) 443-0121

By: Joseph Francis Foye

Publisher's Editor: Randy Baumgardner

This publication was produced using available and submitted materials. The author and publisher regret they cannot assume liability for errors or omissions.

Library of Congress Catalog No. 97-072356
ISBN: 1-56311-505-0
LIMITED EDITION
Printed in the U.S.A.

TABLE OF CONTENTS

DEDICATION

This book is dedicated to the Blessed Virgin Mary,
the Queen of the Most Holy Rosary,
the Mother of God and Our Mother in Heaven.

Father Anthony M. Patalano, O.P.

HOLY ROSARY PRIORY & CHURCH

375 Northeast Clackamas Street
Portland, Oregon 97232
(503) 235-3163

June 1997

Dear Brothers and Parishoners,

When I arrived in 1991 to assume the duties of prior and pastor of Holy Rosary Church, I was not aware that this venerable parish would mark her centenary on 28 January 1994. Once I realized the importance of this event, I sought and received advice from my fellow friars, the parish staff and, significantly, dozens if not hundreds of the faithful families who worship here and consider Holy Rosary their home away from home. At the time, approximately 300 families were registered in the parish versus the 1200 now registered as I take my leave.

The consuming question remained: "How should we celebrate the centenary?" I ultimately decided on a three-phase approach, approved by all: First, we would restore and renovate the church. Second, we would consecrate the church (it had not previously been consecrated because it was considered a temporary structure when built – but it was blessed by then-Archbishop William H. Gross, C.SS.R., D.D.). Third, we would record the 100-year history of this beloved church in a bound book and publish it for the edification of present and future generations. Significant interruptions occurred along the way, including a major church fire, but this present publication represents the completion of this last goal.

I am grateful, as I'm sure you will be, for the hundreds of hours Mr. Foye spent researching and writing this book – all of it without any recompense of any kind. It is well done, and I could not have chosen a better person for the task. My gratitude also extends especially to Fathers Charles Hess, O.P., Provincial Archivist, Fabian Parmisano, O.P., Provincial Historian, Fathers Albert Buckley, O.P., and current pastor Anthony Cordeiro, O.P., our parish's resident artist, Roger Smith (who did the cover), and countless others who gladly contributed their time and effort. I know everyone will enjoy this work and I ask that you keep me and those who produced it in your prayers.

As I depart for my new assignment in Los Angeles, I wish to express my thanks to all who generously supported me in my pastoral duties with their prayers, time and treasure during my six-year tenure. We can be proud of all we accomplished together.

Gratefully yours in Christ Our Lord,

Father Anthony M. Patalano, O.P.
Prior and Pastor

HOLY ROSARY PRIORY & CHURCH

375 Northeast Clackamas Street
Portland, Oregon 97232
(503) 235-3163

FOREWORD

Time is a necessary ingredient in all growth, and maturity is always an ongoing process. These hundred years of Holy Rosary history could never have yielded the great storehouse of faith we have today had that faith not been previously refined in the fire of Scripture and Tradition (that is, reason and revelation) for nearly 2,000 years. Its flame was brought to Oregon and handed over to our forefathers in the 1700's. So, in contemplating our history, we reflect upon this inheritance and the lives of some of the great workers, religious and lay, who were involved in the enormous and complex task of creating on this remote Western Frontier an integrated community and culture composed of people from diverse countries, cultures, and continents. These people would encounter crises and conflicts which would occasionally stall, dehumanize, and nearly destroy their efforts, but nothing would cause their resolve to flag. Their good example is their legacy, which deserves recognition and emulation.

Christ's prescription to us for attaining heaven is: "Deny yourself, pick up your cross daily, and follow me." These 100 years of prayer, self-denial, and daily cross-bearing along Christ's narrow course have already brought a little bit of heaven to us still here on earth, here at Holy Rosary. Many parishioners refer to our parish as an oasis in a secular desert that surrounds us. That is a true summation of our situation in 1994, as it was 100 years ago, or nearly 2,000 years ago simply because we are in this world, but not of this world, as befits Roman Catholics at all times and at every place on this planet.

We love this church, our Dominican Friars, and this community of faithful Catholics as deeply as humans are able to love the things given to us by our Creator. We thank God and our forebears for our inheritance. They kept the faith and we resolve to do the same. We pray that the Wisdom of Heaven may guide and direct our future labors as long as we draw breath, for the love of God, for our descendants and for all those pilgrim souls destined to worship God at Holy Rosary in the years to come.

Mike Palmer

Michael Palmer
President – 1993
Holy Name Society

Michael Palmer

ACKNOWLEDGEMENTS

First, I wish to thank God for giving me the mental, physical and spiritual gifts needed to write this book. Oh God, how good you are to me – you have truly given me more in this life than I have ever deserved and I am grateful beyond measure.

There are so many people to thank for the precious help they gave me in writing this history. I shall begin with Father Anthony Patalano, O.P., who gave me the enviable and privileged assignment. I love Holy Rosary Church, so the task was for me, truly, a labor of love. As St. Bonaventure observed: "All things are sweet to holy love." To be completely honest, I would have been very unhappy had the writing chore been given to someone not completely in love with our beautiful church. As G.K. Chesterton once observed: *"You cannot love a thing without wanting to fight for it."*

Father Patalano also gave ample proof of his love for this church. His legacy speaks for itself as we daily gaze with awe at the beauty this good and holy man left behind. Father would be joyously received should God deign to return him to us as pastor.

I considered the moving of the church from NE 11th and Multnomah Streets to its present location a key and interesting event but could find no photographs depicting the move. I first asked an artist friend to make a drawing I could use in the book, but he said he was incapable of such fine art. Father Patalano found a capable man right in the parish – Roger Smith. Roger did such a fine job that I put his drawing on the cover of the book. I will always be grateful to Roger for his dedication to that task.

I read many books in my research and I am grateful to the authors of those books bearing on the history of the parish. The books and their authors are listed in the footnotes. Of great significance were the books written by Father Stan Parmisano, O.P., Provincial Historian of the Western Dominican Province, who wrote the fascinating *"Mission West: The Western Dominican Province 1850-1966,"* Father Charles Hess, O.P., Archivist, Western Dominican Province, who spent hours going through documents on file at the Province with me and provided interesting anecdotes. Father Wilfred P. Schoenberg, S.J., the dean of Catholic historians in the West, also provided sound advice and great encouragement. His many works were invaluable, among them *"A History of the Catholic Church in the Pacific Northwest"* and *"Those Valiant Women."* Ellis Lucia and Arthur H. Clark, both wrote books on Ben Holladay. They provided the interesting background of our first lay benefactor.

The editor of the *Catholic Sentinel*, Robert Pfohman, several years ago, opined that he thought I was a capable writer. I think this compliment, unsolicited, gave me the confidence I required to proceed with the writing of this book. The hundreds of *Catholic Sentinel* articles were of inestimable value.

Dozens of priests, nuns and parishioners – too numerous to mention – were kind enough to review the original manuscript and correct my many errors. To all of them I remain humbly grateful.

My thanks also to Chris Michel and Linda Kaiser who did beautiful work in designing the pages and cover of the book, and to my publisher, Turner Publishing, especially Randy Baumgardner, for their fine work.

Lastly, my undying gratitude to my lover, my pal, my adorable and lovely wife of 18 years, Sharon, who taught me how to operate a computer. She also put up with my messy office (and scattered papers on the dining room table), and provided patience, love and support in full measure whenever I needed it. And my wonderful son, Mark, who reviewed the book and provided dozens of excellent suggestions. Please, God bless everyone who helped me.

Joseph F. Foye
Joseph F. Foye
Holy Rosary Parish

Most Rev. Francis Norbert Blanchet, D.D.
1795-1883

Archbishop of Oregon City
1846-1880

Most Rev. Charles John Seghers
1839-1866

Archbishop of Oregon City
1880-1884

Most Rev. William Hickley Gross, C.SS.R., D.D.
1837-1898

Archbishop of Oregon City
1885-1898

Coat of Arms
Archdiocese of Portland

CHAPTER

1

1873-1893

BEGINNINGS SHROUDED IN MYSTERIES

To Catholics, the creation of any new church and parish is no small gift from the Almighty Who, in His infinite wisdom, fashions events refreshingly designed to prove, beyond any reasonable doubt, that truth is stranger than fiction. This real-life drama about the first centenary life of our beloved Queen of the Most Holy Rosary Church provides sufficient evidence for that assertion.

BIG BEN HOLLADAY AND GOD'S LITTLE ACRE

This astonishing story actually begins on March 3, 1873, when "renowned frontiersman" Ben Holladay gave Block Number 119[1] in Portland to The Most Reverend Francis Norbert Blanchet, the first Archbishop of the Oregon Province. Block Number 119 was situated between N.E. 10th and 11th Avenues, and between N.E. Multnomah and Wasco Streets.[2] The deed stipulated that the "property was never to be used for anything but for church, charity, or school, etc., purposes under pain of reversion to the grantor."[3]

BISHOP SEGHERS IS MURDERED

Seven years after Ben Holladay gave Block 119 to the Church, Archbishop Blanchet resigned[4] and his Coadjutor Archbishop, Charles John Seghers, replaced him. Seghers, who had previously been bishop of Vancouver Island, Canada, possessed an enduring love for Alaska and its unchurched natives. Alaska came under the jurisdiction of the Vancouver see. He yearned to return to Alaska and establish missions there, so he applied for transfer back to the See of Vancouver in order to renew his work in Alaska. When Pope Leo XIII approved the move, Seghers resigned as Archbishop of Oregon City in 1884 and headed for Canada, en route to Alaska.

In the summer and fall of 1886, Archbishop Seghers was on an expedition in Alaska, accompanied by two Jesuit priests, a guide, and an assistant, Frank Fuller, who was suspected of being mentally unbalanced. The Jesuits had previously rejected Fuller's application for the priesthood. On Sunday morning, November 28, Fuller, in a fit of insanity, shot and killed the archbishop with the archbishop's own 44-caliber Winchester rifle. The two Jesuit companions of Seghers also suspected that Fuller had earlier killed their guide, who had disappeared. Fuller was subsequently convicted of manslaughter. Meanwhile, the Archdiocese of Oregon City was still in possession of Block 119.

BISHOP GROSS AND BLOCK 119

Most Reverend William H. Gross, C.Ss.R., Bishop of Savannah, Georgia, was promoted to the Oregon see February 1, 1885, replacing Archbishop Seghers. In November of that year, Archbishop Gross sent a letter to the Dominican Province in California asking that Province to provide a German-speaking Dominican priest to serve the needs of the burgeoning German population in Portland. Block Number 119 figured greatly in his plans. He would offer that property to the Dominicans as an inducement for them to come to Portland for the purpose of "erecting a modest church" thereon.[5]

TWO DOMINICAN PROVINCIALS PASS AWAY OVER BRIEF PERIOD

Archbishop Gross possessed patience, piety and fortitude in full measure. He would need these virtues aplenty as he proceeded with his plans. Communications were anything but rapid on the Western Frontier in the 1880s. A letter might take six months to reach its destination (if it reached it at all), depending upon the weather, Indian raiding parties, train and stage holdups, internal theft, incompetence, illiteracy and a host of other calamities which frequently conspired to impede the postman "from the swift completion of his appointed rounds." To make matters worse in this case, two Dominican Provincials, who could have expedited the response to Archbishop Gross's request, died within a brief period of time. The first Dominican's Superior to whom Archbishop Gross had written in 1885, The Very Reverend Sadoc Francis Vilarrasa, O.P. died in 1888, and his successor, Father Vincent Francis Vinyes, was "immediately felled by a stroke" and incapacitated for a long period of time before he died in 1892.[6]

Meantime, Archbishop Gross, undeterred, continued his written dialog with the Dominicans, seeking to stimulate concrete initiatives aimed at fulfilling his earnest desire of having the Dominicans "labor to build up and increase love for the Blessed Mother of Our Lord Jesus. [For] no greater good can be done a people than to introduce this Blessed – this channel of all grace – into their hearts and homes. Moreover, I am persuaded that wherever Mary comes – She brings Jesus with her."

THE DOMINICANS ARE COMING!

Dominican Father John Pius Murphy, O.P., who would become the provincial for the Western Dominicans after the death of Father Vinyes, began responding to the overtures of Archbishop Gross. However, across the Atlantic, "the changing of the guard was also taking place at the same time in Rome" A new Master General was being elected to lead the Dominican Order. Father Murphy would consult with the new Master General prior to firmly committing the resources of the Dominicans to the service of those souls in Portland.

By November 1891, fully six years after Archbishop Gross penned his first letter to the Dominicans, Father Murphy, as the Vicar General of the Western Province, would be en route to Portland to consult with His Grace. Prior to his departure from California, Father Murphy received from Archbishop Gross another hand-written letter; which read in part:"…please…keep the object of your visit a secret – I have many reasons for this request…"[7]

SOME INTRIGUING QUESTIONS

"The answer is the question," a philosophical imperative, declares that every answer provokes another question in our endless quest for truth. It applies at this point in this engrossing story, as several questions queue for answers, answers designed to draw us out of the shadowy perimeters of this story and into the center of a real-life drama.

For example, who was Ben Holladay and why did he deed his property to the Catholic Church? Was Ben's wife murdered? What was Archbishop Gross's background? Why did this third Archbishop of Oregon, a Redemptorist, favor the Dominicans over his own Redemptorists in granting land to build a church in Portland? Why, in his very first letter to the Dominicans, did Archbishop Gross write: "… were I to introduce the Redemptorists here, it might cause unpleasant consequences. I will probably at some other time offer my confreres a foundation in some part of my diocese distant from Portland."?[8] And, when informed that the Dominican Vicar-General would be arriving soon, why did Archbishop Gross, in a letter dated November 4, 1891 write: "Please… keep the object of your visit a secret – I have many reasons for this request."?

We shall address these questions and offer some plausible answers in Chapters 2, 3, and 4 which report on the lives and activities of Ben Holladay, Archbishop Gross, and Father Murphy respectively.

NOTES TO THE TEXT

1 Other accounts mistakenly refer to this as Lot Number 191; however, plat maps at the Oregon Historical Society, 1230 SW Park Avenue, Portland, Oregon 97205 confirm 119 to be the correct block number.

2 A multi-storied parking garage for the Lloyd Center shopping mall now occupies that block (in 1994).

3 See March 6, 1898 letter w/attachments from Portland Attorney M.G. Munly to Father Pius Murphy in the Archives, Western Dominican Province, San Francisco, California.

4 Archbishop Blanchet was very ill; he died June 18, 1883.

5 See Appendix 1 for the full contents of the letter.

6 Letter dated August 3, 1972, from Sister Veronica Lonergan, O.P., to Father Kieran Healy, O.P., file in the Archives, Western Dominican Province, Oakland, California.

7 Appendix 1 contains the full contents of the letter.

8 See Appendix 1.

14

Benjamin 'Big Ben' Holladay,
benefactor (c.1885)

BENJAMIN 'BIG BEN' HOLLADAY
BORN 1819 – DIED 1887

ONE LAYMAN CONVERT'S CONTRIBUTION TO HOLY ROSARY'S AND THE PACIFIC NORTHWEST'S HISTORY

No rendering of Holy Rosary Church's history would be complete without recognizing the name of Benjamin "Big Ben" Holladay, our first benefactor, who contributed to the archdiocese the plot of land on which our church was first erected in 1893. These few pages are not meant to build up or tear down his character, but to introduce him and express our gratitude for his generosity. Not to do so would be a callous act of disloyalty. He experienced a great deal of disloyalty during his lifetime, as well as immediately thereafter, and needs no more from those to whom he gave a portion of his possessions.

Moreover, Holladay's life is truly a compelling story, as well as an appropriate introduction to the Portland of the last half of the 19th century, which gave birth to Holy Rosary Parish. Catholics of mature perception might learn some important lessons from the life of Holladay who, with a name like Benjamin and standing 74 inches in height, was a natural to be tagged "Big Ben" after the bell in Parliament Tower, Westminster Palace, in London. He was the embodiment of an entrepreneur few, if any entrepreneurs, before or since, matched in heroic, hands-on accomplishments. Ben, a strapping, sandy-haired Kentuckian with little education, was born and reared in a log cabin by sober, hard-working farm people. He was at home whether by a prairie fire playing poker with Indians and stagecoach drivers or dining next to the President in Washington.

Holladay was born near Blue Lick Springs, Nicholas County, Kentucky on October 14, 1819.[9] He had five brothers and four sisters and, at an early age moved to Weston, Missouri, near Fort Leavenworth. Though of humble origins, he possessed great confidence, uncommon conviction and immense vitality. While still a teenager, he had already acquired and ran a store, hotel, saloon, and post office. He also got to know the soldiers returning from the frontier to Fort Leavenworth, across the river from Weston, and listened attentively to their tall tales of travels in the West. Their exploits intrigued him and the promise of great adventure and generous rewards on the frontier attracted him like a moth drawn to flame.

HOLLADAY BUILT THE OVERLAND STAGE

Holladay built the Overland Stage from small beginnings, ultimately sold it to Wells Fargo for over $2,500,000, and came to Oregon a rich man in the 1860s. Here in Portland he imported 400 Chinese "coolies" from California and built a railroad from Portland to Roseburg, gaining thousands of acres of free land from the government in the process. He owned the greater part of East Portland and his properties became known as Holladay's Addition. He built a fleet of 51 sternwheelers and steamboats which plied the Willamette River, erected a distillery, founded a newspaper, and built a trolley line in downtown Portland.

A TRAGIC FAMILY LIFE

Though Holladay's professional life was singularly successful, his family life became entrapped in tragedies. His first marriage was to Notley Ann Calvert, in Weston, Missouri. Her father was a judge, and direct descendant of George Calvert, the first Lord Baltimore and founder of the Maryland colony. In the eyes of Ann's parents, Big Ben Holladay was "rough-hewn, unshaven, illiterate; vulgar trail trash. He had no knowledge of drawing-room manners and graces."[10] Ben and Ann eloped when she was 15 and he was 20 years old. Their marriage produced seven children.

It was a family history too incredibly sad for words. Ben Holladay would outlive Ann and all of those children by fourteen years. Two died in infancy, another was killed in a gun accident in San Francisco at age 8, a fourth died from illness in New York City in 1860 at the age of three; a pregnant daughter expired on a train near Chicago at age 22, allegedly due to a miscarriage; a son who drank too much died in Hong Kong at the age of 23; and another alcoholic son died in Washington. D.C. at age 30.

Ben spent most of his time pursuing projects in the West. Ann preferred the East. Apparently a high-roller and party-giver who could spend money as fast as Ben Holladay could make it, she died at the Ophir Palace in White Plains, in 1873, at age 49. Ben and his wife had not seen each other for some time. Their marriage had died a spiritual death. In an ironic twist of fate, on the same day of her death, September 18, 1873, as if by omen that all was coming to a close, Wall Street's Black Friday and the resultant "Panic of '73" paralyzed the country, signaling the end of Ben's remarkable financial empire.

BEN MARRIED AT IMMACULATE CONCEPTION CHURCH

A little over a year after his first wife's death, Ben Holladay, now age 55, exchanged the vows of matrimony with Esther Campbell, age 25, daughter of a pioneer mission worker. Esther met Ben through her sister's husband, Sam Smith, an employee of Ben. It was an idyllic May-September romance, he being thirty years her senior.

Page 320 of the marriage registry at the Cathedral of the Immaculate Conception (St. Mary's),[11] NW 18th & Couch Streets in Portland, reads:

On the nineteenth of October 1800 and seventy four, a dispensation of Disparitatis Cultur having been granted by his Grace the Archbishop Fr. N. Blanchet, we the undersigned Pastor of Portland, Oregon, have received the mutual consent of marriage between Ben Holladay of this city, widower of [blank space] on the one part; and Esther Hedwige Campbell of this parish, daughter of age of Hamilton Campbell and Harriette Biddell on the other part, in the presence of Sam Smith and Mrs. Maria Smith.

    [Signed]
    G. F. Fierens, Pastor.

Since the record stated that a dispensation had been granted (for one party being non-Catholic) and Esther was listed "of this parish" it is assumed that Esther was Catholic and Ben non-Catholic in October 1874 when this marriage took place. The marriage produced two children, Ben Campbell Holladay, and Linda Holladay.

BEN A "CATHOLIC CONVERT"

A small notation on a genealogical chart on file with the Oregon Historical Society in Portland, identifies Ben as a "Catholic convert."[12] When and where he converted was not shown.

BEN'S DEATH RECORDED

In the "Saga of Ben Holladay," (page 348) the author wrote: *"Ben Holladay died on Friday evening, July 8, 1887, at 7:50 p.m. Next day De Lind's Undertaking Parlors provided him with the finest casket in stock. On Sunday evening he was taken for the night to the Stark Street home. Next morning High Pontifical Mass was sung at St. Mary's Cathedral in the same block, with its twenty thousand-dollar stained glass windows given by Ben Holladay…"* Page 7 of the Record of Interments at St. Mary's lists Ben's age as "59 years" at the time of his death.[13]

HOLLADAY A MORAL MAN

J. V. Frederick, Ph.D., Northwestern State College, Alva, Oklahoma, wrote the book "Ben Holladay – The Stagecoach King,"[14] in which he commented:

"With all his 'manly vices' Holladay never made the mistake of including immorality among them. He was loyal to his family at all times, and was never associated with vice. When Holladay Street in Denver became known for its vice and could no longer be looked upon as an honor to the man for whom it was named the city changed its name to Market Street.

"Up to the time of his retirement from the stagecoach business Holladay was not a faithful church member or attendant, though

his first wife had been a devout Catholic. He was generous to all churches, believed in them, and practiced many of their precepts. He was especially generous and loyal to his friends. General Doniphan, who had known him from boyhood, wrote of him, that he may have had some faults, but 'desertion of his friends was not one of them.' He was often pleased to turn business deals to their profit."

Ben Holladay's death truly marked the end of an era in Portland, and what historical essays say about Ben Holladay is an important aspect of the past. But what really counts in living is what God knows about us and what we know about ourselves – the ultimate truths. These truths are points to ponder in conducting our lives, for their content either stamps or cancels our passports to heaven.

SUSPICIOUS DEATH OF BEN'S SECOND WIFE

Ben's second wife, Esther, died on April 5, 1889, at age 40, within two years after she had buried her beloved plainsman.

She was buried beside him.[15] Their son, Ben Campbell Holladay, claimed to his dying day, that Esther had been poisoned by schemers intent on taking over Ben's estate. Recorded events back up the son's claim. Maybe she was and maybe she wasn't, and perhaps such questions are best left to the Almighty, but forensic medicine being what it is today, perhaps an exhumation may one day take place to settle the matter. Eventually, the truth will win out – and that is an absolute!

We conclude this chapter on Ben Holladay with reference to the words of Shakespeare: "The evil that men do lives after them. The good is oft interred with their bones." Ben was our brother as well as our benefactor and our spiritual lives have been enriched and nourished through the church built on the property he gave to us. We are grateful and express our gratitude for this gift of land out of the goodness of his heart. "May his soul and the souls of all the faithful departed, through the mercy of God, rest in peace. Amen."

NOTES TO THE TEXT

9   According to Ellis Lucia on page 10 in his book *The Saga of Ben Holladay*, Hastings House Publishers, 1959.

10 Page 37, *The Saga of Ben Holladay*, by Ellis Lucia, Hastings House, Publishers, N.Y. 1959.

11 Researched by volunteer Charles Donahe, October 31, 1994.

12 Researcher Charles Donahe searched the files of St. Mary's but found no record of Ben having been baptized in that parish from the time of his marriage up to the time of his death, July 8, 1887.

13 If, in fact Ben was born on October 14,1819, as recorded by biographer Ellis Lucia, he would have been 67 and not 59 years old at the time of his death.

14 Sub-titled *A Chapter in the development of Transcontinental Transportation*, The Arthur H. Clark Company, Glendale, California, 1940 (page 274).

15 They were first buried in the old St. Mary's Cemetery on SE Stark St., which became the site for the new Central Catholic High School so, in 1937, their caskets were disinterred and transferred to Mount Calvary Cemetery, where they repose today, beneath a ten-foot-high granite tombstone bearing both their names.

William Hickley Gross, C.SS.R.,
Third Archbishop of Oregon City.

CHAPTER
3
1885-1898

ARCHBISHOP WILLIAM HICKLEY GROSS, C.SS.R.
THIRD ARCHBISHOP OF OREGON CITY

More proof positive that God raises up great men in times when the Church needs them most is found in the life of this "grandson of an Irish patriot who had been exiled in 1798."[16] Archbishop Gross was born June 16, 1837 in Baltimore. Like his saintly predecessor, Archbishop Seghers, Archbishop Gross was "first of all, a man of God, not an ambitious or career man...he was a bookish man and loved to discourse on the theology of St. Thomas Aquinas."[17] This love of St. Thomas and his teachings, coupled with his love for Our Blessed Mother, made this Redemptorist a defacto Dominican, and he would turn to the Dominicans, "the Hounds of Heaven," for assistance in feeding the "sheep of his flock." His was a decision that would introduce great religious men and women, lovers of Christ, into the city of Portland, where these servants of the Son of God would build and sustain a devout religious community that would last at least one hundred years, and give promise of enduring until the end of time.

GROSS THE "LIFE OF THE PARTY"
A short biography of Archbishop Gross, written in September 1986 by the Very Reverend Gregory Moys, Chancellor, Archdiocese of Portland,[18] mentions the fact that William Gross "was considered by his seminary classmates as 'the life of the party' during recreation periods and was a spiritual man devoted to both prayer and studies."

WILLIAM THE FIRST
William Gross was installed as Archbishop of Oregon City[19] at the Cathedral of the Immaculate Conception in Oregon City on May 23, 1885, preceding by one hundred years another William, William J. Levada, who carried the crozier from 1986 to 1995. Gross was the quintessential bishop, possessed of far more learning and experience as a bishop than either of his two predecessors when they had assumed the bishopric in Oregon. For one thing, Archbishop Gross had been installed as Bishop of Savannah in 1873, (the youngest bishop in the United States at that time) so he already had 12 years' experience as a bishop before the beginning of his tenure in Oregon in 1885, at the age of 47.

FATHER GROSS AS CHAPLAIN DURING CIVIL WAR

Nor was Gross a stranger to "man's inhumanity to man," as recounted in Archdiocesan Father John R. Laidlaw's book "The Catholic Church in Oregon and the Work of Its Archbishops":[20]

On March 23, 1863, during the Civil War, Father Gross was ordained a priest. He was first stationed in the Redemptorist House in Annapolis, Maryland, where he offered himself as a chaplain in the Union Army in that area. His truly Catholic spirit as a priest of God is made strikingly clear in this story. In the vicinity of Annapolis, a savage battle was fought between the Union and the Confederate armies. During a pause for care of the wounded on both sides, the young Father Gross offered his spiritual aid to the wounded and dying soldiers. Given a Union pass for that purpose joined with a warning from the commander of the dangers involved, he set forth on his mission of mercy and religion.

While caring for the Union wounded in a secluded wooded area, he met some Confederate soldiers who asked his business. At the point of their rifles, he showed them his Union Army pass and offered to help any soldiers. Quite promptly he found himself escorted with great respect to the Confederate hospital, where he cared for the wounded and dying to the best of his ability. Conducted back to the Union lines, he reported to the Union commanding officer, who praised him greatly for his courage and devotion. From that time on until the end of the war, he engaged in conducting missions in the North and South alike.

ARCHBISHOP GROSS – MAN WITH A MISSIONARY SPIRIT

His native intelligence, formal education, and twelve-year tenure as Bishop of Savannah notwithstanding, Archbishop Gross experienced some misgivings about taking over the see of Oregon, as expressed in this letter to another Redemptorist:[21]

Now when I turn to Oregon, I turn to one (diocese) which I regard as a great field yet uncultivated, a great missionary life full of poverty, privations, and very hard work. Oregon has a population of only 90,923 according to the census of 1870. It can in no way compare with Georgia in material prosperity at present or in prospects for the future.

I consider therefore if I go to Oregon, I leave a very fortunate, prosperous and well-to-do diocese where everything has now been put on good footing; and in going to Oregon, I go to the life of a missionary among a scant and rude population, among Indian tribes, and where everything is to be built up…but such a life as Oregon offers makes me desirous of going to it. You know that I am a missionary by vocation…I am still young (almost forty-eight years old), in most robust health, and can preach three and four sermons a day without over-taxing myself.

Hence I say that it is in reality not a promotion, but a yielding of a better for a harder and more toilsome position. It strikes me that therefore I can in all conscience accept the position and transfer to Oregon.

"KEEP THE OBJECT OF YOUR VISIT A SECRET…"

As recorded in Chapter 1, Archbishop Gross wrote a letter,[22] dated November 4, 1891 to the Dominican Vicar General of the Western Dominican Province, Father John Pius Murphy O.P., which is quoted:

Rev. Very Dear Father:

On reaching house last evening from a country mission – I received your welcome letter. I will certainly be in Portland from the 14th to the 23rd of November and shall be most glad to see you. Please however – keep the object of your visit a secret – I have many reasons for this request. Excuse haste, for I am excessively busy.

Yours in Christ Jesu Maria.

The sentence "Please however – keep the object of your visit a secret – I have many reasons for this request." piques one's interest. Bishops, of course, can be classified as religious entrepreneurs who are forced to juggle many issues at a time, not allowing major issues to overshadow one another and thereby compound the problems they already have. Such juggling summons the demand for some degree of confidentiality.

A plausible explanation for Archbishop Gross's request for secrecy can be found by examining the happenings in the archdiocese at that time. In the first place, Archbishop Gross was a Redemptorist priest. Ordinary citizens might think that politics is a pointless pastime participated in only by the secular world, playing no part in archdiocesan affairs, but this is fallacious thinking. Politics, being an integral part of social interaction, plays no small part in the affairs of an archdiocese or any other cultural activity. Several political factors present themselves in the environment under consideration. Consider this quote from the book "These Valiant Women," a history of the period we are examining:[23]

"THE REDEMPTORISTS ARRIVE"

Meanwhile, the archbishop's [Gross's] fellow Redemptorists arrived in Portland on July 5, 1890. Four priests, including the superior Father Charles Sigle, and two brothers from the Baltimore province, were welcomed by His Excellency [Gross] and assigned to a mission center in southwest Portland, formerly the southern part of St. Lawrence parish. The new Redemptorist parish was given the title of St. Alphonsus, who was the founder of the Redemptorist Congregation…But nothing turned out right…The archbishop, it was reported, tended to interfere in Redemptorist personal matters, which pleased no one…Finally convinced that the Portland parish was hopeless, they moved to Seattle in May 1891, leaving the archbishop high and dry in southwest Portland, not to mention leaving the holy rule of the sisters in a limbo of uncertainty.

New Prelates Practice Prudence

Whenever a priest of a religious order is elevated to the rank of bishop, and is then appointed to a new diocese, priests, religious, and employees of the church within that diocese naturally wonder to what degree the ministrations of this new prelate will affect their own ministerial concerns. Might the prelate to their detriment, for example, start importing clergy and religious of his own order, and subsequently show favoritism towards these confreres?[24] Would the new order finally rule over them and the entire archdiocese, not allowing them to conduct their own affairs with the same amount of autonomy they had experienced in the past? These and other questions do arise, and from the perspective of the "appointed one," it is easy to understand why he might bend over backwards to prove his impartiality, (often-times overreacting in the process, and making life miserable for the members of his own order who are in the diocese).

The alternative – to do nothing – is, of course, always appealing, but should a suspicion of favoritism enter the minds of his subordinates, they might sabotage his goals (even unconsciously), solidarity, and the bishop's peace of mind. So the prudent prelate usually gives ongoing and ample evidence of his fairness.

Whatever the circumstances in this case, Archbishop Gross wanted to discuss the plans for the new foundation with Father Murphy in person, and in secret, ensuring that the importation of the Dominican foundation would succeed and not be a repeat of the fiasco that had befallen the Redemptorist foundation.

It must be remembered that Gross initiated the whole process six years earlier, in 1885. So two things were at stake, his six-year investment of time and energy, and a free gift of land in an area that was growing. Gross was sure the Sons of St. Dominic would sow good seed in this fertile land, making well-spent his investment of time and treasure. On the other hand, his brothers, the Redemptorists, might not have packed their bags and left six months earlier had they been aware of this free land destined for the Dominicans. It's possible that, had they known, they may have mounted a campaign in the chancery to capture the land for themselves. Having bigger fish to fry at the moment, the "Archbishop" would want to avoid such a collision course.

Another Reason for Secrecy

Surely, too, it must also have crossed Archbishop Gross's mind that Father Murphy, a very shrewd Irishman en route from California, could come upon the Portland scene and announce to the wrong people that he was the advance man for the Dominicans, only to be told by a local agitator that Portland was a precarious place for a new foundation to be rooted. "Do you know what happened to the Redemptorists, Father Murphy? They only lasted 10 months! Gross hounded them to death and they up and left six months ago." No, Archbishop

Gross was playing it smart. He was not about to have his six-year quest for the Dominicans turn to dross over loose lips. Secrecy would be the key until the die was cast and his crown jewel, the Dominicans, was firmly set in the archdiocesan tiara.

More on the Murphy – Gross Connection

It is apparent from the letters exchanged between Archbishop Gross and Father John Pius Murphy, O.P., that they met in Portland in November 1891, and had come to a meeting of the minds over the establishment of a Dominican Foundation in the City of Roses. Nevertheless, this new marriage was still in the planning stages. Though the two men might have arrived at a "gentlemen's agreement" concerning the creation of the foundation, Father Murphy was no novice. He would reduce everything to writing and first approach his community in California with a formal proposal. Their recommendation then had to go to the Father General in Rome for final approval, this being a momentous move for the Order. All of these communications would take time, and Dominican caution would prevail. This caution, in the long run, would serve the Dominicans well, especially after they became settled in Portland and the crozier was passed to Archbishop Christie upon the death of Archbishop Gross.[25]

Archbishop Gross's Ultimatum

God knows Archbishop Gross displayed the patience of Job in this affair. He had initiated this whole process six years earlier, in a letter dated September 28, 1885. As ten months slipped by after the above November 1891 meeting with Father Murphy, Archbishop Gross, like Job, became anxious and decided to nudge Father Murphy on with a not-so-veiled threat to seek another religious order if the Dominicans were not soon forthcoming with an agreement. Laying down the gauntlet, he gave the Dominicans an ultimatum, shown in this letter to Father Murphy dated September 25, 1892:[26]

V. Rev. P. V. (sic) Murphy, O.P.
V. Rev. Dear Father:

About one month from the present date, I shall go to New York in order to attend the meeting of the Archbishops of the United States. It will be an excellent opportunity for me to procure religious communities for my diocese. I hope therefore that the proposal made by me to have a foundation of your most esteemed community in Portland and for which I have been waiting so very long to hear something definite, may without further delay be decided. I am most anxious and will to have your fathers in Portland, but the spiritual interests of the people, for whose souls I have to answer, are suffering.

I cannot delay any longer. I have been more than seven years the Archbishop of Oregon – and no church of regulars yet in Portland.

In going to New York and the East, I can personally call upon the superiors – and thus have an opportunity for securing a religious community as will not easily present itself. I am still most desirous to have a foundation of your fathers in Portland, but if by the time of my departure for New York (the 24th of October) Your Reverence be still unable to make any measures for the proposed foundation in Portland, you will not take it amiss that I avail myself of my journey to the East, and secure some other community of regulars. It will however gratify me greatly if your Reverence will [be] able to take the definite measures for a foundation in Portland.

I recommend myself to your prayers – and am in the Name of Jesus,

> *Yours truly,*
>
> *[signed]*
> *+Wm. Gross*
> *Archbishop. Oregon*

It is likely that Father Murphy had written a letter which was en route as the above letter was being mailed if one considers the following letter from Archbishop Gross dated October 3, 1892, eight days later:

J.M.J.
V. Rev. Dear Father:

I have just received your most welcome letter and its pleasant contents have filled me with joy. I thank God and His Immaculate Mother that a foundation of your esteemed community in Portland has been definitely settled – and in a short time will be a 'fait accompli.' I hope that your reverence will receive the expected letters from Rome before my departure from Portland for New York. I cannot say how long I may be detained in New York – tho' I shall endeavor to return as soon as possible. I will however leave all views with V. Rev. F. Fierens – my Vicar General – who will be authorized to arrange matters with you, in case of my absence. I do not wish that my absence should be a cause for further delay to the foundation.

I know by experience, how true it is that the devil and his agents raise up fearful opposition to every undertaking for God's glory. Indeed, I am almost afraid to commence a new work – as somehow new crosses are sure to come.

But after the storm comes the calm. Let us place this new work for the glory of Her Son in the hands of the ever Blessed Virgin. For I

know that there is no order which so earnestly strives to spread devotion to that Sacred Mother of God as the Institute of St. Dominic.

I recommend myself to your prayers – and am – in the Name of Jesus,

> *Yours truly,*
>
> *[signed]*
> *+Wm. Gross*
> *Archbishop. Oregon*
>
> *V. Rev. P. Murphy, O.P.*

But the protracted correspondence would continue, as in this letter to Father Murphy from Archbishop Gross dated April 9, 1893 at Sublimity, Oregon testifies:

J.M.J.
V. Rev. Dear Father:

Your most welcome letter came to hand just as I was about to leave Portland for this little town. I thank God and Our Dear Lady of Perpetual Help that at last my long and greatly desired wish to see a foundation of the Sons of St. Dominic in my archiepiscal city is now to be so soon realized.

I am particularly delighted to think that there will be in Portland a religious order that will in such an especial manner labor to build up and increase the worship of the Blessed Mother of Our Lord Jesus. No greater good can be done a people than to introduce this Blessed – this channel of all grace into their hearts and homes. Moreover, I am persuaded that wherever Mary comes – She brings Jesus with her. I shall be in Portland in two or three days – and shall remain at home until you come.

Praying that Our Immaculate Queen will take in her own spotless hands this foundation which is to be all for her glory – I am – most devotedly

Yours in the Name of Jesu –

> *[signed]*
> *+Wm. H. Gross*
> *Archbishop. Oregon*
>
> *V. Rev. P. Murphy, O.P.*

NOTES TO THE TEXT

16 *A History of the Catholic Church in the Pacific Northwest 1743-1983* by Wilfred P. Schoenberg, S.J., Pastoral Press, Washington, D.C., 1987 (page 300).

17 Ibid.

18 Contained in a booklet *Fratres In Unum*, celebrating the installation of His Excellency, The Most Reverend William J. Levada, S.T.D. as the Eighth Archbishop of Portland in Oregon.

19 Later to become the Archdiocese of Portland.

20 Exposition Press Inc., 325 Kings Highway, Smithtown, N.Y., 1977, (page 16).

21 From the book *These Valiant Women* by Wilfred P. Schoenberg, S.J., published by the Sisters of St. Mary of Oregon, 440 Southwest 148th Avenue, Beaverton, Oregon 97007, 1986 (page 96).

22 Originals of correspondence sent to the province are contained in file XI 405:1-5(A) at the Province Headquarters in Oakland, California.

23 Page 133, *These Valiant Women* by Wilfred P. Schoenberg S.J., History of the Sisters of St. Mary of Oregon 1886-1986, printed May 1986, Western Lithograph at Portland in Oregon.

24 These might have been Archbishop Gross's concerns when he wrote in Appendix 1 "…Portland is my place of residence and were I to introduce the Redemptorist here, it might cause unpleasant consequences. I will probably at some other time offer my confreres a foundation…"

25 Archbishop Gross died November 14, 1898.

26 Original on file in the archives of the Western Dominican Province, Oakland, California.

Holy Rosary Church's founder,
Father John Pius Murphy, O.P.

FATHER MURPHY BUILDS A CONVENTUAL CHURCH[27]

JOHN PIUS MURPHY, O.P. – FOUNDING FATHER OF HOLY ROSARY

Comparisons as to efforts expended by men and women in historical enterprises are oftentimes odious for they risk being invidious, but it is an acceptable risk in this case to declare John Pius Murphy, O.P., the "Founding Father of Holy Rosary Church." Not only because he maintained lengthy correspondence with Archbishop Gross for several years, and personally undertook the concrete tasks of building the church and the first rectory. But, for whatever economic, legal,[28] political and public relations reasons, he moved the church and first rectory ten blocks prior to their near completion, installing them in their final resting place, and demonstrating that no obstacle was too big for him to reach his goal. The church and new rectory repose at this same location to this day: 375 Northeast Clackamas Street, between Northeast Union Avenue[29] and Third Avenue in Portland, the front door to the church facing NE 3rd Avenue, and the front door to the rectory facing Clackamas Street.

As far as Archbishop Gross was concerned, Father Murphy came as the White Knight of the Dominicans, culminating nearly eight years of correspondence between the order and the archbishop, whose obvious love for Our Blessed Mother and confidence in the Dominican ability to spread the good news about her and the Rosary sustained him for all of those years. These two Irish-Americans would make a good team.

Assuredly Father Murphy was the right man for the job. Though he may have left his heart in San Francisco, he brought with him to Portland an imagination blessed by grace and buttressed by a keen brain and manly vigor. He was a mature age 49 when he reached Portland, and had been a priest for almost 30 years. Born in Quebec, Canada on June 23, 1844, he had been received as a postulant in the Dominican Order at the tender age of 12, and was admitted to the novitiate at Benicia, California on July 2, 1859. He professed his simple vows on August 4, 1860 at age 16, and his solemn vows three years later at age 19. As a 21-year-old he accompanied the Provincial of the Dominican Order, The Very Reverend Sadoc Francis Vilarrasa, O.P., on a trip to Europe, so he was far from unsophisticated in his view of the world. Father Murphy became the first prior of St. Dominic's Church in San Francisco in February 1876, and prior at Benicia in 1891. He served as Vicar General of the Province in 1892, so he also had some solid experience as a leader and administrator. Some of his beginnings are obscure but a lot is still known. Photographs show he was a stocky man of medium height, slightly rotund, balding, a man with a direct gaze and wizened eyes, and a cigar smoker. He died at St. Dominic's in San Francisco March 28, 1921 at age 76, having served God for over half a century.

The following is quoted from an article in the *Catholic Sentinel* of September 7, 1893:

TWO BLOCKS FOR ONE
A TRANSFER OF PROPERTY FOR CATHOLIC CHURCH PURPOSES
Several years ago the late Ben Holladay deeded to the late Bishop Blanchet of the Catholic Church and successors in trust for the Church, a block of land #191,[30] in what is now known as the Holladay Addition.

The provision of the deed was that the property was to be used for no other purpose than as a site for a Catholic Church or school and parochial residence; and, in the event of the property being disposed of by the Catholic Church, or used for any other purpose than that set forth in the deed, the property was to revert to the owner or his heirs.

Last winter, Reverend Father Pius [Murphy], the head of the Dominican Order of California, came to this city for the purpose of erecting a church and monastery similar to that of the Order in San Francisco. There being no Father of the Dominican Order located in the Northwest, and the Archbishop being desirous of having a House of the Order located in the city, he offered the above-mentioned block for this purpose. It was accepted by Father Pius [Murphy] and work was commenced about two months ago on the building.

After the death of Ben Holladay, the large tract, now known as Holladay Addition, passed into the hands of a syndicate, and was sold in lots, with the provision that no portion of the tract should be used for other than residence purposes.

The proposed erection of the church buildings was in violation of the contract made between the syndicate and the purchasers of the property adjacent to the church block, and in order to avoid litigation growing out of the matter, the syndicate offered two blocks of land, Nos. 67 and 68 on Union Avenue, in exchange for the one held by the Church authorities.

This offer was accepted, and a temporary structure will be erected on block 67 [31] to be used as a church. A permanent parochial residence will also be erected adjoining the church building. Later a permanent stone edifice, similar to that of the Order in San Francisco, will be erected, when the temporary church structure will be used as an assembly hall and for Sunday School purposes. It is expected that at least three of the leading priests of the Order will be stationed in Portland.

HISTORY OF GOOD DEEDS
The deeds to the properties involved (Blocks #119, #67 and #68) were of course at issue in these transactions. Here's how they were handled according to a white sheet (undated and author not identified) on file in the Dominican Archives in Oakland.

Block 119, Holladay's Addition: This property was first conveyed by Oregon Real Estate Company to F.X. Blanchet, (Vol V, Page 111) on March 3, 1873 [by Ben Holladay]. The deed conditions were that the property was never to be used for anything but for the church, charity or school, etc. purposes under pain of reversion to the grantor.

Construction of a church and rectory were commenced sometime in the late 1880s (sic) and due to protest of certain residents in the area, a transaction was consummated whereby Oregon Real Estate Company conveyed by deed to Archbishop Wm. H. Gross Lots 67 and 68, Holladay's Addition by deed recorded in Book 199, page 404 on Aug. 17, 1893, and Archbishop Gross then reconveyed Block 119 to Oregon Real Estate Company under date of 8/18/93 (Vol. 199, page 432).

By deed recorded August 18, 1893, Archbishop Gross conveyed Blocks 67 and 68, to John Pius Murphy, O.P., at a stated consideration of $20,000.[32] It is my understanding that the church and rectory buildings were then moved from Block 119 to Block 68.

Articles of Incorporation for Holy Rosary Church of Portland, an Oregon corporation, non-profit, were filed and dated Feb. 21, 1898, and the incorporators were: Very Rev. John Pius Murphy, Provincial; Very Rev. Lawrence Breen, Prior and Rev. Edward Warner, O.P. Procurator. Capital assets stated were $20,000 – a non-profit corporation.

New articles of Incorporation were filed and dated Feb. 11, 1899 with the same principals and stated assets and other statistics as the previous articles.

By deed recorded Feb. 16, 1899 John Pius Murphy, O.P. Provincial, conveyed Block 68 to Holy Rosary Church of Portland, an Oregon corporation [page 74, Book 256, Record of Deeds, Multnomah County].

It appears that, in about 1908, Holy Rosary Church, Community and Parish, were cited for a Beneplacetum.

The deed records then show the conveyance of Block 212 from Moon[33] Estate Company to John S. Rice, of City and County of San Francisco, Calif. (Book 565, page 112 of deed records). I am informed that there is a John S. Rice, now deceased, listed in the Province Directory.

By deed recorded 2/27/14 John S. Rice conveyed Block 212 to Holy Rosary Church of Portland, an Oregon corporation, and the witness signatories appear to be A.L. McMahon and W.T. Lewis, acknowledged in San Francisco by Notary James McCue.

By deed recorded 5/5/15 John Pius Murphy conveyed Block 67 to Joseph G. Rourke.[34]

In 1916 by deed recorded 11/28/17 Joseph G. Rourke conveyed Block 67 to the Province.

A school was built on Block 212 in 1923, and the original mortgage was placed on the property with the Hibernia Bank of San Francisco in the sum of $45,000, and there showed a series of 7 other short term mortgages, which the bank advises all have been paid in full, and the records destroyed. The mortgage incidentally also encumbered Block 68.

This is all the information I have in my files.

What follows was contained in a letter[35] from (Miss) Patricia Brandt, 910 N.W. 31st, Corvallis, Oregon 97330, who is not further identified, to Bishop Francis Leipzig, Calaroga Terrace, 1400 N.E. 2d, Portland, Oregon and dated January 15, 1975:

MURPHY'S HOLE
Around the turn of the present century, small boys in East Portland delighted in playing games in a large excavation at the corner of Multnomah and East 10th St. For a long forgotten reason, the place was called Murphy's Hole. This is the story on Murphy's Hole.

When Ben Holladay's financial empire was at its height, he donated to Archbishop Blanchet and his successors a block in Holladay's Addition on Multnomah and E. 10th St. Neither Archbishop Blanchet nor Archbishop Seghers ever made use of the land, but in 1893, Archbishop Gross found opportunity to use it to entice the Dominican Order to Oregon.

By July, 1893,[36] [Fr. John Pius Murphy, O.P.] of San Francisco had arrived in Portland to supervise construction of a Dominican monastery. A large basement was dug, and the frame of the building began to rise on [Block 119] of Holladay's Addition. In mid-August it was announced that the buildings were nearly completed. The chapel faced on E. 11th St. and was 110 by 52 feet with a 29 1/2 foot ceiling. The chancel was to be semicircular, and over the main door was a gallery. Adjoining the church was to be the two story residence for the Dominican Fathers. There were 14 rooms, besides closets and a basement. The buildings were low, severe, unornamented, but of substantial construction. Half the block was covered with buildings and plans were to enclose the whole block.

As soon as construction began, neighbors in Holladay's Addition began to protest. After Holladay's death in 1887, the Oregon Real Estate Co. had been incorporated to sell the property. There was a clause in their contract which stated that churches, stores, and saloons were to be excluded. More and more vigorous protests arose from those who had bought and built in the area as they saw the Dominican buildings nearing completion. To avoid trouble, the

A ROSE IS PLANTED IN THE CITY OF ROSES
To get the ball rolling (and later the church and rectory on logs to roll them to their new location) Father Murphy engaged the services of a general contractor named Lionel D. Deane who, when the work was finished, presented the following invoice to Father Murphy:

CHURCH BUILT FOR $22,300
CONTRACTOR'S INVOICE FOR BUILDING HOLY ROSARY
Lionel Deane presented the following invoice to Father Murphy, April 9, 1894:

"This is to certify that I have expended the following sums for the erection of a Church residence and other structures on Block #68, Hollidays[40] Addition, Portland, Oregon:

Surveyor	$ 30.00	
Brick layer	3022.00	
Lumber shingles etc.	1819.85	
Mill Work	2735.70	
Labor to 15 Feb '94	4360.75	unpaid
Painting	840.00	$104.00
Plumber	2760.00	321.85
Plasterer	1700.00	105.00
Blacksmith	190.25	
Hardware & nails	457.60	
Electricity	400.00	34.25
Stained glas	555.40	
Tinner	238.50	
Sheathing paper	49.50	
Cement steps	40.00	
W. shades	36.00	
Light fixtures	200.00	285.50
Moving7	50.00	
Sundries	42.20	
Expenses incurred since 15 Feb	21.85	
Fuel	22.50	
Total	**$20,272.10**	**$850.55**

In addition to the above I have disbursed the following sums:

Insurance for 3 years as $10.000	250.00
Street improvements block #119	825.95
Architect's fee	860.00
Drayage, steamer charges	82.65
Total	**$ 2,018.60**
Receipts to date	22,300.00
Expenditures to date	22,290.00
Balance on hand	**$ 9.30**
Moneys necessary to complete payments	
$850.55 plus $70.00 due Archt. =	920.55
Cash on hand =	9.30
	$ 911.25

Respectfully submitted:

[signed]
Lionel D. Deane

Subscribed and sworn to before me, [signature] E.C. Masten, a Notary Public for the State of Oregon this 10th day of April A.D. 1894.
[signed] E.C. Masten
[SEAL] Portland, Ogn. April 10, 1894
Notary Public for Oregon

[Scribbled notations]	$22,300.00	church
	911.00	house
	23,211.00	**Total**
	20,000.00	Two blocks
	$43,211.00	

real estate company offered to the Dominicans [Blocks] 67 and 68 in Holladay's Addition – if they would give up all claim to Block [119] and move their buildings to the new place. Reluctantly, Fr. Murphy agreed.

As August of 1893 drew to a close, there was feverish activity at the new building site at the corner of Union Ave. and [Clackamas] St. A large crew of men and teams were excavating the foundation. Fr. Murphy bustled about directing the work. On Aug. 31, the slow move of the building frames began. At that time it was disclosed that the frame buildings were intended to be temporary and that a permanent structure of stone would be erected later. When the stone church was built, the frame structure would be used as a church hall.

Curious Portlanders watched the progress. By Sept. 7 the frame was as far as E. 6th, and on Sept. 12, 1893, the church building and residence were placed on their new foundation between Union Ave. and E. 3rd [church facing 3rd and rectory facing Clackamas].

HOLY ROSARY DEDICATED ON JANUARY 28, 1894[37]
Fr. Pius [Murphy], O.P., Provincial of the Dominican Order on the Pacific coast, came from California to attend the dedication on Jan. 28, 1894. At that time, the church, designed by L.D. Deane, was described as being built in Italian renaissance style. And so Holy Rosary parish was founded. Fr. Murphy went back to San Francisco, not realizing that he was to leave his name on that delightful Portland landmark, Murphy's Hole, first – and very temporary – home of Holy Rosary Church.

OREGONIAN ARTICLE ON DEDICATION OF HOLY ROSARY
Page 8 of *The Morning Oregonian* dated Monday, January 29, 1894 reported:

NEW CHURCH DEDICATED
The new church of the Dominican order on Clackamas street and Union avenue was dedicated with impressive ceremonies yesterday morning. The services were conducted by Most Rev. Archbishop Gross, assisted by Very Rev. M.G. Van Scramm of Vancouver; Rev. Father Pius, O.P. (sic) the provincial of the Dominican order on the Pacific coast; Rev. Father Aerden, O.P. of Martinez; Rev. Prior Rielly,[41] (sic) O.P. of St. Dominic's church, San Francisco. Rev. Father Brean [42] (sic), O.P.; and Rev. Father McGovern, O.P. of Portland, and several other members of the local clergy. The impressive dedicatory ceremonies of the Dominican order were performed, and were witnessed by several thousand people. Archbishop Gross preached a sermon, in which he gave a brief history of the order and expressed his gratification at having it represented in Oregon.

The church is in the style of the Italian Renaissance, from plans drawn by Mr. L.D. Deane. It is a neat, comfortable edifice, with good acoustic properties, and is large enough to accommodate the newly formed congregation for several years to come.

The Dominicans are a religious order, and their mission is that of preachers. Portland is the only city in Oregon in which they have located. They have many churches in California, and some rank among the handsomest in that state.

Masses will be celebrated in the new church every Sunday at 8:30 and 10:30 a.m. and vespers at 7:30 p.m.

FIRST DOMINICANS ASSIGNED TO HOLY ROSARY
REV. JAMES BENEDICT McGOVERN, O.P,
FIRST SUPERIOR OF HOLY ROSARY 1894-1895
Father McGovern was born in Ireland on December 3, 1836. He emigrated to the United States around 1841 on the death of his parents, and lived with relatives in Ohio, where he attended the Dominican Fathers College at Somerset. He was received as a Dominican postulant in February 1853, and admitted to the Novitiate July 22, 1853. He was ordained on May 2, 1863, at age 26. His previous assignments took him to London, Canada, St. Vincent's, New York, St. Dominic's and other houses in California before he began his tenure as superior at Holy Rosary on February 1, 1894. He served here for one year and then became Prior at St. Dominic's in San Francisco in January 1895, a position he held until his death. He died at St. Joseph's Hospital in Stockton on September 21, 1918, at age 71.

AN INTERESTING "STORY OF GRACE" [43]
One of the Dominican priests who served at Holy Rosary with Father McGovern was Father James Henry Aerden, who came as a Dominican from the province in Belgium to be a missionary on Vancouver Island, B.C., where he had some sort of falling out with Bishop Demers, who had invited him and later suspended him. Father Aerden, apparently dejected, left Canada and went to the gold country in California, to work in the mines at Marysville. One Sunday at Mass, he realized that the preacher giving the sermon was not accurate in what he said so, after Mass, Father Aerden went back to the sanctuary and talked with the preacher. The preacher soon realized that Aerden was also a priest and he contacted Archbishop Alemany of San Francisco about Aerden. The archbishop, in turn, contacted Father Vilarassa, the Dominican Superior of California. Father Aerden was soon back to work, performing priestly functions in Benicia. During this period there were only 60 priests in all of California; only five of them Dominicans. Thanks be to God, Father Aerden went on to become a most effective Dominican, building the first St. Bridgit Church (since torn down and rebuilt) in San Francisco. He attended the January 28, 1894 dedication of Holy Rosary, and he died March 2, 1896 as rector of Martinez, at age 72. He had been a priest for almost fifty years.

FATHER PETER ALPHONSE RILEY, O.P.

Father Riley, a native of San Francisco, served with Fathers Aerden and McGovern in Portland in 1894, and returned to serve from 1915-1924. He, too, had a vast amount of experience, having been prior of St. Dominic's in San Francisco. He died October 24, 1932 at age 77. He had served God as a priest for 48 years.

REV. PATRICK THOMAS AQUINAS FITZSIMONS, O.P., REPLACES McGOVERN 1895-1896

Father Fitzsimons was also born in Ireland, at Caven, on July 26, 1842. He was admitted to the novitiate December 8, 1864, professed his solemn vows December 8, 1868 and was ordained in 1871 at age 29. All of his assignments were at Benicia and San Francisco before coming to Portland as pastor around January 1895. He died at St. Mary's Hospital, San Francisco, November 8, 1897, at age 55.

FATHER JOHN BENEDICT O'CONNOR, O.P.

Father O'Connor was another native San Franciscan born there December 23, 1865. He was ordained a Dominican September 17, 1890, and so was a young priest serving at Holy Rosary in 1895. He went on to become Prior of Benicia (twice) and San Francisco. He died January 31, 1935 at age 69, having served God for 44 years.

FATHER ROURKE BAPTIZED IN CHURCH BUILT BY FATHER AERDEN

Father Joseph Gregory Rourke, O.P., an assistant at Holy Rosary in 1895 and 1896, was born June 20, 1870, in San Francisco and baptized at St. Brigid's, built by Father Aerden in 1864. He was ordained at St. Mary's Cathedral in San Francisco, April 25, 1894, so had been a priest for only a year when he came to Portland. He served all over California and was prior of the Immaculate Conception Priory at Ross when he died September 27, 1943, at St. Mary's Hospital in San Francisco, just seven months shy of his Golden Jubilee.

REV. THOMAS BREEN, O.P., THIRD PRIOR AT HOLY ROSARY 1896-1899

Father Breen was born June 7, 1864 in San Francisco. He was admitted to the novitiate at Benicia November 25, 1880, professed simple vows May 25, 1882, and solemn vows October 20, 1885. He was ordained in 1888 at age 24. He served in Benicia until coming to Portland in 1895 as Vicar. He died April 11, 1907 at St. Joseph's Hospital in San Francisco, at age 42.

From the March 19, 1944 parish digest comes this account of Father Breen:

FIRST SUNDAY SCHOOL AND ROSARIANS
To Father Breen goes the credit of organizing the first Sunday school, almost immediately after the dedication of the church. At first, classes were held at 2:30 p.m., but this was later changed to the period following the 8:30 Mass.

Some of the teachers called at the children's homes to take them to instructions. When the number of children attending these classes increased, two Sisters from Stanton Street took charge until Holy Rosary School was opened.

The Rosarians also owe their origin to Father Breen. He entrusted them with the direction of the Rosary Procession held on the first Sunday of each month. In these processions, five Rosarians carried the banners.

In connection with the Rosary, it is noteworthy that our daily recitation of the Rosary in the church is an unbroken tradition dating from the very beginnings of Holy Rosary.

REV. JAMES REGINALD NEWELL, O.P.

Father Newell served at Holy Rosary from 1897 to 1899. He was born in Brown County, Ohio, January 22, 1849, went to Woodchester, England, as a Postulant, and studied at Louvain, Belgium. He was ordained June 10, 1876, and went on to become Prior at San Francisco after leaving Holy Rosary. He was a priest for 55 years and died April 28, 1932, at age 83.

HOLY ROSARY FORMED AS A CORPORATION IN OREGON IN 1898

As the following articles of incorporation show, Holy Rosary Church became incorporated in the State of Oregon February 21, 1898:

ARTICLES OF INCORPORATION OF HOLY ROSARY CHURCH PORTLAND, OREGON[44]
We, the Very Rev. John Pius Murphy, O.P., Provincial, Very Rev. Lawrence Breen, O.P., and Rev. Edward C. Warren, O.P. Procurator, being officers and trustees of Holy Rosary Church of the City of Portland, Multnomah County, Oregon, regularly appointed and elected in conformity with the doctrines, canons, teaching and discipline of the Roman Catholic Church, and the constitutions, rules and regulations of the Order of Preachers founded by St. Dominic, do hereby make and subscribe these written articles of incorporation of said Holy Rosary Church and associate ourselves together for this purpose under and by virtue of section 3303 of "Hills Annotated Code of Oregon," and the amendment of said act approved Feb. 25, 1889.

The name assumed by this Corporation shall be "Holy Rosary

Church," and the duration shall be perpetual.

II

1st. To preach the gospel of Jesus Christ according to the doctrines, teaching, canon and discipline of the Holy Roman Catholic Church, and the Constitutions, rules and regulations of the Order of Preachers founded by St. Dominic, which are hereby referred to and made a part hereof; and to be affiliated and associated with the other institutions of said Order of Preachers on the Pacific Coast according to said Constitution, rules and regulations.

2nd. To live in community, and to educate and train youth and to prepare and fit them for community life and membership in the said Order of Preachers as clerical and fraternal members under the said Constitutions, rules and regulations of said Order of Preachers.

3rd. To promote and maintain works of charity, education and the worship of Almighty God.

4th. To acquire, receive, hold, manage and dispose of money and property in trust for said church, and for the promotion of its objects in accordance with said Constitutions, rules and regulations.

III

The estimate value of the property and money possessed by said church at this time is $20,000, and the sources of revenue and income are pew rents, legacies and devises of money and property.

IV

The title of the officers making these articles are Very Rev. John Pius Murphy, O.P., Provincial; Very Rev. Lawrence Breen, O.P., Prior, Holy Rosary Church; Rev. Edward C. Warren, O.P., Procurator. The organization of Holy Rosary Church is, under the Constitutions, rules and regulations of the Order of Preachers as founded by St. Dominic, at present, in the formative stage; and while the present form of organization continues, the successors of the above named officers shall in accordance with said Constitutions, rules and regulations, be chosen by appointment by the superior officers of said Order of Preachers.

When the organization shall be established by a permanent foundation under said Constitutions, rules, and regulations, the successors of the above named officers shall be elected as follows: The said Provincial every four years; and said Prior and Procurator every three years, in accordance with said Constitutions, rules and regulations. Vacancies occurring from any cause during the term to be filled by election or appointment according to said Constitutions, rules and regulations.

In witness whereof, the said John Pius Murphy, Provincial, Lawrence Breen, Prior and Edward Warren, Procurator, have hereunto set their hands and seals in triplicate this 21st day of

February, 1898.

> *In the Presence of:*
> *Henry Bolton*
>
> *(signed)*
> *John Pius Murphy, O.P., Provincial*
> *M.G. Munly*
>
> *(signed)*
> *Lawrence Breen, O.P., Prior*
>
> *(signed)*
> *Edward C. Warren, O.P., Procurator*
>
> *State of Oregon*
> *SS.*
> *County of Multnomah*

This is to certify, that on the 21st day of February, A.D. 1898, before me, a Notary Public in and for said County and State, personally appeared the within named Very Rev. John Pius Murphy, O.P., Provincial, Very Rev. Lawrence Breen, O.P., Prior, and Rev. E.C. Warren, O.P., Procurator, who are personally known to me to be the persons and officers who signed the foregoing articles of incorporation, and acknowledged to me that they executed the same for the uses and purposes therein set forth.

In Testimony Whereof, I have hereunto set my hand and Notarial Seal the day and year last above written.

> *Henry Bolton*
> *Notary Public for Oregon.*
> *[NOTARY SEAL]*

The above is a true copy of the original. C.V. Lamb

Judge M. G. Munly
Mails Deeds to Father Murphy

Though Blocks 67 and 68 were conveyed from Archbishop Gross to Father Murphy August 18, 1893, as previously recorded under deeds, apparently the actual deeds never changed hands. Perhaps the Archbishop was holding onto them until he received the $20,000. In any case, Judge M.G. Munly, who handled legal matters for Holy Rosary, wrote the following letter to Father Murphy on March 6, 1898, six years after the original conveyance:

Very Rev. Dear Father:

I enclose you herewith a deed of Block 68 Holladays Add. Portland for your signature. It should have the signatures of two witnesses to your signature. You should sign the deed "John Pius Murphy, O.P." opposite the pen scroll at the first place for signature and acknowledge the same before a Notary Public. These are all of the formalities necessary.

I send you also the deed from the Archbishop to yourself. I believe this is according to my instructions.

I wish to thank you on behalf of Mr. & Mrs. Barron and Mrs. Munly and myself for the lot of beautiful medals and Agnus Dei which were in the envelope you gave me. We all appreciate them very much. Your "Klondike" message on the envelope is not unheeded and we feel hopeful that through your good prayers our undertakings in the North may succeed.

I have been delayed in sending off this deed by a protracted trial in which I have been engaged for more than a week, besides being "laid up" for a few days.

I trust you are well and will be glad to hear from you, and see you soon again.

> *Sincerely yours,*
>
> *[signed]*
> *M.G. Munly*

JUDGE MICHAEL G. MUNLY
A FIGHTIN' IRISHMAN OF THE CHURCH MILITANT

Holy Rosary's lawyer went by the initials "M.G." as was common in those days. He came to the City of Roses in 1883, and joined Holy Rosary when the church was built ten years later. Since both of his parents came from Ireland, there was little doubt that he and Father Murphy would hit it off. The following biography,[45] summarizes Munly's life up to 1890:

MICHAEL G. MUNLY, ex-Judge of the Circuit Court and a successful practicing attorney of Portland, Oregon, was born September 22nd, 1854, at Carbondale, Lackawana County, Pennsylvania. He is a son of Michael Munly, a coal miner of that state, and of Bridget Munly, who is still living. The elder Munly came to America from Ireland in 1846, his mother is also from Ireland preceding him in 1832, the parents settled in Pennsylvania, where Judge Munly was born and when old enough attended public

Judge M.G. Munly

and private schools of his native place. He subsequently became principal of a public school in Scranton, Pa., from 1875 to 1882, while occupying this position he studied law, and in April 1882, he was admitted to the bar at Lackawanna County. Mr. Munly remained but a short while in Pennsylvania and in Jul, 1882, he went to Oregon. For the first six months he engaged in the strenuous occupation of "cow punching" and roughing it in the cattle business. Coming to Portland in the spring of the year following, he worked in a wholesale drugstore for a while. In October 1883, he was admitted to the practice of law by the bar of Oregon and practiced his profession alone, also doing newspaper work at Portland, and becoming Editor of the "Catholic Sentinel," the leading Catholic Journal of the Northwest. He continued in journalism with success from 1886 to 1890 and in the fall of that year sold out his interest in the Sentinel and devoted his attention to his law business.

As editor of the *Catholic Sentinel*, Munly took on all comers, but especially those Oregon newspapers which attacked the Church he loved. Munly also provoked several newspapers by constantly attacking the public school system. According to historian Wilfred P. Schoenberg, S.J., Munly identified the school system variously as "*wicked, godless and even the tools of Satan*". In his characterization of public schools, Munly was "echoing the words of the hierarchy, especially Archbishop Seghers and Bishop Brondel." Father Schoenberg thought these attacks were counterproductive: "*In the long run, Catholic hostility to public schools was a mistake. It created a backlash that influenced several generations in Oregon, where there was so much animosity toward parochial schools that the outcome of the Oregon Compulsory School Bill of 1922 [see chapters 6 and 8] was all but inevitable, once it appeared on the ballot.*"[46]

Father Schoenberg's diagnosis requires a second opinion. One need only survey the anti-Catholicism extant in the public square, even including that component called "education," since the founding of the Republic. At base we have witnessed a war between the Catholic view of man as opposed to the liberal view of man. The Church recognizes man as possessed of Original Sin who daily combats the Devil. This man's human nature has a permanent, unchanging essence, corrupt to some degree, and with limited potential. Liberalism, on the other hand, holds that there is nothing intrinsic to the nature of man that makes it impossible for human society to achieve the goals of peace, freedom, justice and well-being that liberalism assumes to be desirable and to define 'the good society,' and furthermore defines "human nature as not fixed but plastic and changing; with no pre-set limit to potential development."[47]

Catholics, at bottom, believe man can become saintly through prayer and the grace given to him by God; in this, his transformation comes from within – but he can never become a perfect man because perfection belongs to God alone. Further, so long as there is sin in the world, the world will suffer from its effects. Liberalism believes that the imposition of laws and rules and continuing dialog and consensus-building will gradually transform sinful man to live in peace with his neighbor. Catholics believe we can know truth through Jesus Christ Who is "the Way, the Truth, and the Life." But when it comes to truth, Liberals are in a quandry, as expressed here by James Burnham:[48]

Liberalism is committed to the truth and to the belief that truth is what is discovered by reason and the sciences; and committed against the falsehoods and errors that are handed down by superstition, prejudice, custom and authority. But every man, according to liberalism, is entitled to his own opinion, and has the right to express it (and to advocate its acceptance). In motivating the theory and practice of free speech , liberalism must either abandon its belief in the superior social utility of truth, or maintain that we cannot be sure we know truth. The first alternative – which would imply that error is sometimes more useful for society than the truth – is by no means self-evidently false, but is ruled out, or not even considered seriously, by liberalism. Therefore, liberalism must accept the second alternative.

We thus face the following situation. Truth is our goal; but objective truth, if it exists at all, is unattainable; we cannot be sure even whether we are getting closer to it, because that estimate could not be made without an objective standard against which to measure the gap. Thus the goal we have postulated becomes meaningless, evaporates. Our original committment to truth undergoes a subtle transformation, and becomes a committment to rational and scientific process itself: to – in John Dewey's terminology – "the method of inquiry."

[The liberal, the unbeliever in absolute truth, nevertheless contradicts himself with the statement: "there is no such thing as absolute truth" – which statement is itself an absolute.]

The public school system in the U.S. gradually got worse as time went on. John Dewey [1859-1952] had a profound effect on its ultimate backrupty. His pragmatism, insightful Catholic parents learned long ago, is now the politically-correct view espoused by the National Education Association (which controls what is taught in our schools). That liberals have and have always had a self-serving agenda antagonistic toward (and frequently hostile to) historic Catholic teaching is self-evident. No parent would object to tried and true theories related to reading, writing, and arithmetic, but the inculcation of alien thought, including "values clarification," "situation ethics," and instruction in (and promotion of) the use of condoms, in lieu of abstinence remain to this day "wicked, godless and even the tools of Satan." Sadly, with respect to sex education, the same holds true for the teaching in some Catholic schools, – so much so that home schooling is slowly becoming commonplace in devout Catholic communities.

Schools, of course, were only part of the complex conundrum of inter-religious cooperation, and, each melee took on a life of its own. The anti-Catholicism of the *Christian Herald*, for example, published in Monmouth in 1883, declared:[49]

A Church pointed out by the Spirit of God as the Man of Sin whose coming is after the working of Satan, with all the power and the signs of lying wonders, the Babylon of Revelation and the Mother of Harlots; a Church whose purpose is to rule the world by temporal power, who opposes American liberty, and seeks to overcome our common school system; a Church who virtually repudiated Christ and the apostles…a Church who destroyed the Bible, established the Inquisition of the Dark Ages; a Church in short whose whole history is one of superstition and corruption from top to bottom.

Another newspaper, the *Sunday Examiner*, with which Munly did editorial battle, also took the sting of Munly's pen in 1890, as Munly was leaving the Sentinel:

Ambrose Bierce of the Sunday Examiner *greets Mr. Pixley on his return to this city, after an absence of several weeks: "Glad to see you back, Mr. Pixley – how's Satan?"*[50] Munly always gave as good as he got, and once wrote of *The Oregonian*: *"A minister of San Francisco recently lectured on the subject of 'The Devil and Literature.' He must have read* The Oregonian."[51]

MUNLY'S OBITUARY
The *Catholic Sentinel* of November 1, 1923 reported on Munly's death:

JUDGE MICHAEL GEORGE MUNLY
In 1886, Munly became editor and principal owner of the Catholic Sentinel *devoting four years to editorial work. In 1892 he was appointed Judge of the Circuit Court by Governor Pennoyer. In 1894 he failed in the election to the bench largely because of the activities of the A.P.A. In 1909 Mr. Munly was democratic candidate for Mayor of Portland. In the following year he was elected a member of the Portland School Board, the first Catholic*

to become a member of the Board in 30 years. He was associated with Holy Rosary Church since the coming of the Dominican Fathers to this city.[52]

THE MUNLY-BARRON CONNECTION TO HOLY ROSARY AS TOLD BY PARISHIONER EDWARD MICHAEL FERGUSON

Ed Ferguson[53] is today a daily communicant at Holy Rosary. His roots in the parish extend back to the turn of the century when his great grandmother, Ann Elizabeth Nixon, came to Oregon as a widow around 1868 from Fitzwilliam, New Hampshire via Boston, Massachusetts with two small girls who later became: Mary Elizabeth Nixon Munly, wife of Michael George Munly, referred to above; and Elizabeth Nixon Barron, wife of James T. Barron.

Michael and Mary Munly had a daughter, Anna Munly. Anna married Vance Thomas Ferguson, a non-Catholic, in the Holy Rosary rectory July 7, 1920, and Ed was born to them a year later, on April 20, 1921. So Michael and Mary Munly were Ed Ferguson's grandparents. Mary Munly died in 1933, when Ed was age 11. Michael Munly died in 1923 when Ed was only two years old, so Ed knew his grandmother quite well, but not his grandfather.

Ed Ferguson's father converted to Catholicism at age 55. Ed himself married Catherine Alice Niedermeyer, daughter of B.E. & Tessie Niedermeyer and granddaughter of Joseph and Mary Niedermeyer.

Elizabeth Nixon Barron married James T. Barron, who came from a wealthy family in San Francisco, and was President & Chairman of the Hibernia Bank of Portland. Both the Barrons and Munlys were great contributors to Holy Rosary, and one can understand why loans on property were arranged with the Hibernia Bank – the Barron connection.

THE PROLIFIC FERGUSON-NIEDERMEYER CLAN

As explained, Ed Ferguson married Catherine Niedermeyer. (Catherine's grandparents, Joseph & Mary, were also great contributors to Holy Rosary.) Ed recalls distinctly standing in front of the church watching Joseph Niedermeyer giving out cigars because his wife had just given birth. Joe was then age 52 and his wife, Mary, age 49. Ed stood there with his grandmother, Mary Munly, who turned to his great aunt Elizabeth Barron and said: "Look at him giving out cigars. You'd think he'd be ashamed of himself being a father at age 52!"

Catherine Niedermeyer's parents had 15 children and 100 grandchildren, and Ed and Catherine Ferguson eight children: Michael, Cathleen, Margaret (Peggy), Thomas, Patrick, Mary Elizabeth, Joan (deceased), and Kieran. They also have 28 grandchildren (as of May '92). Cathleen Ferguson Barron currently a parishioner, carried on the tradition by having nine

children of her own with Jeff Barron (no relation to Hibernia Bank Barrons): Damian, Anne Marie, Patrick, Dominic, Michael, Jeffrey, Rachael, John and Matthew.

PEALING OF THE BELLS NOW SILENCED
BELLS HAVE BEEN TRADITIONALLY CALLED
VOX DEO (THE VOICE OF GOD).

Ed Ferguson lived on East 11th Avenue near Holy Rosary in the 1920s, and remembers the the tolling of the bell, which hung from a bell tower standing near the side exit of the church now occupied by the parking lot. A Dominican brother rang the bell, fifteen minutes and again five minutes before the beginning of Mass. Portland later passed a city ordinance outlawing bells, and the tower, being in need of repairs anyway, was dismantled. But Ed remembers it well. He could hear it from home. Asked what he liked most about Holy Rosary, where he's been a member for over 70 years: "It's more of a home to me. I get warm thoughts of my grandmother, and the bell, and coming to pray at Holy Rosary gives me a feeling of contentment. It is home."

"No man is an island, entire of itself; every man is a piece of the continent, a part of the main…any man's death diminishes me, because I am involved in mankind; and therefore never send to know for whom the bell tolls; it tolls for thee."

John Donne[54]

ED FERGUSON'S STORY ABOUT THE VAGABOND

Ed recounts a story he heard from his aunt. One Sunday, Father Joseph Damien O'Brien, O.P., was on the pulpit giving a sermon. A short, wiry, sometimes snappish Irishman, occasionally a little brusque in his communications with others, Father O'Brien observed an inebreated local character – a Mr. Hughes – with long, flowing white hair, pose upon the floor of the vestibule. Mr. Hughes then sashayed down the center aisle to the horrified stares of the congregation. When he reached the altar rail, he threw open his arms and loudly proclaimed: "I am Jesus Christ!" to the wide-eyed gaze of Father O'Brien and the stunned silence of the congregation. Father O'Brien yelled to the ushers, "Get this man out of here."

The discombobulated Father O'Brien, in turning to leave the pulpit, slipped and fell on the steps before the altar, landing with his Dominican habit wrapped around his legs. A parishioner, Mr. Delahunty, a few pews back chuckled in a deep, audible voice, "Ha, ha, ha" no doubt happy to see Father taken down a peg. Father O'Brien arose, straightened out his clothing, returned to the middle of the altar, faced the shocked congregation and declared: "He who laughs last laughs best." The congregation broke up in laughter, and Mass proceeded.

MR. DELAHUNTY'S WILL

Though Mr. Delahunty's "Ha, ha, ha" may give one the impression that he was somewhat insensitive, it is likely that he and Father O'Brien were close enough so that his chuckles were mutually understood male banter. It is undoubtedly true that Mr. Delahunty and his wife both loved Holy Rosary, as indicated in this letter from the pastor, Father Thomas A. Feucht, O.P., to The Very Reverend Joseph J. Fulton, O.P., Dominican Provincial, dated March 4, 1955:[55]

If you recall we spoke of a will coming our way when you were here. Mr. Delahunty left $375,000.00, one hundred thousand going to relatives but the remainder, about $275,000, to be divided. Holy Rosary School will get 1/36 and then another 1/12th, half of which is to be used for students studying for the priesthood from Holy Rosary, the other half to educate the children of the parish. In all we figure the total amount coming to us will be about $30,000. A tidy little sum. His wife left $2,100 to the Church.

Father Joseph Damian O'Brien, O.P.

REV. THOMAS JOSEPH PAUL HENRY, O.P., FOURTH PRIOR OF HOLY ROSARY 1899-1903

Father Henry was born September 10, 1863 at Linden, California and was received as a postulant on January 25, 1889, and was admitted to the novitiate May 5, 1890. He took his solemn profession September 23, 1894 and was ordained December 21, 1895. He became vicar at Portland in 1899, and died July 31, 1919 at age 55.

THE FIRST CHOIR AT HOLY ROSARY

When Holy Rosary was celebrating its Golden Jubilee, this item appeared in the April 2, 1944 edition of the *Parish Digest*:

On the occasion of the dedication of the church, the singing for the Mass was provided by the Choir of Immaculate Heart Parish, under the direction of Professor Millner of Portland High School. Professor Millner borrowed the organ from Immaculate Heart Church, and brought it to Holy Rosary in an express wagon, because Holy Rosary had no organ at that time. Mr. J. F. Barron presented the first organ to our church.

Following is the first choir, 1894: Father Warren, director; Mamie Rice (Carroll), organist; Father Breen, Father O'Connor, Lizzie Sharkey (Heeran); Sadie Sharkey (Striker); Josephine Mahoney; Jennie Munk (Hayes); Nora Sullivan; Mr. Dave Morris; John Sharkey; Frank Sinnott.

The first High Mass sung by our choir took place on Easter Sunday, March 25, 1894. The choir sang the Aloys Wuerth Mass in C and the M. Labat Regina Coeli.
The choir was augmented at times by singers from other districts of the city. Among these were: Mrs. John Burnes, Nell McEntee (Eilers), Amanda Zan Coman, Mrs. Colton and Mrs. Hogan. Mrs. John Burnes was director when Father Warren was called to other duties. Succeeding directors in order were: Mr. E. C. Masten, Prof. Lucien Becker and Mr. John J. Darby.

Other choir members at this time (identified in the April 23, 1944 Parish Digest): *Dr. Walker (bass), Mabel Waller (contralto), Kathleen Walsh (soprano), Leo White (bass), Mrs. R.S. Whitmore (soprano), Jack Wildman (tenor), Ben Winneman (bass) and Dom. Zan (bass).*

1894 PARISHIONERS WHO SURVIVED TO CELEBRATE OUR GOLDEN JUBILEE[56]
The Parich Digest dated March 19, 1944 honored the following jubilarians who had remained with the parish for over 50 years. This additional biographical information was furnished in the March 26, and April 2, 1944 editions of the Digests.

MRS. MARY BACCARICH was born of James Crine and Mary McDonald in Seefin, Ireland. She was married to Frank Baccarich at Astoria, Oregon, by Father Dermond, and moved to Holy Rosary in 1894. Mrs. Baccarich has two sons, John and George, and two daughters, Margaret and Theresa. She is a member of the Altar Society.

MISS KATHERINE DOWD, a native of Portland, was born of James Dowd and Katherine Hurley. Her three sisters are Miss Agnes Dowd, Mrs. Charles Wentworth, and Miss Frances Dowd. She has one brother, Thomas Dowd. Since moving to Holy Rosary, in 1892, Miss Dowd has been a member of the Rosarians, the choir, the Rosary Confraternity and the Altar Society. At present she is the treasurer of the Altar Society.

MRS. HARRY HAYES (JENNIE E. MUNK), is a native of Portland, born in the territory of Holy Rosary Parish of James H. Munk and Teresa Goodman. She has a brother and a sister deceased, Edwin J. and Maud, and a brother and a sister living, Annie T. Woodruff and John C. Munk. Mrs. Hayes was married at Holy Rosary Church in 1918. She is a member of the Altar Society and taught Sunday School in Holy Rosary before the Sisters came.

MR. HARRY HAYES. Canadian by birth, Mr. Hayes is the son of John Hayes and Mary Foskin of Dundas in the Province of Ontario. Of his two sisters, one, Mrs. Annie Hughes is deceased, and the other, Mrs. Henry Hellendorn, is a member of Holy Rosary Parish. Mr. Hayes came to Holy Rosary in 1890 and has lived here continually except for his time of service in Manila during the Spanish American War. In 1918 he married Jennie E. Munk at Holy Rosary.

MISS ELIZABETH MCMAHAN is a native of Portland. Her parents were Michael Joseph McMahan and Elizabeth Burke. Her family includes two brothers living, Joseph and Frank, and four sisters deceased, Madeline, Alice, Marguerite and Mary. Miss McMahan is a member of the Rosary Confraternity, the Altar Society and the choir.

MR. FRANK MCMAHAN was born in Adams, Mass., of Michael Joseph McMahan and Elizabeth Burke. He has a brother and a sister living, Joseph and Elizabeth, and [four] sisters deceased, Alice, Marguerite, Mary [and Madeline]. His family moved into the territory of Holy Rosary Parish in 1882. In 1915 in Holy Rosary Church he married Mary Josephine Riel. Mr. McMahan was a member of the old choir, and is at present a member of the Holy Name Society.

MRS. BENJAMIN NEER was born in Youngstown, Ohio, the daughter of David Morris and Rebecca Williams. Her brothers and sisters are: Sister Mary Amata, O.P., Mrs. Minnie Jones, Mrs.

May Schoenfeldt, Myrtle Morris, Lina Morris, and Arthur Morris. Mrs. Neer came to what is now Holy Rosary Parish in 1886; she married Benjamin H. Neer in 1899. Her daughter Marion is now Mrs. Frank L. Mariman.

MRS. CARLOTTA O'CONNOR was born in Napa Vine, Washington, the daughter of James H. MacDonald and Mary Jane Cutting. She has one brother, Henry D. MacDonald, and four sisters: Katherine and Isabelle Mac Donald, Mrs. Marian Donohoe and Mrs. Agnes Mattingly. Married to Michael O'Connor at Napa Vine, she came to Holy Rosary as a June bride in 1894. Her children are: Muriel (Sister Merwina, of the Holy Names Sisters), Ronald C., Raymond M., Carlotta A., Vincent K., John Malcom, Thomas Claude, and Margaret Mary. Mrs. O'Connor is a member of the Rosary Confraternity and the Third Order of St. Dominic, and was president of the Altar Society for eight years.

MRS. MARY SCHOENFELDT was born at Youngstown, Ohio, the daughter of David Morris and Rebecca Williams. Her brothers and sisters are: Sister Mary Amata, O.P., Mrs. Minnie Jones, Mrs. Benjamin Neer, Myrtle Morris, Lina Morris, and Arthur Morris. Mrs. Schoenfeldt came to the district of Holy Rosary in 1886; she married Charles Schoenfeldt in 1898. Her son is Arthur Morris Schoenfeldt. Before the Sisters came, Mrs. Schoenfeldt taught Sunday school.

MRS. SARAH SHEEHY is a native of County Clare, Ireland. Her parents were John Hogan and Mary Smith. She was married at Old Saint Mary's Cathedral to James Sheehy, and moved to Holy Rosary in 1892. Her children are: Marguerite, Robert, and James and Colonel Wyville Sheehy, U.S.A. Mrs. Sheehy is a member of the Rosary Confraternity, the Altar Society, and the Third Order of St. Dominic. Her brothers and sisters are: John, Michael, James and Timothy, Bridget, Margaret, two Marys, Norah, Anna, Kate, Agnes, and Josephine.

MRS. MARGARET TRACY was born in Decatur, Illinois, daughter of Dennis Corcoran and Bridget Degin. She has one brother, William Corcoran, and one sister, Elizabeth. Married to Edward Tracy in the old Cathedral (Third and Stark Streets), she came to Holy Rosary in 1891. Mrs. Tracy is a member of the Altar Society (of which she was president for ten years), the Rosary Confraternity and the Third Order of St. Dominic. She has been a member of the Sewing Circle for over 30 years.

MRS. AGNES WINNEMAN, daughter of James Sweeney and Mary Orr, was born in Steubenville, Ohio. She has one brother, Charles Sweeney. Mrs. Winneman came to Holy Rosary in 1895; her husband was the late Bernard H. Winneman. Mrs. Winneman has served as a member of the Altar Society and is also a member of the Rosary Confraternity.

Notes to the Text

27 The word "conventual" simply denotes a church which is not a parish church, but more a monastery for monastic or religious life, and is distinguished by "community living" as opposed to "solitary living."

28 Though speculation has since surfaced that anti-Catholicism was involved, the writer found no evidence of it; but it is quite true that anti-Catholic organizations were active and many people in the general population mistrusted or hated Catholics. As for the erection of churches in the area, the following notice appeared on page 8 of The Oregonian dated July 13, 1893: "The United Presbyterian Church of the East Side has just let the contract for the erection of a church building on its lots in Holladay's Addition, on Grand Avenue and Wasco Street. The structure will be frame and will cost when completed about $5,000." Also, the Holy Rosary Church bulletin of January 9, 1944 declared: "When the work of construction [of Holy Rosary] was nearly completed, the first obstacle was encountered, in the shape of an ordinance forbidding the erection of a church or public building in that section."

29 Union Avenue has since been renamed Martin Luther King Boulevard in honor of the renowned black civil rights leader.

30 Numbers are transposed; correct number is #119.

31 Church and rectory were erected on Block #68. Fr. Agius sold Block #67, south of #68, to Mr. Lloyd of Lloyd Center, who sold it to the Upjohn Company, which now occupies it.

32 As earlier reported, the Dominicans were to receive the land free but, apparently, when the two-blocks-for-one transaction took place, the Dominicans received free only the one block promised (which turned out to be #68, the church block) and agreed to pay Archbishop Gross for the second (i.e. adjoining block #67, which was first used for a baseball field, then in 1946 was sold to the Lloyd Corp. which, in turn, sold it to the Upjohn Company, the present owner).

33 Correct spelling is "Noon."

34 In all likelihood he was Father Gregory Joseph Rourke, O.P., the Provincial Procurator at the time.

35 Contained in the archives of Holy Rosary Parish.

36 Several factual errors occur in the original article, replaced here with brackets containing the correct information.

37 Now the feast day of Dominican Saint and "Angelic Doctor" Thomas Aquinas (1225-1274).

38 Mr. Deane designed the buildings as well.

39 Contained in Provincial Archives, Oakland, California.

40 Holladay's name would frequently be misspelled "Holliday."

41 Father Peter Alphonse Riley, O.P., who was Prior of St. Dominic's at the time and later served at Holy Rosary 1915-1924.

42 Thomas Lawrence Breen, O.P.

43 As told to the author by Father Charles Hess, O.P. Provincial Archivist, Oakland, California.

44 Copied from the original on file in the Archives of the Western Dominican Province, Oakland, California.

45 Quoted from page 99, *Defender of the Faith, The History of the Catholic Sentinel 1870-1990*, by Wilfred P. Schoenberg, S.J., Oregon Catholic Press, Portland, Oregon, 1993.

46 page 101, ibid.

47 Page 51-53, *Suicide of the West* by James Burnham, 1964.

48 Page 74, *Suicide of the West*.

49 page 86, ibid.

50 page 104, ibid.

51 page 102, ibid.

52 From page 1, Col. 5, *Catholic Sentinel*, November 1, 1923, reporting on the death of Michael G. Munly.

53 Edward Michael Munly Ferguson died at age 72 on October 22, 1993. A concelebrated Mass of Christian Burial, held Monday, October 25 at Holy Rosary, was attended by hundreds who loved him, including this author, in a fitting send-off to a great and good man.

54 Devotions upon Emergent Occasions [1624], John Donne.

55 On file in the Dominican archives, Oakland, California.

56 The author expresses sincere gratitude to Father Arthur Morris Schoenfeldt, CSC, now at the University of Portland, for providing the long-lost Parish Digests quoted here and in Chapter 10 of this book. See entry for his mother, Mrs. May Schoenfeldt, a Golden Jubilarian which follows.

57 This was obviously meant to mean the geographical area, since the church was not opened until 1894.

58 Marriages were not allowed at Holy Rosary until it became a parochial (i.e. parish) church in February 1908. The first couple married at Holy Rosary Church – on 29 June 1908 – were Stephen J. Riordan and Grace M. Conlon, parents of parishioner Mary Riordan Boland, spouse of Francis Boland. Father Albert Sadoc Lawler, O.P., the pastor, officiated.

59 The same Father Arthur Schoenfeldt, CSC, University of Portland, who furnished the 1944 bulletins from Holy Rosary, from which information on the jubilarians is here quoted.

Archbishop Alexander Christie (right) with Father Henry Humbert Kelly, O.P., Pastor/Prior of Holy Rosary (circa 1913).

CHAPTER

5

1901-1910

HOLY ROSARY BECOMES A PARISH
WAS IT WON IN A POKER GAME?

Holy Rosary started out as a conventual church – a mission – as mentioned in the preceding chapter. Fifty years later, on the occasion of Holy Rosary's Golden Jubilee, Father C. V. Lamb, O.P., who had left Holy Rosary in 1913 after nine years of service, would be quoted in the Parish Digest of February 6, 1944 as follows:

The Holy Father himself [Honorius III] gave St. Dominic's priests the title of Preachers, giving the Order the privilege that was formerly reserved to bishops. When we came here [to Portland] it was therefore understood that we would not take care of a parish, but would be a mission to assist the people and parishes by preaching and hearing confessions and promoting devotions, especially the Rosary. But the Archbishop and his priests thought it best for us to accept a parish, and so, to please them, our superiors agreed. Without relinquishing any of our rights as a missionary church, we assumed the obligations of a parish, in 1909.[60]

BISHOP LEIPZIG'S INTERESTING MEMORANDUM
The following memorandum, written by retired Bishop Francis Leipzig and contained in the files of the Archdiocese of Portland, points to the beginnings of our history as a "parish."

FORMATION OF THE DOMINICAN PARISH – HOLY ROSARY, PORTLAND OREGON
Originally a priory for many years after it was established in the [18]'90s. Father William Daly, pastor of Immaculate Heart, was called out frequently on sick calls to that area whereas the people attended services at the Priory.[61] On one occasion Father Daly was called during the night to bring the sacraments to a very ill woman. Next to the candle in the sick room he saw a picture of a Dominican priest, possibly Father O'Brien. By accident Father Daly knocked the picture off the table and was very much embarrassed. Here was a woman who never went near Immaculate Heart but always went to the Dominican's Priory, but on the other hand, when she needed the sacraments the pastor of Immaculate Heart was called. So in thinking the incident over the next day he went up to Archbishop Christie and felt there should be some geographic parish lines established. That was a reason no doubt, that Holy Rosary Parish was established. So instead of being just a priory for the Dominican Fathers, it became a parish. (This from Monsignor Murnane).

POLITICS, POKER AND HOLY ROSARY PARISH

Father Lawrence E. "NBA" Banfield, O.P., who once coached kids in basketball at Holy Rosary School (see Chap. 10), and who is still today a dynamic speaker on the Dominican Preaching Band, has served the Western Dominican Province for many years.[62] A tall, lean, vigorous, crafty, and witty silver fox, and raconteur of great renown, he relates "the rest of the story" (of our becoming a parish) as told to him by diocesan priest friends who were alive at the turn of the century, and with whom he also played poker.

It seems that a group of diocesan priests customarily relaxed Sunday evenings playing a little poker when, one night, one of them, (Father William Daly?), was called away from the game to bring the sacraments to a woman – thus interrupting the game. Upon returning to the game, he said words to the effect: "We're going to have to do something about those Dominicans; they'll have to take on a greater share of the workload. I'm going to talk to the archbishop about this."

Call it coincidence if you will, but here is a quote from Father Schoenberg's great book[63] partly describing Portland's Archbishop Alexander Christie and his leisure pursuits:

"...Tall and rangy, impressive and orotund of address, with pawky humor, he was more at ease with his priests taking innocent (or perhaps not so innocent) delight in cheating a bit at poker and purloining any loose cigars that might be around. A man's man. The severance of Baker [Diocese] from his sheepfold doubtlessly caused him tears of anguish..."

DID OUR BLESSED MOTHER INTERVENE?

Was His Excellency at the poker game that night when Father Daly was called away, thus disrupting the game? Was the decision to make Holy Rosary a parish a done deal before the cards of the last hand were dealt? Perhaps Our Blessed Mother paid a brief visit to the game on our behalf that night, motivated by a profound and tender concern for us, and gave the gamblers food for thought in full knowledge that we, her future lost sheep, would be in dire need of a good parish after the Vatican II conclave! Maybe we actually won Holy Rosary Parish in a poker game; it would certainly be a scintillating expression of Mary's love for us! No matter how the deal was struck, we have to consider it a great stroke of good fortune for the future parishioners of Holy Rosary.

HIGH DRAMA SURROUNDED ESTABLISHMENT OF HOLY ROSARY AS A PARISH – A POST-POKER GAME GAMBIT?

But the narrative history behind our becoming a parish has another delightfully interesting twist; and it goes to show that a man who cheats at poker, no matter how innocently, bears watching! On this occasion, His Grace "pushed the envelope

too far" as the saying goes. On February 23, 1905, Archbishop Christie, then serving his seventh year over the metropolitan see, like a confident Catholic holding four aces, wrote a letter in his own hand to Very Rev. Pius Murphy, O.P., Holy Rosary's Founding Father who, at this point in time, was serving as Provincial of the Province. Archbishop Christie's letter, really a rather grim ultimatum, is quoted as follows:

Dear Rev. Father:
The large number of Catholics in the vicinity of your church in Portland makes it necessary to establish a parish and also a parish school. I subjoin the action taken by our Diocesan Consultors regarding the establishing of this parish.

EXTRACT FROM COUNCIL PROCEEDINGS:
*In regard to the Rev. Dominican Fathers in Portland, it is the consensus of the Council that the Most. Rev. Archbishop write the Very Rev. Provincial of the Dominican Fathers in California, and again request him to accept a parish and build a school **and, if he does not accept this, to write to another Religious Order to accept this offer.** —from the Council held Feb 16, 1905.*

*You would have the best parish in Portland in a very short time. **You understand that in accepting this parish you will be governed by the statutes of the Archdiocese; and, therefore, conform to all diocesan laws and regulations: the same in fact as all other parishes in the Archdiocese.***

I would be pleased to have you visit Portland and see for yourself what a splendid parish you would have if you accept our offer.

However, if you cannot come, please inform me, as soon as possible, what you intend doing regarding this proposition.

The time is at hand when we must take action and establish this parish.

Asking God to bless you, I am yours very truly in Christ –
[emphases added]
                                                    +A. Christie

The Dominicans had been operating independently of the chancery for 11 years, in accordance with a prior agreement made with Archbishop Christie's predecessor, Archbishop Gross, "under the constitutions, rules and regulations of the Order of Preachers founded by St. Dominic" as stipulated in the Articles of Incorporation of Holy Rosary (see Chap. 4). So Archbishop Christie's new initiative fundamentally altered that prior agreement.

The Archbishop's mandate having been duly noted, the Dominicans' displeasure likely proceeded through the stages of curiosity, outrage, sorrow, triumph and finally merriment as they presented their response to this usurpation (and expressed threat by the Archbishop to have them either comply with his wishes or be replaced by another religious order). The Dominicans' response would take almost three years but, backed by Rome with a Beneplacitum,[64] would consummate a final agreement far different from that proposed by Archbishop Christie.

Though the archbishop wrote the music to the song they would ultimately sing together, the Dominicans wrote the words. Quoted here are the final articles of agreement approved by the Dominican Master General and the Sacred Congregation for Religious Affairs in the Vatican dated February 15, 1908:[65]

FINAL ARTICLES OF AGREEMENT REACHED BETWEEN DOMINICANS AND ARCHBISHOP CHRISTIE

Entered into the fifteenth day of February of the year nineteen hundred eight by the Most Rev. Alexander Christie, D.D., Archbishop of Oregon City and the Very Rev. Arthur Laurence McMahon, O.P., Vicar General of the Dominican Congregation of California.

Whereas the Most. Rev. Alexander Christie, Archbishop of Oregon City desires the Community of Holy Rosary, belonging to the Dominican Congregation of California, and canonically established in the City of Portland, Oregon, to accept the care of a parish to be described below and to be known as the parish of Holy Rosary.

And whereas the Dominican Community of the Holy Rosary possesses a conventual church which the Most. Rev. Alexander Christie, Archbishop of Oregon City desires shall serve as the church of the parish offered, and enjoys all the canonical rights, and privileges of exemption in the administration of its property, that are peculiar to canonically erected communities of regulars.

It is agreed between the Most. Rev. Alexander Christie, Archbishop of Oregon City, and the Very Rev. Arthur Laurence McMahon, O.P., Vicar General of the Dominican Congregation of California that

*1. In accepting the parish offered by Archbishop Christie, **the Dominican Community of the Holy Rosary shall in no way surrender its canonical rights, and privileges of exemption in the administration of this property and shall continue to enjoy, uncontrolled as at present, all the revenues of the church to which the parish is to be annexed.***

*2. It is agreed that **in lieu of a percentage of the revenues of the church** to be paid to the Archbishop of Oregon City as a cathedraticum, **such as is paid by the administrators of churches that are merely parochial, there shall be given for diocesan purposes, an annual donation on a basis of fifty cents for every family in the parish** (emphases added).*

3. It is agreed that the Dominican Fathers of the Holy Rosary Community in the administration of this parish, shall in all other respects be governed by the diocesan laws; and, specifically, that they shall render to the Most Rev. Archbishop of Oregon City, yearly or whenever required, an account of the spiritual administration of this parish and that they shall announce and take up in their church the usual diocesan collections as ordered by the Archbishop.

4. It is agreed that, until such a time as the Catholic population East of Sixteenth Street, North, in the City of Portland, shall increase to such an extent as to warrant the formation of a new parish in that section of the City, and the erection of a new parish church in the neighborhood of Twenty Eighth Street, the limits of the parish of the Holy Rosary shall be as follows: Sullivan's Gulch from the Eastern City boundary line to the Willamette River; the Willamette River to Tillamook Street; Tillamook Street to Union Avenue North; Union Avenue North to Eugene Street; Eugene Street to East Seventh Street North; East Seventh Street North to Thompson Street; Thompson Street to the Eastern City boundary line; Eastern City boundary line to Sullivan's Gulch: but that the increase of Catholic population East of Sixteenth Street North shall warrant the formation of a new parish in that section of the City, the Eastern boundary line shall be Sixteenth North. The establishing of the new parish east of Sixteenth Street to be left to the judgment of the Archbishop of Oregon City.
Signed in duplicate at Portland, this fifteenth day of Feb., 1908.

> *[signed}* *[signed]*
> *Archbishop Christie* *Arthur Laurence McMahon, O.P.*
> *Archbishop of Oregon City* *Vic. Gen. Calif.*

In accordance with the above articles of agreement, I hereby give over to the Dominican Community of the Holy Rosary the parish of the Holy Rosary in the City of Portland.
Signed in duplicate at Portland this fifteenth day of Feb., 1908.

> *[signed]*
> *Archbishop Christie*
> *Archbishop of Oregon*

In accordance with the above articles of agreement, I hereby accept for the Dominican Community of the Holy Rosary, the parish of the Holy Rosary.

> *[signed]*
> *Arthur Laurence McMahon*
> *Vic. Gen. Calif.*
> *Signed in duplicate at Portland this fifteenth day of Feb., 1908.*
> *[Archbishop's Seal]*

So, in this final hand of poker, the Dominicans held an unbeatable royal high straight flush to Archbishop Christie's four aces and, no doubt, their gratitude would match archdiocesan gloom over this whole affair.

ARCHBISHOP CHRISTIE'S BACKGROUND

Ed "Van" Vancoelen, now age 93, an acolyte for the archbishop at morning Masses at the Cathedral, described Archbishop Christie as a holy man. Archbishop Alexander Christie, D.D., stood about 6' 6" tall, was very imposing and very dignified. He invited Van to join him for breakfast after each Mass, and he told Van, then a youngster, that he should always wear a collar and tie. Van, who lived in Holy Rosary rectory in those days, recalls that the Archbishop also regularly came to Holy Rosary for confession.

According to Holy Rosary Parish administrator Richard Unger, whose father was Archbishop Christie's chauffeur, the archbishop had been a Shakespearean actor before he converted to Catholicism late in life; further, he had been a priest for only five years before becoming a prelate. So to some degree the archbishop's inexperience, combined with his artistic temperament, touches on this high theater. Had he greater knowledge and understanding of Church administration – and perhaps a little less flair for the dramatic – he might not have acted in such a peremptory manner on the advice of his "Diocesan Consultors." It is not as though he were dealing with a new and inexperienced "order of regulars." The Dominicans are the *"first religious order properly so called [they were established in 1216]…The Friars Preachers were…[and still are] an army of priests, organised under a Master-General in provinces, and ready to go wherever…needed, without any obligations of stability to this house or that, owing their stability, not to any particular house, but to the order and will of their superior"*[66] [one reason we discover our own parish priests gone for weeks on end, sometimes to different continents]. In short, the Archbishop's direct threat to the Dominicans' mission in the City of Roses was the equivalent of David taking on Goliath, with Goliath holding the slingshot. The final resolution to his unfortunate course of action must have caused him considerable consternation and embarrassment. Unger said that, during his later years as archbishop, he was practically paranoid about signing papers.

PARISHIONER NAMED KNIGHT OF ST. GREGORY BY POPE PIUS XI

Mrs. Anna Gertrude Miller Morris, now a youthful 93, became a member of Holy Rosary with her parents in 1902, and she recalls Father Lawler as "a wonderful man." Gertrude's father, John P. Miller, a German immigrant, came to Portland in the 1890s and couldn't get work because businesses in general would not hire Catholics; nevertheless, he eventually got into the lumber and building business and built many of the Catholic churches in the Portland area, for which work he was named a Knight of St. Gregory by Pope Pius XI in 1923. They lived three blocks from Halsey and two blocks from the river in the area now occupied by the Memorial Coliseum.

Gertrude's mother, an immigrant from Luxembourg, like her father, was a devout Catholic and, long after Gertrude and her three brothers and two sisters grew up, whenever the sons and daughters visited their parents' house, their mother insisted that they all kneel in the kitchen (dirty dishes or no) and pray the Rosary before leaving for their own homes.

Gertrude moved from the parish to Milwaukie in 1912 but retained fond memories of Holy Rosary and Fathers Lawler, O'Brien, and Shaw whom she described as wonderful priests. She referred to Father Agius as a "honey" and said, in later years, she attended one of his retreats at McKenzie Bridge.

First Pastor/Prior Albert Sadoc Lawler, O.P.

HOLY ROSARY RECTORY RAISED TO STATUS OF PRIORY

The Centenary[67] edition of the *Catholic Sentinel* contains the following:

Holy Rosary was established as a parish, in the charge of the Dominican Fathers, in February, 1908, by Most Reverend Archbishop Christie. The first pastor was Very Rev. A.G. Lawler, O.P., who has been a local superior since 1903. Early in 1909, the local house was raised to the dignity of a priory, with Father Lawler as the first prior. The community had received sufficient members for the choral recitation of the Divine Office and other community exercises, hence the change in status.

So in 1909 Holy Rosary became the first Dominican Parish and Priory in the Northwest. It would remain a Priory until 1935, when it was again reduced to the status of a house due to the diminished presence of priests [caused most likely by the closure of Aquinas School and the departure of those priest-teachers from the priory].

ROSARY SUNDAY PROCESSION
A GLORIOUS TRADITION AT HOLY ROSARY

Holy Rosary Sunday has long been a tradition at Holy Rosary, celebrated by a procession of priests, nuns, parishioners, and children, all decked out in their "Sunday best" around one or more city blocks, praying the Rosary led by the pastor.

OTHER HOLY ROSARY ACTIVITIES AND
TRADITIONS IN THE EARLY 1900S

Becoming a parish and priory were not the only church happenings in the early 1900s. Numerous activities and traditions were established, many still in practice today.

Rosary Sunday procession (c. 1914) led by Fathers Lawler and Kelly.

The interior of the Holy Rosary Church as it appeared around 1914.

HOLY ROSARY DOMINICAN MISSIONARIES
RIDE THE RAILS IN THE FIRST CHAPEL CARS

On May 10, 1869, officials hammered in the "golden spike" joining the Central Pacific and Union Pacific railroads at Promontory, Utah, marking the completion of the transcontinental railroad. Within 10 years, Father Francis Kelly of the Catholic Church Extension Society would convert 72-foot-long Pullman cars into chapel cars, with built-in altars and pews capable of seating 50-65 people; amenities included sleeping quarters, a kitchen and dining room for the priests. The Catholic Church Extension Society spearheaded this innovative method of reaching remote settlements with these "messengers of light and love." Archbishop Christie was an enthusiastic supporter of this Catholic outreach effort, and several priests from Holy Rosary rode the rails. Unfortunately, the specific efforts expended by the Dominicans at Holy Rosary were not found by this author; however, a note contained in the provincial archives [from Holy Rosary Prior Arthur Townley, O.P. to the Provincial, Father McMahon] said: *Fr. McDevitt... is going to the Chapel Car.* On page six, section 3 of the 90th Anniversary of the Catholic Sentinel, dated October 6, 1960, in an article entitled "Holy Rosary Church Center For Dominican Fathers," it was noted: *Father Augustine Naselli, O.P., also brought the light of Catholic truth to remote regions from a railroad chapel car.*

HOLY ROSARY DOMINICANS
SERVED CONVENT OF THE GOOD SHEPHERD

Quoted from parish bulletin dated April 23, 1944 filed in the parish archives:

Today, "Good Shepherd Sunday," so called because in the Gospel read at Mass Our Lord speaks of Himself as the Good Shepherd, brings to mind that our Golden Jubilee Year also marks the fortieth year of our service at the Sisters of the Good Shepherd.

The Sisters trace their origin back to a foundation established in 1641 at Caen, France, by Saint John Eudes: The Sisters of Our Lady of the Refuge.

The Sisters of the Good Shepherd are a branch of this Society, established at Angers in 1835 by Mother Mary Pelletier, recently canonized.

Though cloistered, the Sisters, with their industrial school, render to society a service that is highly esteemed by all who have at heart the interests of young womanhood.

In 1902, a convent of the Good Shepherd was opened here in Portland at 20th and Irvington Streets. The Dominican Fathers were given the charge of serving the spiritual needs of the institute in 1904. This charge the Fathers willingly undertook and fulfilled, even though it involved a long trek, often over snow and ice, to give the Sisters a 6:30 Mass each morning.

The present convent on North Dekum Street was opened in 1917, and the Dominican Fathers continued as chaplains. Nearly every one of the Fathers stationed at Holy Rosary has at one time or another had occasion to exercise his sacred ministry on behalf of the Sisters and girls of the Good Shepherd Convent and Saint Rose's Industrial School. All speak of this duty as a valued privilege.

This year we pray especially that in the years to come we may continue our association with this edifying community, lending a priestly hand in its noble work.

"I AM THE GOOD SHEPHERD. THE GOOD SHEPHERD
GIVETH HIS LIFE FOR HIS SHEEP"
(John: 10.11)

FIRST SACRAMENT OF CONFIRMATION AT HOLY ROSARY

According to the January 30, 1944 parish bulletin, recounting the history of the parish: Following are the names of those who received the Sacrament of Confirmation at its first administration in Holy Rosary Church, June 24, 1909, by the Most Reverend Archbishop Christie:

THE BOYS: *William Lansing, S. Laidlaw, James Joseph Sheehy, Bernard Eugene Niedermeyer, Wyville John Sheehy, Raymond Francis Delahunt, James Francis Keating, Robert E. Joseph Manning, Clement John Sharkey, Lawrence George O'Halloran, John Walter Fish, James Daniel Doyle, Bernard James Esch, Percival Lawrence Brown, Frederick W. Walter Schade, Gerald Hubert Conway, Cyril Alfred Niedermeyer, Frederick Joseph Niedermeyer, Raymond Vincent Johnson, Thomas Burke Calvin, Henry James Hawley, Graham Patrick Sharkey, Reuben Robert Smith, William Aloysisu Kennedy, Frank Benedict Wochinck, Edward Timothy Hogan.*

THE GIRLS: *Elizabeth Mary Helen Hawley, Cecilia Veronica Wochinck, Olivetter Cecilia Fleury, Mary Veronica Lavin, Evelyn Catherine Cecilia Keating, Beatrice Damien O'Brien, Muriel Aurelia Genevieve O'Connor, Grace Frances Sweeney, J. L. Frances Bonneau, Hazel Virginia Johnson, Julia Veronica Keeney, Margaret Mary Tierney, Catherine Laurencia Southard, Julia Anna Cosgrove, Virginia Agnes Brown, Madeline Rose Brown, Lucille Isabella Delahunt, Margaret M. Cecilia Maginnis, Mabel Catherine Hughes, Blanche Catherine Kennedy, Mary Agatha White, Celeste Catherine Smith, Josephine Andrina Hoben, Pearl E. Cecilia Williams, Celonise Anna De Grandpre, Marion Catherine Martin, Nellie Anastasia Glennon, Elizabeth Catherine Hogan, Frances Mary Corbett.*

THE SPONSORS: *For the boys: Mrs. M. J. Munly and Mr. D.A. Morris; for the girls: Mrs Mary Munly and Rebecca Morris.*

Sponsor David A. Morris

CHANGES IN THE CHURCH COMPLETED

The Catholic Sentinel of May 14, 1908 reported (on page 5):
The concrete wall in front of the church has just been completed, while in the Sanctuary may be seen hand-carved brackets for the statues of St. Dominic and St. Thomas, and new candlesticks for the High Altar.

A program found in the archives of Holy Rosary lists the following activities and parishioners partaking in the Rosary Sunday Procession of October 6, 1907.

Cross bearer...R. Sheehy
Acolytes.................................John Barry and John Lavin
Rosary Banner..A. Sweeney
Tassels...........................John Sheehy & Jas. Maginnis
Altar Boys

Banners of the Five Joyful Mysteries
Miss K. Dowd, Marshall

1. Annunciation.....................................Irene Sweeney
   Children in white
2. Visitation..Miss Nita Philip
   Children in white
3. Nativity.......................................Miss Frances Houck
   Children in white
4. Presentation...............................Miss Frances Schade
   Young Ladies of the Rosary Confraternity and Junion Rosarians in white.
5. Finding in the Temple.......................... Miss C. Higgins
   Senior Rosarians and others in white.

SECOND DIVISION
Mrs. E. Tracy, Marshall
Banners of the Five Sorrowful Mysteries

1. Agony...Miss Florence O'Brien
   Ladies of the Third Order of St. Dominic
2. Scourging.......................................Miss Grace Sweeney
   Ladies Altar Society
3. Crowning with Thorns..........................Miss M. Sheehy
4. Carriage of the Cross....................Miss M. McMahon
   Ladies of the Rosary Confraternity
5. Crucifixion...................................Miss Mamie Dunn
   Ladies of the Rosary Confraternity and others

FIRST HOLY NAME SOCIETY IN OREGON FORMED AT HOLY ROSARY

The following is quoted from a parish digest dated April 23, 1944:[71]

The first records of the Holy Name Society of the parish open with its reorganization in 1910.[72] On January 10 of that year, ten young men met in the Fathers' House. They were: Thomas Dowd, Thomas Hughs, John Lavin, Ed. Leonard, William Sheahan, Frank Sweeney, Robert Sheehy, A. Sweeney, Thomas Banzer, and Fred Donnerberg.

Discussion during the meeting centered about the principle aim of the Society: the promotion of reverence and love for the Holy Name of God.

As a special work, the group selected providing for ushers at all the Masses.

Mr. William E.P. Sheahan was unanimously elected president of the Society; Mr. Thomas Banzer, vice-president; Mr. A. Sweeney, secretary.

Father C. V. Lamb, O.P., was appointed spiritual director by the Very Rev. Father Lawler, O.P.

Appointments were made for the ushers at the Sunday Masses; the Wednesday before the first Sunday of each month was adopted as the regular meeting night; and after a brief talk on the spirit of the Society by Fr. Lamb, the meeting was adjourned.

Other members included in these first records, besides those already mentioned, are: George Donnerberg, Joe Donnerberg, Tracy Higgins, Arthur King, and Elmer Littlejohn.

Father C. V. Lamb, O.P., was appointed Spiritual Director by the Very Rev. Father Lawler, O.P.

THERE WAS NO SECOND HOLY ROSARY CHURCH IN PORTLAND

It is important at this juncture to correct an error in recorded history reported on the front page of the April 14, 1910 edition of the *Catholic Sentinel*[73] as follows: *"Dominican Fathers to build a new Holy Rosary Church, and present church to be made into a school. Present church built in 1894. The second Holy Rosary Church erected in Portland by the Dominican Fathers was dedicated by Archbishop Christie."* The Holy Rosary Church alluded to in this article was dedicated by Archbishop Christie, but it was located in Vancouver, British Columbia, not Portland. Our church today is the same one built by Father John Pius Murphy in 1894, and blessed (but not dedicated because it was considered a temporary structure) by Archbishop Gross on January 28, 1894.

Notes to the Text

60 The year was actually "1908;" since the articles of agreement were signed February 15, 1908.

61 "Mission" better describes the church & rectory; it became a priory in 1909. Prior to 1908 (when it became a parish in the proper sense) Holy Rosary was within the territorial jurisdiction of Immaculate Heart Parish. Parishioner Irene Stopper Kutcher recalls Father Daly was beloved by all. He died suddenly, right after celebrating Easter Sunday Mass in 1934; the church could not contain the multitudes who went to his funeral Mass.

62 Pastor and Prior Anthony Patalano recorded in the Sunday Bulletin of September 29, 1991: "Father Banfield was first assigned to Holy Rosary as his first assignment after he was ordained back when the earth's crust was still cooling." Poor Father Banfield gets "no respect" at Holy Rosary! But Father always gives as good as he gets, so don't feel too sorry for Father Banfield. Feel sorry for Father Anthony, who is sure to receive his comeuppance when he least expects it!

63 *A History of the Catholic Church in the Pacific Northwest – 1743-1983*, by Father Wilfred P. Schoenberg, S.J., The Pastoral Press, Washington, D.C., 1987.

64 Beneplacitum literally translated means "Well pleased . . ." In short, the Holy See was pleased with the past performance and future promise of the Dominicans in the City of Roses.

65 This same year, 1908, "The United States and England, long under the jurisdiction of the Congregation for the Propagation of the Faith as mission territories, were removed from its control and placed under the common law of the Church." See page 121, 1989, *Catholic Almanac*, Our Sunday Visitor, 200 Noll Plaza, Huntington, Indiana 46750 .

66 From *A Popular History of the Catholic Church*, by Philip Hughes, New York, N. Y.: The Macmillan Co.1947.

67 *A Supplement to the Catholic Sentinel*, Portland, Oregon, May 4, 1939, covering *100 Years of the Catholic Church in the Oregon Country*, page 24.

68 Among other things, six or more priests present are required for a mission to become a priory.

69 This author expresses sincere gratitude to Bradley Collins, Editor, The Catholic Church Extension Society, 35 East Wacker Drive, Chicago, Ill. 60601 for the material he furnished on the Chapel Cars.

70 Bishop Francis P. Leipzig wrote a book *Extension in Oregon*, contained in the archives of the Archdiocese, which gives a fairly comprehensive history of the Chapel Cars in the Pacific Northwest.

71 Vol II, No. 52.

72 Other accounts still extant and incorrect show its formation in June 1912.

73 And contained in item 1065, page 200, of *A Chronicle of the Catholic History of the Pacific Northwest 1743-1960*, by Wilfred P. Schoenberg, S.J., printed February 1962 by the Catholic Sentinel Printery at Portland in Oregon.

School days, school days,
Dear old Golden Rule days,
Readin' and 'ritin' and 'rithmetic
Taught to the tune of a hick'ry stick.
You were my queen in calico,
I was your bashful, barefoot beau,
And you wrote on my slate: "I love you Joe"
When we were a couple of kids.[74]

Holy Rosary's First School (c. 1912).

HOLY ROSARY SCHOOL

Editor's note: We here interrupt the chronological history of Holy Rosary in order to give the history of our school its own chapter.

The story is told of a fifth-grade Catholic boy sitting on a chair in a parochial school office with a cut on his leg being treated by a nun, on her knees before him, her veil concealing her face from his vantage point. He looked down and thought: This mysterious woman, ever vigilant, like my mother, so willing to heal my wounds. "Why do you do this for me, sister?" he asked, "It was my fault." She kept working. "It doesn't matter whose fault it was, Timmy," she said. She continued at her task. Even more perplexed but inquisitive, Timmy boldly asked: "Why are you a nun, sister?" This time she looked him in the eye and said: "I'm a nun so I can help you to grow up and be a strong, educated, intelligent and caring Catholic man."

No devout Catholic man or woman, whether priest, religious or lay person, doubts the profound and positive influence of the Catholic nun, who has for centuries provided to the laity the truths of the faith – to boys, girls, young adults and adults in the many classrooms of the Church Universal – helping them to grow and be strong, educated, intelligent and caring adults; no less so than that did the Apostles provide the seeds of faith to the souls of the Early Church. Indeed, a good case can be made that the departure of so many nuns from our Catholic school system in the United States, after Vatican II, caused the downturn of new vocations in the Catholic Church in America. Nuns, early on, had an uncanny knack for glimpsing future priests inside of boys and future nuns inside of girls. These holy women, by their own excellent example, wise counsel, and gentle nudging encouraged these children to seriously consider the pursuit of religious life. Evidence of their success is overwhelming.

Former Holy Rosary pastor, Father Paul Duffner, O.P., now Director of the Rosary Confraternity, who in 1990 celebrated his Golden Jubilee, attributes his own priestly vocation to the Dominican Sisters who taught him in grades one through 12 in the rural community of Jacksonville, Illinois, during and following the Great Depression.

THE DOMINICAN SISTERS OF MISSION SAN JOSE, CALIFORNIA[75]:
A community with papal approbation (1922) under the title of Queen of the Holy Rosary. In 1876, Sister Maria Pia Backes accompanied by Sister Mary Amanda Bednartz and Sister Mary Salesia Fichtner came to San Francisco, California, from Holy Cross Convent in Brooklyn, New York at the invitation of Joseph Sadoc Alemany, Dominican, and first archbishop of San Francisco. The Brooklyn community had been a foundation of the ancient convent of Holy Cross in Regensburg, Bavaria, in 1853 and during the ensuing years became the parent

community of twelve independent congregations of Dominican Sisters in the United States.

The San Francisco community, after twelve years under the jurisdiction of New York during the administration of Archbishop Patrick Riordan, became autonomous, establishing the first motherhouse in San Francisco with Mother Pia elected as first prioress general. In 1906 the motherhouse was transferred to Mission San Jose on the historic ground behind the Franciscan mission founded by Father Fermin Lasuen in 1797. Before the end of the nineteenth century the community's foundations extended from Oregon to Southern California and during the first decade of the twentieth century to Germany and Mexico. In 1907 the sisters' Constitution received the Decree of Praise from the Holy See and in 1922 final approbation.

In 1992, the community under its superior general, Sister Renilde Cade, numbered 343 professed sisters, who staff one college, six schools, 24 elementary schools and two resident institutions in the United States, ten foundations in Mexico, and one in Germany. Allied to the community's corporate ministry of Christian education are members serving the Church in adult education, parish and hospital pastoral care, college campus ministry, detention ministry, social justice ministry, social work, nursing, and internal ministries.

DOMINICAN SISTERS HEAD WEST TO CALIFORNIA – THENCE TO PORTLAND, OREGON

Mother Seraphina Maerz and four companions – Sisters Dominica Klein, Hyacintha Schneider, Ambrosia Niedermeier, and Francisca McCarthy – from this congregation came to Portland in 1888, during the tenure of Archbishop Gross. On September 3, 1888 they used the basement of St. Joseph's Church, at N.W. 15th and Couch, to teach 49 pupils. They then established and administered the new school, which opened in March 1890, and was transferred to the parish in 1893. St. Joseph's School closed in 1920 due to shifts in population; however, in the interim, the Dominican sisters also served as teachers for the first school at Immaculate Heart Parish at North Williams Avenue and Stanton Street, where they lived in St. Dominic's Convent, which housed the sisters teaching at both schools.

Since there were no bridges across the Willamette River in this area at the time, the sisters who taught at St. Joseph's took the ferry, for which there was no charge, back and forth across the river every day (journeying from Immaculate Heart to St. Joseph's and back).

HOLY ROSARY BUYS PROPERTY FOR SCHOOL

On December 9, 1911, Holy Rosary Church purchased Block 212[76] (including lots numbered 1 to 8) from the Noon Estate Company of Oregon, which was represented by its president, Emily J. Noon and its secretary, Viola Noon Currier; with John S. Rice, representing the Province: total payment for the property was $35,144.11 ($34,000 plus taxes, realtor fees, filings etc.). Located on the property was a three-story frame house with an address of 208 NE Weidler. The house, referred to thereafter as the Noon House, would be our first Holy Rosary School and, after a new school was built, a convent for the nuns who taught there.

HOLY ROSARY SCHOOL OPENS

On September 3, 1912, our school opened with 43 pupils. The first four sisters were: Sister Mary Amanda (Meyers) (1912-1917), the first principal, Sister Mary Amata (Morris) (1912-1922), who taught first and second grades, Sister Mary Seraphica (Boehm)(1913-1923), who taught third and fourth grades, and Sister Mary Loretto (Schafer)(1914-1917), who taught fifth and sixth grades. The first music teacher was Sister Mary Aloysia (McSweeney)(1912-1915), and the first "house sister" was Sister Mary Afra (Jager)(1917-1922).[77]

A contract drawn up between the sisters' Congregation of the Most Holy Rosary, Mission San Jose, California and Holy Rosary Parish stipulated that the sisters would receive a salary of "$30 a month for a year of ten months, or of $25.00 for a year of twelve months, to be paid quarterly," and "All tuition fees collected from the pupils shall be given to the Pastor. All moneys received for extras, music, painting, etc. shall be the exclusive property of the sisters." The sisters would also "be prepared to teach Sunday school and take charge of Sodalities if desired to do so by the Pastor."

In the beginning, the sisters teaching at Holy Rosary resided at their convent, St. Dominic's, on N.E. Stanton Street. It was here in 1911, in a room on the first floor of the convent, that the sisters opened Immaculata Academy, "A Day School for Girls," where many of the Holy Rosary girls completed their high school education, "with special courses in music, art, and sewing."

Dominican Sister
Emilia Aloysia Techtman, O.P.

Dominican Sister Emilia Aloysia Techtman came to Portland from Wisconsin as a child, graduated from Immaculata Academy in 1934, and entered their Dominican convent in July 1934. Now "up in years" but delightfully young at heart and quick of mind, she wears the Dominican habit as proudly today as she has over these 58 years. Today she teaches CCD at St. Therese Parish in Portland, is a writer, and one of the five Dominican Sisters of Mission San Jose (O.P.) left in Portland. She recalls the hardships suffered by the early sisters:

SISTERS WALKED TO SCHOOL – ONE HOUR EACH WAY

Before the convent was opened at Holy Rosary, they walked for about one hour each way, from St. Dominic's Convent (which opened in 1888) on NE Stanton Street to Holy Rosary, in all kinds of weather. Rain-repellent clothing was not available in those days so, when it was rainy and cold, their habits were soaked by the time they got to school. And they were so cold it almost made them cry. One of the Dominican brothers at Holy Rosary, Brother John Leo Haggerty, who was always such a hard worker, would have a crackling fire going in the school stove by the time they arrived, and they would stand around the stove and warm themselves front and back and dry their clothes before the start of class. After teaching all day, they took the long walk back home to NE Stanton.

New Holy Rosary School built in 1923, SW corner of Weidler and Third Avenue

MOTHER GENERAL FINDS THE GOING ROUGH

"One time," Sister Emilia laughs, *"Mother General Bernadina was visiting Portland and staying at the convent on NE Stanton, when she expressed the desire to visit the sisters in the classrooms at Holy Rosary School, unaware of the distance involved. After walking for a half hour, the Mother General complained of fatigue and asked whether they would have to walk all the way back. 'Yes, Mother General,' replied one of the nuns with her, 'but we don't have to teach all day like the other sisters.'*

NEW SCHOOL BUILT IN 1923

The *Catholic Sentinel*, dated August 10, 1923, contained a brief article stating that "The cornerstone of the new school [and hall] of Holy Rosary parish was laid last Sunday afternoon with Archbishop Christie officiating." Sister Emilia added that this was done in the presence of "a number of the reverend clergy" and was witnessed by "a large assemblage of parishioners and visitors."

"When the new school was built at Holy Rosary," she advised, *"the sisters turned the upper floors of the old school – the Noon House – into a convent, thus ending their daily trek to NE Stanton."* Understandably, they considered this new arrangement a little bit of heaven on earth.

PUPILS REPULSE KKK

Sister Emilia recalls that she was in the second grade (at another school in Portland) when the Ku Klux Klan surrounded Holy Rosary School, behooded in their white coneheads on horseback, a composite of the Four Horsemen of the Apocalypse. The Klucker hoodlums were bent on scaring innocent kids and their teachers. *"They were mounted on horses and had their sheets and hoods on, trying to intimidate the children."* But upper graders and brothers, John and Bill Daskalos, class of '33, would not be intimidated. Sister chuckles: *"They picked up rocks and threw them at the feet of the horses, causing the horses to rear up and almost dislodge their riders. And one of the mothers pulled the hood off the head of one of the KKK men and recognized him as her milkman."* Sister Emilia makes her well-manicured hands into a fist, and punches the air: *"The riders were soon galloping across the Broadway Bridge with the Daskalos brothers and some other Holy Rosary School kids in hot pursuit, pelting the ground with stones."*[78]

Sister continues: *"The father of the Daskalos boys was from Greece and their mother was from Ireland"* and, with this introduction, relates another humorous episode: *"One day Sister Honorata McEntee was teaching civics, and explaining the need for the police to have search warrants, when one of the Daskalos boys piped up and said, 'The police didn't have a search warrant when they raided my father's still. They walked right in and confiscated everything.' The class and later on the other sisters broke up laughing over that disclosure.*

"The Daskalos family lived in a big house on the corner of NE Weidler and Vancouver Avenue, which is still there today. Later they moved to a farm and invited all of the sisters out to the farm once a year for a big feast, which we all looked forward to with great relish."

Sister Emilia also remembers our own Father Dominic Hoffman – now in residence at Holy Rosary – when he was an Associate Pastor back in the forties and would come across the street to teach the religion class. After a few classes, he asked Sister Eileen to sit in the back of the room to keep the kids from becoming too unruly. *"He was such a gentle man, the kids took advantage of him, and he had a hard time keeping control of the class, but he knew Sister Eileen would have no trouble at all."*

On one occasion, when a new sister was assigned to the school, one of the third-grade boys said to another *"We have a new sister,"* to which the other replied: *"No. It's the same sister, only she's got a different face."* On another occasion, a new pupil, observing one of the sisters write for the first time, exclaimed in amazement: *"She writes just like we do,"* perhaps assuming that the saintly sisters suddenly appeared at the school from somewhere in outer space.

"The Happiest Years of My Life."

Sister Emilia's wholesome face responds as she evokes nostalgia; she smiles and, as she gazes into the past, a bit of moisture wells up in her twinkling eyes: *"My years at Holy Rosary from 1944 to 1950 were the happiest years of my life – we were all Dominicans – one big, happy family! Of course mowing the grass in front of the convent was not fun because of the steep grade – and we had an old push mower – but what wonderful years! When the convent closed, Father Feucht gave all of the furniture and furnishings to the sisters."* Thank you so much Sister Emilia – for everything!

Meeting Room Finished in New School

A notice in the Parish Digest of April 23, 1944 read:

The meeting room in the school building is now finished. We are especially grateful to Mr. Jake Yager, Mr. Joseph Schmitz and Mr. A. M. Jorgensen for the many hours of labor they put into making it such a really fine room – it once being unfurnished and full of all sorts of odds and ends. Drop in an see it.

Sisters Tie Tin Cans to Wedding Car

Parishioner Irene (Stopper) Kutcher tells this entertaining tale of her post-wedding activities on August 19, 1941. Irene's aunt was Sister Superior Callista (Stopper), the sister of Irene's father. In those days, according to Irene, the nuns were not permitted to attend weddings, so after she and John Kutcher were married at Blessed Sacrament Church, they drove over to Holy Rosary School so that Sister Callista could see Irene in her wedding dress. While they were in conference with Sister Callista, Sister Mary Dominic and Sister Jerome sneaked out of their classrooms, rummaged through the trash barrels, and found some tin cans which they linked together with string and tied to Irene and John's wedding car, parked on the street.

After this visitation, John and Irene drove off, the tin cans clattering over the streets and the school kids cheering, while John and Irene, convulsed in laughter, returned their friendly waves and those of the amused pedestrian onlookers, who were signaling their loving congratulations from the nearby sidewalks. Irene said it was a memorable ending to a brief visit with Sister

Callista, and proof positive that those loving nuns had a great sense of humor. Irene's husband, John, a member of the Oregon National Guard since 1934 and now called to active duty, would soon transfer to Europe via Fort Lewis, Washington and Fort Dix, New Jersey for service in World War II, with warm thoughts of a splendid wedding day, due in no small part to the sisters and kids at Holy Rosary School.

Parishioner Remembers School Days

Parishioner Jim Bobzien is tall and ramrod straight with an athletic build and a quiet, sincere, unassuming manner. This 1941 graduate (aided by his lovely wife Jacqueline) wrote the following memoir in May, 1992 about his school days at Holy Rosary:

Holy Rosary Parish School was a wonderfully small institution when I entered the fifth grade in 1937. There were about 75 students. I remember Sister Mary Dominic as our principal. I understand she is still quite busy with the Dominicans in the Bay Area (my younger sister, Mrs. Delores Huwaldt still corresponds). There were two grades in each room. I'm sure this was an interesting challenge for all the nuns. Sometimes we would get sixth grade geography in the fifth grade!

The school ground faced Second Avenue and was on quite an elevated lot. It had a few large apple trees on the perimeter, probably the remnants of an old orchard.

Our football-baseball athletic field was a block south of the church where the Upjohn Company now stands. This was a challenge for Sister Mary Dominic. She came out to the corner of Third and Halsey and rang a big brass bell at 1:00 p.m. to summon us back from lunch play a block away. When the bases were loaded, we were not too prompt in returning to school. Then we heard from one of the priests on a very threatening note.

We had a large gym/auditorium which was used day and night during rainy times. This was also a bone of contention because of the added electric bill for our late-night basketball. Father was pressed for funds in those times [in the middle of the Great Depression]. But he thought the higher costs worth it to keep us off the streets. He was, of course, right.

Father "N.B.A." Banfield [see Chapter 10] was our basketball coach; really very athletic and very good with a basketball.[79] I believe it was either Father Banfield or Father Joe Agius who determined that the fights on the school grounds would best be settled in the gym. To that end, a set of boxing gloves was acquired. By way of rule, when a scrap broke out we were marched to the gym and put on the gloves. It was good, clean fun – a few bloody noses and puffed up lips, but no lawsuits in those good old days.

Holy Rosary as a riverside school had a good ethnic base, a United Nations of Czechs, Irish, German, and Italians. Names I recall: Guenero, Oreskovich, Ligatich, Walsh, Bell, Coyle, Carovonich, Pezzel, Elich, Lennon, Frange, Erskine, Brosterhous, Renner, Lorimor, Barrett, etc. Trivia – the Renner family had a famous uncle: Lawrence Welk

Holy Rosary Hall was used for our Calaroga Club dances on Friday nights quite often. Father Joe Agius guided our football games – six-man, no pads, on hard dirt.

Father McMullen was the first pastor I recall. Father McDermott was my religious instructor and he had a profound influence on my life-long outlook in what was really important in life. His battle cry was "just be always good!" – really basic philosophy. Any old time parishioners would remember Father McDermott's booming voice when he sang "O Salutaris"[80] and "Tantum ergo" at Benediction.

Father Lindsey, a huge Irish priest, was head of the Holy Name Society. Attendance was very good once he horse-collared you. In those days, the dads and sons always attended the Holy Name Mass and had breakfast together. Quite nice!

The Dominican sisters were housed on campus in the convent on the southeast corner of Second and Weidler Streets; their convent and courtyard part of the school complex. Most of the bottom floor served as music classrooms, predominantly piano.

During the summer months I served at the 8:00 a.m. Mass quite often. It seemed like most of the other boys had jobs or were vacationing; also I lived close to the church, on First and Hassalo. I really enjoyed these opportunities because of the beautiful courtyard on the north side of the church, where the parking lot and parish center are now. It had several huge king apple trees bordering Third Street. The apples were so large that the single apple Father gave me after Mass was enough for my mother to bake a fair-sized apple pie. Gravel paths wandered through a pretty landscape of small trees, shrubs, and a flower garden to a shrine on the northeast corner of the lot. Most mornings several priests would be walking these paths reciting the Divine Office.

The interior of the church had pretty frescos painted on a semi-curved ceiling. The old main altar was quite nice with the usual old-style trappings. The most recent bell tower was removed some time ago as it was not very stable. I do miss hearing the bell toll for Mass.

As an added thought I should mention that Fathers McClory and Banfield were special to my sister Dolores Huwaldt. Father Banfield once rescued my sister from being expelled from Immaculata Academy for placing the Infant Jesus on the donkey at Christmas. Father Banfield explained to the good sisters that Jesus probably did ride a donkey so it was not a sacrilegious act.

The devoted and saintly Dominican sisters at Holy Rosary School gave me the basic building blocks to enter and be successful in other schools and career paths. Moreover, they helped infuse in me a rock-solid faith. I shall always be in their debt.

In ending, my wife Jacqueline and I have both been long-time parishioners of Holy Rosary. We were married here in 1948 by Father Feucht. We love our Dominican priests and our parish!

MORE GOOD TIMES AND GRADUATION

Mary Lou Moser Byrne (class of 1936) of Bellevue, Washington furnished a beautiful photograph taken of the students who were in school in 1913. She recalls a humorous episode relating to her friend and classmate Alice McGrath. Sister Amanda to Alice: "Ask the housekeeper if Father Olsen has any laundry to be done." Alice's translation of that request to the housekeeper was: "Does Father Olsen have any dirty habits?" Thank you for going out of your way to send us the photograph and the memories Mary Lou!

Kathleen Lavin (a 1925 graduate) and Florence McEachern (a 1926 graduate), both of whom are still hail, hearty, and full of fun, spent several days compiling lists of names of students who attended Holy Rosary School over the years. We are so grateful for all of their work!

Kathleen invited this author and Florence to her lovely apartment in NE Portland. She lives on the second floor and you feel like you're in the middle of a forest when you look out the living room window facing the center court of the complex. It's a lovely place for a lovely lady. Kathleen's tranquil face glowed as she smiled and we all took a trip down memory lane, recalling past events at Holy Rosary School: "On the first day of school," said Kathleen, "we were shy two desks and one chair desk, so sister had Catherine Coyle and me squeeze onto one chair. Catherine and I sat together all day. We had a good time and it was a wonderful way to begin the first day of school." Father (Pastor) Olsen stood at the back of the room.

Florence laughed aloud remembering how inquisitive the girls were about the secluded sisters on the second floor and what they did when they weren't teaching. She recalled that the girls' bathroom was on the second floor of the Noon House (then the school convent) and that, during lunch period, they'd go to the second floor saying they had to go to the bathroom, "just so we could look through the keyhole into the kitchen, where the nuns were enjoying their lunch – but nothing interesting ever happened." "We used to call Sister Seraphica "Sister South Africa," Florence laughed, "and years later Sister came into a doctor's office where I was working and we chatted. I asked her if she knew what we called her behind her back." Sister Seraphica gave her a knowing smile and replied: "Of course – Sister South Africa." Florence chuckled: "Which only goes to show that the sisters had not only eyes in the back of their heads, but ears as well!"

Florence's mother was a cook at the rectory for several years, and she remembers that her mother was never allowed to enter the dining room or any other part of the rectory outside the kitchen, from which she passed meals to the priests through a sliding partition.

A GRATEFUL SISTER SUPERIOR
WRITES TO THE DOMINICAN PROVINCIAL

Sister Seraphica taught at Holy Rosary School for over a quarter of a century and was also the Sister Superior from 1930-1936 and 1944-1948. Her thoughts about Holy Rosary were recorded in a letter, dated April 24, 1946, which she sent to Very Reverend B. Blank, O.P., Provincial of the Western Dominican Province:

Dear Father,

That you have written such nice replies to our good wishes to you at Christmas and Easter time, also in reply to our expressions of sympathy on the death of our good Father McDermott and Father Owens, I feel encouraged to write to you.

I wish to thank you in the name of the sisters and the parishioners for giving to Holy Rosary the choicest gift you ever could bestow on a parish – good, holy, zealous and self-sacrificing priests.

Father Agius has done wonders with his good, holy assistants, Father Feucht and Father Condon, to bring a high spiritual and family-like parish standard. What a grace for all of us.

You may think I am saying too much, but too much cannot be said, when one has been here since 1913 and gone through hills and valleys, thick and thin, joys and sorrows.

The people are delighted and more than happy. No one hears the good that is being done and the good said about our Dominican Fathers more than we sisters. Their good example is inspiring. A little secret. I have more love of God now than I have ever had in my life, due to the good example and brotherly love of the good Fathers you have given us.

I am only a poor little superior at Holy Rosary Convent so I can speak for all of the sisters for they all would say what I am saying, but they do not know that I am writing this kind of letter to you.
The Fathers, if not otherwise busy, always take part in the devotions, Masses, etc., and kneel in the church. The people remark about it and love it. It inspires them to devotion and to become better.

Fr. Feucht has charge of the altar boys. A boy told me that he was going to be a Mass server. I told him when he serves he should fold his hands like Father Feucht, it looks so respectful. He said "Yes sister and Father Feucht looks like he is full of grace." I asked him

what made him say that. He said: "I think that when I see him."

We can say that of all the Fathers here, Thank God, and thank you for following the inspiration of the Holy Ghost in giving us Father Agius as pastor and his good zealous helpers.

Enough, I think you understand. Now that I have written this letter to you I feel that I have done what my conscience has prompted me to do for the past few years. This is a long letter, Reverend Father, but I have not the ability to express in short sentences.

God love and bless you in your many responsibilities. We all pray for our Dominican Fathers.

> *Respectfully, gratefully and humbly,*
> *I am your devoted Sister in St. Dominic*
> *[signed]*
> *Sister M. Seraphica*

LEO WHITE

Leo White, God rest his soul, graduated in the 1918 class at Holy Rosary. When interviewed shortly before his death,[81] he recalled that Sister Seraphica was a disciplinarian, a kind and gentle one, and not easily fooled. He remembers that someone set the clock ahead one hour hoping to get out of school early, but Sister noticed it immediately. "*She spilled the beans to Sister Mary Amanda, who was then principal,*" he smiled. Leo also recalls staying after school one day and being fascinated at overhearing another sister speaking German to a man who came to the school to repair the radiators. Leo also remembers his namesake, Brother Leo, who made the fire for the nuns, rang the bell every day, and always worked at full pace on the parish grounds.

"*In the early days,*" he relates, "*we kids had lots of fun on the Willamette and Columbia Rivers. In the summertime, they erected swimming tanks which water passed through, the lips of the tanks surrounded by huge pontoons, which were attached to the banks of the river. The pontoons kept the tanks afloat. It cost five or ten cents to swim, and that included a locker. In the winter, we skated on the Columbia at least once or twice, and they drove horses across the frozen Willamette in the 1920's.*" Leo, who lived at NE 10th & Tillamook in the early days, also remembered seeing riders of the KKK openly galloping down the streets with their sheets and hoods on while he was walking to Benson High School – "*Morons who thought they owned the streets.*"
Leo's wife, who died in 1966, was Kathleen Conner, also a Holy Rosary School graduate. Leo and Kathleen had eight children and they were proud of them all – "*none of them in jail,*" Leo laughed: Jack, Dick, Kathleen, Francis, Fred, Tom, Dan, and Patricia "*who was born on the last day of the year. I almost missed out on a New Year's Eve Party.*" Leo's daughter, Sister Francis, has been a nun for 30 years with the Holy Child Order (SHCJ).

HOLY ROSARY SCHOOL CLOSES

June 1955 marked the end of an era. The school closed for good on the recommendations of Sisters M. Callista Stopper and Redempta Prose. They had observed drastic demographic changes and noted the following factors leading to their recommendation :[82]

1) *The rapid industrialization in the areas of Holy Rosary and Immaculate Heart Parishes;*

2) *The opening of all eight grades at Saint Anthony's Parish and the effect on Holy Rosary's student body [editor's note: 36 pupils were bussed from Saint Anthony's to Holy Rosary].*

3) *The location of Father Schmitz's new school which was in the parish where the sisters recently purchased property for their new high school (Marycrest)…the area is rapidly developing and the new parish (St. Therese) includes seven public schools with thirteen first grades in its boundaries.*

4) *Plans are being made right now for this area and unless we take the opportunity offered us now, we shall lose this district to another Order or Congregation. Such a situation would, of course, prove embarrassing for our high school. Also, it seems illogical to cling to two dying parishes and lose the opportunity to begin in a young and developing area.*

5) *Father Schmitz's plan, to begin with only the first and second grades, seems to allow us time to staff the school gradually – a condition doubtless necessary in our present critical shortage of teachers. We feel that this is an opportunity we cannot afford to lose. And since no more sisters can be spared for Oregon at present, we ask permission to attempt to accommodate ourselves to this opportunity with the number of sisters we have here for the time being.*

This chapter on Holy Rosary School covers the years 1912-1955 from the viewpoint of the school and was inserted at this point for the sake of cohesiveness with respect to the history of the school. We return to the regular history of the parish beginning with the years 1911-1920 in the following chapter.

School children celebrate Holy Rosary's Golden Jubilee (1944) by reenacting the events of 1894-1944.

Left to Right

Dominican Sister Modesta Bauer

Dominican Sister and former
Principal Sister Anthony Rusting

Dominican Sister Celestine Stiebritz

Left to Right

Dominican Sister Genevieve Duffy

Dominican Sister Callista Stopper

Dominican Sister Marcella Ashton

Left to Right

Dominican Sister Peregrina
Henglberger – "cook"

Dominican Sister Bernice Sherlock –
"Art Instructor"

Dominican Sister M. Rosalia Monaghan

Left to Right

Dominican Sister and former
Principal Angela Marie Boedigheimer

Dominican Sister Emilia Techtman

Dominican Sister M. Valeria
Cummings

1st row: Dominican Sisters Mary Michael Phipps and Rose Mary Hennessy.
2nd row: Bonaventure Fritz, Ancilla Althaus, fnu. Fidelis and Celestine Stiebritz.

Dominican Sisters Amata Morris, Callista Stopper
and Seraphica Boehm.

Following are two stanzas from a poem written
by Catherine de Hueck Doherty,[83]
contained in an article by Patricia Treece
in the September-October 1992 edition
of *Catholic Heritage*[84] magazine, a fitting tribute
to the nuns who served at Holy Rosary,
and all nuns everywhere:

A nun is a woman of the water and towel
Constantly kneeling before Mankind
to wash its tired feet.
A nun is a prayer – Everlastingly
lifting her arms to God
For those who don't

Dominican Sisters Jerome Delsman,
Angela (Eileen) Molahan and Julia Perez.

Dominican Sisters Lioba Doehman, fnu. Aquinato and fnu. Dolorosa.

Left
First graduating class (1917)
at Holy Rosary School.
Girls (left to right) areMarie
Sytryker, unknown, Carolot-
ta O'Connor, unknown,
Annamarie McCormack and
Beatrice White. Fathers
Sylvester Chamberlain, O.P.
(left) and Stanislaus Olsen,
O.P. are shown with the
boys, not identified.

Jim Bobzien [class of '41] mentioned earlier in this chapter, wrote the
following poem in fond memory of Holy Rosary School, on the
occasion of the school reunion held in 1994.

ODE TO HOLY ROSARY

by Jim Bobzien

Remember Holy Rosary and little children down the hall,
Remember Holy Rosary and the Nuns that stood so tall,
Remember Sister Julia who had the candy store,
Remember then at recess time your pennies she'd implore,
Remember Holy Rosary and the portico so dry,
Remember that's where we were marched in damp November skies,
Remember our Priest's instruction class on Monday afternoon,
He gave us all the basic Truths that some forgot so soon,
Remember when the bell would ring and we were called to learn,
Those were the lessons we tried to grasp for grades we had to earn,
Remember down the street we went to the playground south of church,

Right
Holy Rosary's 1952 graduating class
shown with Father Thomas Feucht, O.P.
1st row (left to right) Darryl Christman,
Patricia Macabeo, Sonjia Brooks, Bar-
bara Britt, Mary Mulvey, Robert Bley-
thing; 2nd row: Elharsel Lewis,
Kaye McDonald, Joe Clark, Fr. Feucht,
Lewis Day, Nancy Connolly, Stephen
Pongracz; 3rd row: Susan Hyde, Harley
Frisby, Kenneth Hoff, Andrew Johnson,
Caroline Pupil, and Freddia Brooks.

Left
Holy Rosary's 1929 graduating class shown with Rev. Father F.A. Pope. (left to right) lst row: Christiana Daskalos, Lillian Darby, Mary Plescas, Elisabeth Silva and Ermith Phinney. 2nd row: Earl Kelly, Tony Faber, Bernie Tobkins, Ed Scherfen, Fr. Pope, William Dixon, Vincent Byrne, and John Conchuratt. Photo furnished by Mr. Vincent Byrne.

Baseball, football, no holds barred, we played on barren earth,
Remember Sister Superior in stately habit garbed,
We dared not test her wrath for long if we should leave the yard,
Remember all neat uniforms and salt a pepper cords,
To keep them clean and patched with care was all we could afford,
Remember Palmer writing drills and ovals oh so round,
The Sisters took great pains to make our learning most profound,
Remember well those Christmas plays when you wore angel wings,
And how Sisters cringed in fear for words we didn't sing,
Remember all the friends you made, it seems so long ago,
These are the folks around you now, tell them all "Hello"

Above
Holy Rosary's 1930 graduating class shown with Rev. Father F.A. Pope. The class included Irene Morell, Madeline Conner, Basil Byrne, Geraldine Brifey, Eileen Langman, Florence Tobkin, Ambrose Tobkin, George Swanson, James Courtney, J. Mackey, Virginia Eivers, Bernard Leonard, George DeCamp, George Gould, Fred Eilers, Edward Hoerner, Alfred Illk, Regan McCoy, Joseph Staudenmaier, Kathleen Darby, Frances DeCamp, Margalee Holmes, Dorothy English, Anna Plecas, and Mary Reilly.

Left
Holy Rosary School pupils put on a Christmas play in 1943.

NOTES ON THE TEXT

74   Refrain from *School Days* by Will D. Cobb & Gus Edwards, 1904.

75   Taken from the *Catholic Encyclopedia* and furnished by S. Evangela, O.P., Mission San Jose, California by letter dated March 15, 1993.

76   Warranty Deed 49468 recorded December 15, 1911, Book 565, Page 172, Multnomah County Book of Deeds, Portland, Oregon. A Chinese restaurant and parking lot now occupy that space.

77   Names kindly furnished by Sister Evangela, O.P., archivist for the Dominican Sisters, Mission San Jose, California. See Appendix 5 for a complete list of sisters who taught there and the names of the graduates.

78   Joe Mayer, who grew up in the rectory from 1914-1942 (his mother, Anna, was housekeeper until 1958) related that the KKK once burned a cross on the school grounds.

79   The January 9, 1944 Parish Digest reported: "Holy Rosary, thanks to Father Banfield, has three basketball teams." Father Banfield is also a good golfer as this author discovered while playing with him, and parishioners Paul Wolf and Joseph Mayer (class of 1931) at Glendoveer Golf Course in Portland in June 1992, during one of Father's short vacations from the Dominican Preaching Band – and he still has a great sense of humor.

80   Dominican and Doctor of the Church, Thomas Aquinas, composed the hymns *Verbum supernum* and *Pange Lingua* still today known more by their last verses *O Salutaris* and *Tantum Ergo*.

81   During the interview, Leo knew he had terminal cancer, but he never mentioned the fact. He died November 12, 1992, in Portland.

82   See *A history of the schools staffed by the Dominican Sisters of Mission San Jose, California: 1945-1982* by Sister Mary Catherine Antczak, O.P., a thesis deposited at Loyola Marymount University, Los Angeles, California on May 14, 1985.

83   See Chapter 11, which recounts Catherine's life at Holy Rosary as head of the Stella Maris House, circa 1956-1968.

84   A publication of Our Sunday Visitor, 200 Noll Plaza, Huntington, IN 46750-1696, page 63.

Photo of student body at Holy Rosary School, 1913, furnished by Mrs. John O. Byrne, then Mary Lou Moser, shown far left, 2nd row, with big white bow in her hair. Pastor H. H. Kelly, O.P. standing left rear. John O. Byrne was also attending but absent on this day.

Father A. S. Chamberlain, O.P. (c. 1925)

CHAPTER

7

1911-1920

CATHOLIC HISTORY IN OREGON FROM ANOTHER PERSPECTIVE

In the second decade of the 20th Century, Holy Rosary Church was one of 120 Catholic churches in the whole of Oregon,[85] a state not always hospitable to Catholicism. The following passage is quoted from the Centennial History of Oregon[86] covering the years 1811-1912:

The Catholic population of Oregon are maintaining two colleges of the university class, as universities go in Oregon, Columbia University of University Park, and Mount Angel of Marion County. And in addition to this literary and religious organization the church recognizes with favor the following fraternal, if not secret, organizations which neither Protestants nor sinners may join, to-wit: Catholic Order of Foresters; Catholic Knights of America; Young Men's Institute; Ancient Order of Hibernians; Knights of Columbus

One wonders whether the author was writing tongue-in-cheek in this caricature of the Church. No doubt a small dose of anti-Catholic bigotry percolated in the pen of this compiler of Oregon history as he wrote those lines which, if true however, assure us that, since sinners were not allowed to join those Catholic organizations, the membership was composed of hermetically sealed saints, an enormously intimidating prospect not only for Protestants, but for Catholics alike. Did he not know that the Pope himself is considered a sinner like the rest of us, and that the Pope would be the first to admit that he, too, must tread carefully the same straight paths we all must navigate in order to enter that narrow gate spoken of by Christ?

Lost in this one paragraph of Oregon history is the eternal message that the Catholic Church and all of her associations and members exist to wrest men and women everywhere from the power of sin, and that the existence of our institutions would lack in pertinence for Catholics and in credibility for all Christians were sinners not allowed to join. In 1992, Catholics would not be allowed to join, for example, certain prison ministries because they were not "born again," which only goes to show that there is no such thing as a sleeping Satan who, always wide awake, has for eons exhibited his own cunning manifestations of the supernatural all over the globe.

Compare the above historical reference with the following, which that author wrote concerning the history of Presbyterianism in Oregon, contained in that same volume:[87]

Here is the genuine article, carrying the reader back to 1638 when Sir Henry

Wotton, a favorite of James VI of Scotland, wrote in one of his letters that he was sorry to hear of new "oathes in Scotland between the Covenanters, who they say will have none but Jesus Christ to reign over them." Oregon has but one Covenanter minister, and one church of the covenant, organized December 2, 1911; but it would be a blessing to the state if there was one such church of these sturdy Covenanters on every hill top, and in every valley of the state.

U.S. ANTI-CATHOLIC ROOTS ALSO FOUND IN MASONIC-MORMON TRADITION

The bond between Masonry and Mormonism is described in a book about the Mormon founder: *No Man Knows My History – the Life of Joseph Smith, The Mormon Prophet* by Fawn M. Brodie[88] a former member of the Church of Latter Day Saints. The bonding of these two movements did not bode well for Catholics, considering the fact that both had axes to grind against the Catholic Church. Smith was born on December 23, 1805 and he died on June 27, 1844, at a time when the Mormons were being driven out of the eastern seaboard and were heading west through Illinois to find their promised land, as foretold by Smith. Brodie writes of Joseph Smith:

Early in the writing [of the Book of Mormon] *Joseph vigorously attacked the Catholic Church. The prophet Nephi was made to have a vision in which he foretold the stage of America in the last days. Then, he said, the scourge of the land would be "that great and abominable church…the whore of all the earth…whose foundation is the devil."* [89]

Later on, Smith found solace and soulmates among the Masons, whose abracadabra (secret names handshakes, passwords, and oaths etc.) intrigued him, so much so that he made them a part of the Mormon liturgy. On page 280 of *No Man Knows My History* Fawn Brody writes that Joseph Smith's:

interest in Masonry became so infectious that many Mormon elders hastened to follow his lead, and within six months [Smith's] *lodge had 286 candidates compared to only 227 lodge members in all of Illinois.*

> "…Blest are you when they insult you and persecute you and utter every kind of slander against you because of me. Be glad and rejoice, for your reward in heaven is great." (Matthew 5:11-12)
>
> but
>
> "…Let not your heart be troubled, neither let it be afraid." (John 14:27)

HOLY NAME SOCIETY BEGUN BY DOMINICANS IN 1247

The Holy Name Society's Dominican background has its roots in a document dated October 12, 1274. It was a decree from Pope Gregory given to the then Dominican Master General John Garbella, O.P., now known as Blessed John of Vercelli (after a town where John came from in northern Italy). In giving the decree to John, the pope declared:

> *"Very dear son, we enjoin upon you and the friars of your Order to urge the people to show greater reverence for the Holy Name of Jesus…at the pronouncing of that Name everyone should bow his head…"*

The Dominicans at Holy Rosary traditionally have been the spiritual directors not only of our parish Holy Name Society (founded in 1910) but of the Metropolitan Holy Name Union (consisting of all local parish societies) as well. The "Personal Record" of Father Edwin Stanislaus Olsen,[90] O.P.S.T.L., on file in the Dominican archives of Oakland, California, notes that Father Olsen "established and was Diocesan Director of the Diocesan Union of the Holy Name Society for two years." Throughout the world, Dominicans have been leaders and advisors to the national and international Holy Name Societies as well.

PARISH HOLY NAME SOCIETY IN 1912[91]
JUDGE MICHAEL MUNLY ELECTED PRESIDENT

The Holy Name Society at Holy Rosary Church met on June 18, 1912, according to a bound book found in the church's archives. Thirty five men attended the meeting. The minutes of this meeting are quoted:

This meeting was called to order by the Rev. Spiritual Director, who explained that, at the initial meeting held on Sunday, June 2, a committee was appointed to meet Tuesday evening June 11 for the purpose of suggesting names of members for the various offices of the Society. Mr. Larkin, as chairman, was then asked for a report of the committee's action and he submitted the following names:

For President	Judge M. G. Munly
" V. Pres.	Mr. C. P. McGinnis
" Treas.	Mr. J. C. Larkin
" Rec. Secy.	Mr. M.E. Fitzgerald

Upon motion, Mr. J. Frank Sinnott was appointed to act as temporary secretary of the meeting; and there being no response to the request for further nominations, upon motion of Mr. Morris the nominations were closed, and the secretary was instructed to cast the unanimous vote of the meeting for Messrs Munly, McGinnis, Larkin, and Fitzgerald for offices as recommended by the committee.

Upon taking the chair, Mr. Munly gave a brief outline of the origin and history of the Holy Name Society, its blessed founder, the lofty purposes for which it was organized, the great good it has achieved in past centuries, and the pressing need in our times for a society of this character to stem the evils of profanation and blasphemy; and as a public profession of faith in the divinity of Christ – with regard to which there exists so much of doubt and misbelief amongst sectarian denominations.

It was unanimously agreed that the next meeting should be held two weeks from the date of this meeting, for the purpose of perfecting matters of organization, when adjournment for the summer season would be considered.

At this point the president asked to be excused and Mr. McGinnis as vice-president became the presiding officer.

The chair suggested the appointment of a committee to formally present for adoption at the next meeting, a constitution and by-laws together with some recommendations as to the manner of raising funds, etc. A motion to this effect was offered by the spiritual director which was carried, and the following committee was named by the chair:

> *Father Kelly* [Humbert H. Kelly, O.P. – Pastor]
> *Mr. J. Frank Sinnott*
> *and M. G. Munly*

Concerning the founding of the Metropolitan Holy Name Union, the *Catholic Sentinel* of November 22, 1917[92] had this to say:

METROPOLITAN HOLY NAME UNION FORMED
A meeting was called three weeks ago of all the pastors of this city and vicinity by request of Archbishop Christie. Twenty pastors gave immediate response and assembled at the Priory of the Dominican Fathers at Holy Rosary Church. At this time there have been Holy Name Societies established in about twenty-five parishes. A meeting of the executive board will be held November 23 at the Priory of Holy Rosary Church.

First quarterly meeting will be held in the Cathedral Hall, Dec. 9th. This will be the formation of the Diocesan Union Society. After the meeting, a parade of delegates will march from the Hall to the Cathedral, there to assist at Forty Hours Devotion.

WHETHER TO BUILD A NEW CHURCH
As previously indicated, the church which still stands today was originally meant to be a temporary church; therefore, discussions about erecting a new church surfaced in almost every decade after the church was built in 1894. For example, in a letter dated December 10, 1913,[93] the pastor, Father Henry Humbert Kelly, O.P., and with parishioner Michael Munly (see Chapter 4) were urging the provincial to buy the stone of the *"old library of Portland which they are tearing down"* [on the corner of Broadway and Stark]. The approximate price would be $10,000. Father

Kelly added, *"I have been speaking to some of the people, and they told me their donation was ready as soon as we started, and that there would be no trouble to get the others to come through as soon as we started to build."*

In a letter dated December 16, 1913, to the provincial, Mr. Munly concurred *"This building is all of cut stone. The foundations are of granite and the superstructure is of buff sandstone. The building is about 143 feet by 66 feet."*[94] In a follow-up letter dated December 17, 1913, Mr. Munly wrote: *"The stone would cost $7500. Hurley Mason Company [has] proposed to reconstruct the building on your ground for $25,000."* [95]

PRUDENT PROVINCIAL HAS OTHER PLANS
The provincial responded to these overtures in a letter dated January 24, 1914:

"I fully appreciate the need for a new church and school in Portland, but have been hesitating on account of hard times," [but] *"let us go at this carefully in our own way and we shall succeed sooner or later in having a good church which will be within our means."*

Perhaps no one in those days would prophecy that our church would stand so solid up until 1994 and give promise of weathering many more years, due in no small part to the restorative contributions made by the priests, nuns and parishioners across these decades. Since Portland lies on a fault line, scientists have predicted that sooner or later an earthquake will strike Portland. Who knows, we may all one day be grateful that we have a wooden and not a stone church because wooden structures withstand earthquakes far better than do stone structures.

ARCHBISHOP CHRISTIE INTERESTED IN
HOLY ROSARY'S PLANS FOR NEW CHURCH
During this earlier timeframe, the Dominican provincial had been in touch with Beezer Brothers Architects, in Seattle.[96] Archbishop Christie somehow heard this news and it sparked His Grace's interest, as indicated in this curious letter from Beezer Brothers to the provincial, dated October 8, 1914:

Right Rev. Christie has asked us to furnish him (as soon as convenient and practical) a set of blueprints from preliminary plans but under your instructions we cannot do so. We have told his Reverence that you have asked us not to give copies of these plans to anyone…will you please advise us with reference to the Archbishop's request.

Of course, every archbishop is vitally interested in and has a right to know about proposals to erect a new church within his archdiocese. But the question of why Archbishop Christie wrote to the Beezer Brothers in Seattle directly (rather than to the Holy

Rosary Priory – where he frequently went to confession – or to the provincial) to obtain the blueprints was a mystery that did not yield its secrets in other correspondence filed in the archives. From the provincial's point of view, it is probable that the plans for the new church were merely in the talking stage, and he would not bother to inform His Grace about such plans until they were firm, and action taken to implement them imminent.

Six years had elapsed since the Archbishop's 1905-1908 "confrontation," with the Dominicans (explained in Chapter 5) over the governance of Holy Rosary Church as it became a parish. The Dominicans demurred in 1908 (repulsing his threat to replace them if they did not go along with his plans) and, ultimately, Holy Rosary became a parish on Dominican terms with the blessing of the Holy See. This unfortunate incident may have left a bad taste in the mouth of Archbishop Christie, and it is possible that the Archbishop was still smarting over this episode.

Also of relevance was an article which appeared on the front page of the April 14, 1910, *Catholic Sentinel* reporting that Holy Rosary was to build a new church and make the present church into a school. It was during that era "Prior to 1928, for about a quarter of a century, the Sentinel was operated under private ownership," [97] thus not under the direct control of Archbishop Christie (although he did have considerable indirect control). Christie could have read this Sentinel article and assumed that the Dominicans were about to present him with a *fait accompli*, not even giving him the courtesy of approving their plans. Such a presumption could cause him to undertake his own investigation.

Also, and perhaps more significantly, Michael George Munly, the legal counsel for Holy Rosary for several decades, had once been the "editor and principal owner" [98] of the Sentinel. In fact, he wrote articles at least up until 1890, so he had good connections at the paper. Since Munly had also engaged in negotiations for Holy Rosary to possibly buy the stone of the razed "old Portland library," he may have had the news release placed in the Sentinel as a pump-priming gesture, in effect saying "Oh yes, you bet, we are going to build a new Holy Rosary Church. Let's get on with the job."

On April 19, 1914, Archbishop Christie had dedicated the first

Part of 1914 proposal for a new Holy Rosary Church – drawn up by architect Arnold Constable at Beezer Brothers Architects, Seattle, WA – plans were eventually scrapped.

Blessed Sacrament Parish church, with Father B. V. Kelly as pastor, so church architecture was certainly on his mind. Another factor to consider is that Archbishop Christie had, for a long time, been raising funds for building a new archdiocesan cathedral [99] as well as a Catholic university, [100] so he must have had a general interest in building design. And, not incidentally, he may have been concerned about the impact any new Dominican church would have on his own fund-raising efforts within the archdiocesan community.

PLANS FOR NEW CHURCH SCRAPPED

In any case, the whole matter eventually became irrelevant. Though discussions and some fund raising had taken place between 1911 to 1917 within the parish, plans to build a new church were dropped. The provincial had mentioned "hard times" in 1914. Thereafter, war was on the horizon, drawing people's attention and their imaginations overseas. Seed money for the fulfillment of new ideas would, in this wartime buildup and for the immediate future, be hard to come by for projects not relating to the vigorous prosecution of the war.

THE QUEST FOR A CHURCH HALL

The presumption all along among Holy Rosarians was that the standing church would one day be turned into a combination school and parish hall. Therefore, understandably, there remained some unsatisfied parishioners when the plans for the new church were shelved, as indicated in a letter from Father Olsen to Provincial McMahon dated January 14, 1917, which stated: *"Something like building a hall has to be done for there are some who are suspicious of us, thinking we are hoarding money."*

The previous pastor, Father Henry H. Kelly, O.P., had brought up the subject of a new hall as early as April 21, 1912, on which date he notified the provincial of alterations he had to make in the Noon House, [101] for card parties held by the Rosarians and a *"stag party for the men. Ladies will be excommunicated if they appear."* He explained that he: *"Started to build up the Rosarians, and Sunday school [and] put a prize up for the young lady who obtains the most new members…[But we are] handicapped without a hall. The people are getting tired too, giving up their houses for card parties, and I have no place to hold the meetings of the societies. So I do hope we will be able very soon to turn the church into a school and hall."*

Well, a new school was built, and it contained a spacious hall (gym) sufficient for the seating of 400 people to play Bingo or consume corned beef and cabbage dinners during fund-raising events, but all of this would not take place until 1923.

FATHER CHRISTOPHER VINCENT LAMB, O.P., LEAVES HOLY ROSARY

The *Catholic Sentinel* of January 30, 1913[102] reported that Father Lamb was leaving Holy Rosary, "after nine years of service…to take charge of St. Vincent's Church, Vallejo, California." Father was born July 28, 1871 in Vallejo. He received his Dominican habit on May 5, 1890 and was ordained at the Cathedral in San Francisco on December 21, 1895, when Holy Rosary was almost two years old. He served at Holy Rosary from 1903 to 1913, as assistant and sacristan. He had a beautiful singing voice, even in old age, and organized several of the finest boys choirs Holy Rosary ever had. He died at St. Helen's Hospital in Chehalis, Washington, March 6, 1962 at age 90, a priest of deep spirituality for 66 years.

WAR DECLARED APRIL 6, 1917 – CATHOLIC PRESENCE PROMINENT

America, allied with England and France, went to war against Germany, ending the neutrality declared by President Wilson in 1914, and seventy-five men from the parish entered the military in 1917. Over one million Americans would be sent to Europe by July 1918. Hostilities would not end until November 11, 1918, which would become Armistice Day among U.S. holidays, recognizing the service of 4,743,826 military personnel, of which 320,710 were casualties.[103] Immediately after President Wilson's declaration of war, the archbishops of the United States made the following statement (the first religious body in America to do so):[104]

Our people, as ever, will rise as one man to serve the nation. Our priests and consecrated women will once again, as in every former trial of their country, win by their bravery, their heroism, and their service, new admiration and approval. We are all true Americans, ready as our age, our ability and our condition permits, to do whatever is in us to do for the preservation, the progress and the triumph of our beloved country.

CATHOLICS DEFEND THE UNITED STATES

Although Catholics in the U.S. numbered only 17% of the population, it was estimated that between "25% to 35% of the Army was Catholic, and that almost 50% of the Navy was Catholic." These astonishing figures were attributed to the fact that (1) Catholics were taught that patriotism is a virtue, and that they did not need to be drafted but voluntarily joined the fight; and (2) Catholics were generally healthier, more educated, and – due to their religious upbringing – had a lower percentage of social diseases (such maladies disqualified men for military service). Moreover, the values and world view possessed by Catholics allowed them to face life with courage, hence to face death with courage as well. There were eleven Catholic major generals and fifteen Catholic brigadier generals serving the U.S.

Army in World War I. Catholic chaplains accounted for 1026 of the officers, including Father Francis P. Duffy of the famous "Fighting Sixty-Ninth," the Irish regiment from New York City.[105] So, for all anti-Catholics forces to see, yes, Catholics, including their clergy, in all ranks served and died for their country, considering it their patriotic duty to do so.

FATHER (PATRICK) ANDREAS M. SKELLY, O.P.

Father Skelly, a famous author of religious works, served at Holy Rosary in 1912-1913 and again from 1920-23. In one five-volume work entitled Doctrinal Discourses[106] he wrote:

When ex-President Wilson was making his "swing around the circle," which ended so disastrously for himself and his party, before the last presidential election, one of the cities he visited and spoke in was Seattle. The Pacific battleship fleet was in Puget Sound at the time of his visit, and occasion was taken by him to hold a review in Seattle harbor. He boarded the flagship, and the admiral, to grace his presence, gathered together from the whole fleet a picked crew, every man of whom had won honors for efficiency and gallantry during the war. Of that honor crew of 800 men, the cream of the whole Pacific fleet, no less than 600, that is 75 per cent, were Catholics.

The details of Father Skelly's life are sketchy. Official records show he was born July 8, 1855 in County Meath, Ireland, took his solemn profession on December 25, 1881 at the Convent of Sts. Sixtus and Clement in Rome, and was ordained on June 25, 1882. In 1894 he was the Master of Novices at Sts. Sixtus and Clement, and was assigned to San Francisco 1909. He died March 21, 1938 at age 82. He had been a devout priest of God for 55 years.

FATHER CLYDE ALOYSIUS SYLVESTER CHAMBERLAIN, O.P.

Holy Rosary's Father Chamberlain voluntarily entered the Army when military preparedness for war first began in the U.S. The *Catholic Sentinel*[107] reported that Father Chamberlain *"left to take up duties as an army chaplain as early as 1915,"* and a chronology of the parish in the archives of the Dominican province declared that *"75 men of the parish entered the service"* and Father Chamberlain received a *"commission as lst Lieut. Chaplain, U.S.A. He enters service at Vancouver Barracks at Vancouver, Washington. He is sent to Beauregard, Louisana, and assigned Senior Chaplain at Base Hospital. After several months he is transferred to 114th. Ammunition Train, 39th Division, U.S.A. His regiment goes to France and he sees service in the Field of War. He returns with his regiment to the U.S., arriving at New Port News, Jan. 31st, 1918."*

FATHER CHAMBERLAIN'S BULLET GOES ASTRAY

Father Chamberlain taught at Aquinas School while serving at Holy Rosary. He was a heavyset man, overweight, and had a penchant for gadgets. One time, while tinkering with a revolver, he fired it accidentally and the bullet went through the closet of his room into the closet of the room next door, piercing the suit of Brother Francis, for whom he had to purchase a new suit. Father Chamberlain was born August 25, 1881 in Jacksonville, Illinois. He received his habit at Benicia, November 1, 1904, was ordained in Washington, D.C. June 24, 1910, and died at St. Dominic's in San Francisco December 30, 1957, at age 76. He was found dead on the floor by the elevator outside the refectory, after celebrating Mass and having breakfast. The fathers and brothers prayed the Salve Regina by the body of their deceased comrade.[108]

FLU EPIDEMIC CLOSES CHURCH – PRIESTS READY TO HELP!
An effective flu vaccine had not yet been developed when a flu pandemic engulfed the world in 1918, killing an estimated 20,000,000 world wide and 548,000[109] people in the U.S. alone (vs. 53,513 U.S. military killed in *all* of World War I). Portland was not spared. Pastor and Father E.S. Olsen, O.P., sent letters to all of the parishioners because of the *"protracted closing of the Church,"* ordered by medical authorities. In his letter,[110] Father Olsen notified everyone that:

First of all we wish to let you know that we have you in mind constantly during these trying times, still mindful of your sons and brothers in the service, and making daily commemoration of you in the Holy Sacrifice of the Mass, that the scourge of the prevailing sickness may spare you. Moreover, the Rosary is recited every evening to win the intercession of the Mother of God, the Queen of the Holy Rosary, for you. May She throw the Mantle of Her protection over your homes.

Secondly, understand that we priests are at your service in sickness. We are ready to minister to you no matter what the danger may be. We shall come to you at any time of the day or night. Don't delay. If, after taking all human precautions and having turned your hearts and raised your souls to God, the affliction does strike you, send for the priest. Telephone East 1754 or Home phone C 1028.

This coming Thursday is the Vigil of All Saints Day and it is a day of strict Fast and Abstinence. Friday is the Feast of All Saints, a Holy Day of strict obligation. Owing to the closing order of the Board of Health, no public Masses will be said. We shall be saying Mass at the hours of six, seven and eight o'clock. At home, unite yourselves spiritually with the Priest saying Mass at those hours. Let the Father and Mother gather the children together and all say the Rosary in the evening. (You may eat meat on Friday, the feast of All Saints).

Saturday is All Souls Day, on which by means of Holy Mass commemoration is made of all the Faithful Departed. Every Priest has the privilege of saying three Masses that day and for all the Faithful on condition of confession and Holy Communion, a Plenary Indulgence may be gained as often as they make a visit to the church, from noontime of All Saints to midnight of All Souls Day. ENCLOSED YOU WILL FIND AN ENVELOPE AND PAPER IF YOU DESIRE TO HAVE YOUR DEPARTED RELATIVES AND

FRIENDS COMMEMORATED ON ALL SOULS DAY. A Mass will be said every day during the month of November for those on the list, so be generous in your donation.

Finally, will it be asking too much of you to contribute in a lump sum for Church support what you would have given each Sunday had there been public services? Our only means of support is what you in your generosity give us. We are at the present time paying interest on $25,000, part of the purchase price of the school property. Monthly payments of about $125.00. We must support the Sisters with their salary of $100.00 also, each month. The closing of the Church puts us face to face with actual necessity. HELP US GENEROUSLY.

> *Dominican Fathers,*
> *E.S. Olsen,[111] O.P., Pastor*

Parishioner Gertrude (Miller) Morris recalls that the flu epidemic had hit Portland like a blizzard, and she estimated that about 25,000 people were infected. She herself was struck down and had a temperature of 106-degrees, with no antibiotics available. Her hearing was so badly damaged as a result, that she had to wear a hearing aid after 1938. She remembers that the basement of the auditorium was filled with felled patients. And where Holladay Park Hospital is located today,[112] the government had started to build a veteran's hospital, but sold it before its completion; it then became Hanneman Hospital and, subsequently, Holladay Park Hospital. The basement portion of that hospital contained about 2500 people downed by the flu, and "people were dying like flies." As earlier stated, according to the 1992 World Almanac, an estimated 20,000,000 people world-wide died in this pandemic.

FATHER REGGIE LEWIS, O.P.
THE GREATEST PREACHER OF THE PROVINCE
During this timeframe Father Reggie Lewis served at Holy Rosary. He was from a wonderful San Francisco family. His brother, Ray, also a Dominican had been ordained early (privately) because of tuberculosis and sent to a T.B. hospital in Deming, New Mexico. In the words of Father Charles Hess, O.P., Provincial Archivist, Father Reggie Lewis was "according to tradition, the greatest preacher in the Province. They say that even the choir boys listened to him." And from Father Gregory Anderson, O.P., formerly of Holy Rosary: "the greatest preacher the west ever produced. He could mesmerize little kids."[113]

Reggie died of bleeding ulcers while in his 50s. Another brother, Bill, was the builder of St. Dominic's Church in San Francisco, and a fourth brother, Louie, was a waiter at the St. Francis hotel. At Father Ray's 40th anniversary as a Dominican, his friends threw a huge party for him at Eagle Rock, California, (planned in private for fear he wouldn't be around for the 50th) smuggled brother Bill down for Ray's celebration and the brothers were able to renew their brotherly love during this festive occasion.

WAR OVER – HOLY ROSARY CELEBRATES SILVER JUBILEE

A Silver Jubilee brochure, written by then-pastor Edwin Stanislaus Olsen, O.P., nestled in the church's archives, provides a wonderful glimpse of what was on his mind in those days:

JUBILEE GREETINGS

"I am the mother of Fair Love and of Fear and of Knowledge and of Holy Hope. In Me is all grace of the way and of truth; in Me is all hope of Life and Virtue." "I was exalted like a rose plant in Jerico"

Dear Parishioners, Friends and Lovers of Holy Rosary Church: We have gathered together, Priests and People, to celebrate the twenty-fifth anniversary of the establishment of our Church of the Queen of the Most Holy Rosary. It is our Silver Jubilee. Let us approach with a clean conscience and in the fullness of Faith to the Throne of Grace that we may receive aid in the seasonable time for the Jubilee takes upon itself something of the Sabbath or Rest of the Lord during which we must give our mind and heart to Him in worship and praise.

May God the Father look down upon us with pleasure considering us His children, indeed. May God, the Son Incarnate, open to us all the Treasure of Love of His Sacred Heart. May God, the Holy Ghost, the Spirit of Love, sanctify our souls and be diffused in our hearts. And may the Blessed Mother, Queen of the Holy Rosary, intercede for us all as we turn to God to win His Blessings in this our Silver Jubilee in the Church which bears Her Glorious Name.

We Dominican Fathers have been established in your midst for the past twenty-five years. We have erected a Church, under the glorious title of the Queen of the Most Holy Rosary. To it you come to worship the Almighty God. In it some of you have been married. At its Altar you have received for the first time, and so many times since, the Body and the Blood of the Lord, Christ Jesus. From this Church

your dear dead mothers and fathers and children and friends and relations have been buried. Here you have come with the burden of your sins and your troubles, and have found relief. Here you have listened to the Word of God, unfailingly preached to you. Here, in God's Province, lies the way of your salvation. Your souls are in our hands. Before God, we hope that our ministrations have not been unavailing; that the life which is in Christ Jesus, the Lord, has been planted in your souls; that we have led you, as a flock, into the pastures of plenty; that we have, indeed, declared to you and made known the Glory of the Name of the Son of God and have glorified the Wonderful Mother of this self-same Christ. We have stood in your assemblies and have preached Christ and Him Crucified, and our every effort has been to make you understand that the Mother of Christ is the Mother of Fair Love, and of Fear and of Knowledge and of Holy Hope; that in Her is all Grace of the way of Truth; in Her is all hope of life and of virtue.

As Dominican Fathers, having the care of your souls, we are bound by the Tradition of seven centuries of Dominican life to uphold the Name of God and His Son, Christ Jesus, the Lord and the Fair Name of His Blessed Mother. Such preaching and ministry have begotten for the Church hundreds of Saints and Beatified.

And most appealing to you who read this, the greatest number of the Beatified of the Order were lay-women, members of the Third Order of St. Dominic. They came from every walk of life, were trained by the Dominican Fathers to love the Lord in the Blessed Sacrament, to have a heart ready for fellowship in the sufferings of Christ. There were virgins and widows, daughters of Emperors and Kings and daughters of the poor; young girls and aged women, like little Blessed Imelda and Blessed Mary Mancini. There were Doctors, Lawyers, University men and ordinary everyday working men. They were folks just like ourselves.

A brochure written by pastor Edwim Stanislaus Olsen, O.P. to celebrate the Silver Jubilee.

A Treasure of Promises Kept

They were made Saints by the self-same Blessed Sacrament of the Body of the Lord Christ. Their hearts ever enshrined the fair ideal of womanhood which is in the Mother of God. Possibly the only thing which keeps us all from becoming Saints, such as they are, is the lack of that which stands out so prominently in all their lives, the love of suffering in compassion with the sufferings of Christ. They seemed to seize on the text of St. Paul: "It is given to you not only to believe in Him but also to suffer with Him." So ardent were they in compassionating the pains, for more than eighty Dominicans are credited with receiving the Sacred Stigmata, or the wounds made by the nails and spear and thorns in the Feet and Hands and Side and Head of Our Lord.

The same sanctity may be ours. If we persevere in our devotion to the Blessed Mother and to the Blessed Sacrament we may grow to love his Cross and all that it means in suffering. We have a special title to the patronage of the Virgin Mother, in so far as our Church is dedicated to her honor as Queen of the Most Holy Rosary. She has taken root here amongst an honorable people, the Rose of Sharon and the Rose Tree of Jerico established in this City of Roses.

St. Dominic, the Holy Patriarch, is looking down upon us. He has been in Heaven for 694 years, and has never failed in the promise he made when dying, that he would be a Father indeed to his brethren doing his work.

Round about him are his great Saints. They are our Brothers and our Sisters. A whole army of glorious souls, who have washed their stoles in the Blood of the Lamb, and follow Him whithersoever He goeth. They were clad in white because they were worthy. This great cloud of witnesses to the Sanctity of St. Dominic, will, if we turn to them now, pray for us, and together with their Father, will raise up in Heaven the glorious praise of Mary in the Salve Regina, Hail Holy Queen. One fancies that the choirs of Heaven will cease their singing: O Clemens, O Pia, O Dulcis Virgo – Oh Clement, Oh Loving, Oh Sweet Virgin Mary. Then the full chorus of Dominican Saints and Blessed saved will plead for us with Her: Dignare eo laudare Te, Virgo sacrata, da illis virtutem contra hostes tuos; make them worthy to praise Thee, Oh Holy Virgin, give them power to conquer thine enemies. And she, benignant Mother, will turn to Her Divine Son and ask the Grace for us; that His truth may be made to prevail amongst men; that the life of his Grace he established in the hearts of all men; that in a multitude of Saints His Name and that of His own Blessed Mother shall be glorified.

In God the Father and the Lord, Jesus Christ, Grace be to you and Peace. We give thanks to God always for you all, making a remembrance of you in our prayers without ceasing; being mind-ful of your faith, and labor, and charity and of the enduring of the hope of our Lord, Jesus Christ before God, our Father. Knowing, brethren, beloved of God, your election, for our Gospel hath not been unto you in word only, but in power also, and in the Holy Ghost, and in much fullness, as you know what manner of men we have been among you for your sakes. And you became followers of us and of the Lord, receiving the Word in much tribulation with joy of the Holy Ghost. So that you were made a pattern to all that believe.

As we were approved of God that the Gospel should be committed to us, even as we speak, not as pleasing men but God who proveth our hearts. For neither have we used at any time, the speech of flattery, as you know; nor taken an occasion of covetousness, God is witness; nor sought we glory of men, neither of you or of others.

Whereas we might have been burdensome to you as the Apostles of Christ we became as little ones in the midst of you as if a nurse should cherish her children; so desirous of you we would gladly impart to you not only the Gospel of God but also our own souls, because you were become most dear to us.

You know in what manner, entreating and comforting you as a Father doth his children, we testified to everyone of you that you should walk worthy of God who hath called you unto His Kingdom and Glory.

Therefore we also give thanks to God, because, that when you had received of us the word of the hearing of God you received it, not as the word of men but, as it is indeed, the Word of God.

WHAT IS OUR HOPE, OR JOY, OR CROWN OF GLORY? ARE NOT YOU, IN THE PRESENCE OF OUR LORD JESUS CHRIST AT HIS COMING? FOR YOU ARE OUR GLORY AND OUR JOY. (St. Paul, Thessalonians, ch. 1.)

We feel that this testimony of St. Paul may be applied to you of Holy Rosary Church and we are thankful and grateful to all who in the past Twenty-five Years have so whole-heartedly co-operated with us. God's best blessing be yours.

DOMINICAN FATHERS OF HOLY ROSARY CHURCH
By E.S. Olsen, Pastor.

QUEEN OF THE MOST HOLY ROSARY PRAY FOR US

This ends this chapter which closes the second decade of this century.

NOTES TO THE TEXT

85 In 1785, 125 years earlier, according to Bishop Carroll, there were only 23,000 white Catholics in the U.S., administered to by 34 priests (see page 71, *The Faith of Millions*, by Rev. John A. O'Brien, Our Sunday Visitor, Huntington, Indiana, 1974). Great testimony to the growth of the Catholic Church here.

86 Page 586, Vol I, 1811-1912 on file at the Oregon Historical Society, Portland, Oregon.

87 Page 584, ibid.

88 Second Edition, Knopf, 1971.

89 1 Nephi, Chapters 13 &14, Book of Mormon.

90 Prior and Pastor at Holy Rosary from 1915 to 1921; president of Aquinas College, and residing at Holy Rosary 1923-1924; and in residence (also ill and convalescing) at Holy Rosary 1929-1932.

91 See Appendix 4 for names of Society members found in Society records, which are incomplete.

92 Page 4, columns 6 and 7.

93 Contained in the files of the Western Dominican Province (XI: 40601).

94 Our standing Holy Rosary church is 110 X 52 feet, so there would have been brick to spare.

95 As previously noted the cost of the original church construction (of wood) was $22,300, so it appeared that if he could get a stone church erected for this price, Mr. Munly was a shrewd horse trader.

96 They had, during March in 1911, built the side altars; and the outside steps (of wood) for $175.

97 Page 38, *The Centenary, 100 years of the Catholic Church in the Oregon Country*, Supplement in the *Catholic Sentinel*, Portland, Oregon, May 4, 1939.

98 The front page of the *Catholic Sentinel* of November 1, 1923, reporting on his death, stated: "In 1886, Munly became editor and principal owner of the *Catholic Sentinel* devoting four years to editorial work.

99 Groundbreaking for the new cathedral took place June 7, 1925, two months after Archbishop Christie's death – see page 536, *A History of the Catholic Church in the Pacific Northwest*, by Jesuit Father Wilfred Schoenberg.

100 In 1901 he had bought Portland University (now the University of Portland) from the Methodists and renamed it Columbia University. It was undergoing expansion during Christie's tenure.

101 Which was opening this same year to house the first grade school.

102 Page 4, column 6.

103 Page 702, *The World Almanac and Book of Facts*, 1992. Numbers of Catholics involved was not mentioned.

104 Page 232, *Our Catholic Heritage*, Albert J. Nevins, M.M. Our Sunday Visitor, Inc. Huntington, ID 46750, 1972.

105 Pages 232-235, *Our American Catholic Heritage*, ibid.

106 See pages 264-265 Vol. 5, published by Dominican Fathers, Aquinas College, Portland, OR, 1924.

107 Front page of May 2, 1915 edition.

108 Information relating to Father's death was furnished by Father Charles Hess, O.P.

109 Page 445, *The World Almanac and Book of Facts*, Pharos Books, New York.

110 Original, undated, in file XI: 40601, Dominican Provincial Headquarters, Oakland, California.

111 Father Olsen later had both legs removed due to diabetes.

112 The June 30, 1994 *Oregonian* reported the hospital closed its doors and was put up for sale.

113 According to a contemporary, Father Gregory Anderson, O.P.

114 For the years 1894-1919 furnished by "Agnes Dowd, 917 N.E. Hazelfern Place" – whose name is penned on it.

Teen members of the Calaroga Club on bicycle outing (c. 1936). Left to right: Bernard "Benny" Leonard, Virginia McCarl, Margaret Leonard, unidentified, Nellie Kenna (kneeling), unidentified, Eddie Owens, Pete Guerra and Ed Hoerner.

THE ROARING TWENTIES

As the third decade of the 20th century dawned, Holy Rosary was in financial difficulty, but it would weather the crisis through the generosity of its people.

TITHES LAW IMPOSED FOR THE YEAR 1921

The *Catholic Sentinel* dated March 3, 1921 contained the following:[115]

Father [Very Rev. E.S.] Olsen announced that the burden of carrying a $36,500 debt on the school is intolerable and, a new school being a necessity in a short time, the old school and the block between East Second and East Third and Halsey and Weidler must be liquidated. Father Olsen also told the people that the Dominican Order had purchased two blocks and built the present Church and priory over 27 years ago at a cost of $42,800, and that when the Archbishop gave the Dominicans the parish he enjoined upon them the maintenance of its school.[116] Consequently a third block was purchased and it is to pay for this school and this alone, that the tithes law has been imposed for this year."

This write-up is rather confusing. Archival records indicate the property, *including the Noon House,* was purchased for $35,144.11 in 1911, and that this same property was not *liquidated* but *mortgaged* "with the Hibernia Bank of San Francisco in the sum of $45,000" to build the new school, in 1923. The *Catholic Sentinel* dated March 10, 1921 reported:[117]

Holy Rosary Parishioners Pledge $20,000. Collectors at Mass Receive over $13,000 in promissory notes. Last Sunday $5,000 was raised, so they have a total of $18,000. At least $36,500 must be raised to pay the debt incurred in buying the block of land and building which now inadequately house the Holy Rosary Parish and School.

FATHER EDWARD A. MCDONNELL CELEBRATES FIRST MASS

On July 9, 1922, Reverend Edward A. McDonnell[118] celebrated his first solemn Mass at Holy Rosary, his home parish. He had been "recently ordained in the East[119] after studying for the past ten years at the Dominican House in Washington, D.C. He left this week for the South, and received his appointment from the Dominican Motherhouse in California." He was the son of Holy Rosary Parishioner Florence McDonnell.

Christian Brothers Business College which Holy Rosary Dominicans took over and re-named Thomas Aquinas School (1922-1927)

CHRISTIAN BROTHERS – DOMINICAN CONNECTION

The two Dominican co-founders of the Province of the Holy Name of Jesus in California, Jose Sadoc Alemany, O.P. and Sadoc Francis Vilarrasa, O.P. figured greatly in the later coming together of the Holy Rosary Dominicans and the Christian Brothers of Portland. Alemany and Vilarrasa were Catalans from northeastern Spain. They had previously studied together before coming to the U.S. Alemany was appointed Bishop of Monterey in 1850, while Vilarrasa took up the work of forming the Dominican Province in California. Three years after his appointment to Monterey, Alemany was named Archbishop of San Francisco. It was in this capacity that Alemany used his influence, after several years of personal and written pleadings, and a personal visit with Pope Pius IX,[120] to have the Christian Brothers establish a foundation in California. And it was Oregon's third Archbishop, William Gross, CSsR, who persuaded both the Christian Brothers (in 1886) of California and the Dominicans (in 1893) of California to establish foundations in Portland.

DOMINICANS OPERATE AQUINAS SCHOOL 1922-1927[121]
TO STAVE OFF JESUIT INTRUSION INTO THE NEIGHBORHOOD

We are grateful for this account of Aquinas School (then situated between NE Clackamas & Wasco and between NE Grand & Sixth – front facing west on Grand) written by Bro. Stephen Meriwether, O.P., in March 1980, and contained in the archives of the Western Province (paragraphs not in quotes are the words of Brother Meriwether):[122]

In the face of mounting debts, a decrease in available teaching brothers, and tepid support from Archbishop Christie and the parochial clergy of Portland, the Christian Brothers announced their intention to close Christian Brothers College in Portland. The college, located at Grand Avenue and Clackamas Street in the Holladay Addition of

Portland, was opened in 1907 by the Brothers of Christian Schools, who operated a school in Portland as early as 1886. Christian Brothers College offered both classical and commercial instruction to young men throughout the Portland area.

As early as 1920, rumors were circulating that the Christian Brothers soon planned to close their college or sell it to the Jesuits, who were supposedly looking for a school site in Portland. This news sent shock waves through the Dominican community at nearby Holy Rosary Parish. Arthur L. McMahon, Provincial of the Western Dominicans, summed up these fears in a letter to the fathers at Holy Rosary:

"I hope that Archbishop Christie will not allow the Fathers (Jesuits) to take the place without making restrictions as to a public oratory, if he allows them to take it at all. Unless he places a restriction they will have the right, once they are established, to have such an oratory. As you know, they would make the most of their opportunity to draw the people to it, regardless of Holy Rosary."

In the summer of 1922, Provincial McMahon made a last attempt to prevent the Jesuits from obtaining Christian Brothers College. Father McMahon proposed using the college building as a grade school for Holy Rosary Parish until the Christian Brothers would have enough teaching brothers to reopen the college in two or three years. In a letter to Brother Joseph [F.S.C.], Superior of the Christian Brothers, Father McMahon wrote:
"we might arrange with you and the Archbishop to use your building for the parochial school until you will be prepared to resume your work there, thus saving you the taxes that you would have to pay if the building were not to be used for school purposes, and saving the Archbishop the embarrassment of turning to those whom he really does not wish to have there."

In his reply, Brother Joseph was generous in his praise for the Dominicans: "Nevertheless we do not look to the Dominicans, always uniformly kind to us, or to others to inconvenience themselves in the premises." The Christian Brothers had decided to leave Portland and put the college up for sale. Archbishop Christie promptly wrote to Father McMahon proposing that the Dominicans should acquire Christian Brothers College for the bargain price of $45,000 of which the Archbishop and the pastors of Portland would contribute $21,000 – an offer earlier made to the Christian Brothers.

The ghost of the Jesuits continued to haunt Father McMahon, who wrote one week after receiving the Archbishop's proposal:

"He (Brother Joseph) does not mention the Jesuits by name, but he seems to mean that they intend to sell to them.

"In Portland I found that the Jesuits were going about saying that they were to have the place. It seems clearer than ever that we were in jeopardy, that our very existence in Portland was at stake. The Archbishop feared that they would first buy, and then get Rome to say that they should open the school regardless of the wishes of the ordinary and of his clergy…

"The matter has been thoroughly thrashed out in my own mind and with the Portland Fathers, and I can see only one thing to be done, that is that we should take the school. If we do not, the Jesuits will, and then we might just as well 'shut up shop' as to try to hold the people of the parish. We couldn't exist."

With Archbishop Christie's blessing and the encouragement of Portland's pastors, the Dominicans took over Christian Brothers College in the summer of 1922. The Dominicans, though unprepared for the task, expected great success and an enrollment of around 200 students. The school was to continue offering commercial as well as classical courses under the new title of Aquinas School or Aquinas Commercial College and High School as it appeared in a brochure printed by Fr. Arthur Townley, O.P., who arranged the details of the school transfer. Somewhat to their displeasure and surprise, Fathers Andrew Skelly, O.P., and Alphonsus Riley, O.P., were assigned to teach at Aquinas School. Father George Sturla, O.P., came down from Seattle to take up the responsibilities of director of the school.

For a little under $1,900 the Christian Brothers sold the desks and equipment of Christian Brothers College to the Dominicans and school was ready for opening day on September fifth with an enrollment of 125 pupils. Brother Joseph closed his affairs in Portland with a frank warning to his successors:

"In our grievance against Portland, on financial grounds and because of broken or diplomatic promises, in particular, our friends the Dominicans must not be made to suffer. We regret that items of this deal may appear like piking, or could appear as such to one

not familiar with the circumstances. I am under instructions from our Assistant Superior; and the further fact enters, viz., that we got so little for nothing and need so much, that we must, at times, be made to appear ungenerous. Our communities that invested money in Portland have just been instructed to close their accounts as an entire loss. Our District Account…which is our novitiate fund…will show a loss of ten thousand. This is what Portland has done for our progress, not to mention that we never received a subject from there, at least not one of proof."

As with the Christian Brothers before, financing Aquinas School was a heavy burden for the Dominicans. By September 30, 1922 Father McMahon had become anxious that Archbishop Christie had made no noticeable effort to secure the mortgage on the school as he had promised to do. Father McMahon wrote to Father Townley in Portland:

"The Brothers are naturally very much provoked after all their trouble over Portland, and I am beginning to feel provoked too. I cannot see any reason for the delay in taking up the note. Certainly there can be none for the utter disregard of others by the Archbishop. I shouldn't be at all surprised if the Brothers would add this to other complaints they have made to the Delegate. Perhaps it will have to go to him anyway. If the Archbishop intends to put off the payment of the $21,000 until he nets it from the pastors, he will find himself in a bad position…And we have our freedom to throw up the school and make it known just why.

"I hate to think that the Archbishop is contemplating such a thing as trying to force us to carry the loan until he gets ready in the uncertain future to pay it, and while carrying it to pay the interest without getting reimbursement for this; but his ways do not look right."

Even when this matter was settled, the Dominicans faced considerable expenses for books and badly needed repairs on the school building. Expenses were higher than expected at the school and revenues in the Province were low in 1922 as Father McMahon noted:

"It is hardly necessary to say that I was very much upset by the amount due, for you (Fr. Townley) led me to think it would be only about four thousand dollars. It is, as you probably know, $6268.63 (as of December 1922).

"However, as to the indebtedness I can understand that while there was so much to be done hurriedly you could not easily keep track of everything. What is to be done now is to pay it off… Expenses for our students have been exceedingly heavy, much heavier this year than ever before; and our receipts have been distressingly low. Through missions we have received an insignificant sum this year."

During the second year of operation a strong effort was made to secure more Dominican teachers in order to cut the costs of lay faculty. As director of Aquinas School, Fr. Edward Stanislas Olsen, O.P., was appointed to succeed Father Sturla. This was not an assignment to Father Olsen's liking, however, as Father McMahon wrote on July 7, 1923:

"Father Olsen was reluctant to take up the work for personal reasons and because he believed that it is not the work of the Order and that it is contrary to its traditions, that we have nothing to gain by it individually or as a province, and that we cannot hope to succeed where the Christian Brothers failed… There came a crisis in the unsatisfactory affairs of the Brothers, and when they decided to leave Portland there developed a crisis for all; we were really not prepared to take up the work last year, but we had to or else let the Jesuits establish themselves within a stone's throw of Holy Rosary."

With Father Olsen came Fr. Christopher Vincent Lamb, O.P., as instructor of physics and chemistry. Shortly, however, Fr. Andrew Hunt, O.P., took over these classes.

The fall enrollment in 1923 was disheartening, only 81 boys in the upper grades and three in the eighth grade, which had to be canceled. Classes were cut to the minimum required for entrance into the University of Oregon in order to cut costs. Father Olsen lamented the lack of Dominicans trained in teaching technique:

"the school is on a shaky foundation if you expect that it would run with anyone picked up at haphazard, such as Father____. True he shows a wonderful and a most commendable spirit in being willing to undertake the work. But that good spirit is not for this business."

By the end of the first term as director of Aquinas School, Father Olsen was convinced that his gloomy predictions had born fruit. Enrollment was down to 70. On March 18, 1924, Father Olsen gave this report to the Provincial:

"The school is too new to have a spirit and esprit de corps. That comes mainly from tradition begotten of years. So there is no holding principle there. And if there is to be a spirit instilled in Aquinas you must provide Professors who are in a better disposition for the work than we, with the exception of Father (Sebastian) Bohan, possess.

"Personally, I just despise the work. My opinion about it may not mean anything to you but when one is in that sort of mind for the sake of the work itself you should know it, and that the work may not fail completely I feel you should provide a new head for it. I am suggesting Father Bohan because of his ability, his willingness, and his studious make-up, his forward planning gift, his years. And mainly because he is interested and young enough to have hopes and ambitions, incidental to youth in the Priesthood, he will have the zeal to make the school go. That zeal and the hope out of which it springs are simply dead within me.

"I said I just despise the work. I do. To me it is the most futile work any Priest can be assigned to. I just don't believe in it. And from observation and inquiries I can venture to say that not fifty percent of the Priests in America really believe in it. And I'll venture a prophecy at the same time. When, as by necessity, the school will have to make an appeal for financial assistance you will find that the Priests of this town and the people of this town are so apathetic and unbelieving that they will not respond. I hope I am not a true prophet in that. And should it come to pass that there will be a great demand for High School education and Aquinas becomes a filled school then you will find, just as the fruit is ripe and ready for picking and the Province has a chance to get some of its money back, the parishes and other interests will establish High Schools, and we will still be holding an empty sack with a hole in the bottom of it."

Father Olsen's objections went much deeper than his personal frustrations with the work; he doubted the very advisability of religious schools:[123]

"if as a child in a grammar school, and as a youth in high school one has been under the care of Sisters and Brothers in our Catholic Schools and then is unable to stand on his own legs in the Faith while at college, then that in itself is sufficient proof that there is something fundamentally wrong with the system. At least this is wrong, the position taken by so many that the parochial schools are the leaven. But the reply to that is easy. Leaven has to be directly mixed with the dough that is to be leavened. The public schools and parochial schools are apart, openly antagonistic on principle and won't mix, and will induce a condition of antagonism that remains throughout life. But if Catholic children mix in with other children in a public school they ipso facto become the leaven. The Faith is allowed right within the camp of the so-called enemy. To say that the Faith of a child is endangered thereby is derogatory of the power of Faith itself. And besides if the custody of the Faith means a battle why not have the child trained and familiarized with the battle."

Without comment on Father Olsen's predictions or sentiments about the value of parochial schools, Father McMahon accepted his resignation and appointed Fr. Sebastian Maurice Bohan, O.P. as director of Aquinas school for the term opening in September of 1924. Father Bohan vigorously set about bolstering the support of the parochial clergy for Aquinas School and attempting to raise funds for the school. Everyone in Portland was cordial and most flattering of the work of the Dominicans at Aquinas, but all had ample reasons for withholding their financial support, just as Father Olsen had predicted they would.

The third year of Aquinas School started with an expanded Dominican faculty, including Fathers Ehrenfried, O.P., Gabriel Knauff, O.P., Dionysius Mueller, O.P., and Antoninus Healy, O.P. Classes opened on September 2, 1924 with an enrollment of only 58 students. This increased to a more respectable 85 by the end of the month, but still far off the goal of 200 and a considerable decrease from the first year's enrollment of 125. Father Bohan offered some explanation of this dismal picture in a letter of September 22, 1924:

"Since the opening of classes I have been trying to discover a reason for the comparatively poor attendance at the school. Two things have helped to do this, at least in part. One is the rumor, of which I told you (Fr. McMahon) when you were in Portland, that the school would not be kept open long. I think that I have gotten this pretty well killed. The other is the unfortunate impression that we are parish priests spending our spare time in the classroom."

To facilitate his work Father Bohan took up a room in the school, walking back and forth each day to Holy Rosary for his meals, Mass and Office. Soon Father Ehrenfried, who taught English, joined him at Aquinas where they worked feverishly to repair the crumbling building and to keep abreast of the mail, grades and report cards. The increased faculty of Aquinas School, assigned to Holy Rosary Priory, raised serious problems between Father Bohan and Father Townley, Prior of Holy Rosary. While the Prior expected that all the Fathers assigned to the parish would assist in hearing confessions and taking outside Mass assignments, Father Bohan objected that this was an excessive burden on men who spent the whole day in the classroom besides outside time spent in preparation. Father Bohan objected that the Prior's heavy handed rule interfered with the operation of the school, undermined the authority of the school director, and led to divided loyalties among the teachers, with the school taking second place to the needs of the parish.

In preparation for the fall term of 1925 Fr. Andrew Pope, Prior of Holy Rosary, was appointed director of Aquinas School while Father Bohan remained to teach Latin and history. Before classes opened in September, however, Father Pope was in turn succeeded by Fr. Thomas Gabish, O.P. who also served as subprior of Holy Rosary Priory. The pattern of falling enrollment continued through this fourth year of Aquinas School, ending the year with only 62 students. This was followed in September of 1926 with a disappointing 78 pupils. The faculty, however, was greatly strengthened by the arrival of Fr. John Owens, O.P. a noted educator, formerly one of the teaching brothers of Lacordaire, and recently President of the Colegio Lacordaire in Buenos Aires, Argentina.

In 1927 Father McMahon suggested a possible remedy to the drooping enrollment using Aquinas School as a pontifical school for candidates to the novitiate. On January 24, 1927 he wrote:

"It has been my conviction for years that when candidates for the novitiate are studying under our Fathers who are training them along with other boys the results will always be better. Fathers teaching only our candidates are very prone to be neglectful. They are stimulated to do their best by parents, and by public

criticism, and by competition. And the boys are more likely to be stirred by the spirit of emulation to strive harder. For in a large number there will be more who stand out and set a higher standard of personal endeavor."

These plans did not materialize, however, and falling enrollment and heavy financial burdens forced the closing of Aquinas School five years after it was taken over from the Christian Brothers. These had been difficult and frustrating years marked by an almost universal inability to raise funds from the community to support the school, rapid turnover of faculty and frequent changes in direction and leadership, viz., four directors in five years through resignation or Provincial replacement. For two years the Holy Cross Brothers operated a high school in the old Aquinas/Christian Brothers College building, but even this school was closed for lack of support.

On December 30, 1932 an arsonist set fire to the abandoned school building. The structure was so heavily damaged that it had to be razed. The property of Block 75, Holladay's Addition, was sold for $15,000 in August of 1935 to Multnomah School District No. 1, ending the Dominican experiment in secondary education in Portland.

ANTI-CATHOLICISM IN 1920s RAMPANT IN OREGON

The Oregon of the 1920s presented a landscape resplendent with Catholic accomplishments in the building of churches, schools, and hospitals proportionally far greater than ought to be expected of so few, continuing a glorious tradition extending all the way back to the Early Church and up to 20th century America, an entire period when Catholics worldwide were by far the greatest (and in some cases the only) leaders in building schools, hospitals, orphanages, asylums, and leper colonies for the poorest of God's poor. And, in particular, long before the state took an interest in these matters in the late 18th century. For example, St. Vincent's was the first hospital in Oregon, opened in 1875.

In Oregon alone in the 1920s, Catholics had eight hospitals and three orphanages, even though the total Catholic population hovered around the 60,000 mark, while the entire population numbered 783,389 [124] souls. Not only that, but the Church had over 100 priests and about the same number of nuns, as well as approximately 6,000 pupils being taught in Catholic academies and schools. The anti-Catholics in the state decided to do something about these latter statistics. But first a little background is in order to cast proper light on the big happenings.

The American flag was given respect by being prominently displayed in the Sanctuary of every Catholic church in the United States. Children in Catholic schools recite the Pledge of Allegiance at the beginning of every school day. The Church encourages the honest payment of taxes, and part of the Holy Name Pledge states:

I pledge my loyalty to the flag of my country
and to the God-given principles of freedom,
justice and happiness for which it stands.
I pledge my support to all lawful authority
both civil and religious.

The Knights of Columbus stand at attention and recite the Pledge of Allegiance to the flag of the United States at private and public gatherings. In short, Catholic Americans should be above suspicion when it comes to loyalty and love of country; and the deaths of hundreds of thousands of Catholic military in all wars tender mute testimony to this record. Even so, this evidence of loyalty would never (and will never) satisfy the anti-Catholic throng, which holds Catholics in high suspicion because of Catholic love of and allegiance to the Pope, and it was a fear of "foreign control" which allowed the forces of bigotry to prevail in the passage of an Oregon law in 1922 mandating that Catholic children attend public schools. The bigots apparently presumed that a good dose of Protestantism, which was rampant in the public schools of those days, would be the appropriate antidote against the perceived "papism" being preached in the Catholic schools.

LAWYER LEO SMITH GREW UP AT HOLY ROSARY

Leo Smith recalls this third decade of the twentieth century quite well. He attended Christian Brothers Business College (which later became Aquinas School), graduating from its grammar school in 1918. He was a member of Holy Rosary parish, and participated in sports sponsored by the parish Holy Name Society. Leo played on the parish baseball, basketball, and football teams in 1922 & 1923. Father Edward B. Kenny, O.P., associate pastor, coached these teams and was the kids' mentor. Father Kenny inspired Leo and the other kids to such a degree that they practiced with great intensity and, in their own weight division, "won everything in the city league." Father Kenny saw to it that the kids got uniforms and he accompanied them on trips, mostly around town, but also once a year to the state penitentiary in Salem, where they played the prison inmates. Father Kenny died February 11, 1925 at age 45. He had been a faithful priest of God for 21 years.

One of Leo's teammates was "Hap" Albers, whose parents owned Albers Milling Company, which local merchants boycotted because the Albers were Catholic. Leo's father, who was in the meat business, was also boycotted by the same merchants for the same reason, as were many other Catholics who dared to enter business for themselves. At the time, application forms for both private or public employment required applicants to state their religious preference. Anyone who did not answer the question was asked point blank: "What is your religious preference?" If you answered "Catholic" you were automatically disqualified. This discrimination in hiring no doubt encouraged many Catholics to become entrepreneurs in their own right.

Leo was born in 1903, so he was a teenager, then a young college student when some momentous events took place, acts which would warn Oregon Catholics to be wary of the people in control of municipal, city, county and state governments. Leo recalled that this anti-Catholicism was rampant in Oregon throughout his young life. The KKK played no small part in stirring things up. This organization started up as a political organization and, in order to incite people and attract a following, they disseminated all sorts of lies about Catholics, who were in the minority.

CONNECTIONS TO LINDBERGH KIDNAPPING

Leo completed his baccalaureate studies at the University of Portland (then known as Columbia). After graduation, Leo and Tom Sisk attended Gonzaga University, which they left for Georgetown Law School. This adds another footnote to parish history. After roommates Leo and Tom graduated from Georgetown Law School, Tom Sisk joined the FBI. J. Edgar Hoover,[125] in 1932, assigned Tom to the infamous Lindberg kidnapping case. Charles A. Lindberg was famous for making the first solo flight across the Atlantic from New York to Paris, a feat which earned him the appellations "Lucky Lindy" and "The Lone Eagle." The kidnapping of his 20-month-old son in 1932 riveted the attention of the nation. Tom Sisk went to New Jersey on a lead and became famous in FBI history when he traced the ransom money back to the kidnapper, Bruno Richard Hauptmann, whom Sisk arrested after Hauptmann admitted culpability. Hauptmann later retracted his statement of guilt to Sisk, after consulting a lawyer, but it was too late. Hauptmann was tried in a "spectacular trial at Flemington, and electrocuted in Trenton, N.J. prison, Apr. 3, 1936."[126] Tom Sisk now lives in Yakima, Washington.

ANTI-PAROCHIAL SCHOOL BILL
VS. THE DOMINICANS AT HOLY ROSARY

Leo Smith returned to Portland after graduation from Georgetown Law School, and took up a law practice. In those days, he recalls, the attack on the Catholic Church, though concealed behind facades of respectability, was nonetheless utterly pervasive. Several organizations hated Catholics, among them the American Protective Association,[127] the Knights of the Ku Klux Klan[128] and, of course, the Scottish Rite of the Freemasons. Members of one were frequently members of another of these organizations. Of course Freemasonry had been condemned by several popes much to the displeasure of its members, and Catholics are still not allowed to join the Masons, despite rumors to the contrary.

Unquestionably, there existed a large conspiracy, including elements outside of Oregon, designed to mount this attack against the Church. A representative of the Scottish Rite Masons from Washington, D.C., William MacDougal, was quoted as saying: *"Oregon has been chosen as the first state in which to try out this bill because she has no foreign element to contend with, and is, more than any other state, purely and fundamentally American."*[129]

In 1922, this triumvirate of the APA, KKK, and Masons, through the initiative process, put on the Oregon ballot a measure requiring that all children in Oregon between the ages of 8 and 16 attend only public schools, effectively putting an end to the Catholic school system in the state. At the same time they printed, distributed and pasted to their cars, bumper stickers saying *"KKK I Salute You."* They had a lot of money and the backing of a candidate for governor, Walter Pierce, from eastern Oregon, who headed the KKK ticket. KKK members got nearly all of the KKK candidates elected, including Pierce, thus controlling the governor's mansion, the Oregon legislature, the Oregon Supreme Court, and many judgeships throughout the state. A large majority of the people voted in favor of this law (115,506 for, 103,685 against) which, it must be added, the local *Journal & News Telegraph* opposed.

A Child is Not a Creature of the State

When the 1922 law was passed, the Sisters of the Holy Names brought suit against the State of Oregon. Catholic lawyers John P. Kavanaugh, Hall S. Lusk and Dan Malarkey constituted the Sisters' legal team. They pleaded the case in the Federal Court in the old Pioneer Courthouse and won. But KKK Governor Pierce appealed the case to the U. S. Supreme Court. Judge Kavanaugh argued the case before the Supreme Court (Hall Lusk wrote the briefs). This violation of Catholic basic rights, known as the *Oregon School Case,* was overturned within three years (in June 1925) by the Supreme Court, which unanimously declared:

"The fundamental theory of liberty upon which all governments in this Union repose excludes any general power of the State to standardize its children by forcing them to accept instruction from public teachers only. The child is not the mere creature of the State; those who nurture him and direct his destiny have the right coupled with the high duty, to recognize, and prepare him for additional duties."[130]

Leo Smith, in previewing this history of Holy Rosary, stated: *"The Supreme Court in this case not only rendered a decision which would prevent bigots from closing private schools, but it also set forth the monumental and very important legal concept of natural law: that the child is not a creature of the state and the parents not only have the right, but the duty to select a school which their child shall attend to prepare such child for additional duties in life. The decision was unanimous and is still the law."*

As time passed, Leo Smith entered politics and was elected to the state legislature, where he served for six years, and where he lobbied for the Archdiocese for no fee. In those days legislators were paid a stipend of $4.00 a day for 40 days and worked free of charge thereafter. They served out of a sense of duty and responsibility to the state and, according to Leo, *"we had some good legislators because they were dedicated men."*

Archbishop Howard gave Leo all of the Archdiocesan legal work. However, Archbishop Howard's successor, Archbishop Dwyer, did not communicate with Leo as Leo expected (*communication* between client and lawyer being the accepted norm from time immemorial). This non-communication from Dwyer leaves a bad taste in Leo's mouth to this day. To begin with, Dwyer had his secretary call Leo to notify him that he could be the legal representative of the archdiocese. Leo consented; however, when Leo later telephoned the Archbishop or sent letters and briefs to Dwyer for approval or comment he got no reply. Finally, in frustration, Leo says, "I wrote and told him I could no longer represent the archdiocese due to a lack of communication." The archbishop gave no response to that communication either, so Leo threw up his hands in frustration and quit, never again to darken the door of the chancery office.

Catholic Kids Allowed to Ride School Busses

Leo Smith remains proud of the fact that while he was serving in the legislature, Oregon state law was amended to allow students attending parochial schools to ride the school busses. Up until that time, regardless of the weather, only students attending public schools could ride the school busses. So Catholic kids trudged through snow, ice and rain while the public school kids looked down on them from the comfort of the school bus. In 1962, the University of Portland awarded Leo an Honorary Degree of Doctor of Law in recognition of his exemplary service to the Church, the Archdiocese, and Catholic families. Leo, who fought for the rights of the children of those families, was proud and pleased to accept the award, which he cherishes to this day, God love the man.

Dominicans at Holy Rosary Not Intimidated

Meanwhile, the Dominican priests serving Holy Rosary during the 1920s were a courageous lot, uncrushable by the KKK or anyone else. To their everlasting credit these friars, under their strong and resourceful pastor and prior, Rev. Stanislaus Edwin Olsen, O.P.,[131] remained unintimidated during these tumultuous times. Father Olsen opened and operated Thomas Aquinas School as well as Holy Rosary School, and erected a brand new grade school with a $60,000 gymnasium during these months when the Oregon law, which would have put Holy Rosary out of the school business, was wending its way through the legal maze that led to the United States Supreme Court. This vile law, passed by the legislature at Salem in November 1922, would have caused the closure of the new grade school being built. This new school opened in August 1923 (see Chapter 6) almost two years before the Supreme Court finally rendered its landmark decision favorable to Catholic education, a decision deemed a disaster by the anti-Catholic bigots in this state and in the entire republic.

Pistol-Packin' Prior Father Arthur Ignatius Townley, o.p.

Surely one of the most colorful characters ever to have served at

Holy Rosary was Father Arthur Townley, O.P., who succeeded Father Olsen and filled the role of pastor and prior from 1922 to 1925. Edward "Van" Vancoelen, when just a boy, lived in the priory in the room next to Father Townley at the time. Van's father made these room-and-board arrangements because Van's mother was ill and unable to take care of Van. Van also attended Aquinas School (and hosed down the restroom floors there) and performed various chores around the priory. He said Father Townley was very good to him. He described Townley as a nervous man, thin, about 5' 9" tall, and impatient to a fault. A concrete example of Townley's impatience, Van recalls, took place one Sunday when the great writer, Father Andreas M. Skelly, O.P.[132] one of Townley's assistants, was preaching at Sunday Mass. Father Skelly authored many books. He was an intellectual whose sermons, according to Van, *"went right over the heads of the congregation."* One Sunday morning, Townley apparently had had enough of Father Skelly's preaching and, right in the middle of Skelly's sermon, proceeded to the altar and resumed Mass, forcing Skelly to leave the pulpit.

According to Van, Father Townley built two more bedrooms on the west end of the second floor of the priory.

PRIOR TOWNLEY'S SAW MILL

What amazes one is Father Townley's avocation and the time he devoted to it. According to Van, Father Townley operated a sawmill somewhere in the state of Washington. At the time, Townley, as prior, was responsible for Aquinas School, and he had been taken to task by the provincial, Father McMahon for underestimating expenses by over $2200, a considerable sum in those days. Perhaps Townley thought he could make up this deficit through a little entrepreneurial effort. Whatever the circumstances, every Monday morning Townley would leave the priory for the sawmill and be gone all week, returning on Friday evenings. So he spent only weekends at Holy Rosary, even though he was prior. Word of Townley's extraofficial activities reached the ears of the provincial, Father McMahon, who summoned him to San Francisco. Rather than face the

Ed "Van" Vancoelen as a young man. As a boy in the 1920s he lived in the rectory.

music in California, Townley took off for Washington in 1925, lived with his mother and ran the sawmill. Sometime thereafter, Townley apparently with a change of heart, went to San Francisco to meet with the new provincial, Very Rev. Pius M. Francis Driscoll, O.P., for reconciliation.

Driscoll was willing to discuss this friar's return to the Dominican Order, but not until Townley had repaid several Holy Rosary parish families money he, Townley, had borrowed to build his saw mill business. Apparently a heated discussion ensued, during which Townley pulled a handgun and shot in the direction of Provincial Driscoll. One doubts that Townley intended to kill the provincial. In any case, the bullet found its resting place in the wall behind the provincial's desk. Later, when a discussion took place concerning the bullet's removal from the wall, Driscoll apparently said words to the effect: "No I want it to remain there to remind future provincials of the dangers inherent in being a provincial."

According to one source, over 30 years later, the repentant Townley returned for reconciliation when Father Joseph John Fulton, O.P. was provincial (1957-60) and *"before his death, Fr. Townley was reconciled to the Church by Fr. Fulton. He is buried in Benicia, with the same type marker the friars have; but he is buried outside the community circle."*[133]

FATHER FRANCIS ANDREW POPE, O.P. BECOMES PASTOR

Father Townley's successor, Father Pope, was one of the most beloved priors ever to come to Holy Rosary. Father Pope was born in Ennismore, Ontario, Canada on March 13, 1884. Father became naturalized in 1925. He had been

Rev. Father Arthur Townley, O.P.

Rev. Father Francis Andrew Pope, O.P. with his choir boys.

trained by the Christian Brothers and at Sacred Heart College in San Francisco. He took the Dominican habit in 1914 and was ordained in the chapel of the Dominican House of Studies in Washington, D. C. on June 12, 1921. He held a masters degree from Catholic University, in D. C. Father "sang like a herald angel" even late in life and organized boys' choirs at Holy Rosary, where he served as pastor from 1925-1930.[134] He was a holy man, a tireless worker and beloved by the parishioners, as this May 21, 1926 letter to the Dominican provincial makes clear:

Rev. J. B. O'Connor O.P.
Dominican Fathers
San Francisco, Cal.

Reverend and Dear Father,

In behalf of the bazaar committee of Holy Rosary Parish, we have been delegated to direct to you the following plea:

Our pastor, Father Pope, has labored hard and well for the interests of Holy Rosary Parish and, during the past year, has made a most remarkable showing in the reduction of the parish debt. You no doubt, dear Father, realize that the burden is what might be called enormous, and our beloved pastor has come to us and has shouldered the responsibilities in a way that can only be done by one bountifully filled with the grace of God, and a firm determination according to the words of scripture "to render unto Caesar the things that are Caesar's and to God the things that are God's."

From the pulpit, little has been said about money, and religion has been foremost in his heart, causing him to be we might say the most beloved pastor we have ever had. In his own quiet way he has conducted the finances of the parish in such a way that we know that his sacrifices have been many, and without question, there is attached to accomplishments similar to his a mental strain that

must be relaxed ere he become old before his years.

It is our wish and plea, dear Father, as representatives of Holy Rosary Parish, that permission be granted our reverend pastor, Father Pope, for sufficient leave from his duties to attend the coming Eucharistic Congress so that he may enjoy a much needed rest to which he is justly entitled. This was the unanimous vote of the committee at a recent meeting and, while over the protest of the pastor, nevertheless, we feel that he is entitled to this consideration. And we as members of his flock entreat you to grant him this leave. A sufficient amount to defray his expenses for the trip has been voted to be withheld from the proceeds of a recent successful bazaar.

As the summer schedule of Masses will shortly be given effect, we feel that for a few Sundays he is absent, the Masses can very well be arranged without any undue inconvenience to the parish. And whatever the inconvenience may be, we are more than willing to cooperate in order that he may have the pleasure of this worthwhile trip.

Therefore, once again, dear Father, let us beseech you to grant our request and sanction the leave of our dear pastor to participate in this wonderful exemplification of Catholicity. As the time is growing short and reservations should be made as early as possible, might we ask you to take action as soon as possible , handling direct with Father Pope to avoid any unnecessary delay.

May the grace of Almighty God be with you is the wish of the members of Holy Rosary Parish, of which we as a committee represent.

(signed)
John Farrell, James W. Mackey
O'Connor Committee

Father Pope had a wonderful vacation with the provincial's blessing; he expressed gratitude to one and all.

MARBLE ALTAR SHIPPED TO
HOLY ROSARY FROM SAN FRANCISCO

The Catholic Sentinel dated July 24, 1930,[135] contained the following brief article: *New Marble altar being erected in Holy Rosary Church, Third and Clackamas Streets, to be used for the first time for Holy Mass on August 3, 1930. The interior of the church is being remodeled to harmonize.* This altar had been in St. Dominic's Church in San Francisco, when that church was destroyed during the 1906 earthquake. Father Pope had the altar shipped by train to Portland in 1927. This altar replaced the old altar which contained reredos.[136] The names of all the people who contributed to the shipping, handling and refurbishing of this "new" altar were inscribed on a scroll which was placed inside the altar. This scroll later disappeared. The altar first abutted the rear wall of the Sanctuary, but was turned around during the liturgical changes of the 1960s.

Our marble altar which was at St. Dominic's in San Francisco
until that church was destroyed in the 1906 earthquake.
Father Pope had the altar shipped to Portland by train in 1927.

THE CALAROGA CLUB[137]

During Father Pope's tenure as prior and pastor, he founded the Calaroga Club, thereby allowing the young people in the parish to enjoy wholesome pleasures such as dances and outings. They also put on plays elegantly scripted by Associate Pastor Clyde Aloysius Sylvester Chamberlain, O.P. who had left Holy Rosary tour here in the parish.[138] The *Holy Rosary Catholic Monthly*[139] noted:

Last Friday was the time of the Halloween party given by the Calaroga club. It was a marvelous success. The decorations and the music was the best in the city of Portland. The Calaroga Club is a society composed of members who do things. The short time that the club has been in existence has shown that the club is the origin of the activities of the parish.

The Calarogan Players, the dramatic unit of the club, have two plays in rehearsal, "Alone," a religious play treating of purgatory, and "The Ghost Story," by Booth Tarkington. The latter, in spite of its uncanny name, is one of the best comedies of the past few years.

"Alone," the other play, by Father Chamberlain, is a religious play THAT IS DIFFERENT. It has for its theme the return of a soul from purgatory. There is no attempt to tax the credulity of the audience. It will be a hardened heart indeed that will not throb the faster at the duel scene, or will not go out in sympathy to the hapless ALONE as she wanders about the scenes of her former life finding that all save the priest and the Little Boy have forgotten her.

When the priest anoints ALONE on the stage, the scene borders on the sublime. Leo White as the Priest rises to the heights of a real artist. Master Paul McGrath in the role of the "Little Boy," acts as though he were a veteran of the stage. Margaret McDowell plays Alone, supported by Jack Gaus as John Poole, George Eilers as Fred Blunt, Rosalie Gobbi as the Mother, Leo White as the Priest, Walter Grant as the Doctor, Paul McGrath as Little Boy, Mary Clare Larkins as Alice Poole, Mary Marcelle Dineen as Poole's little girl, Alice Murphy as the High School Miss, Ambrose Finn as Jones, Joseph McCormick as Epworth, and the Guests in the Garden Scene.

BIGOTS' 1922 ATTACKS HARBINGER OF THINGS TO COME –
PASSAGE OF RELIGIOUS GARB BILL

Logic has little or no effect on prejudice, emotion being the enervating force. So, while celebrating their victory in the Oregon School Case (before it was declared unconstitutional), the bigots turned their wrath against the Catholic clergy and religious who were teaching in public schools. Father Wilfred P. Schoenberg, S.J. relates part of the story:[140]

The state legislature, entirely controlled by Governor Pierce and the Klan…sought other means for satisfying their lusty constituents. They finally seized upon the idea of a "Religious Garb" bill, which they passed on January 31, 1923, with a more than comfortable margin. According to this law, members of religious orders, wearing their customary habits, could no longer teach in public schools. As a result, Sisters of the Holy Names were barred from teaching in St. Paul public school, and public schools in Verboort, Sublimity, and Roy, which had been staffed by the Sisters of St. Mary, were returned to the status of secular schools, despite their entirely Catholic membership and tax support.

ATTACKS AGAINST THE CHURCH CONTINUE AD INFINITUM

The attacks against the Church, which occurred in Oregon and elsewhere, would continue unabated and the Church would still bleed as she was destined to do. The Oregon School Case and

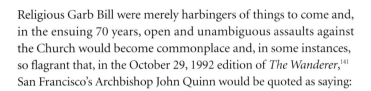
Advertisements in the November 1925 issue of Father Pope's *Holy Rosary Catholic Monthly*.

Religious Garb Bill were merely harbingers of things to come and, in the ensuing 70 years, open and unambiguous assaults against the Church would become commonplace and, in some instances, so flagrant that, in the October 29, 1992 edition of *The Wanderer*,[141] San Francisco's Archbishop John Quinn would be quoted as saying:

If you want to be a Catholic today, you have to be prepared to be ridiculed, to see the Mass and sacraments profaned and ridiculed…There is no longer room for ambiguity. We have to know where we stand, and with God's help we have to stand firm in the midst of these increasing attacks. The Catholic Church, it should be clear, is the one thing in American society which is exempt from the rules of fair play and which can be openly ridiculed and held up to contempt and ridicule.

The archbishop was referring to active anti-Catholic organizations, the media, the movie and music industries and some of their most vocal and prominent idols. But attacks would come from within the Church as well, from cardinals, bishops, priests, theologians, nuns and influential lay Catholics – 'apostates' constantly assaulting the Church by denouncing its teaching and its hierarchy in Rome, recalling the Gospel of Luke:[142]

> *This child is destined to be the downfall
> and rise of many in Israel,
> a sign that will be opposed.*

Archbishop Quinn would remind his listeners and readers of this as well, and give attentive Catholics this profound message:

The path of the Church must be the path of Christ. If Christ had to suffer ridicule and rejection and crucifixion, the Church, too, must suffer ridicule, rejection and crucifixion…I want you to stand with me and to be unashamedly Catholic and to stand firm and coura-geous in the face of the increasing attacks on the Church – that is, on you and me."

Further commentary on the pervasive aspect of anti-Catholicism is not within the purview of this chapter. We are getting ahead of the story. As the Dominican priests and nuns kept their vigilance and struggled to build a healthy and hardy Holy Rosary community in this third decade of the twentieth century, their number was reduced by the untimely death of their eminent colleague, Father Bohan.

FATHER MAURICE SEBASTIAN BOHAN. O.P., DIES AT AGE 34 [143]

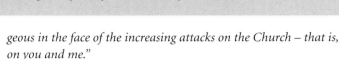

Father Maurice Sebastian Bohan, O.P., died at St. Vincent Hospital in Portland on December 3, 1928. He had been a priest for only 10 years. The cause of death was not given. A native of San Francisco, he studied for the priesthood at the Dominican House of Studies in Benicia, California, then attended Catholic University, Washington, D.C., and the Collegio Angelico in Rome, possessed a licentiate degree in canon law and a lectorate in theology. In addition to teaching at Aquinas School and once serving as its director, he became widely known for preaching missions and retreats and lecturing on the radio under the auspices of the Catholic Truth Society of Oregon, which was founded to combat the efforts of the APA, KKK, Masons and others attacking the Church during this period. He was a prominent speaker on Monsignor Charles Smith's *Catholic Hour*. In addition, he was the beloved chaplain and friend of the Catholic Daughters of America, Court Multnomah No. 270 in Portland. The *Holy Rosary Catholic Monthly* reported:

The funeral services were held in Holy Rosary Church, Wednesday morning December 5th [1928], where a Solemn Requiem Mass was celebrated at 10 o'clock, the Very Rev. F.A. Pope, prior of Holy Rosary, being the celebrant, assisted by the Rev. John A. McKeon as deacon and the Rev. Wm. McClory as subdeacon. The Rev. I.E. McNamee

The 1930 First Holy Communion class. 1st row: (left to right) William Lesac, Donald Walsh.
2nd row: Edward Tobkins, Thomas King, Joseph Illk, Robert Hornsby, unknown.
3rd row: John Oreskovich, Frank Churich, Irene Barrett, Father T.S. Connelly, Patricia Hunt, Michael Pezel, and Joseph Yuskat.

*was master of ceremonies. The Rev. Chas. M. Smith, executive
secretary of the Catholic Truth Society, preached the sermon. The
Most Rev. Archbishop Howard was present in the sanctuary and
gave the absolution. Many of the clergy were present and a host of
friends filled the church during the service. Following the services
here, the remains were taken to Benicia, California, for interment
in the cemetery of the Dominican Fathers.*

NEW ORGAN DONATED TO THE CHURCH

According to a brief article in the *Catholic Sentinel*[144] dated
*February 2, 1928: "A donation of a new organ for the Church has
been announced. The Church has been requested that the name of
the donor be withheld."* [NOTE: *The Parish Digest* dated April 2,
1944 stated that "Mr. J. F. Barron presented the first organ to
our church."].

THE ROARING TWENTIES

This decade, known as the "Roaring '20s," came on the heels of
federal laws designed to do away with the "evils of wine and gin."
On December 18, 1918, Congress passed and sent to the
(then) 48 states for ratification, the 18th Amendment to the
Constitution, prohibiting the manufacturing, sale, or service
of alcoholic beverages. On January 16, 1919, Nevada became
the 36th state to ratify that amendment, which then became
the law of the land. People did not stop their consumption of
alcohol, of course, they merely made their own "bathtub gin"
or frequented one or more of the speak-easies which sprang

up like water lilies and were soon so numerous as to make
Prohibition a farce.

World War I had ended in 1918 and the boys were coming
home. It was a time for celebrating, and a little lubrication by
liquor would make festivities much more enjoyable. Huge profits
would accrue to those who bought whiskey in Canada (which
did *not* have Prohibition) and imported it illegally into the
United States, one of the ways by which many respectable people
acquired huge wealth. By the end of the decade, the people
knew it was farcical to continue this hypocrisy, and Franklin
Delano Roosevelt, the 1932 presidential candidate, made repeal
of Prohibition a part of his platform. The 21st Amendment
repealed the 18th on December 5, 1933, and the party was over.
In reality, the party was over in 1929, when post-World War I
prosperity came to an end and stock prices plummeted on Wall
Street, ushering in the Great Depression. This depression would
last well into the 30s and cause President Roosevelt to resort
to pump-priming the economy to rebuild the American infra-
structure and "put people back to work." There followed a
military build-up, begun around 1938. Eventually, World War II
would soon provide work to practically any able-bodied person
willing to serve in the armed forces or work in a factory. Then
the Japanese attacked Pearl Harbor on December 7, 1941, and
we were at war. This evil event would rebuild the economy to a
scale previously unimagined, and at a cost of $360,000,000[145]
and 1,078,162 American casualties. But let's visit the 30s first.

Notes to the Text

115 Page 1, Col. 1.

116 This cannot be because their was no school at that time. The agreement between the Dominicans and Archbishop Christie (that Holy Rosary would henceforth be a parish) was signed and became effective February 15, 1908. Holy Rosary purchased the school block (212) December 9, 1911. The first school (the Noon House on block 212) first opened September 3, 1912. But it is true that the Archbishop wanted the Dominicans to operate a parish school.

117 Page 1, Col. 4.

118 Father McDonnell gave the retreat when our own Father Paul Duffner, O.P. received his habit in 1934.

119 Taken from *The Catholic Sentinel* of July 13, 1922, pg. 5, col. 2.

120 See page 8, *Called to the Pacific*, by Ronald E. Isetti, F.S.C., St. Mary's College of California, Moraga, CA, 1979.

121 While under the Christian Brothers, it had been variously named St. Michael's School (at SW Fifth & Mill), St. Mary's School (at the Cathedral), Blanchet Institute (again at Fifth & Mill) and, finally Christian Brothers Business College (at NE Clackamas & Grand), according to pages 51 & 52 of their 1886-1911 Silver Jubilee book.

122 Files XI: 40601, and XI: 406:0:2, Dominican Provincial Headquarters, Oakland, California.

123 Editor's note: This was prior to the issuance of Pope Pius XI's *Encyclical Letter on Christian Education of Youth*, dated December 1, 1929, which strongly promoted the "founding and maintaining of schools and institutions adapted to every branch of learning and degree of culture."

124 Page 521, *A History of the Catholic Church in the Pacific Northwest* by Father Wilfred P. Schoenberg, S.J., The Pastoral Press, Washington, D.C., 1987.

125 Hoover once ordered that profiles be made of the finest FBI agents throughout the U.S. The subsequent studies identified only two commonalities among those identified as top agents: they were all Catholic and of Irish descent. Thereafter, he hired mostly Irish Catholics until forced to end this discrimination when new Federal anti-discrimination laws were passed.

126 Page 548, *1992 World Almanac and Book of Facts*, 200 Park Ave., New York, N.Y. 10166.

127 The APA "at its height claimed millions of members… it "sought to repeal naturalization laws, to forbid teaching any foreign languages in public schools, and to tax Church property." Page 169, *Our American Catholic Heritage* by Albert J. Nevins, M.M., Our Sunday Visitor, Inc. Huntington, Ind. 46750, 1972.

128 "By 1925, the Klan claimed five million members," page 170, ibid.

129 Page 522, *A History of the Catholic Church in the Pacific Northwest 1743-1983*.

130 Pope Pius XI quoted this statement in his *Encyclical Letter on Christian Education of Youth*, (St. Paul Editions), December 1, 1929.

131 Father Olsen later had to have his legs amputated due to diabetes.

132 See Chapter 7 for more on Father Skelly.

133 Quoted from a footnote on an undated *List of Pastors – Holy Rosary Church, Portland, Oregon* on file in the archives of Holy Rosary Church.

134 Father Pope's personnel record shows he was an assistant pastor at Holy Rosary for a brief period in August 1933.

135 Page 5, column 3.

136 Webster: "A screen or partition wall usu. ornamental and of wood or stone located behind an altar."

137 No relationship to Calaroga Terrace, which was built many years later. Calaroga was the birth place of St. Dominic.

138 Father Chamberlain's personnel record contains no mention of his WWI service or his two assignments at Holy Rosary, presumably because of clerical omission; nevertheless Holy Rosary Parish bulletins and archdiocesan Catholic directories show such service. See Chapter 7.

139 Published by Father Pope and covering November 1925.

140 Page 527, *History of the Catholic Church in the Pacific Northwest 1743-1983*.

141 A Catholic weekly newspaper, 201 Ohio Street, Saint Paul Minnesota 55107.

142 Words of Simeon at Christ's Presentation in the Temple, Luke 2-34.

143 Some accounts say age 35.

144 Page 5, Col. 1.

145 Pages 699 & 702, *The World Almanac and Book of Facts, 1992*.

Pope John Paul visits our Fr. Hofstee, Chaplain of Tala Leper Colony, Philippines.

DEPRESSION AND THE PRE-WAR YEARS

A FORMER HOLY ROSARY DOMINICAN SERVES LEPERS

A remarkable priest, "a true saint," served at Holy Rosary during this decade: Father Anthony Leo Hofstee. Father Hofstee was born June 30, 1903 in Utrecht, Holland, the son of Dominic and Mary Hofstee. He emigrated to the U.S. and attended St. Mary's High School in Oakland. He was ordained in 1932 and served at Holy Rosary in 1934. Later assignments took him to Berkley, Seattle, and Vallejo. When World War II started, Father Hofstee signed up as a Catholic chaplain in the U.S. Army. His military duties took him to the Phillipines, where he learned about the lepers at Tala. It had a profound effect on him and would change his life forever. After his discharge at the end of the war, he requested and received from the Western Dominican Province permission to open the Tala Leprosarium in the Philippines and serve as its chaplain. Parishioners at Holy Rosary made contributions to his work over the years. Mother Teresa put a stamp on his greatness. We are grateful for the following information from parish bulletins, furnished by two beautiful sisters, daily communicants, long-time Holy Rosary parishioners and living "saints" themselves, Maryetta and Elizabeth Foley.[146]

[Dated 5-27-84] Father Anthony Leo Hofstee, O.P., who was a priest at Holy Rosary in the '30s is now 80 and living in retirement after his 35 years as chaplain and director of the Tala Leprosarium in the Philippines, recently received the first Mother Teresa Award. Mother Teresa flew personally to Manila to present the award named after her, which carried a cash prize of $50,000. In her remarks during the presentation, Mother Teresa said the example set by Fr. Hofstee should be emulated by everyone in order to alleviate the sufferings of the poorest of the poor in the whole world.

[Dated April '86] Word has been received that our Dominican Father, Leo Hofstee, O.P., died at the Chaplain's house in Tala, The Philippines, on Saturday, April 26, 1986. Born June 30, 1903 in Utrecht, Holland, Fr. Leo entered the Dominican Province from Everett, WA. in 1925, and was ordained a priest in 1932. He spent more than 45 years working for and living with the lepers on Tala and it was among them that he spent his last days. In accordance with his wishes he was buried in Tala. Please keep this dedicated man in your prayers: in the minds of many he was a true saint.

Father Hofstee had a twin brother, also a priest, Father G.M. Hofstee, S.V.D., who served as a missionary in India. Father Gregory Anderson, O.P., recalls that *our* Father Hofstee was a "very funny man," and a man "of heroic virtue." He added: "I wouldn't be surprised if he were canonized."

FATHER WILLIAM STANISLAUS McDERMOTT, O.P., BECOMES PASTOR – GOOD COMMUNITY SPIRIT IN THE PRIORY

The Roaring Twenties had ended with a crash, and the United States would suffer through its worst depression in history, ending only when World War II would begin a decade later; but for now things were stable at Holy Rosary.

Father McDermott, who had been serving as a missionary[147] at Holy Rosary for several years, was elected prior in 1930. Born April 5, 1889, he hailed from Butte, Montana, was educated at Mt. St. Charles College in Helena, the capital, received his habit on September 16, 1912, and was ordained May 10, 1918 at the Dominican House of Studies in Washington, D.C. He would move on to become Master of Students and Novice Master at Benicia and Ross during the period 1931-1938. In 1938, he returned as an assistant at Holy Rosary, and remained here until his death October 17, 1945, at age 56, having served God for more than a quarter of a century.

ARCHBISHOP HOWARD ASKS THAT DOMINICAN PROVINCIAL PROVIDE RETREAT FOR DIOCESAN PRIESTS

In a March 1, 1931 letter to Provincial James B. Connolly, O.P., Father William McClory, O.P., wrote:

Last evening the Archbishop called up to ask if you were going to give any retreats. If you are, he would like you to give the retreat to the priests of the diocese. Had he been certain about it, he no doubt would have written directly to you. I told him that I would write you immediately about it. Could you let me know, so that I may convey your message to him. I think it would be a wonderful thing were you to take it…

The retreat begins on the fifteenth of June which is a Monday and continues until Friday.

Everything is going along well here in Portland. Fr. Clyne is very willing and does everything that is asked in a very religious-like way. Rules are being observed as well as usual. Of all the houses that I've been in, Portland is the best. I think that we have observance that compares with any in this Province or any other.

The provincial, in a March 4, 1931 letter replied that he would be pleased to give the requested retreat to the priests of the archdiocese.

FATHER THOMAS STEPHEN CONNELLY, O.P.
(B. DECEMBER 17, 1892 – D. DECEMBER 6, 1965)

Father Connelly succeeded Father McDermott at the helm of Holy Rosary in 1932. He would serve here in that capacity until 1935. Father was born December 17, 1892 in San Francisco, so he was 39 years old when he took over the parish. He was ordained on May 10, 1918 in the chapel of the Dominican House of Studies, Washington, D. C. He was a Latin teacher and had been assistant pastor at Holy Rosary (1924-1925), so all was not new to him.

The Reverend
Stephen T. Connelly, O.P.

Further, he would return to Holy Rosary as pastor (Jan. '47-Sep. '48). He died on December 6, 1965, just shy of age 73. According to sources in the parish, Father Connelly and Catholic Charlie Wentworth, the owner of an automobile dealership in Portland, were fast friends and Charlie provided a free car for the priests every year. According to Father Dominic Hoffman, Father Connelly had a falling out with Archbishop Howard, who wrote a letter to the provincial asking that Father Connelly be transferred out of Portland. Father Connelly served two tours in Seattle.

FATHER FREDERICK BERTRAND CLYNE, O.P.
MOST DECORATED CHAPLAIN OF WORLD WAR I

Father Clyne was born March 23, 1877, so he was in his fifties when he served at Holy Rosary in 1932, 1933, and 1934. He had previously been a pastor of the Dominican parish in Pittsburg, California, and it was rumored that he built the rectory there largely on his winnings from poker, at which he was a whiz. He would go on to serve as pastor at Benicia from 1938-1944. He came from a wealthy and powerful Benicia family and his exploits in World War I were legendary. According to Father Gregory Anderson, O.P., former associate pastor at Holy Rosary and currently serving at St. Jude's Shrine in California, Father Clyne was an urbane, smooth individual, of medium height and build, who once settled an insurrection of soldiers at Plattsberg, New York and, through special acts of Congress, simultaneously held commissions in the Army, Navy, and Marines.

In a letter to the provincial dated October 13, 1918, Father Olsen commented: "*Had a letter from Fr. Clyne at the headquarters of Pershing – he was about to leave that night for the front-line trenches.*" Allegedly, Father Clyne personally captured 17 Germans with an empty rifle and, at the end of the war, he was the most decorated chaplain in the military. Because of his reputation, genius and connections, he was chosen by the California bishops to shepherd through the California legislature a bill to exempt Catholic Schools from taxation. Father Clyne's wealthy brother always provided him with a new Stutz Bearcat car, which he used to chauffeur his altar boys to burials at the local cemeteries in high fashion, much to their delight. He took Father Anderson to lunch at DiMaggio's Restaurant in San Francisco many times. Father Charles Hess, O.P., mentioned that Father Clyne – when Hess was a young priest – also took him to DiMaggio's.

PARISHIONERS PITCH IN TO REDUCE DEBT DESPITE DEPRESSION

The 1930s were depressed times in Portland as well as all over the U.S. and the world. The grand experiment to build up Lloyd Center came to a standstill. Excavation for a grand hotel on the corner of 15th & Multnomah had proceeded before the project was put on hold, so a big hole remained on that corner. The enterprising Lloyd Corporation staff filled the foundation with benches and a stage from which concerts were given. When the economy improved, building resumed. Meantime, fifteen blocks northwest of the site, at Holy Rosary, it was announced in January 1932 that *"the following members of the parish are using a new series of envelopes for their weekly offering. We wish to express to them our sincere thanks for their cooperation:"*

Mrs. I. Albers
Mrs. L. Agusutus
J. Byrne
Mae Caraher
Mrs. A. Charmard
F.C. Collier
Elizabeth Corcoran
Mrs. P. Coyne
Ray Collins
Mrs. R.M. Drake
Agnes Dowd
Mrs. J.L. Day
Mrs. A. Dewar
J.J. Driscoll
T.F. Eilers
Clements Eilers
Wm. Eivers
H.W. Erren
J.H. Faber
J.H. Esch
F.E. Fraights
Mrs. T. Fitzpatrick
Nell Gaffney
E.E. Gambee
E. Gaffney
R. Gobbi
C. Gill
Thos. Gavin
F.J. Harold
Mrs. F. Medernach
B. McCaffrey
E.A. McGrath
Mrs. B. McCaffrey
Ione McCreary
Alice McGrat
James McDevitt
H.A. McMahon
Elizabeth McMahon
J. McMillan
C. McDowell
B.H. Neer
J.L. Neidermeyer
H. Neidermeyer
Mrs. M. O'Connor

Miss H. Albers
Mr. J. Barron
Mrs. W. Alderson
Olive Campbell
F. Charmard
Grace Connelly
Mrs. H. Cruttenden
Mrs. C. Carpenter
A.J. DeRossier
Catherine Dowd
Frances Dowd
Geo. Duggan
M.J. Doyle
Mrs. C. Dashcolis
Geo. Eilers
John Eilers
C.A. English
Emma Erren
Dorothy Faber
Mrs. J. Farrell
Alice Frainey
H. Fenolio
Anna Gaffney
F. Gaunero
Mrs. M. Gobbi
F.S. Grant
A.J. Grobin
E. Montgomery
J.A. Moore
M. Mercier
Don McEachern
Mrs. D. McEachern
D. McCabe
Mrs. M. McCreary
L.M. McPherson
M.D. McMahon
F. McMahon
Mrs. L. McMahon
Grace McDonald
Francis McDowell
C.A. Neidermeyer
J.E. Neidermeyer
J.J. O'Connor
Elizabeth O'Keefe

J.R. O'Keefe
W.E. Pound
Jos. J. Quirk Jr.
Fred J. Rutto
Mrs. S. Richards
C.L. Schoenfeldt
W.E. Sheehan
Mrs. J. Sheehy
Mrs. C. Slater
Grace Sweeney
J.W. Sweeney
M. Slaird
Mrs. M. Hartman
Thos. Healy
F. Hennessey
Lillian Hughes
F.J. Hoerner
Mrs. Illidge
M. Jackson
Mrs. N.J. Kelly
Mrs. C. Kenison
L. King
Mrs. M. Lansing
J.C. Larkins
Ellen Lavin
W.L. Lorimer
E.P. Murphy
J.F. Maguire
B.E. Metzler
M. Muelhberg
Elizabeth Maher
Mary Martin
Mrs. M.G. Munly
Mrs. A. Mayer
T.F. Meager
Mrs. E.J. Tracy
Robt. Tynah
Mrs. G. Veatch
Mrs. M. White
Leo White
Mrs. E. Walsh
J.R. Weich
Lucille Wilke
Helen Zarra
Mrs. Jones
M. Sharkey
Mrs. M. McLoughlin
Shirley Maguire
Helen McRaith
Mrs. C. Hensel
Mrs. Vandal
Mrs. Curley
Mrs. Tipton
Mrs. M. Sells
Marg. Sharkey
H. Kosterman
Mrs. A. Barber
P.G. Moore
Mrs. Oreskovick

Gladys Peterson
J.F. Quirk
G. P. Richsen
Thelma Rutto
A. Sarsfield
Dorothy Scherfren
Mrs. A. Singleman
Mary Sherbert
R.E. Goodwin
Mark Sweeney
A. Sweeney
W. Hartman
H.J. Hayes
F.B. Hughes
E.J. Hughes
T.S. Hogan
Alma Hoerner
Lois Jackson
Mrs. Jackson
J.L. Kelly
Anna King
Guy King
Ed. Larkins
P. Lavin
Mrs. O.M. Lowell
Anna Murphy
R.K. Murphy
J.R. Maguire
D.A. Morris
Mary Maher
Fred Martin
W. Munly
Mrs. H. Manning
J.T. Meagher
Miss C. Meagher
Mrs. Dr. Tynah
J.J. Vossen
B.H. Winneman
Miss B. White
Mrs. W. Walsh
Eugene Walsh
T.F. Weich
W. Williams
Emma Zarra
Thos. Farrell
M.M. Creegan
P. Early
A. McRaith
Mrs. Currier
Miss A. Kelly
Mrs. Lindsay
Mrs. J. Landa
Mrs. Gilrain
Miss A. Leahy
Mary Phillips
Miss K. Weiss
P.J. Bannon
Miss Fay Kennedy

The bulletin recording the previously mentioned names also noted:

CHURCH SUPPORT

Let each member give "according as the Lord has prospered him," is a command to be considered, even as the Ten Commandments. No member of the Church can consider himself or herself a conscientious Catholic if he or she is not willing to contribute a just share towards the support of religion. Let your conscience be your guide, but do not deceive yourself by unbalanced excuses. Whatever it is, give willingly, cheerfully and regularly. We fail to have heard of anyone who has ever gotten rich by economizing on his church contributions nor of anyone becoming a pauper by obeying this commandment.

One would think that any Catholic would indeed feel honored to donate regularly to a work which directly represents God, the Giver of all goods, upon this earth.

We may not all be able to give as large an amount as we would like, but even the widow's mite was acceptable to the Lord.

FATHER LAWRENCE ROBERT "CHICK" LINDSAY, O.P.

Father Lindsay was another priest who served at Holy Rosary for several years in the 1930s. He got his nickname "Chick" from his fellow priests, who jokingly observed that he came from The Chicken Capital of the World, Pataluma, California. Actually, he was born in Rutherford, California. He was an "enormous Scotsman with a great mop of white

Father Lawrence Robert Lindsay, O.P.

hair," had a "deep booming voice resembling that of a carnival barker," and a "delightful man" in the words of Father Gregory Anderson, O.P., Father Lindsay died of a heart attack while taking a shower.

FATHER WILLIAM ROBERT FEEHAN, O.P.

(SHOT IN THE FOREHEAD WITH AN ARROW)

Father Feehan, another popular priest assigned to Holy Rosary in the 1930s (Feb. '35-Oct. '38), was a native of San Francisco, where he was ordained, at St. Mary Cathedral, on June 15, 1929. He was born December 17, 1899, so was age 35 when he first arrived at Holy Rosary. Joe Mayer, who lived in the rectory in those days, smiled and jokingly referred to the "Terrible Tobkins" in connection with Father Feehan. Joe and his friend, Leo Tobkin[148] recall Father Feehan as a fairly good baseball player. Father Feehan headed the CYO baseball team. Joe and Leo were teenagers at the time and the priests and young parishioners

played sandlot ball on the lot south of the church, which Holy Rosary owned in those days. They recalled that Father Feehan's one shortcoming at third base was a weak throwing arm, so they persuaded him to move to the second-base position.

Father Feehan, adored by the younger set in the parish, ran the teenage Calaroga Club, which held dances, put on plays, engaged in outings, and so forth. Leo Tobkin recalls, for example, that the Calaroga Club kids would rent a U-Haul truck, fill it with straw, put an old rug on top of the straw, and drive up to Mount Hood to go skiing – right after Father Feehan, who accompanied them, finished saying the 6:00 a.m. Mass.

Father William Robert Feehan, O.P. (c. 1936)

THE SLINGS AND RUBBER-TIPPED ARROWS OF OUTRAGEOUS FORTUNE

The priests of the parish, particularly Fathers Feehan and Chamberlain, visited the Tobkin house regularly in those days. The Tobkins lived first at 11th & Tillamook and then at 17th & Multnomah. The kids loved the priests, and the feeling was mutual. The family consisted of the parents, Mary and Zeno, a longshoreman, five boys and four girls: Bernard, Florence, Amby, Leo, Paul, Margaret, Edward, Dolores, and Rosemary Tobkin.

On one such visit one of the young Tobkin girls (either Margie or Florence), who was playing with a bow & arrow tipped with a rubber suction cup, took aim and shot Father Feehan on the forehead (whether intentionally or not is still contested – but the clan did not get the moniker "Terrible Tobkins" for nothing). Anyway, they tugged and tugged trying to remove the offensive arrow from poor father's head. This was on a Saturday night. The next morning the Tobkin clan prayed in their usual first-row pew in front of the pulpit, and their guardian angels could see them snickering as Father Feehan gave his sermon – for there in the middle of father's forehead was a round, red spot, plainly visible to all, the remains of father's recent encounter with the "Terrible Tobkins."

Father Feehan went to his eternal reward on April 19, 1963. Provincial Father Joseph Agius was the celebrant at Father Feehan's funeral Mass in Vallejo, California on April 24th. Father Gregory Anderson, O.P. said that Father Feehan was so beloved that two separate funeral Masses had to be celebrated to accomodate the crowds honoring this holy man, who had been a faithful servant of God for 33 years.

NOTES TO THE TEXT

146 Who loaned us a looseleaf binder of church bulletins and newspaper clippings they've saved over the years, tracking the goings-on at Holy Rosary; an example of the on-going love affair parishioners of Holy Rosary have had with their beloved Dominicans.

147 Not all priests residing at Holy Rosary are parish priests, even though they live in the priory. Some are in retirement, while others take on special duties, for example directing the activities of the Rosary Center.

148 Leo's brother Ambrose, Fred Eilers, Bennie Leonard and Ed Hoerner, who graduated from Holy Rosary School together in 1930, still play bridge together every Monday night.

149 No relationship to Calaroga Terrace, which wasn't even planned until the late 1950s.

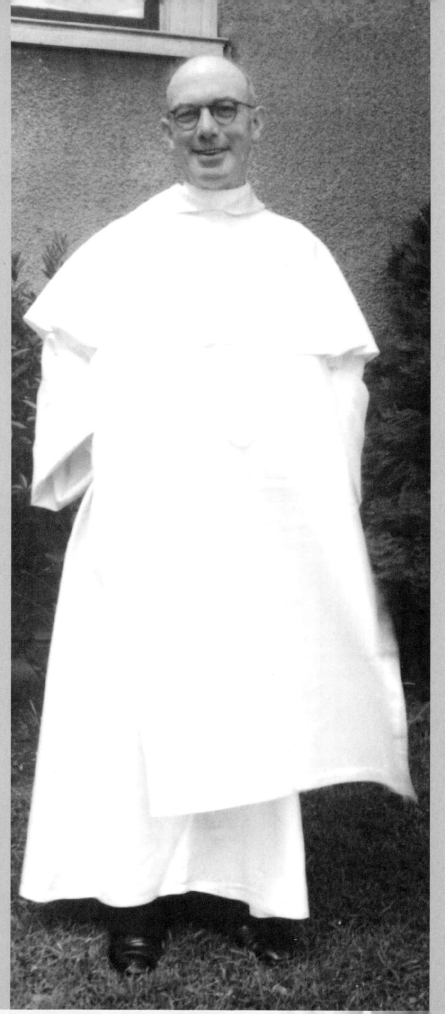

Father Edward
Gerard McMullan, O.P.
(c. 1936)
Pastor 1936-1942

WORLD WAR II AND POST-WAR YEARS
AT HOLY ROSARY

Father Edward Gerard[150] McMullan, O.P., became pastor at Holy Rosary in 1936[151] and would continue his tenure as pastor during the first year of the war, until May 1942, at which time he would be replaced by Father Joseph Agius, O.P., whose earned appellation many years later would be "Mr. Holy Rosary." In the meantime, Father McMullan celebrated the silver jubilee of his ordination with a Solemn High Mass in the church at 10:00 a.m., May 22, 1941. McMullen was a native of San Francisco, where he was born March 30, 1886. He was ordained May 17, 1916 in Washington, D.C. According to Ed "Van" Vancoelen, a parishioner at the time, McMullan was ordered to return to San Francisco during the early part of 1942. He appealed to Archbishop Howard, who appointed him to the post of chaplain at Maryville Nursing Home in Beaverton, Oregon where he remained until his death. So here we inject another bit of Holy Rosary's history for continuity concerning the life of Father McMullan.

> *"Cast me not off in the time of old age; forsake me not when my strength faileth."* (Psalms 71:9).

As the history of Holy Rosary attests, many priests have returned to this parish in advanced age ever to be cared for by the younger lions of the lair, never a minuscule task considering the individuality of those under consideration. Nevertheless, Dominican religious look after one another unto death, and the elderly among them cast away fear of abandonment in the full knowledge of this truth. This is not this author's surmise but his personal observations.

Father Thomas A. Feucht, O.P., pastor from 1948 to 1958, remained in close contact with Father McMullan at the Maryville Nursing Home, and wrote the following in a letter to the provincial, dated October 10, 1950:

Father McMullan is in the hospital again. The doctor told me that his lungs are constantly filling up with fluid. The Archbishop seemed to be in favor of taking him out of Beaverton. As he said, "there is no use precipitating his demise." However, I have reasons to believe that the Archdiocese wants that chaplaincy at Beaverton. The Archbishop implied that he is no longer able to fulfill his duties. However, the Sisters told me that he was always able to say Mass. The greatest difficulty is that he is alone out there. Fr. McMullan told me this afternoon that once last winter he had an attack while walking through the snow and had to crawl on hands and knees to the house or neighbor's house. His doctor stated that within the last several months he has been getting steadily worse.

Provincial B. M. Blank, O.P., in a letter dated October 12, 1950 (two days later) responded to Father Feucht:

Please contact the Archbishop about Father McMullan. If he wishes to remove him I shall do so. It seems to me that his health is not what it should be for such a position. It may well be that he would like to live in your house in Portland or I can bring him to this area. There is a brother in Ross who is an R.N. and takes excellent care of Father Netterville.

Within a little over 30 days, discussion of what course of action to take concerning Father McMullan's future was irrevocably resolved. Father McMullan died. According to Van, (who today lives at the same Maryville Nursing Home) on November 23, 1950, Thanksgiving Day, Father McMullan had gone to dinner at the Holy Rosary rectory, later to return to his little house on the Maryville campus. Within a few hours, he called the sisters and told them he was dying. The sisters notified a priest from the nearby St. Mary's Home for Boys[152] who anointed Father before he died that night at the age of 64. He had been a faithful servant of God for all of his adult life – 44 years. A Funeral Mass was celebrated for Father McMullan at Holy Rosary.

U.S. Enters World War II
Now we return to the 1940s. The Japanese bombed Pearl Harbor, Hawaii on December 7, 1941, "a date which will live in infamy" in the words of then-President Franklin Delano Roosevelt. On the following day, the U.S. declared war on Japan and, on December 11, the U.S. also declared war on Germany and Italy, after those countries declared war on the U.S. Gradually, across America, the smoke of war permeated every home, church, school, business and governmental agency, and the hearts and minds of the American people embraced one overriding goal: win the war. American men and women who now robed themselves in military uniforms would require a vast corps of chaplains to serve their spiritual needs. Past, present, and future Dominicans of Holy Rosary would render honorable service as chaplains in the various branches of the military. These included Anthony Leo Hofstee (U.S. Army); William Aquinas Norton (U.S. Navy); and John Wilfred Ryan (U.S. Army).

Honoring Housekeeper Anna Mayer – "Mrs. Holy Rosary"
But "they also serve who only stand and wait,"[153] and recognition of salutary service would come to a saintly woman greatly loved by priests, sisters, parishioners and Holy Rosary school children, to whom she gave kindness, gentle advice, a little hug, a bandage if necessary, and freshly-baked cookies. She was especially remembered by the black members of the parish, outcasts in subtle ways, for whom she made coffee and cookies after Mass.

On the first of May, a Monday in 1944, Holy Rosary's legendary

Mrs. Anna Mayer (c. 1936) housekeeper (1924-1958)

and beloved housekeeper, Anna Mayer, celebrated twenty years of service to the priests and parishioners of Holy Rosary. No history of Holy Rosary would be complete without recording the deeds of this devout woman. She would serve still another 14 years as seamstress, cook, confidante, secretary, and mother to all, but this was her special day. Typical of the many greetings Anna received was the following handwritten letter from the Provincial, Very Reverend B. M. Blank, O.P., dated April 26, 1944:

Dear Mrs. Mayer:

I am most grateful for your attentive kindness to the Fathers during your many years in Holy Rosary. They have spoken of you on so many occasions throughout the Province.

I hope you will enjoy Monday, and I shall keep you in my prayers.

Sincerely,

(signed)
B.M. Blank, O.P.

Among the other greetings was a fancy silver jubilee card with an image of Christ on silk ribbon, signed "From your boys" (the priests serving at Holy Rosary at the time). Mrs. Mayer was astonished when she opened it, and tears of joy came to her eyes, for it contained four five-dollar bills from her "boys," who themselves received a mere $15.00 stipend each month. Records show the following Dominicans were assigned to Holy Rosary at the time: Joseph M. Agius (pastor), Daniel J. Wolf, Lawrence E. Banfield, and William S. McDermott.

In the mail from St. Patrick's Church, Eureka, Utah came this letter dated May 2, 1944 from Father J. William McClory, O.P.: [154]

Dear Ann:

Already your good friends at 375 Clackamas have endeavored to show their appreciation of your twenty years of service for the Dominican Fathers. There are many other Dominicans whom you have known and whom you have served who were not near enough to have joined in the festivities marking this milestone in your life of faithful service for those who would preach Christ and Him crucified. They too would wish to offer their congratulations even though it has to be done by letter.

Your work, even though it lacks the glamour of the foreign missionary or the great lady whose name may appear many times in the paper as the leader of popular church affairs, even though it has been a hidden life of sacrifice and service, it surely must be pleasing to God. You have aided the servants of Christ to preach the gospel by caring for their natural needs, a very necessary occupation. If a cup of water given in the name of Christ will bring a reward, surely twenty years with those who break the Bread of Life to God's children will bring you a rich reward from the Great High Priest whose ministers we are. May God bless you, may He give you much happiness and good health.

Remember me to Joe and Mary. How about Mary? Aren't you a grandmother yet or a prospective one? I hope Joe is doing well. Has he gone overseas yet?

Wishing you the best of God's blessing, I remain

Your sincere friend in Christ,

[signed]
Father McClory, O.P.

P.S.

Since the Black market will give you only a peek at a pair of nylons for this price, use it for something else. [no amount was mentioned]

Anna also received a beautiful card "A Gift from All of Us," signed by Sisters M. Seraphica, Catherine, M. Kathleen, M. Celeste, M. Julia and M. Anthony of the Dominican Sisters of Mission San Jose who, at that time, were operating Holy Rosary School. The description of the gift was not mentioned.

Another greeting [signature illegible] came from a former Holy Rosary priest then stationed in Seattle:

Hello:

So this is your 20th anniversary since you started throwing pots and pans around at Holy Rosary: and that is a lot of throwing. But it has been a lot of fun, at least some of the time – even most of the time, or has it been all of the time? I like to think the last is nearest the truth. But all of the time you have brought untold happiness to all of the Fathers; and that is what has brought you your greatest joy and happiness, and with it blessings that can't be known here, I am sure.

I have been told that the day is going to be observed in some special way. I should be on hand for that, but I just can't get away: have 50 kiddies to help get ready for their 1st Holy Communion next Sunday, and two Confirmations that I have promised to attend. But I know they will have a grand time, and I will remember you in my Mass in the morning.

Perhaps by this time you are a "grand-ma" and that will help make the day a big one. With every best wish, and my thanks for all you have done for us in the good old days. Will hope to see you soon.

"Sir Boss" [155]

Anna was 48 years old on the occasion of this 20th anniversary. She and her then six-year-old son, Joseph, had come to the rectory to live and work on May 1, 1924, from the coal mines in Wyoming. Anna died in 1973 at age 79. Joe[156] recalls some of the events of living and growing up in the rectory in those days:

JOSEPH MAYER GREW UP IN THE PRIORY (1924-1942)
The expansion of teachers for Aquinas School, assigned to the priory, meant eight and nine hungry appetites for meals, including the parish priests and Brother Leo. This made it necessary for Fr. Townley, then prior, to find someone permanent to do the cooking and necessary shopping. My mother found out about the opening for cook from Catholic relatives in the area and was hired. We were assigned quarters on the first floor of the north side of the rectory.

Shopping was done at N.E. Broadway and Union, at the meat market and drug store. Vegetables were brought three times a week

Joe Mayer with Father G.M. Knauff (c. 1935)

by Joe Amato, who would come driving his horse and wagon down the street, ringing a large bell attached to the front seat. I can still hear him calling to us "Buon giorno, Buon giorno"(good morning), and it wasn't long before he taught me to say in Italian the names of the various vegetables.

What a busy place the priory was with all the fathers in the house. To hear them chanting their prayers in the hall before going to the refectory for meal brought goose bumps in a hurry.

It wasn't long before the Aquinas teachers felt they needed recreation, so they decided upon a tennis court. On the north two-thirds of the church block was an orchard with varieties of cherry and apple trees, with one peach and one pear tree. The old bell tower stood in about the center with a small tool shed surrounded by lilac bushes slightly

to the west. This shed provided an excellent place to play games and hide out. When the decision was made to build a tennis court, the shed was the first to go. What a sad occasion for me as a child.

Then came the axes, shovels, wheelbarrows and eager hands, and it wasn't long before a full tennis court with a white banded net and dirt floor was complete. At the south end, where the church stood, was erected a steel pole barrier with mesh to keep tennis balls from bouncing off the church or hitting people walking along the path. Almost as suddenly as it began, the court was abandoned when Aquinas School closed in 1927.

Brother Leo was just like an old shoe: well worn, dependable, an all-around handy man. When the radio became the rage, Brother Leo made radios for the fathers and gave us our first introduction to the wonderful programs of Amos & Andy, the famous Hoot Owls (skits, talks, etc.,), and others. Our first radio was a little box with crystal rock, wire pointer and head piece, all hand made by Brother Leo. What a wonderful event.

The basement of the rectory was the work shop for Brother Leo and he would let me help him when he would make hosts for Communion at Mass. First he would make up the dough, then pour it into a flat grill with a gas burner underneath. He would then pull down a hinged cover which would flatten the dough as it baked. When the sheets of dough were done we would use a hand cutter to individually cut out each rounded host. It took quite a while to make up a week's supply of hosts.

During the depression years, the number of fathers stationed at Holy Rosary varied from five to seven and my mother would ensure that the meals were well cooked and adequate. These years also brought many transients knocking at the back door asking for something to eat. She always found a way to put something on a plate for them. If there was anything to be done, raking, weeding, sweeping, etc., she would have them do this work, so that they would feel that they had earned their meal.

Mrs. Annie Foster, who lived on Victoria Street nearby, used to do all the laundry in the basement for the fathers. She came once a week. Charlie Wentworth had the Nash dealership on E. Burnside, and he provided sedans for the priests. Some of the pillars of the church I knew in those days, in the 1930s and '40s were Bob Rengo, Wilford Lorrimer, Lee Riordan, Matt Creegan, Stan Brosterhous, Joe McDowell and his sister Anne Marie, the Mary McCormick family that lived across the street from the church, Mark Sweeney, who also lived nearby, Joe Fritz and Frank Eixenberger.

Leo Tobkin and I served as altar boys right up until the day I joined the Air Force in World War II.

Joseph Mayer

The winds of World War II came and, on March 16, 1942, Joe enlisted in the Air Force. He subsequently entered pilot training, became a commissioned officer, and flew B29s over Europe. But to this day he cherishes those fond memories of growing from childhood to manhood among the wonderful Dominican priests and nuns who served at Holy Rosary during those three-plus decades.

Brother Leo Haggerty (1926)

HOLY ROSARY MEETS ITS HISTORIC RENDEZVOUS WITH A GREAT JUBILEE

On Sunday, May 29, 1942, Father Joseph M. Agius, O.P. took over the duties of pastor for the first time.[157] This man of great spirituality, learning and know-how came at a proper time to prepare the parish for its Golden Jubilee, which would be celebrated within two years. This son of St. Dominic was destined to become Provincial of the Western Dominican Province from 1960 to 1964, but his job for now would be to increase spirituality within the parish and, not incidentally, get Holy Rosary out of debt by the year of its jubilee celebration. To this latter end, Father Agius published the following undated "We have a dream" bulletin (long before the phrase was used in the 1950's civil rights movement):

QUEEN OF THE MOST HOLY ROSARY PRAY FOR US

Dear Parishioners and Friends:

Two weeks ago it was called to our attention that January 28, 1944 will mark the fiftieth anniversary of the establishment of our church as Queen of the Most Holy Rosary. It will be our Golden Jubilee. Surely that ought to be a grand occasion for all of us! We hope to make it so.

Have we dreamed a dream?

We are well aware of the debt on the school ($37,800), and we see quite clearly that both the church and school stand in need of repair and paint, and yet...here comes the dream...

We should like very much to celebrate our Golden Jubilee free from debt and with our church and school looking as fine as possible.

What do you think?
Have we dreamed a dream?

Please let us know your ideas on the matter and, if you believe the dream has a chance of coming true, please feel absolutely free to tell us of any plans you think will help towards such a realization.

We intend to keep your ideas and plans, and then, most likely in September, to discuss them in general assembly, with the intention of arriving at some definite scheme of action. In the meantime, let us pray to Mary, Queen of the Most Holy Rosary, that she may help us to make our Golden Jubilee dream come true.

With kind personal regards, we remain,

The Dominican Fathers

[The Golden Jubilee booklet is reprinted in Appendix 6.]

Priests and Parishioners Hold Novenas for Parishioners Serving in the Military
(HELD ON THE WEDNESDAY OF EACH WEEK AT 7:45 P.M.)

The 1944 Parish Digests[158] dated below contained these notices concerning scheduled events for that week:

(Jan. 9). This week pray especially for John Hofstee, Paul Tobkin, Bernard Tobkin, Robert Niedermeyer and Robert Fleskes. Special prayers are asked for Don Legrand, wounded in the battle of Tarawa, now in San Diego Naval Hospital.

(Mar. 19). Pray especially for: Frank Church, David P. Kemp, Donald Lickel, Frank Rawlinson, and Milton Lennon. Father Banfield will speak on: HOW TO CONFESS.

(Mar. 26). Pray especially for: Thomas Jorgensen, Donald Jorgensen, Herrold B. Graves, John Joseph Graves and Ralph R. Smith. Father Banfield will speak on: DOES SORROW TAKE AWAY SIN?

(Apr. 2). Pray especially for Leo Campbell, William Adkisson, William Phinney, William Maxwell and Matt Kuzminich. Father Banfield will speak on: CALVARY THE CLIMAX OF SIN.

(Apr. 23). Pray especially for: John J. McCarthy, George Swanson, Jack Gavin, Courtland McMahon, and Melvin Swanson.

Choir Reorganized

The Parish Digest dated April 23, 1944 contained the following announcement:

TWO YEARS AGO Mr. Albert Hunt reorganized the choir with the following members: Elizabeth McMahon, Mary McLaughlin, Patricia Hunt, Ronald Bergeron, Mrs. Briggs, Mr. and Mrs. Legrand, Mrs. Bobzien, Mrs. J. Murphy, Mrs. K.A. Tormeehlen and Mr. Albert Hunt.

Christmas Party for Kids Held in December 1943

From the Parish Digest dated January 9, 1944:

Since it is "better late than never," we now want to thank: (1) Santa McDermott and his "Reindeer Committee" who put on such a fine Christmas party for all of us; (2) Santa McDermott, the Sisters and the Mothers' Club for giving the children their Christmas party; (3) the Altar Society ladies for cleaning and decorating the Altars for Christmas and all during the year; (4) Mark Sweeney for setting up and taking down the Crib and for being "on deck" the entire Christmas season and for his continual helpfulness; (5) the Mothers' Club for purchasing the gravel for the school yard and some dishes for the kitchen; (6) ALL of you for your constant and loyal support; (7) the good people whose deeds we never hear of, or who, in our rush, may be overlooked. THANKSAMILLION!

The Parish Digest of March 19, 1944 honored the following members of the parish who had been members for 50 years:

Miss Katerine Dowd, Mrs. Harry Hays, Miss Elizabeth McMahan, Mr. Frank McMahan, Mrs. B. H. Neer, Mrs. M. H. O'Connor, Mrs. Charles Schoenfeldt, Mr. William Sheahan, Mrs. James Sheehy, Mrs. M. Thompson, Mrs. Margaret Tracy, and Mrs. B.H. Winneman.

Father Lawrence E. Banfield, O.P.

Father Banfield was one of the most popular priests ever to serve at Holy Rosary (see Chap. 6). He entered the Dominican Order at Ross, California in 1935, completed his seminary training at St. Albert's College in Oakland, and was ordained in 1941. He came to the parish in 1944 at age 29 and served here until 1948. He loved working with kids. A natural athlete, he formed baseball, softball, football, and basketball teams in the parish.

Father Lawrence "NBA" Banfield, O.P. (1996)

The Parish Digest of January 9, 1944 contained this entry:

Holy Rosary, thanks to Fr. Banfield, has three basketball teams. The high school boys who lost their first game 32-31 play here Monday night at 7:30. The grade boys open here Thursday against Immaculate Heart, 4:30. The girls play next week.

And from the Parish Digest dated March 19, 1944:

We are pleased to see Father Banfield and the boys from the school cleaning and mowing the playing field.[159] *We promise them suits for their softball team!!!*

Also, from the Parish Digest dated March 26, 1944:

Our Catholic Charities collection amounted to $189.22. We have been given back forty per cent of this, or $74.69. Since we may use this money for "organized parish sports for boys and girls," we shall let Father Banfield use it for the boys and girls of our school.

Father Banfield claims he is a native of an Indian village – Chicago! – however, he was raised in a small town in Wisconsin and Washington, D.C., the son of a military doctor. He is a first-rate preacher and, at age 80 in 1994, gave a ten-day Novena at Holy Rosary. He has spent decades as a member of the Dominican Preaching Band, living out of a suitcase and traveling all over the United States and Canada. He once served as an instructor in homiletics in the Dominican seminary, and has also preached in foreign countries as a guest preacher for the U.S. armed forces. He was awarded the honor of Preacher General by the Dominican order, the highest honor for a preacher. He loves Portland, and especially its golf courses, and resides here when not on the road. He once said that when he dies "I want to be carried out of Holy Rosary in a pine box with all the kids singing Ave Maria at the top of their lungs."

GIFTS TO DOMINICAN NOVITIATE
Letters dated June 9, 1948, found in the archives of the Western Dominican Province in Oakland, California, recorded the following gifts "For a Father's room at the novitiate:"

Mr. and Mrs. Joseph Niedermeyer – $250
The Sheely Family – $350

ATTACK ON CATHOLICS DIRECTED AT POPE PIUS XII
Post-war evaluations overwhelmingly confirmed the patriotism of American Catholics; no one could seriously accuse Catholics or Catholicism of being un-American. However, the Church's enemies, undeterred, pointed their cannons of contempt at Pope Pius XII, claiming that he abetted the Holocaust by not speaking out against Hitler – a lie decades would not erase[160] in this revisionist history of World War II, even though the truth was

overwhelming. Such lies should rise or fall on empirical evidence. One example: the leading scholar of the Holocaust in Hungary, Jeno Levai, proclaimed that Pope Pius XII "did more than anyone else to halt the dreadful crime and alleviate its consequences." And Israeli diplomat Pinchas Lapide wrote: "The Catholic Church under the pontificate of Pius XII was instrumental in saving the lives of as many as 860,000 Jews from certain death at Nazi hands."[161]

Truth being wedded to charity and greater understanding to true love, perhaps the most poignant witness to Pius XII's heroic stance was Chief Rabbi Emilio Zolli who served in Rome during the Nazi occupation. His first-hand account was summed up in these words: "no hero in all of history was more militant, more fought against, none more heroic, than Pius XII." Rabbi Zolli was so convinced of the Catholic Church's possession of truth and its solidarity with Jews that he himself converted to Catholicism, and took the Pope's name as his baptismal name.

MORTGAGE BURNING
Father/Pastor Joe Agius was unable to fulfill his dream of having the parish free of debt during the Golden Jubilee celebration in January 1944; however, he accomplished that task a little over two years later. The April 14, 1946 Parish Digest announced: "At long last we are out of the debt that plagued the parish for so many years. Thanks be to God! And a thousand thanks to a great little parish whose members and friends have been so loyal and generous all through the years."

On Rosary Sunday, October 6, 1946, a Solemn High Mass was held in the church. A special bulletin also announced that day as also being "MORTGAGE-BURNING DAY," inviting all parishioners to the school hall after Mass – "Come and see the mortgage go up in flames." Ushers distributed at Mass a flyer with the drawing of a hand holding a match to a scroll with the word "mortgage" written on it. Archbishop Howard officiated at Mass and there followed the annual Rosary Procession. Then everyone adjourned to the school hall where the actual burning took place and refreshments served between 4:00 and 6:00 p.m. The senior choir led in the singing of the following songs:

Good-bye Mortgage
Holy God We Praise Thy Name
A Perfect Day

As the song title proclaimed, it was a "perfect day," in the continuing celebration of Holy Rosary's 50th Jubilee, begun two years earlier.

"And thou shall sanctify the fiftieth year, and shalt proclaim remission to all the inhabitants of thy land: for it is the year of jubilee. Every man shall return to his possession, and everyone shall go back to his former family." (Lev. 25:10)

PARISH DIGEST PUBLISHES POEM BY SISTER M. REYNOLDINE, O.P.

IN THE CARPENTER'S SHOP

Each day to Joseph's shop there came
A troop of eager boys,
And in the lead was Mary's Son,
With broken bits of toys.
The wooden goat grew legs again;
The woolly sheep, a tail;
The puppy's ears were mended quite
By Joseph's magic nail
Dear Carpenter of Nazareth,
Our broken hearts we bring.
Oh, won't you make them new again
And give them to the King?

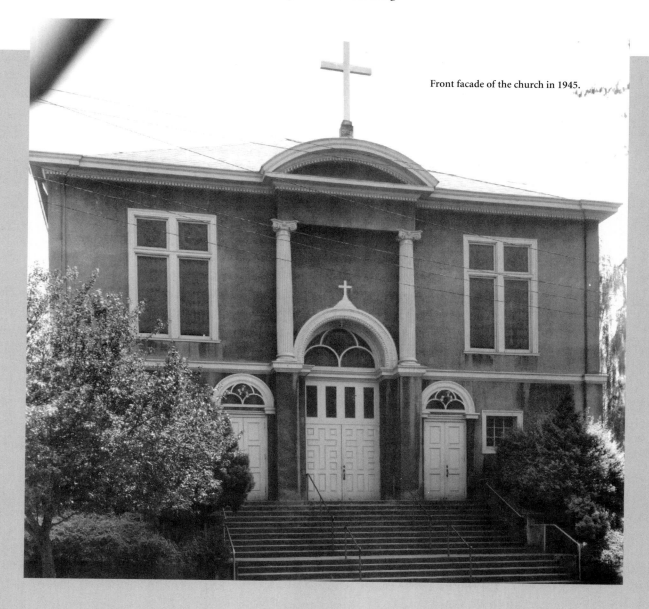

Front facade of the church in 1945.

FIRST HOLY COMMUNION

The parish bulletin dated May 2, 1948 showed the following children were to receive their
First Holy Communion that day at the 8:30 a.m. Mass:

John Banzali	Freddie Mae Brooks	Carol Marshall
Edwin Bauder	Katherine Fairbanks	Clarissa Martinez
Alice Brooks	Mary Theresa Larison	Marjorie Rausch
Louise Brooks	William McAllister	Dorothy O'Hare
Leo Fritz	William Strawder	Dennis Coffey
Janice Clow	Cecil Hodges	Sidney Doll
	Mary Clapperton	

Rosary Sunday Procession – 1943.

Joe Mayer as a young boy living in the rectory with Dominican Fathers, left to right, Thomas S. Connelly, Albert "Pat" Healy, and G.M. Knauff (ca. 1925).

Dominican Fathers, left to right, Thomas S. Connelly, William McDermott, William J. McClory, and Joseph M. Agius (c. 1943).

NOTES TO THE TEXT

150 His obituary card showed his religious name as Gerald, but archival records show Gerard. Some documents also spell his surname McMullen; however, the official record shows it spelled McMullan.

151 He had previously served as assistant pastor here from November 1927 to February 1931.

152 St. Mary's Home for Boys was five minutes away; whereas Holy Rosary was anywhere from 45 minutes to one hour away.

153 This line is from John Milton's poem *On His Blindness* [1652].

154 He had previously served at Holy Rosary (1929-1931 and 1942-1943) and would return to Oregon to serve as chaplain at the State Penitentiary in Salem from 1951-1961, and also spend his final days here before his death at Holy Rosary on January 28, 1972 at age 80 (see Chapter 13).

155 According to Joe Mayer, "Sir Boss" was Father Thomas S. Connelly.

156 Joe's sister, Mary, and his estranged father remained in Wyoming.

157 He would serve as pastor until 1947, then return and serve as associate pastor, 1968-1970, again as pastor 1971 & 1972, as associate pastor from 1968 to 1970, and be in residence from 1973 to 1983 as Director of the Rosary Confraternity – a total of 19 years at Holy Rosary.

158 We express gratitude to Father Schoenfeldt of the University of Portland who provided these lost copies of Parish Digests. Father's great grandparents David Morris and Rebecca Williams were some of the first parishioners at Holy Rosary, and they contributed generously of their time and treasure to the new church.

159 It was located on the block south of the church, today occupied by the Upjohn Company.

160 In the January 25, 1995 New York Post, Rabbi Marvin Hier proclaimed in part: "For every [Catholic] pastor…who died en route to Dachau…there were dozens of other prelates – from Pope Pius XII down – who at best looked the other way [and] were bystanders rather than activists, and sometimes assisted the Nazis in carrying out their Final Solution."

161 Quoted from page 10, Vol. 21, No. 10, December 1994, *Catalyst, Journal of the Catholic League for Religious and Civil Rights*, 6324 W. North Avenue, Milwaukie, WI 53213.

Our Lady of the Rosary restored, painted by parishioner Mary Van Buren.

CHAPTER

11

1951-1960

DYING AND NEW BEGINNINGS

Job rent his garments, shaved his head, and fell down upon the ground and worshipped: "Naked came I out of my mother's womb and naked shall I return thither. The Lord gave and the Lord hath taken away. As it hath pleased the Lord so it is done. Blessed be the name of the Lord." (Job 1:21)

HOLY ROSARY A DYING PARISH?

Chapter 6 records the rationale of Sisters Callista and Redempta relating to the closing of Holy Rosary School in June 1955. These sisters' observations about Holy Rosary being a "dying parish" were unquestionably valid. In fact, several knowledgeable priests commented that the Western Province had considered closing down the church as well. The Lloyd Corporation and other large businesses were buying up land and houses all around the parish area, and a new shopping mall would take up entire blocks, placing Holy Rosary in the center of it all. In the process, Holy Rosary's parishioners moved on. Archival records maintained at the provincial headquarters in Oakland, California show that the number of families registered at Holy Rosary went from a high of 250 in 1939 to only 29 families in 1953. And parishioner Larry Johnson, who occasionally had Associate Pastor Father Pat Healy to dinner in those days, stated that the parish had been reduced to five registered families by late 1955. So Holy Rosary Parish likely had the dubious distinction of being the smallest parish west of the Mississippi, if not in all of North America.

HOLY ROSARY SCHOOL A PRIVATE SCHOOL?

The pupil population reached a high of 200 during the years immediately preceding Holy Rosary School's closing, dropping to 172 in 1954. So there were 38 fewer students in the school than Holy Rosary would have in its CCD program in 1992 (i.e. 210). It is also important to note that only 27 percent of the student body belonged to the parish, the remainder being non-Catholic or from other parishes.[162] These demographic changes had the effect of negating the charter of Holy Rosary as a parish school, teaching Catholic youth and serving the needs of the parishioners. It had become, rather, another private school essentially serving non-Catholic families in the general area of the parish, captive to their stability, and at a time when nearby parishes were slowly building their own schools. To add to the conundrum, Holy Rosary parishioners with children were moving away from the area.

BLACK PUPILS IN THE MAJORITY

Father Feucht took a census of the parish in 1950 and, in a March 8 letter to the provincial, reported:

The Holy Name men are just about finished taking up a census… We have about 155 children in school. The largest group comes from St. Rita's Parish. There are only 49 children in our school who come from within the boundaries of our parish. Twenty eight of these are Negro, of which fifteen are Catholic, and four to be baptized soon…When the Negroes start moving things will really be bad.

In retrospect, Catholics should be proud of the fact that, considering the racial climate of the 1950's, when the KKK was still active in Portland, with discrimination common and its opposition weak, 39 percent of Holy Rosary's school children were black. This sent the racists the alarming message of the Church's ongoing mission to accept into its most intimate folds, all people, drawing no lines against ethnicity, race, nationality, color or creed. It would be yet another excuse to stir up anti-Catholic sentiment in the community.

WHY BAD THINGS SOMETIMES HAPPEN TO GOOD PEOPLE

In his bestselling book *Crossing the Threshold of Hope*[163] His Holiness John Paul II observed that *"The history of salvation is also the history of man's continual judgment of God,"* a judgment to which man is entitled. This is so because God created man as *"rational and free, thereby placing Himself under man's judgment."* The closing of Holy Rosary School was judged wrong by some and looked upon with no inconsiderable consternation by others (Why was God allowing this to happen?). But true believers, no matter what occurs along the way, always look at individual events in the overall context of God's plan for their lives. Did this closing occur because God had greater designs for the parish in the future? Could this evil produce an even greater good from God in actuality? Hindsight and solid theology regarding God's designs always give affirmative answers to these questions; because God only allows evil to happen so that a greater good may come about. In this case, the closure of Holy Rosary eventually resulted in the emergence of three new schools: Saint Anne, Saint Joseph, and Saint Therese.

OLD SCHOOL/CONVENT OCCUPIED BY THESPIANS

An added bit of history concerning the Noon House comes to us from parishioners Larry Johnson and his wife Beth, two lovely people in love with each other and with Holy Rosary. After the Dominican Sisters moved out of the Noon House in 1955, it lay deserted, disheveled, and ready for razing, but still sufficiently sound to serve as a home, providing that generous amounts of elbow grease and some replumbing, rewiring, and carpentry were vigorously applied. Larry and Beth, a young married couple at the time, were willing to undertake those chores and make this house a home, as well as a rehearsal studio for the plays they

performed, mostly on weekends. They approached the pastor, Father Thomas Aquinas Feucht, O.P., with their proposal, and he agreed to rent it to them for about $20.00 a month, with the caveat that they would be responsible for maintaining it and expect no help from Holy Rosary in its upkeep.

Larry, a self-described "cradle Catholic"[164] and an actor and director by profession, had attended the University of Portland, from which he received a B.A. and B.M.E. and, later on, a master's degree in theater. He taught speech and drama at Marylhurst College, and math and mechanical drawing at the Northwest Technical Institute. Beth worked as an assistant to the personnel manager at Roberts Brothers department store.

Larry would procure a play, for example "The Four Poster," and either he and Beth or another couple, Dick and Electra Fair, would rehearse in the Noon House and later on give live performances at various parishes. They would charge the buyer a fixed fee for performing the play and it would be up to the buyer to sell the tickets and bring in the audience.

During the dog days of summer, Larry occasionally raked the leaves in the orchard which occupied what is now the parking lot on the north side of the church, and the pastor, Father Feucht, would come out of the rectory with a cold beer and hand it to Larry to slake his thirst. He and Father Feucht would occasionally sit on the stoop, or under the canopy of apple trees with apples the size of softballs, drink in the beauty of the orchard, and discuss the affairs of the parish which, *"very poor"* at the time, resembled a spent candle ready to relinquish its rays. Larry was intensely impressed with this humble priest, "a nice guy from Idaho," a "simple and good man," whose brother was also a priest.[165]

Larry and Beth, God bless them, subsequently adopted and reared four children.

FATHER THOMAS FEUCHT, O.P.,
KEPT THE PARISH INTACT AND DOMINICAN SPIRITUALITY ALIVE

Dominicans like Father Feucht would keep the parish intact in the worst of times, for they belong to a brotherhood attuned to the teachings of St. Thomas. They were not obtuse pilgrims journeying through a world about which they knew nothing. Imbued, as they were in abundance, with a faith far too sophisticated for worldly interpretation, they could never be intimidated or lured by the seductive fear of foreboding; for they knew all things are liable to perpetual changes yet remain under God's providence, reason enough to cast away fruitless cares. They willingly and joyfully, as today their followers do, pass along this message to all willing to listen. They give the laity strength and resolve unimagined before it was infused by these men dressed in black and white and possessed by the love of their Creator. One of St.

Father Thomas Feucht, O.P., pastor, with the First Holy Communion class in 1952.

Thomas's first principles (out of ten) was "You cannot give what you do not possess." They possessed faith and so were able to share it in abundance.

These soldiers of Christ, despite their predicament of poverty would "put on the armor of light," "put on the Lord Jesus Christ,"[166] and cast off thoughts of impending doom, knowing full well that "All things have their season" including "A time to be born, and a time to die." But it was *not* Holy Rosary's time to die. Holy Rosary had been humbled, but it still remained under the protective care of the Mother of God, who had her own designs for this "dying parish" in the forthcoming decades, which now appeared to be approaching at warp speed.

[From Chapter 6: *And Sister Seraphica suggested to the little boy who was to be a Mass server: "You should fold your hands like Father Feucht," and the boy replied, "Yes sister, and Father Feucht looks like he is full of grace." She asked what made him say that, and the boy replied: "I think that when I see him."*]

FATHER MARTIN MARK DONNELLY, O.P.

One of Father Feucht's popular assistants during the years 1951-55, was Father Martin M. Donnelly, O.P., who was in his early 30s at the time, and had been ordained only three years earlier, on June 12, 1948. Father Donnelly served as a chaplain to several hospitals in Portland, and he also taught philosophy and theology at Marylhurst. He also served as a chaplain at the

Oregon State Prison. Sometimes he joked that he would break curfew and sneak into the rectory after hours, explaining to Larry and Beth Johnson that, on such occasions, he would wait until truck drivers shifted gears so that he could enter the priory without being discovered by Father Feucht.[167] Father Donnelly had a fine speaking voice and did a lot of radio work. The May 24, 1951 *Catholic Sentinel* reported: "*Father Martin Donnelly, assistant pastor of Holy Rosary Parish, will commence a new series of broadcasts each Sunday night on the general subject of the Rosary, commencing this Sunday, May 27, [1951] over station KBKO.*"

Father Lawrence Banfield, O.P., recalls Father Donnelly with fondness, and remembered he also taught at high schools in Los Angeles and Vallejo, California. Father Donnelly left Holy Rosary to become Pastor and Prior of Blessed Sacrament Church in Seattle, Washington.

Parishioners Larry and Beth Johnson still keep in touch with Donnelly, and remember vividly that he was eagerly sought after for confession, retreats and visitations to hospitals; and will long be remembered by the many men and women he brought into the faith (Beth was one).

Boom and Bust in Parish Area During World War II – Bigotry Besieged the Black As Well As the Catholic Community

The United States Navy needed ships after America entered World War II, and Portland would become a shipbuilding center, with the Kaiser Company on Swan Island taking the Northwest's lead in this industry. With so many local workers serving in the military, the

"*Kaiser Company recruited workers from the East and South, bringing them to Oregon on trains dubbed 'Magic Carpet Specials.' Many black people were recruited and came, attracted by the promise of good jobs and high wages. Estimates vary, but between 20,000 and 25,000 black people came to Portland in the early 1940s; white migration to Portland was about 100,000.*"[168]

Portland was not prepared for these breathtaking changes. Blacks had constituted a small "shadowy" minority in the city, and now they were a "brilliantly observable" minority. Some people in the Rose City resisted these changes and a spiral of hate spread through the town. The scorn previously heaped on Catholics was now leveled at blacks. So black Catholics bore both burdens. Jim Crow signs sprang up in restaurants and saloons, and Portland's Mayor Earl Riley declared: "*Portland can absorb only a minimum of Negroes without upsetting the city's regular life.*"

The black people had come at the behest of the shipbuilders, who had said nothing about race or religion in their recruitment literature, yet:

"*Initially, job opportunities were a disappointment to the black workers. When they applied for jobs in the shipyards, they were told that nothing was available, and many help wanted notices specified "white only." Although the Kaiser Company had promised good jobs, local unions resisted integration, a prerequisite for skilled jobs under the closed shop system. One union leader, Tom Ray, boss of local 72 of the Boilermaker's Union, said he would "pull the place down" rather than give black people equal job rights at the Kaiser Portland shipyards. After pressure from the NAACP, the Kaiser Brothers, a federal inspection team and a reprimand from President Roosevelt, the unions compromised and more skilled jobs were opened to black workers, but only for the duration of the war.*"

When the war ended, the bigots lowered the boom on the black workers who

"*had no job security or seniority, and most were fired. In 1947, three months after one-third of the city's twelve thousand black workers lost their jobs, Julius A. Thomas, Industrial Relations Director of the National Urban League, came to Portland voicing the frustrations of the black community and classifying Portland as 'just like any southern town...the most prejudiced [city] in the west.'*"

Hostility towards these newcomers was not limited to that found in the white community because "*there was an increase in racial tension, and hostility between 'new' and 'old' blacks. The power structure in the black community changed, and some former leaders, accustomed to dealing with the white power structure as members of a tiny minority were labeled 'Uncle Toms.'*"

To make matters worse, the Vanport Flood, which occurred on May 30, 1948, dispossessed "*about 18,500 people including 5,000 blacks*" who were living in the Vanport housing projects: "*all available housing was pressed into service, and many of the black people who were left homeless were taken in by families in the metropolitan area. While many of the stranded white families were able to leave town, black families, many subsisting on welfare and unemployment, did not have the financial resources to settle elsewhere.*"

Holy Rosary's Closed Convent Becomes Stella Maris House – Furnishes Aid to the Black Community for 12 Years

Larry and Beth Johnson lived in the Noon House for about a year when Baroness Catherine de Hueck Doherty came to their attention. Catherine, who had been born in Russia, was the subject of an article entitled "Canadian Messenger of the Sacred Heart" by Mary Lewis Coakley.[169] This article, condensed in the October 1992 issue of Catholic Digest, recounted her work among the poor in Canada and the United States where, in New York, she met and married Eddie Doherty, then a nationally famous newspaper reporter. Catherine brought this fallen-away Catholic back to the Church and into her arms. They were married in 1943. Both were prodigious writers and separately authored many spiritual books, among them: *Desert Windows, A Hermit Without a Permit* (by Eddie Doherty) and *Coming Home and The People of the Towel and the Water* (by Catherine) – all by Dimension Books, Denville, New Jersey. Catherine had the following books published by Ave Maria Press, Notre Dame, Indiana: *Poustinia, Fragments of My Life*, and *Not Without Parables*.

> "I begin to see how true it is that God shows no partiality. Rather, the man of any nation who fears God and acts rightly is acceptable to him."
> (Acts: 34-38).

Stella Maris House Under Direction of Catherine De Hueck Doherty

Catherine, who had also founded a lay secular institute, the Madonna House Foundation in Canada, was looking for quarters in Portland to accommodate her ongoing ministry, dedicated to serving the black community in Northeast Portland, when she became acquainted with Larry and Beth Johnson, who willingly surrendered the Noon house to her with Father Feucht's blessing. Being on the edge of the black community, the Noon House was an ideal location for then-imaginative outreach programs, which had the backing of Father Feucht and were partially supported by Holy Rosary Church. Subsequently, Catherine, with the blessing of Archbishop Howard and Father Feucht, renamed the Noon House the Stella Maris House, whence she served the poor in the area, especially the poorest of the black population, fighting to see that black people might receive the benefits of black-white cooperation in general, and Catholic care in particular. She fought hard on getting Christ's black brothers and sisters emergency supplies and medical treatment, their just desserts from within a system skewed by racial hate.

Later in that period Jean Fox took over as Catherine's director of the Stella Maris House, which also became the center for the Young Christian Student Movement, as well as the Charismatic Renewal movement. It was a beehive of activity, and many of those "busy bees" would bug resolute racists outraged by these "insurrectionist" activities on behalf of the black families residing in nearby neighborhoods.

The Stella Maris House served the black community for about twelve years, from those same rooms where black mothers and fathers (and some of their children) had first learned reading, writing, and arithmetic under the careful tutelage of the Dominican sisters.

After twelve years of marriage, Catherine and Eddie Doherty agreed,[170] at his request, to live a life of celibacy. Eddie, whose brother was a priest,[171] then studied for the priesthood and was ordained in the Melkite Rite in 1969. Eddie died in the 1970s

and Catherine in 1985. May God love them and keep them both. Catherine's good works throughout the United States and Canada earned her pontifical medals from Rome, and the Pius X Award from the Martin de Porres Society for her contribution to interracial justice, not only in Portland but at other locations as well, including New York City's Harlem District.

Pride and Prejudice

We Catholics in particular, if we are to preach and practice the good news in truth, must avoid the siren calling us away from the virtue of love towards the vice of racial discrimination defined, partly at least, as *"allowing one's choices to be shaped by personal likes and dislikes, jealous love of one's own family, group prejudices, culturally established patterns of bias, and so on."*[172] We are not only disavowing Christ in succumbing to such vice, we are disobeying the Golden Rule and many other teachings of Christ in Scripture which define our duties in truth: Dt 10.17-19; Mt 22.16; Mk 12.14; Lk 20.21; Rom 2.11; Gal 2.6; et al.

"Those who cannot bring themselves to do this must reject the gospel, whereas anyone who accepts the gospel is required to live in a new way, with new values, which Jesus both teaches and exemplifies (see Mt 5-7)."[173]

Only God knows what interracial bridges were built during these twelve years of collaboration between Holy Rosary and Stella Maris House. Ultimately, only God cares about and tallies such outcomes. The overriding point of reference is that we members of the human race, in all of our variations, are *exiles* in this world. Sin is not a part of human nature because it is *contrary* to human nature. Sin is only consonant with fallen nature, which we all have in common. Consequently, we must *all* carry our crosses, whatever our pedigree, and we may do so either joyfully or hatefully; it's our free choice. One important truth we know from Christ: each of us carrying our cross selflessly makes it lighter; therefore, selflessness in carrying our crosses ought to be our *natural* inclination in seeking the *supernatural*.

Another thing we all have in common is this quest for the *supernatural*, a quest implanted by God into our very being, continually stirring our imaginations. And there it shall repose until we are blessed to venture through that narrow door and permanently possess the Beatific Vision. At that divine moment we will no longer be the "poor banished children of Eve."

> *His mother and his brothers arrived, and as they stood outside they sent word to him to come out. The crowd seated around him told him, "Your mother and your brothers and sisters are outside asking for you." "Who are my mother and my brothers?" And gazing around him at those seated in the circle he continued, "These are my mother and my brothers. Whoever does the will of God is brother and sister and mother to me."*
> (Mark 3:31-35)

CLOSED HOLY ROSARY SCHOOL AND A FIRST FOR MENTALLY RETARDED

After the closure of Holy Rosary's "new"[174] school in 1955, Father Feucht taught adult education classes there, and then the school was used to develop a prototype for a pilot program involving mentally retarded children, according to parishioner Margaret Peterson who, in a letter to the parish, said the program *"was the brainchild of Mrs. Irene Dardick and Miss Doris Donnel, both Jewish women. I'm sure it was the first effort of its kind in the city, state, county – in the church or community – and was purely volunteer. My beloved twin sons attended… It was the first day program they knew, as there were no 'special' classes in public or private schools then. I doubt any rent was charged by Holy Rosary, but it was a big blessing to many parents like myself!"* Thank you, Margaret, for this footnote, for it provides another interesting dimension to the lives of those loving people who participated in our parish history.

Several years thereafter the old convent and school were razed to accommodate plans for a Catholic retirement community, ultimately named Calaroga Terrace (see Chap. 12). Holy Rosary Church still retained, and does to this day, title to Block 212 on which the school and convent sat. This property is now leased to the owners of the Roadway Inn chain which, in turn, sub-leased part of their lease to the Golden Palace Chinese restaurant.

THE BLACK CHAPEL, FRANCISCA GABRIEL AND THE STATUE OF ST. MARTIN DE PORRES

Parishioner Francisca Gabriel came to Holy Rosary in 1949 from St. Lucia, West Indies (via Puerto Rico). She went to the Congress Hotel in downtown Portland but was refused a room "cause they did not like blacks." She spoke Creol French at the time, but not much English. A black hotel worker named Ralph contacted parishioner Charlie Royer, who introduced her to Holy Rosary and to another black woman, Doris Reynolds, from Jamaica, with whom she took up residence.

Francisca was forced to deposit $5,000 with the Immigration and Naturalization Service. It was assurance that she would be self-supporting – and refundable once

Statue of Saint Martin de Porres
purchased by parishioner Francisca Gabriel.

she had become settled. When she later qualified to withdraw the money, she earmarked it for the statue of a black saint. This all occurred around 1962, the year the wonder worker of Peru, Blessed Dominican Martin de Porres (1579-1639), was canonized by Pope John XXIII. So Francisca settled on this saint. Father/Pastor William Aquinas "Wild Bill" Norton ordered the statue on her behalf and, when it came, she also purchased a small altar for the statue.

SAINT MARTIN DE PORRES STATUE WAS FIRST VENERATED AT A DAY CENTER NAMED AFTER THIS SAINT.

Black Catholics were not joyfully received by all in the area churches, including some bigots at Holy Rosary in the late 1940s and early 1950s. So blacks gathered at the Saint Martin Day Center, located on the corner of Williams Avenue and E. Broadway, which housed the Saint Teresa Chapel. Diocesan and Dominican priests said Mass in this chapel for black people. According to Francisca, when then-pastor Father Thomas Aquinas Bernard Feucht, O.P. heard that blacks felt like outsiders at Holy Rosary, he visited the St. Martin Day Center and personally urged all of the blacks at the center to begin attending Mass at Holy Rosary, which they did. Father Feucht would, in no uncertain terms, rebuke any parishioner who protested.

When our church was renovated in 1994, the altar which Francisca had purchased was moved to the parish center, where it served as the altar for Mass. This same St. Martin de Porres statue now has its own niche on the north wall of the church near the side entrance.

Francisca speaks fondly of Father Feucht, who served as pastor from 1948 to 1958 and again from 1974 to 1975. Father Feucht "carried food to the poor," especially black people and procured for Francisca an interpreter, Margaret Seal, to help Francisca study for the citizenship test. Father also acted as a witness at Francisca's swearing in. Francisca smiled as she recalled the day in 1954 when she became a citizen. The judge at the hearing said *"In all my years in this court I have never had a Catholic priest act as a witness. You must be real special."*

THE ROSARY VS. SCIENCE – A TALE WORTH TELLING

Our own Father Paul A. Duffner, O.P., former pastor and now Director of the Rosary Confraternity, related this delightful story in May-June 1992 issue of his monthly periodical "The Rosary – Light & Life:" [175] It is inserted at this point for its poignancy vis-a-vis the Rosary's influence at Holy Rosary Church, in a world where science is god.

Over a hundred years ago a university student found himself seated in a train by the side of a person who seemed to be a well-to-do peasant. He was praying the Rosary and moving the beads in his fingers.

"Sir, do you still believe in such outdated things,?" asked the student of the old man.

"Yes, I do. Do you not?" asked the man.

The student burst out into laughter and said, "I do not believe in such silly things. Take my advice. Throw the Rosary out through the window, and learn what science has to say about it."

"Science? I do not understand this science? Perhaps you can explain it to me," the man said humbly with tears in his eyes.

The student saw the man was deeply moved. So to avoid hurting the man's feelings any further, he said: "Please give me your address and I will send you some literature to help you on the matter."

The man fumbled in the inside pocket of his coat and gave the boy his visiting card. On glancing at the card, the student bowed his head in shame and became silent. On the card he read: "Louis Pasteur, Director of the Institute of Scientific Research, Paris."

HOLY ROSARY, THE ROSARY CONFRATERNITY, AND RADIO ROSARY

Clearly the most defining and shaping characteristic of the Dominicans is their devotion to the Rosary. From their waists hang the beads and crucifix, dark and stark against their white linen habits, announcing to the world their belief in the power of the Angelic Psalter. Original credit for the praying of the Rosary resides with, of course, Our Blessed Mother. Yet, "A few ancient but authentic stories about the Holy Rosary" [176] give the background for its introduction into the world by the Dominicans, whose brothers in the Western Dominican Province made it a wellspring of prayer at Holy Rosary parish. The parish took to the air waves and brought this Psalter of Jesus and Mary [177] to thousands of homes in the Pacific Northwest and, with the cooperation of the Rosary Confraternity, to millions of families worldwide, thereby exceeding Archbishop Gross's fondest dreams.

MORE ON PASTOR AND FATHER THOMAS AQUINAS FEUCHT, O.P..

In May 1944, Father Feucht was tapped by the Provincial for assignment as associate pastor to Pastor Joseph M. Agius, O.P.

The Rosary Center, headquarters of the Rosary Confraternity, catercorner from the church.

Here he remained until 1949, when he assumed the role of and served as pastor until 1958, when he was replaced by Father William A. Norton, O.P. Father Feucht also headed the Western Dominicans' Rosary Confraternity [178] in California in the 1970s. In 1975 when he was again dispatched to Holy Rosary, he requested and received permission to move the Confraternity to Portland with him, intending to be both pastor of the church and director of the Confraternity at the same time, even though the Confraternity would have no direct relationship with the church, the Confraternity being a separate apostolate. The resultant approval marked a marriage made in heaven, and California's loss would be Portland's portion. It remains here today, once again headed by its founder in the Western Dominican Province, Father Paul Duffner, O.P. [179]

ORIGIN OF RADIO BROADCASTS TRACED TO "A FEW PRAYERFUL WOMEN"

We ought to recognize the intercession of Our Blessed Mother in our affairs. Historical evidence of her help exists in the Herculean happenings at Holy Rosary Parish in the 1950s due to the praying of the Rosary.

According to Bishop Leipzig: [180] *"The seedling of this Radio Program was planted by a faithful group of women who, in 1950, met in homes to encourage the recitation of the Rosary. They were first known as the Fatima Group and then later as the De Montfort group…Mrs. Alice Bowman, Mrs. Margaret Brandes, Mrs. Grace Cole, and Mrs. Delores Plasker. These women, and others, made a single broadcast on station KPOJ, Oct. 7, 1950, [181] and thereafter approached Archbishop Howard for permission to have regular broadcasts. He agreed but asked for a regular sponsor. The Archdiocesan Holy Name Union [which was organized at Holy Rosary in 1917] agreed to sponsor the broadcasts and has since been assisted by many parishes and Catholic organizations, including the Knights of Columbus, Catholic Daughters of America, and the Catholic Foresters."*

RADIO STATION KBKO BROADCASTS ROSARY

On May 15, 1951, the "Daily Rosary for Peace" was being broadcast over KBKO "each Tuesday, Wednesday, and Thursday at 6:45 p.m." [and] *"public response to the Rosary broadcast…exceeds that received for any program over that station, according to Gordon Bambrick, one of the station owners…James R. Lynch, president of the Holy Names societies, states that voluntary contributions are being received which practically assure change to daily broadcasts in the next month…"* [182]

HOLY NAME MEN AND FATHER FEUCHT JOIN FORCES – RADIO BROADCASTS EMANATE FROM HOLY ROSARY CHURCH

Blessed John of Vercelli, sixth Master General of the Dominican Order founded the Confraternity of the Holy Name Society in 1274. Historically, Dominican pastors devote a great deal of effort in establishing societies at new parishes, and sustaining them once in place. The Society has been active at Holy Rosary since at least 1910, and in 1917 the Metropolitan Holy Name Union, then consisting of 25 parish branches, held its first meeting at Holy Rosary. The Dominicans of Holy Rosary have been their chaplains for decades. Father Feucht and the men of the Holy Name would spearhead a drive for a daily broadcast of the Rosary:

"The men of the Holy Name Union began to dream of a daily Rosary broadcast which was realized on June 26, 1951, over station KBKO. In August 1951, Father Thomas A. Feucht, then pastor of this parish and now residing here as provincial director of the Holy Rosary [Confraternity], thought that greater reverence would be shown if the Rosary were recited in a church. Archbishop Howard [agreed and designated] Holy Rosary Church because of its name and central location." [183]

On September 23, 1951, the daily Rosary for world peace began after Father Feucht delivered a 15-minute talk on devotion to the Rosary, preaching the praises of Mary, after which he led the first daily Radio Rosary from the church at 7:00 p.m. over station KBKO.

Many beautiful weddings took place at Holy Rosary including this 1953 wedding of Irene Loumer to Thomas John Faherty.

A Great Milestone in the Praying of the Rosary

Within a quarter of a century, in October 1976, Holy Rosary would be the second church in the United States[184] to have broadcast the Rosary for twenty five years, which witnessed over 228,725[185] people praying the Rosary at radio broadcasts emanating from Holy Rosary Church.

"All ages to come shall call me blessed…"[186]

Marian Year Pilgrimage to Holy Rosary (1954)

When Marian years occur, Catholics partake in pilgrimages to distant places. However, a report of a different pilgrimage is here quoted from the July 29th edition of the *Catholic Sentinel*:[187]

"One hundred automobiles with 320 persons left Sacred Heart Church on Wednesday July 21, making the Marian Year pilgrimage to Holy Rosary Church in Portland, Oregon. The daily Rosary led by Father Paul, OSB, was recited at 6:45 in Holy Rosary Church. Benediction followed. The group is planning another pilgrimage in October."

And from the September 22, 1954 *Catholic Sentinel*:

"The Holy Name Society and other Catholic groups will observe the fourth anniversary of the Daily Rosary broadcast – on Sunday evening, September 25 at 6:15 in Holy Rosary Church. During four years the Holy Name men and other Catholic groups have taken turns reciting the Rosary over Station KVAN from the Holy Rosary Church in this city. During the past four years it is estimated that 43,000 people have come to the Holy Rosary Church for the broadcasts. According to a survey, 25,000 persons from Clark County, Washington and the metropolitan area listen to the program…very many listeners are non-Catholics."

In December 1958, according to the *Catholic Sentinel*,[188] the Holy Name Society spearheaded

"a new method of financing broadcasts of the Radio Rosary for Peace. About $1,500 a year is needed to pay the costs of the Rosary broadcasts which are daily at 7 p.m., except on Sundays when the time is 6:45. The radio station KWJJ broadcasts the 'Radio Rosary for Peace' which has been on the air for seven years."

Father Albert Antoninus "Pat" Healy, o.p., Dead at Age 63

Father Healy came from the "auld sod," having been born in Sligo, Ireland, January 24, 1896. He was yet another Dominican who would return to Holy Rosary to die. He returned[189] in April and died in June 1959. Father "Pat," as he was popularly known, stood about 5' 8" and possessed generous jowls and a little tummy to boot. With his protruding and smiling blue Irish eyes he resembled, "a wise, innocent, and beneficent frog," in the words of Beth Johnson.

Father Pat "cleaved the universe" in giving his final blessing after Mass, and always did the "profound bow" of the Dominicans prior to leaving the sanctuary. "He was a great confessor," recalls Larry Johnson, "and a great example of Dominican spirituality. He was an awfully good and holy man, and preached those wonderful sermons you don't hear any more." [Except at Holy Rosary]. Larry chuckled: "Father Pat loved Oregon and once said, feigning humorous regret: 'I just know they're going to bury me in that hard ground in Benicia.'" Father Pat's prophecy was fulfilled in due time.[190]

The effects of Father Pat's sense of humor reached beyond the confines of the Beaver State down to the provincial house itself in California. Father Charles Hess, O.P., Provincial Archivist, said he thought it was Father Healy who, when he was in Portland, often started innocent rumors with the connivance of his fellow priests at Holy Rosary, and they'd make bets on how long the rumor would take to descend on the provincial headquarters, become properly corrupted, and wend its way back to the Holy Rosary rectory with a visiting priest from another part of the province. Apparently, Father Pat provided endless fodder for this rumor mill. "Did ya hear that all the priests were invited to dine with the governor?" "Did ya hear that a parishioner left a million dollars to the parish?" Eventually, of course, those of more mature perceptivity soon became uncomfortably aware that they were being had; thereafter, future news out of Holy Rosary in Portland was heard with a wan smile and a shaking head filled with suitable skepticism.

A priest who knew Father Pat at St. Dominic's described him as a "gentle, quiet man who was wonderful preaching to children." Another, more recently, remarked: "He was a good man, I liked him."

Father Pat died, after a long illness, June 14, 1959, at Providence Hospital in Portland, the day he was celebrating 36 years in the priesthood, having been ordained June 14, 1923. His obituary, taken from the June 18, 1959 edition of the *Catholic Sentinel* is quoted:

"Requiem Mass for Father Albert Healy, O.P., 63, of Holy Rosary Church, was offered Tuesday morning at Holy Rosary Church. Interment will be at the Dominican Cemetery in Benicia, California. Father Healy died Sunday at Providence Hospital after a long illness. He was born in Ireland January [24], 1896. He died on the 36th anniversary of his ordination to the priesthood.

"He was a teacher at the old Aquinas High School in Portland in 1924 and served there several years before going to San Francisco. He returned later to Holy Rosary parish for about ten years and was in San Francisco again for eleven months before returning here in April. Father Healy was a teacher at Villa St. Rose in Portland for several years. He also taught at the Dominican House of Studies when it was situated in Benicia, California. He was prior and parish priest at St. Dominic's in San Francisco for a number of years."

REQUIESCAT IN PACE

Neither history nor historians close the book in the life of one man. That right is reserved to God, who closes the book at the Final Judgment. Father Healy was well aware of this finality. May God have mercy on the soul of this faithful servant of Christ, and another Irish priest who served here in the 40s and 50s, and the summer of 1982: Fr. Patrick (Bernard) Condon, whose obituary, taken from the October 1986 edition of the *Irish Herald*, San Francisco, follows:

WELL KNOWN CALIFORNIA PRIEST
ONCE SAVED THE LIFE OF DE VALERA[191]

"In Spokane, Washington, on August 22 [1986],[192] the death took place of Fr. Patrick (Bernard) Condon [O.P.], a native of Clonmel, Co. Tipperary [Ireland] where he was born on January 8, 1904. He was ordained in St. Mary's Cathedral, San Francisco, on June 13, 1942, by the late Archbishop Mitty. His last assignments as priest were at the Immaculate Conception Church, Republic, Washington, and Mission Church, Curlew, Washington, near the Canadian border. Before joining the priesthood Fr. Condon held an executive position with a railroad company.

"According to family friend Margaret Lomacin, Fr. Condon was involved in Ireland's fight for freedom as a young man. He was awarded a medal by the late President de Valera whose life he was instrumental in saving by leading him to safety through the Comeragh Mountains of Co. Waterford during the war with Britain.

"During his priestly career Fr. Condon served many years in California where he was responsible for building a church and school at Antioch. He rebuilt Our Lady of Limerick Church, Glenns Ferry, Idaho, and St. Brigid's Church, Bruneau, Idaho, and served as pastor[193] in Holy Rosary Church, Portland, from 1944 to 1947 and again from 1956 to 1957 and during the summer of 1982.

"He was well known up and down the west coast as a retreat master, convent chaplain, pastor and builder. During one of his visits to Ireland, Fr. Condon brought back to Glenns Ferry a statue of Our Lady from the Dominican Church in Limerick. Fr. Condon was buried on August 25 at the Dominican Fathers Cemetery, Benicia, California."

Father Condon was the subject of the following three Holy Rosary bulletins during his 1982 summer service at Holy Rosary (bulletins kindly furnished by parishioners Maryetta and Elizabeth Foley). The bulletins are quoted below:

"[**7-18-82**] We are pleased to have Father Patrick B. Condon, O.P., who is helping out during Fr. Buckley's absence. Fr. Condon is a former pastor, prior, and retreat master, and a native of Ireland."

"[**8-29-82**] Holy Rosary Parish has indeed been blessed in having

Father Patrick Bernard Condon, O.P., help us out this summer. Some of you old-timers may remember that Father Condon was assigned to Holy Rosary Parish from 1944 to 1947, and again in 1956 and 1957. His presence at Holy Rosary has been most welcome. His spirituality, his inspiring sermons, and his gracious demeanor, have been greatly appreciated by both the Priests and lay people. Father Condon will leave tomorrow for his duties in Cottonwood, Idaho, as Chaplain of the Benedictine Sisters, at St. Mary's Hospital…We wish him well in his new assignment, and hope that he will come back again, and renew his acquaintances and friendships at 'Good Old Holy Rosary.'"

"[**9-5-82**] *Fr. Bernard Condon, who replaced Fr. Buckley this summer, was stricken with severe shortness of breath at Grants Pass en route to California. The condition proved to be a mild thrombosis of the heart, but fortunately the heart was not damaged. He remains in Southern Oregon Hospital, Grants Pass, for observation and thanks you for your prayers."*

[We recall Sister Seraphica's letter, dated April 24, 1946 (Chapter 6): "…*Father Agius has done wonders with his good, holy assistants, Father Feucht and Father Condon, to bring a high spiritual and family-like parish standard. What a grace for all of us…*"]

In a letter dated October 9, 1944 Pastor Joseph M. Agius, O.P., wrote to the provincial:

"*Father Condon is fitting in nicely. He is a genuine priest, a wonderful community man, an excellent subject, liked by all…it will be a pleasure to have him in our midst. He preached his first sermon at Holy Rosary last Friday; it was quite all right, sincere and to the point. Comments were favorable. May I say for myself, Father, that it is a relief to work with such a man.*

I wonder if you would let Father Condon be Procurator here at Holy Rosary. He can handle the job all right, and doing so would let Father McDermott be free to carry on his parochial work."
[The provincial approved this request].

> *May your soul be secure in heaven*
> *A minute before the devil knows your dead.*
> —An Irish Proverb

ORIGIN OF THE SHRINE OF OUR LADY OF THE ROSARY

Father Feucht wrote the following letter, dated January 14, 1955, to the provincial, Father Joseph J. Fulton, O.P.:

Since the Rosary has been broadcast from Holy Rosary Church, there has been a growing interest throughout the City of Portland to build a shrine here in Holy Rosary Church, to the Blessed Mother. The work is being backed entirely by the Diocesan Holy Name Society. Plans have been drawn by the architect and estimate given: $6,000.00. This would include a general renovation of the

Pastor William A. Norton, O.P. receives new statue of Our Lady of the Rosary for shrine built by the Diocesan Holy Name Society.

Father Fulton approved of the work and, four years later, this article appeared in the *Catholic Sentinel*:[194]

"A new shrine and statue at Holy Rosary Church, N.E. Third and Clackamas, Portland will be blessed by Archbishop Howard Friday night, Nov. 6. The blessing will take place after a 6:15 p.m. Mass offered by the Very Rev. Joseph J. Fulton, O.P., provincial of the Dominican Fathers. The statue, carved of wood and painted, was ordered from Rome eight months ago and has just arrived, Father William A. Norton, O.P., pastor of Holy Rosary Church, said. It depicts St. Dominic at the feet of the Blessed Virgin, receiving from her the Rosary."

SIGNIFICANCE OF SYMBOLS IN OUR LADY OF THE ROSARY STATUE
The significance of the dog, the globe, and the flaming torch in our Lady of the Rosary Statue would be explained by Father Anthony Patalano, O.P. pastor and prior, in the church bulletin dated July 12, 1992:

"Within the past few months, several people in the parish asked me about the little dog that is portrayed in the statue of Our Lady of the Holy Rosary. This "pooch" is one of the major symbols of Dominican heraldry. According to legend, Saint Dominic's mother, Blessed Joan of Aza, had a dream while she was pregnant that she gave birth to a dog, who, when coming out of the womb, immediately began running around the world brandishing a flaming torch in its mouth. Weird dream you say! Not really, when you consider this was a time when people put a lot of emphasis on interpreting dreams. Even in our own day, people keep dream journals and much has been written on the interpretation of dreams.

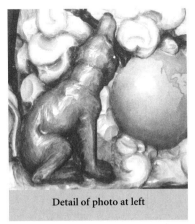

Detail of photo at left

"As for the little dog, the torch and the globe of the earth, the explanation is simple. The dog is the symbol of fidelity. The torch is the light of the Gospel. This little dog, who represents Saint Dominic and the Order of Preachers (Ordinis Praedicatorum) which he founded, would be faithful in preaching the good news of Jesus Christ throughout the world.

Sanctuary, and especially of the side altar. I will send you a copy of the plan as soon as they have smaller ones printed.

I do not know whether this plan will meet with your approval or not. Of course the entire expense of this project will be raised by the Diocesan Holy Name, and will be of no expense to us. They had hoped to have it finished by the 31st of May, the new feast of the Blessed Virgin.

You know, I wish that someone were Pastor here with a little sense of organization. It seems that I let a lot of opportunities slip through my hands. Novenas etc. should be started here.

Sincerely in St. Dominic

[signed]
T.A. Feucht, O.P.

"Sometimes Saint Dominic is portrayed with an eight-point star. This too is based on legend. It is said that when he was brought to the font to be baptized, the eight-pointed navigators' star came down from heaven and rested on his forehead. What does this mean? Simply that Saint Dominic was favored by God to do something special in the Church."

Holy Rosary on the Verge of Abandonment?

Even though the praying of the Rosary was beginning to attract new parishioners, the church itself was badly in need of repair, as recalled in this letter from Mary Loomis dated January 19, 1993:

"Our first impression of Holy Rosary Church in the late '50s was that it was on the verge of abandonment. It was dark, dingy, and seemed spiritless. The pews were coated with a very dark varnish, and I believe that the floors were bare wood. Then Father Norton arrived with spirit. I recall entering the church and facing stacks of floor tiles in boxes. Worshippers were given the opportunity to provide tile for the aisles – at a dollar a tile. Pioneer Square [195] *must have gotten the buy-a-brick idea from him! Of course complete restoration was under way (the understanding among the few parishioners was that the parish was broke). Father intended to provide an inviting church for the 'parish' of people employed in the immediate north-east area. A lack of funds presented him with a challenge not an obstacle. I believe that his sister provided more than a little 'seed' money to get this project going, but it didn't take him long to find local arms to twist. He wasn't afraid to take on a grand project, and had the ability to make others want to help him see it through. (If you didn't want to, you did it anyway). He was always so cheerful and positive about his projects. How could they fail? And they didn't.*

"The interior of the church was painted a pastille salmon pink at this time, and this is worthy of mention because of the 'raspberry' brouhaha which occurred when redecorating was necessary some years later. Father consulted with Kay Matschiner about the repainting. Kay was an old time parishioner (since birth) and a truly dashing woman with great style and taste. Well, they had the church painted raspberry red. As people entered the church on the Sunday after it was painted you could literally hear the gasps. Father heard about that. So the next Sunday he announced that he would poll the congregation on their feelings about the paint job, and if the majority disliked it, it would be repainted. Secret ballots were cast at every Mass, and the raspberry walls were saved. Of course, the grumbling was pretty well dissipated by the opportunity to have one's say. And the church was gorgeous.

"Other things that Father Norton did:

1) *Constructed the St. Dominic Chapel Shrine and commissioned the hand-carved statue. Also the St. Joseph statue.*

2) *Reduced the size of the pulpit. It was originally much taller.*

3) *Added the St. Martin [de Porres] Chapel. This statue was originally in the back of the church. When Blessed Martin was canonized, Father made a special place for him.*

4) *Initiated the construction of Calaroga Terrace. In a brain-storming session with Father about ways to develop the parish, I mentioned the possibility of locating some retirement housing on land already owned by the parish. You can see that that little seed flourished.*

"Our family's favorite Father Norton story is about a conversation I had with him shortly after we met. Our oldest children were about ten and eleven years old at the time and were serving Sunday Mass at Holy Rosary. Father wanted them to be available for daily Masses, but I explained that I didn't have a car available during the week, and their bicycles needed repair, so they just couldn't make it during the week. (We lived a good distance from the church). Out came his fat black wallet, 'How much will it cost to fix the bicycles?' he asked. The bikes got fixed, and the boys were faithful servers for many years. Our four other sons also were servers and we had someone (actually a pain) on the altar until we moved from the parish in 1980.

"The enclosed card shows the raspberry walls – and also the dollar-a-tile aisle! Father Norton was a natural leader – never any doubt about who the boss was – but he would be remembered best as a person who met every challenge, whether refurbishing old buildings or counseling people in their darkest hours, in a positive and practical and Godly way."

More On Father William Aquinas "Wild Bill" Norton, o.p.

Father Feucht had many times expressed the desire that someone with "a little sense of organization," and a "little more dynamism" would take over as pastor. This wish was fulfilled when the provincial assigned Father Norton to assume the duties of pastor in 1958. At the close of an October 9, 1958 letter to the provincial (The Very Reverend Joseph J. Fulton, O.P.), Father Norton stated *"This parish is very poor but I have raised over $2,000 so far."* [196] He soon had many projects on the front burner: paving the parking lot ($8600), redoing the confessionals ($700), painting the church ($1,000), etc. for a total bill of a little over $11,000. In his usual fashion, he would "go for broke," and the healthy parish he had at the end of his term would prove him right. At the close of that same letter he wrote:

"I just did what I KNEW should be done and what I feel SURE would meet your approval because I am confident that you know I am doing my level best to save this parish and to make it clean, comfortable and reasonably beautiful for the people and for the priests in the rectory. Trust me and you will not regret it. I suppose I cannot say 'obediently yours' but I will say GOD BLESS YOU!"

Original grotto of Our Lady of Lourdes was located at the north end of the parking lot before being moved to its present location in 1958 by stone-mason and parishioner Stan Brosterhous.

PARISHIONER STANLY BROSTERHOUS REBUILDS SHRINE TO OUR LADY OF LOURDES

The hard-driving new pastor would put in a parking lot as soon as possible. Part and parcel of Father Norton's plans for the new parking lot included the tearing down and discarding of Our Lady of Lourdes shrine which then occupied the north end of the apple orchard (on the south side of Halsey, facing the church) where the entrance to and exit from the present lot are now located. Stan, a stone and bricklayer by trade, recognized the beauty of the rocks and stones that formed the nooks, crevices, and crannies of the shrine, and set about salvaging it all. He prevailed upon Father Norton to give him four days to dismantle the pile of beautiful dry-rocks, relocating them so that the removal of the orchard and the leveling of the ground for the parking lot could proceed.[197] He then recruited as many Holy Name Society men as he could muster, and moved the entire pile of stones to the north wall of the church, out of the way of the parking lot construction crew, and proceeded with this massive project. Stan said:

"I wanted to do something for Our Blessed Mother. If you lay two ton of stone a day you're doing well. So when you lay 100 ton you're talking 50 days. Rocky Butte quarry and Joe Marsden either donated the rocks or sold them to us at discount. Columbia Brick donated the sand and cement. Also, we defrayed the cost with corned beef or ham and cabbage dinners in the school gym. We had a gas range with six burners and a large grill. The men did all the work and the school girls waited on tables, where we sat 400 people. Sometimes we served 600 to 1000 people beginning at 1:00 p.m. Father Agius started Bingo. Sometimes the jackpot got as high as $1600 to $1700 on a 'black-out.' Frank Eixenberger and I traded

places calling Bingo. It brought in a badly needed $15,000 a year to the parish. Portland Mayor Dorothy McCullogh Lee attended the games. Later, when she closed down the games with a city ordinance, we called her 'Nasty-Nice Dorothy.'"

Stan and parishioners Dan Caven and Lee Riordan, and other members of the Holy Name Society, set about rebuilding the shrine, mixing the cement and building it up stone by stone, evenings and weekends, all the while pursuing their own jobs during the day. It took almost a year, but with hard work and true grit they finally completed the shrine that now adorns the north wall of the church today.

On one occasion, Stan observed water at the foot of the shrine and asked Father Norton where it came from. Father, chagrined, said he had installed new plumbing because he wanted water flowing over the feet of Our Blessed Mother. Stan was livid because this flowing water could cause the shrine to disintegrate. Stan talked over the problem of Father Norton's "meddling" with Architect Francis Jacobberger, who told Stan to tell Father Norton that no other architectural changes could take place without first consulting Jacobberger. Stan passed the message and Father Norton graciously complied with this advice from the experts. One year later, the following notice appeared in the November 19, 1959 edition of the *Catholic Sentinel*:

"A new outdoor shrine of Our Lady of Lourdes at Holy Rosary Church, NE 3rd and Clackamas, Portland, was blessed recently by the Very Rev. Joseph J. Fulton, O.P., of San Francisco, provincial of the Dominican Fathers for the Pacific region. The shrine depicts the Blessed Virgin Mary appearing to Bernadette."[198]

The new grotto was blessed by Provincial Father Joseph Fulton, O.P. in 1959.

Stan, born October 24, 1906 in Dogden, North Dakota married Jetta Irene Beach, who was born in Wichita, Kansas November 17, 1908. They came to Holy Rosary in 1942 from Bend, Oregon. They were close to Pastors Agius, Feucht, Norton and Cassidy. On their 50th wedding anniversary, June 27, 1978, they renewed their marriage vows at Holy Rosary, in a ceremony led by Father Feucht, with Father Agius assisting. After the ceremony they drove to Welches Golf Course near Mount Hood for breakfast. Father Agius accompanied their party, but Father Feucht was not strong enough to make the trip. Stan and Jetta are a wonderful couple, God love them.

Stonemason Stanly Brosterhous admires his work two decades later (1978).

ANTI-CATHOLIC BIGOTRY TRANSFORMED FROM IRRATIONAL TO PARTLY RATIONAL DURING HOLY ROSARY'S 100 YEARS

Anti-Catholic bigotry neither abated nor disappeared in the intervening years. With the election of Catholic John F. Kennedy to the presidency in 1960, that old irrational fear of the Pope living in the White House and secretly running the country was expressed *ad nauseum*. It soon became self-evident, however, that the Pope had little or no influence on the Kennedy presidency (devout Catholics said of Kennedy: "Johnnie we hardly knew ya."). But, in at least one dimension, irrational fear turned to rational fear as the sexual revolution of the nineteen sixties began its destructive journey through the soul of America.

The "free-sex liberators" were rightfully convinced that the Catholic Church would be the greatest obstacle to their "successful" revolution. The Church was an obstacle then and would be "a sign of contradiction" for the ensuing decades as adulterers, homosexuals, abortionists, sex-education enthusiasts, and euthanasiasts (an unheavenly host controlled by Satan himself) combined to tear down the Church in the United States.

"Tear down" is no exaggeration. For example, pioneer abortionist Bernard Nathanson, after he had a change of heart, frankly admitted that he and his colleagues had been party to detailed plans to deliberately attack the Catholic Church, and had used their influence, with any group that would listen, to achieve that goal. And so the bigotry and blindness, this time, would be more rational than not, and continue to the end of the century. But first let us visit the 1960s.

NOTES TO THE TEXT

162 Taken from extant school rosters on file at Holy Rosary Priory.

163 Page 61, Alfred A. Knopf, New York 1994.

164 His sister has been a Benedictine nun for 55 years.

165 Urban Feucht, O.S.B. And two of Father Feucht's sisters were nuns: Sister Rose Marie, O.P., & Sister Dolorosa, O.S.B.

166 Romans 13:11-14.

167 Father Donnelly, a faithful priest for 25 years, later left the priesthood and married, but was reconciled with the Church, and is today a devout Catholic.

168 Italicized paragraphs in this section of this chapter are quotes from the Winter 1994 issue of *Oregon History Magazine*, published by the Oregon Historical Society, 1200 SW Park Avenue, Portland, Oregon 97205, and are excerpts from *A Peculiar Paradise: A History of Blacks in Oregon*, by Elizabeth McLagan.

169 661 Greenwood Ave, Toronto, Ont., Canada M4J 4B3.

170 Norma Monahan, a delightful and saintly woman and full-time volunteer at the Rosary Confraternity, was personally acquainted with Catherine, who volunteered this information.

171 And writer, according to Father Lawrence E. Banfield, O.P.

172 *The Way of the Lord Jesus, Volume One, Christian Moral Principles* by Germain Grisez, Franciscan Herald Press, 1434 West 51st Street, Chicago 60609, page 212, (Aided by Basil Cole, O.P., Western Dominican Province, et al.).

173 Ibid, page 534.

174 The original school was the Noon House, which then became a convent for the Dominican Sisters, after the new school was built in 1923 (see Chapter 6).

175 Vol. 45, No. 3 – A Western Dominican Publication, P.O. Box 3617, Portland, Oregon 97208.

176 Taken from pages 18 & 19 *The Secret of the Rosary* by St. Louis De Montfort, translated by Mary Barbour, T.O.P., Bay Shore, N.Y. 11706, 1954.

177 So named "because it has the same number of Angelic Salutations as there are psalms in the Book of Psalms of David," page 25, ibid.

178 Our own Father Paul Duffner, O.P., had earlier founded this chapter of the Confraternity in California.

179 This apostolate was established over 500 years ago by the Holy See as a world-wide prayer movement.

180 Taken from speech delivered by Bishop Francis P. Leipzig on the occasion of the 25th Anniversary of the Radio Rosary, Holy Rosary Church, September 23, 1976.

181 *Catholic Sentinel*, September 18, 1958.

182 *Catholic Sentinel*, May 24, 1951, page 1.

183 From speech delivered by Bishop Francis P. Leipzig on the occasion of the 25th Anniversary of Radio Rosary, Holy Rosary Church, September 23, 1976.

184 St. Francis of Assisi Church in Rochester, New York, had their first radio broadcast on March 4, 1950, according to Bishop Leipzig.

185 Taken from speech delivered by Bishop Francis P. Leipzig on the occasion of the 25th Anniversary of the Radio Rosary, Holy Rosary Church, September 23, 1976. Untold millions of Rosaries have been prayed as a result of these early efforts.

186 Luke 1:48.

187 Page 4.

188 December 11, page 10.

189 He had previously served at Holy Rosary: 1924-1928 and 1949-1955.

190 According to Father Charles Hess, O.P., Dominican Historian and Archivist at the Oakland Provincial Headquarters, all deceased Dominicans of the province, are buried at Benicia, except two: Fr. Anthony Leo Hofstee, O.P., who wanted to be buried with the lepers he served at Tala in the Phillipines, and a brother, a widower when entering the order, who wanted to be buried next to his deceased wife.

191 Father Gregory Anderson, O.P., who knew him, said "Barney" had been a messenger for the I.R.A. as a boy, and loved to sing all 130 verses of *The Soldier's Song* during recreational periods at the Province.

192 Archival records of the Dominican Province, Oakland, show he died at St. Joseph's Hospital, Chewelah, Washington where his sister, Sister M. Humilitas, O.P., was serving at the time.

193 Actually, he was associate pastor. Father Joseph Agius, O.P., was pastor from 1944 to 1947, and Father Thomas Feucht, O.P., was pastor from 1949 to 1957. In the summer of 1982, Father Gerald Buckley, O.P., was pastor.

194 Dated October 29, 1959, page 1, column 5.

195 Pioneer Square in downtown Portland is an open-air square, paving for which consisted of bricks paid for by donors who had their names inscribed on them.

196 Stan Brosterhous said Father Norton's family "had money" and that they had oftentimes helped Father Norton in his various pursuits, including the purchase of the Our Lady of the Rosary Statue which, the Holy Name Society funded. Father Norton was the spiritual director of the Holy Name Society at the time.

197 In a letter to the provincial, Joseph J. Fulton, O.P., dated October 9, 1958, Father Norton wrote: "The paving of the new parking lot is finished," so most of this activity took place in the spring, summer and fall of 1958.

198 The shrine has been desecrated several times. One time, someone stole the statue of Bernadette. Later, some demented person damaged the face of Our Blessed Mother.

Father Florent Gutierrez Martin, O.P. before the 1971 Christmas chreche.

POST-VATICAN II LITURGICAL CHANGES
(MET WITH DOMINICAN MODERATION)

"Unless the Lord build thy house, they labor in vain who build it."
(Psalm 126)

FOREVER ANCIENT – FOREVER NEW

Beginning in the 1960s and lasting at least into the 1990s, the Catholic Church in America experienced a sea change as instructions on the new liturgy slowly trickled down to the dioceses and parishes throughout the United States, and the potency of the new reformers would pulsate outward through every nook and cranny of the Church, and into the minds and hearts of Christ's sheep. The modernists' "renewed" church would not be as envisioned by the Council, i.e. Roman Catholicism's old wine contained in fashionably new decanters. Vatican II designed it that way, but the modernists made the "old wine" a foul brew offensive to the tastebuds of the faithful. Hot-beds of sedition captured and corrupted Bishops' conferences, Catholic universities, theological associations, priests' senates, the Catholic press and other levers of power.

All of the modernists' gambits would corrupt the Church, for the devil himself hid in the implementation of the Vatican II directives. The liturgy became increasingly innovative, a "show" in many instances, an occasion for mourning. To the poor souls in the New Church, the Old Church became unrecognizable, and their anguish heartfelt at this perplexing turn of events. Some of the changes occurred by happenstance, while others were the fulfillment of detailed and deceitful plans imposed by an apostate clergy, religious and laity, wrought through national and international networking. "What's going on in the Church?" the sheep would ask themselves and others, as they slowly became engulfed in constant change and cockamamie notions that gained momentary currency. Answers would come years later.

"WE OVERCAME THEIR TRADITIONS, WE OVERCAME THEIR FAITH."

Psychotherapy and reliance on the expertise of faithless flakes played no small part in the destruction of several Catholic religious orders in the Catholic Church in America in the 1960s. The Latin Mass, a bi-monthly magazine[199] published a special edition in 1994 which featured an interview of Dr. William Coulson who, with Psychologist Carl Rogers, lit the fires of rebellion which cremated those orders. One of the first orders selected for the Rogers-Coulson therapy was The Immaculate Heart of Mary nuns in California. Through the use of non-directive counseling, small "encounter" groups, "sensitivity training" and other techniques employed in humanistic psychology, these two psychologists (along with a cadre of 60 facilitators) were responsible for the IHM nuns reducing the number of their schools from 60 to one school. And of the 560 nuns who participated in this "therapy," "within a year after our first interventions, 300 of them were petitioning Rome to get our of their vows."

Holy Rosary Becomes a Magnet Parish

Surely some souls never recovered from the battering they received, and they left the Church with their personal demons. Others perserved in the hope that things would improve. In this milieu, the liturgical changes at Holy Rosary would be characterized as moderate. The astute Dominican priests – at least at Holy Rosary – deftly avoided the banal and profane and held onto the sacred and solemn. As a consequence, this "dying" parish became a magnet parish to pious Catholics from throughout the archdiocese and beyond, re-attracting former parishioners long gone from the old eastside areas, as well as wandering souls from distant cities in southern Washington and the lower Willamette Valley in Oregon, who found out through word of mouth that Holy Rosary possessed what they were seeking: some remnant of Roman Catholic tradition.

These were not people of frivolous mind in matters of redemption or the finality of the four last things (death, judgement, heaven and hell). They would cleave to their own private perception of what God wanted of them and, when they found Holy Rosary, the parish began a period of resurgence which would continue unimpeded up to its centennial celebration and beyond. Our Blessed Mother would see to it that this "dying" parish with five families would explode into a vibrant parish with more than 900 families, administered to by Friars who had been faithful to her, her Son, and His Vicar, and the air would be charged with activity as generosity goaded the imagination of these "refugees" eager to serve. These new parishioners at Holy Rosary possessed a delicate balance of faith and understanding undergirded by a keen need to worship. What did these formerly beleagured Catholics want? Simply put, they wanted to be "Roman Catholics." Anything else would be a form of spiritual suicide. Some people inside and outside the Church branded them as "old fashioned," "straight-laced" and "not with the program," but they would hold to their vision of how a prayerful soul should lovingly respond to God in His house of prayer.

Parish Prayer to the Mother of God

Upon reflection, most parishioners would doubtless attribute the good fortunes of Holy Rosary Parish to the maternal presence of Mary, to whom this community has prayed daily and with fervency since its founding. In May 1961, for example, the parish celebrated the 10th anniversary of the Rosary for Peace radio broadcasts which, in thirty years, would culminate in the incorporation, in Portland, of the first lay-sponsored radio station in the United

States, its call letters being KBVM (for Blessed Virgin Mary). Holy Rosary priests, beginning with Father Paul Duffner, O.P., have served as spiritual advisors to the Radio Rosary (originally broadcast from inside Holy Rosary Church on local radio stations KBKO, KVAN, and KWJJ).

Among the lay heroes of the Holy Name Society involved in the founding of Radio Rosary were: James Lynch, Joseph McCully, John Layman, Henry Becker, John Nelson, John Petrusich and Leo Greiner.

Ten Years – 3,000 Broadcasts – From Holy Rosary Church Celebrated

On May 15, 1961, the founders of Radio Rosary celebrated the 10th anniversary of the program,[200] noting that *"more than 3,000 broadcasts have been made with more than 100,000 persons participating in prayers at Holy Rosary Church,"* and *"Thousands of inquiries concerning the Rosary and the Catholic Faith have been received as a result of the broadcasts, and many converts to the Church have been attributed to them. Hospitalized people and other shut-ins make the Radio Rosary a part of their everyday routine."*

Plenary Indulgence Gained for Souls in Purgatory

On September 23, 1961, Father Stanley Parmisano, O.P., conducted the annual Rosary Novena, which ended October 1. *"Through a special privilege granted by the Holy See, all who visit Holy Rosary church from noon Saturday, Sept. 30, until Sunday evening, Oct. 1, may gain a plenary indulgence for the souls in purgatory for each visit, by saying six Our Fathers, six Hail Marys and six Glorias for the intention of the Holy Father.[201] All priests of the archdiocese have been invited to attend the Mass, to march in procession, and to be guests, with Archbishop Howard and Bishop Leipzig, at a brunch in the rectory hall after the ceremonies."*

Approximately 1500 People Attend Celebration at Holy Rosary Church

On October 1, 1961, Archbishop Edward D. Howard and Bishop Francis P. Leipzig of Baker joined Holy Rosary clergy and hundreds of parishioners and other faithful in yet another celebration of the 10th Anniversary of the Radio Rosary. Archbishop Howard celebrated at the 12:10 p.m. Mass, and Bishop Leipzig gave the sermon.

An outdoor procession followed the Mass, at which the Algera Chorale of Marycrest High School sang. A priest led the Rosary for the procession from the pulpit over loudspeakers installed outside the church. Archbishop Howard and Bishop Leipzig marched in the procession "preceded by priests and a Knights of Columbus honor guard." Benediction and the distribution of blessed roses followed the procession, in which "marchers carried banners depicting the 15 mysteries of the Rosary." "Bishop

Howard paid tribute to the members of the Holy Name Society for the work they [had] done in sponsoring the program."[202] These prayers and observances brought peace and tranquility to the parish for several years, but the winds of change would carry the spectre of modernism, if only briefly, into the Holy Rosary priory in the years ahead.

FATHER WILLIAM AQUINAS "WILD BILL" NORTON, O.P.

Father William A. "Wild Bill" Norton, O.P. was the pastor at Holy Rosary during the early 1960s (his tenure actually began in 1958 and he served until 1964). The vibrant and irrepressible Father Norton earned his moniker, "Wild Bill" the hard way, with an Irish flair for feats of derring-do, mainly driving fast cars at high speed, and having a bigger-than-life imagination, as well as the brains, brashness, and resolve to execute his plans with dispatch. His passion rarely ebbed. He was a street-wise ex-seaman, who had served in the U.S. Merchant Marine prior to 1928. He also served as a chaplain in the U. S. Navy during World War II (1941-46). This 'Hound of Heaven' had the face of a bulldog with a tenacity to match. He was ordained as a Dominican August 18, 1934, and remained a breathless messenger of Christ for 44 years before his death on October 2, 1978, at the age of 78.

Father Gregory Anderson, O.P., Associate Pastor at Holy Rosary in the 1980s, recalls driving north from San Francisco with Father Norton at the wheel in the 1950s, before the interstate freeways were built. Norton, coursing over hills traveled by logging trucks, pressed pedal to the metal, passing those six-wheelers on narrow turns with perilous drop-offs and, at the same time, singing or telling stories while Father Anderson's knuckles turned white holding on to the dashboard and door handle. "He was something else," said Father Anderson, "a real character in a class by himself, who lived life to the fullest."

We extend our thanks to Susan Schulzke, who was the parish secretary for ten years, for memories of her encounters with Father Norton:

FATHER NORTON'S MOUSE TRAP

In the summer of 1963, I found my way to Holy Rosary Church to see a priest about becoming a Catholic. The pastor, Father Norton, was out hearing confessions so the cook asked me into the kitchen to await his return.

Father Norton came and talked to me quite a while, then suggested I attend his classes. The first thing I remember was a little mouse going around Father's feet as he was teaching. I guess he saw a strange look on my face and, all the while knowing the mischievous mouse was at his feet, asked me if I had a question. All the class laughed when I told him I had a 'thing' about mice. After taking a second class, I was baptized on December 14, 1963.
A few months later, in 1964, Father called me and asked if I would

like to work for the Dominicans. My first job was sitting by the front door to answer phones and doors. One day a man in shorts and tee shirt rang the bell and said he wanted to go to confession. I told him he would have to make an appointment. He said: "I am a priest." I was shocked and told him I couldn't tell that by the way he was dressed. He came after that with collar and properly dressed (and we later became friends). I believe Father Norton was in a convalescent home[203] *after he had a stroke. It was amazing how well he got around in his electric wheel chair, helping all the people he could.*

During this time the main altar, which had come from San Francisco to Holy Rosary, was ruined when it was turned to face the people. At about this time Mass was said in English. Father Curtin had a time at first because he talked so fast. A few other priests came but did not stay long, so I don't remember much about them.

FATHER NORTON BUILDS PARKING LOT

Father Norton's imagination occasionally engaged his impatience, but quiet traits of tenderness overcame accompanying tirades. He had sufficient charm to talk birds out of trees, and though he would agree with Joyce Kilmer that "Only God can make a tree," he saw the orchard next to the rectory as an impediment to parish growth in a time when more and more people were taking up their love affairs with automobiles, himself included. Some also said he did not like mowing lawns and this was a way to get out of that boring duty – but that was not the case. In any event, one of his first acts was to cut down the orchard and pave it over to make a parking lot; thereby, would-be parishioners could park their cars and have easy access to the church. Even though some parishioners had moved from the area during its industrialization and lived in other parishes, they still attended weekly Mass at Holy Rosary; and more would come because they now had a place to park – "if you build it they will come."

FATHER NORTON PLANS A RETIREMENT FACILITY

Father Norton was responsible for *promoting* the idea of building Calaroga Terrace,[204] a retirement facility across the street from the church of this "dying" parish. He convinced the Western Dominican Province, then under the able leadership of Father Joseph Agius, who had been pastor at Holy Rosary from 1942-47, to help back his impressive plans.

Father Norton figured that, through a planned marketing campaign, elderly Catholics in Oregon and other places could be convinced to move to this retirement facility, to which Holy Rosary would provide chaplains and celebrate Mass in a chapel on the premises or across the street in the church proper. Then, if all worked well, Calaroga Terrace would provide a steady pool of parishioners for the coming decades. A mounting sense of greatness and excitement permeated the community when the ground-breaking took place.

The *Catholic Sentinel*, dated December 26, 1963, gave this account:

Plans were revealed here this week for construction of a 14-storey retirement home, to be completed by early 1965 on a location across the street from Holy Rosary parish church and sponsored by the Dominican Fathers of the Holy Name province covering the 13 western states, including Alaska and Hawaii.

At the same time, directors of University Senior Citizens, Inc., which had been the sponsoring group for the University Tower,[205] announced that they were pledging their cooperation and support to the new Dominican sponsored project.

The new project will be known as Rosary Tower, a name chosen by Fr. William A. Norton, O.P., Holy Rosary pastor, and will occupy the block bounded by NE 3rd and 2nd Avenue and Clackamas and Halsey Street. It will form the initial segment of the $50 million Coliseum Garden development[206] which is being planned for a large area east of the Memorial Coliseum by Theron L. Hedgpeth, a leading developer and builder of similar projects in the western states from Santa Rosa, Calif.

Hedgpeth, in Portland last week, stated that 'my associates and I welcome this sincere expression from the sponsors of University Tower and hope that the hundreds of persons who looked to University Tower for security and happy retirement will find it, at an early date, in our Dominican-sponsored facility in Coliseum Gardens.'

Associated with Hedgpeth in many of his projects have been the Utah Construction and Mining Company and the Henry C. Beck company.

Charles E. Royer, executive director of University Tower and now affiliated with development of the new project, said 'tremendous interest' has already been shown in Rosary Tower 'from many of the people who had been interested and paid deposits on apartments in University Tower.'

Advantages of the new project, he said, included location – with proximity to downtown, Lloyd Center, the Coliseum and Holy Rosary church and the stepped-up completion date.

'Excavation and construction will be underway in two or three months at most,' he stated. 'Completion and move-in date is guaranteed for early 1965.'

Royer said also that the new facility would include 'the most comprehensive medicare program of any retirement facility in the country.'

He said one or two members of the directors' board of University Senior Citizens will serve on the board of the Dominican-sponsored facility.

In announcing the termination of plans for the University Tower project, Father Paul E. Waldschmidt, CSC, president of the University of Portland, said new Federal regulations 'would require an entirely new financing plan to proceed' with the campus-based project.

'Rather than this, we have preferred to cooperate with the new development, which we feel will substantially answer the purposes for which the University Tower was conceived. Since the construction contract has already been let, the facility can be completed sooner, to meet the needs of the many persons who desire assured retirement living in a Catholic atmosphere.'

Father Waldschmidt and Paul F. Murphy, president of the University Senior Citizens board, have notified directly all persons who have indicated interest in University Tower of the change in plan. They have recommended that they consider the new development.

Father Joseph M. Agius, O.P., provincial of the Dominican's Holy Name Province from Oakland, Calif., and a former pastor of Holy Rosary parish here, announced in Portland this week that the province has entered into a long-term ground lease agreement to the north of Holy Rosary Parish, at NE 3rd and Weidler, site of the parish hall and former school building.

Royer said this building is being extensively remodeled to accomodate construction and sales offices for Rosary Tower. It will also house four fully furnished model apartments, constructed to provide a 'dimensional view' which will be open for public inspection in late January or early February [1964].'

Royer said the new Rosary Tower will comprise studio, and one-and-one-half and two-bedroom apartments.

Hedgpeth is expected to reveal details of the complete Coliseum Gardens development within a few weeks.

[As Father Cassidy commented in his remembrance of this venture: *The building was built and then little by little the province pulled out of it – because the original idea didn't sell too well* (i.e. affordable housing for retired members of the Third Order of Dominicans, as well as other parishioners)].

FATHER NORTON DEPARTS HOLY ROSARY

According to the April 10, 1964 Sentinel, Father Norton was transferred to the Dominican provincial house in San Francisco to become director of the Third Order of St. Dominic (now known as Dominican Laity). "Several hundred parishioners and friends honored Father Norton at a reception April 5 in the Coliseum Gardens office building."

REVEREND FRANCIS FELIX CASSIDY, O.P. SUCCEEDS FATHER NORTON
From October 1964 to June 1970, Father Cassidy, in many ways an exact opposite in personality to Father Norton, served Holy Rosary parishioners as their pastor. The exuberant Father Cassidy provided this interesting information about his journey to Holy Rosary:

The following are just a few thoughts I was asked to "jot" down by Father Anthony in regards to "my stay" at Holy Rosary Church in Portland. Patalano

1) *In case I "lose you" it was a great time – really a thrilling time, because "Vatican II" was just getting started, with all of its new ideas!!*

2) *Father Agius was the provincial and he asked me to go to Holy Rosary as pastor. I had been to Mount Angel for one excellent year (1947-1948) before I went into the novitiate. However, I did not know where Holy Rosary was located in Portland.*

I drove a red Dodge car "dead head" to Portland (to save money!) and arrived in early October 1964 – on a dark, cold night about 8:00 p.m. I looked over the vast city (population 400,000 at the time) and then asked a gas station man how to get to the church. He directed me across a bridge and then he told me to turn left. I did what he told me, and started passing empty lots and warehouses…a rather poor part of the city. Then I saw the rectory and church in the middle of more empty lots, and I said to myself "No wonder Father Agius sent me here."

I was received well by Father Barnabus Curtin and Father Kieran Healy, and enjoyed the community and the "warm" look of the house and the simple church.

Susan Schulzke was the bookkeeper and receptionist (and cook at times)…she was outstanding! (Her late husband had a floor covering company and she knew the business world). She was more or less a recent convert by Father Bill Norton, O.P.

3) *Archbishop Howard was in charge and he was very kind to me. He gave an order that all altars must face the people by November 29th, 1964…English was being worked into the Mass more and more.*

4) *That "order" from the archbishop was carried out in this way: Father Healy and I removed the wooden altar that St. Martin de Porres was on and then we put it in front of the main altar!! We placed it between the altar rail. It fitted very well, and looked fairly good with its wooden "ribs" (that St. Martin Shrine cost $10,000).*

5) *The next thing we needed was a microphone system, so the people could hear us from that altar. We bought a second-hand one from a salesperson who worked for Jantzen, Inc., the sports clothing manufacturers, because we did not have very much money at that time.*

6) *We decided among ourselves that the altar was too low, and so we brought in experts on the liturgy and they said they would draw up plans so that the marble altar could be used to face the people (that advice only cost $400 – another expense for us on our low income). The altar came up from St. Dominic's in San Francisco on the train, and so we "knew" it could be moved again!! (My Mother and Father were married before that altar in San Francisco!). They were thrilled to see it again, in Portland!!!*

7) *The same company that built the hall (Brockamp & Jaeger, Inc.) guided us through all of this, and we were able to complete everything (in 1965 and 1966) as one sees it today (although someone said they are going to move the tabernacle to a different place this year – 1992).*

8) *Susan Schulzke's brother-in-law put in the red carpet in the Sanctuary, but since we had so little money we left the table in the body of the church.*

9) *The next project that we did was to paint the church two-tone gray, and put a new roof on the church and rectory.*

10) *Since we did not have much money Father Healy and myself and two Protestant ministers and about 10 college kids from Portland State University Newman Center (under Father Healy's direction) did the work. The Newman Center is now Koinonia House – and recently celebrated its 25th anniversary. It took us from Monday to Friday, working eight hours a day under the direction of a union painter. (He really worked us!) One girl, Sandy Knudsen, became a baptized Catholic and was married by Father Healy…the painting experience really "got to her!."*

Those simple words speak volumes about this magnificent priest of great sanctity and humility. He was truly loved during his tenure as pastor. People kidded that Father Cassidy was born with a smile on his face and nothing in life has erased it. No doubt he'll give St. Peter a big smile when he saunters through that "narrow gate" a "minute before the Devil knows he's dead." In a September 14, 1992 letter, in response to one by this author, who asked him about things accomplished and people and episodes remembered, Father Cassidy wrote:

1) *Father Healy, O.P. – "TOPS!" – we laughed a lot and worked a lot together. I gave him full free time to work at "Koinonia House," but he helped us too with his preaching (and painting of the church and house).*

2) *Father Barney Curtin, O.P. – a real fun person – loved to go across the street and come back with a pizza, etc. A good preacher – also the new liturgy changed!!! Father Ward (the provincial) told him to shave off his beard – a traumatic experience for him (and us). "Signs of the times" he obeyed!*

3) *Father Martin Gutierez, O.P. – a real character, brilliant and worked hard on his English sermons and Spanish Mass (former professor at St. Albert's) – but slowly got to enjoy the busy parish life. He died at Holy Rosary preparing a sermon.*

4) *Father Agius, O.P. – "TOPS" – a good friend. Had lots of ideas regarding "Radio Rosary," "Holy Name Society," and "Calaroga Terrace." A champion!!! He helped Calaroga Terrace get started and had an office there…also served the people as chaplain.*

5) *The 75th anniversary of Holy Rosary was fun and low key – a Mass of thanks. It snowed! The Radio Rosary every night, live from the church. It was great!!! The Holy Name men did a great job under John Petrusich. Archbishop Howard prayed the Rosary on every First Friday. He loved it and said: "We'll never know how many people we might have helped through the Radio Rosary…it's a tremendous prayer – a good summary of our faith."*

6) *The full construction of "Calaroga Terrace"…a thrilling and successful venture!!! I went to some big meetings. Father Norton wanted to build a two or three story building ("home") for retired Third Order people on that property, across from the church. The idea exploded and Mr. Hedgepeth, Utah Construction Company, built a 17-story "home." Ha! Ha! only a few Third Order people could afford to get in!!! But Father Norton (and I'm sure Father Agius) had the original idea!! A great vision!! Wow!!*

The building was built and then little by little the province pulled out of it – because the original idea didn't sell too well. For many years the provincial came up for the meetings every six months. I think it was a great addition to the neighborhood – everything started to go up after it was built…motels, etc;…and the whole area changed. I think all the land was ours (with a school building on it) – I do not know who took it over. They had a good group of people on the board.

7) *A great Altar Society (Rose Brogna – a good helper) – all were excellent workers.*

8) *Father "Wild Bill" Norton – a great priest and person and character!!! He drove very fast and "wild." He also had "wild" ideas. He paved over all of the rose garden and that was "wild," except people came to church, because we now had a parking lot!! He did the same thing at St. Mary Magdalen's in Berkeley, California!!!*

9) *I taught and heard confessions at Marylhurst College, took care of Holladay Park Hospital, helped at the Grotto from time to time, also at Good Shepherd Convent. Also helped at St. Michael's downtown*

often. Went to Providence and St. Vincent hospitals when asked.

10) *I think you can see how happy I was to serve at Holy Rosary. Father Louis Robinson, O.P. died in our mission in Chiapas, Mexico (age 35 years old) and I went there 6/1/70.*

FOLK SONGS AT HOLY ROSARY?

In a letter to the provincial dated January 16, 1966, Father Cassidy, as pastor, commented that "the music commission" gave a "green light" to students singing "folk songs" during Mass, and that, as a result, "Fr. [Kieran] Healy was happy."

STATUE OF OUR LADY OF CHARITY

An unsigned and undated notice (probably from a prior church bulletin) on file in the archives of Holy Rosary Church, is quoted:

OUR LADY OF CHARITY We are asked from time to time what is that small statue of the Blessed Virgin just to the left of the Blessed Sacrament altar. It is a statue of Our Lady of Charity, also called Our Lady of El Cobre. The Blessed Virgin under this title is the patroness of Cuba.

It seems that in the year 1604 some men in a small boat were caught in a storm in the bay of Nipe – off Cuba, and were fearful of drowning. They prayed to the Virgin Mary for protection, and as they were rowing along with things getting out of control they found floating in the water a small statue of Our Lady similar to the figure near the Blessed Sacrament altar. They reached the shore safely, and attributed their safe return – which they considered miraculous – to Our Lady.

This statue is still venerated in a beautiful church in El Cobre, Oriente (Cuba), and is a veritable national shrine. In 1916 Benedict XV, at the petition of a large number of Cubans, declared "The Blessed Virgin Mary of Charity, called El Cobre, the principal patroness of the whole republic of Cuba." The feast is celebrated Sept. 8th, the birthday of Our Lady.

Some 11 or 12 years ago, when Fr. Florent Martin Gutierrez, O.P. was living here at Holy Rosary, a Mass was celebrated each month in Spanish for Spanish-speaking Catholics – most of whom were Cubans. It was at that time that this statue was purchased. The plaque beneath the statue reads: "Our Lady of Charity of El Cobre, Patroness of Cuba, has been acquired with the contributions of Cuban refugees residing in the State of Oregon. April 1970." [207]

The 1970s would be even more exciting as the next chapter illustrates.

NOTES TO THE TEXT

199 Published by the Foundation for Catholic Reform, 1331 Red Cedar Circle, Fort Collins, CO 80524-9998.

200 Article, page 11, *Catholic Sentinel*, May 11, 1961.

201 Article, page 4, *Catholic Sentinel*, September 14, 1961.

202 Article, page 1, *Catholic Sentinel*, September 28, 1961.

203 At Siena House in Oakland (residence Mountain View) where he delighted the old folk.

204 See Mrs. Mary Loomis's letter in Chapter 11, wherein she mentioned to Father Norton, during a brain-storming session with parishioners, the possibility of erecting retirement housing on property owned by Holy Rosary – as a means of developing the parish. So Mary is credited with originating the idea.

205 A retirement residence affiliated with the University of Portland.

206 Coliseum Gardens, a huge development, never got off the drawing boards.

207 Apparently the above notice appeared in a church bulletin in 1981 or 1982. Father Florent Martin Gutierrez, O.P. served at Holy Rosary from 1967 to 1973.

Parish center – 1997

NEW PARISH CENTER BUILT
CHURCH ATTRACTS MEN AND WOMEN DESIRING "ROMAN CATHOLIC" WORSHIP[208]

A BURGLAR IN THE BASEMENT

Susan Schulzke, mentioned in Chapter 12, the housekeeper in the priory during the '60s and '70s, recalls that one of the priests used to slip his shoes off and read at night. One night he heard a noise in the basement of the church and went to investigate. Sure enough, someone had broken in and was stealing candle and poor-box money. The thief promptly pounced on the poor priest, bopped him on the head, and stole off into the night. It was only one among a prolonged series of thefts which would occur during that time, including the purloining of a precious oriental rug (which had been donated by a parishioner)[209] from the sanctuary, several flower pots, and other salable items which, in earlier days, would have been left untouched in the sure knowledge that no thief, not even the meanest, would steal from the House of God.

A CATHOLIC DOG DOESN'T PRAY BUT STOPS THIEVES

Susan wrote: *"In the early '70s, Father McClory, Father Curtin, Father Martin, Father Agius, Father Healy, Father Arnheim and Father Curran lived in the rectory. They were quite a diversified bunch. Then there was 'Thumper,' a lonely dog given to Father Cassidy. He was trained by Dr. Florence Beardsley who lived at Calaroga Terrace. She tried to teach him to pray, but after much effort decided she could not teach him to pray because she was a Protestant and he was a Catholic dog."*

Father Felix Cassidy wrote: *"Thumper was really smart. A sort of a shepherd dog. The priests liked him. We did not have any robberies after we got him! A successor of Saint Dominic's, Father General Fernandez, once visited and he did not like dogs, so we hid Thumper in a bedroom. Sure enough, Father went to take a 'siesta,' opened the door, and discovered Thumper. Really funny! Later I arranged for the Dominican Sisters at Marycrest High School to meet the Father General and one of the sisters sang a Spanish song for him. That made him very happy and was a nice ending to his visit."*

THE BIGGEST ATTEMPTED BURGLARY OF ALL

Burglary and larceny, while issues requiring attention and resolution, were not events of elephantine proportions. There were larger issues to face for the "diversified bunch" at Holy Rosary Rectory in 1971, as well as at other rectories in the entire Western Dominican Province and, for that matter, the entire Catholic Church in America,[210] whose ecclesiology, liturgy and subsequent outlook would be fundamentally altered by a larcenous new modernism which would seek respectability, as well as new adherents, by proclaiming itself to be the authentic voice of Vatican II. Entire books have been written to explain this phenomenon.[211] Modernism will be merely touched upon (but cannot be fully explored) within these pages to give the reader a sense of the anguish felt by devout Catholics (on account of this plague) during the three decades leading up to our centenary celebration, and why these sheep were so grateful to have had their Dominican shepherds, a blessing giving them ample cause for joy at their centenary celebration, over and above the mere passage of one hundred years.

THE FIVE HORSEMEN OF THE SUPREME PONTIFF AND HOW WE KEPT THE "PEARL"

Five Dominicans of truly great spirituality reigned at Holy Rosary for several years in the seventies (at the precise time they were needed): Father Paul Duffner, Father Colin Vincent McEachen, Father Dominic Hoffman, Father Thomas Feucht, and Father Joseph Agius. Father Duffner served as pastor. Individually and collectively, they formed a formidable wall no Modernist was able to breach.

Father Dominic M. Hoffman, O.P.

These great men knew, spoke and extolled the Word of God, unequivocally taking on all erstwhile "expert" comers who would attack the Pope or the Church. Sunday bulletins, or inserts within them, covered a wide range of topics (avoided at many Catholic church pulpits, when Modernism became the false god). What the Magisterium of the Church said, they would defend, with a vehemence – to the death. No topic was taboo in outlining the Magisterium's teachings: contraception, abortion, homosexuality, ordination of women, sex education and so forth. They preached simply, with outstanding clarity, unequivocation, and theological soundness: the true "facts about Planned Parenthood," the myth of "population explosion," Marxism, the immorality of such TV programs as SOAP, and a host of other moral issues, urging parishioners to take a moral stand and make their feelings known to government officials, newspapers, and sponsors of products on radio and TV.

FATHER FEUCHT DEAD AT AGE 65

Father Feucht was destined to serve at Holy Rosary for a total of 20 years (1944-58) and (1974-80), ten of them as pastor and, in the end after heart surgery, as director of the Rosary Confraternity, which post he was filling when he died, at age 65, in a Portland hospital. Parishioners prayed the Rosary for him on the eve of a funeral Mass celebrated in June 1980 at his favorite sanctuary in the City of Roses, Holy Rosary Church. He was born July 9, 1914 at Culdesac, Idaho and attended St. Albert College in Oakland. He was professed as a Dominican Sept. 14, 1934, and he was ordained June 3, 1939, in St. Mary Cathedral, San Francisco. He was first assigned to Holy Rosary at age 29 (in 1944) under a man frequently referred to as "Mr. Holy Rosary," Father Joseph Agius, who taught this young priest the ropes. There's little doubt that, by now, they both reside in heaven for having fought "the good fight of faith."

FATHER AGIUS – "MR. HOLY ROSARY"

Among the wisest Dominican shepherds to serve at Holy Rosary was Father Joseph Mary Agius, O.P. (God rest his soul.) He was born on April 9, 1905 in San Francisco, and died there March 10, 1989. Father Gerald A. Buckley, O.P. (who served as pastor from 1981 to 1984) called Father Agius "Mr. Holy Rosary." This appellation is natural enough considering the fact that Father Agius spent 19 years at Holy Rosary, as pastor (1942-47, 1970-72), associate (1968-70), and director of the Rosary Confraternity (1973-83). He was provincial of the Western Dominican Province from 1960 to 1964. His middle name is evidence of his love for the Mother of God, a Church treasure to be shared: "For where your treasure is, there will your heart be also." (Mt. 6:21). Sharing this treasure would consume over half a century of his time on earth.

Father Agius grew up in Petaluma, California, was half Italian and half Maltese in descent, small in stature, with a prominent nose and direct gaze, and always erect and dignified. His preaching was marked by the careful enunciation of cogent thought, and always orthodox. His closest comrades among the Dominicans were men renowned for their orthodoxy: Fathers C.V. McEachen, Tom Feucht, Paul Duffner, and Dominic De Domenico. In a letter[212] to this author, Father Buckley wrote:

"Fr. Duffner and his predecessor, Fr. Tom Feucht, were both staunch defenders of Catholic orthodoxy, to a degree that they, together with the ever-present and sometime pastor Fr. Joseph Agius, definitely gave Holy Rosary its character as a very conservative parish. I myself, who did not see myself as pastor, was sent 'kicking and screaming' (an exaggeration of course) by Fr. Paul Raftery, the provincial, to Holy Rosary to 'move it along a bit.' I am quite conservative myself, although a little bit to the 'left' of those gentlemen. Given the leaning of the community, as well as my own theological commitments, I did not really succeed in 'moving' us on much, certainly not in the progressive sphere…"

A SIGN OF CONTRADICTION
Jesus said to his disciples: *"I have come to light a fire on the earth. How I wish the blaze were ignited! I have a baptism to receive. What anguish I feel till it is over! Do you think I have come to establish peace on earth? I assure you, the contrary is true; I have come for division. From now on, a household of five will be divided three against two and two against three…"* (Luke 12:49-53).

Christ's "division" would occur close to us here at Holy Rosary.

"RENEWAL" OF HOLY ROSARY THE GOAL OF THE DOMINICAN MASTER GENERAL?
But the move to make Holy Rosary more "progressive" did not begin with Father Buckley's assignment to the parish in 1980. In August 1971, the priory "household" was divided, over issues now obscure. This division was sufficiently serious to require the visitation of the provincial, Father Paul Scanlon, O.P. to Holy Rosary. On the "progressive" side was Father William Barnabas Curtin, O.P., who, in a letter dated August 23, 1971 declared to Father Scanlon:

Fathers Joseph Mary Agius, O.P. (left) and
Colin Vincent McEachen, O.P., 1968

Dear Paul:

I am sincerely sorry about the bitterness that surrounded our community meeting last week. I think that you realize that I appreciated as fully as anyone the complex points of view involved and the relative principles of the contending parties. I want peace as much as anyone, but peace is too big a sacrifice to make where there is a surrender of our precious newly found rights and freedoms involved. I felt that I could only bring the maximum pressure to bear for my case, as the other party apparently did as well. I cannot but feel that you sold out to expediency where a firm stand and the overriding of local authority, however difficult this may be, was required.

I can't let it go with the impression that you were neutral and refused to take sides. You clearly took the side of backing local authority, "stet authoritas," any sentiments to the contrary notwithstanding. Even if you argued with Father Agius, your argument was very weak compared to what it should have been. Even considering the vast pressures of your office, I feel that an injustice was involved. The wider this is known in the Province, the deeper our divisions will be.

I am enclosing an editorial that was printed in the Catholic Sentinel recently. I think that it wraps it all up nicely from my point of view. I want to insist again that I am sorry that no true dialogue between the parties resulted from your visit. I genuinely feel that this was not predominantly my fault and that I tried to be open to the views of the other side.

If we are going to have the renewed confidence in the religious life of which you have spoken, it can only be where the intrinsic rights and freedoms of the subject are defended courageously by higher authority when these are infringed on the local level. With every best wish, I am,

Fraternally in Christ,

[signed]
William B. Curtin, O.P.[213]

P.S. What are we to think of the Wadsworth Statement on Preaching signed unanimously by Council members from three Provinces? Is it something platitudinous, utterly without meaning in terms of concrete application? So far it sounds like so much hot air, "flatus vocis."

P.S. I recall that when the Master General was here for the great reform a few years back, he left explicit instructions about St. Dominic's and Holy Rosary, and I think that the latter, in the detailed plans, was to become a Priory and selectively cultivated. Perhaps if you could find these papers and their exact prescriptions, you would have a mandate for the renewal of Holy Rosary from the highest authority of the Order. It would be strong support for such a renewal and you could put more men in Holy Rosary and have them elect a first man.

WESTERN DOMINICAN PROVINCIAL
RESPONDS TO PROGRESSIVE PRIEST'S COMPLAINT

In responding to Father Curtin's letter, Provincial Paul Scanlon, O.P. wrote this letter to the entire priestly community at Holy Rosary.[214]

August 23, 1971

Dear Fathers:

I would imagine that our meeting last week was as frustrating to you as it was to myself and Father [Peter] Curran. Having had a chance to mull the matter over in my mind a bit, I would like to share a few thoughts with you.

In a sense, as Father Agius pointed out, the situation of the community is a microcosm of the situation of the Church at large. That is, there is a strong drawing up of positions on one side or another and very little desire to yield one's position in any way. On the one hand, it is probably good that people are defining their positions and estimating what it is that they stand for or against. Any attempt, as was evident in Portland, to find a middle ground or compromised position, or even a discussion of points of difference, comes to a standstill. Yet the Church, nor the Order, nor the Parish at Portland can continue if the only way in which unity can be found is to avoid discussions of issues that are at the very heart of Religious Life and the running of the Church.

What strikes me is that none of us ever sat down and asked 'What does the Lord want for Portland?' And so the question became a matter of political positioning, each party trying to overpower the other and/or undermine it by allegations and criticisms. I see no solution in the future for this type of problem, whether it be at Portland or elsewhere, unless the community involved is humble and willing enough to ask the Lord for his solution. Although I would hope, I would not expect, that the community as a group could pray together for this solution. I mentioned to Father McClory that I had spent a great deal of time in prayer before coming to Portland. I had also asked the people at the House of Prayer to make this one of their special intentions during the summer. What

I realize is that more prayer is needed on the part of the people at Portland, rather than what one group or another may want. I realize all of this may sound pietistic, and yet I am willing to take the chance of being criticized for that approach. But I firmly believe, and am most sincere in saying this, that we have failed because we have not allowed God to work in and through us in this problem.

To allow one side or another to take charge of the Parish and see the other side depart from the community may seem like a victory for one side or another. However, I cannot see that it is really a victory, for it merely avoids the problem rather than solves it, and communities that are too homogenous end up by being closed in upon themselves and stagnate rather than grow. Father Curran will summon a meeting of the Personnel Board as soon as possible and we will try to solicit their help in approaching this question, so that by the time the Provincial Council convenes at the end of September we will be able to nominate a Pastor.

> *Yours in St. Dominic*
>
> *[signed]*
> *Paul Scanlon, O.P.*
> *Provincial*

FATHER WILLIAM MCCLORY, O.P. DIES AT HOLY ROSARY

In 1971, Father William McClory, O.P. returned to Holy Rosary to finish out his pilgrimage on earth. In his active days, he had the look of one of those 1930s priests out of central casting in Hollywood: over six-feet tall with the physique of a fighter, a square jaw, an intelligent face, and a direct no-nonsense gaze that would not be lied to. This real-life prison chaplain walked the final steps to the death chamber with many a repentant convict while serving as the Catholic chaplain at the State Penitentiary in Salem from 1951 to 1961, a position for which he was paid. Parishioner Stanly Brosterhous related a story that made the parish grapevine in those days. Reporters were witnessing the death of an infamous prisoner who was writhing in the gas chamber before death. These press reps found the prisoner's contortions amusing and began to laugh and tell jokes. Father McClory, who was present, towered over them with his tall frame and in righteous anger admonished them for their wanton display of disrespect for human life in general and this man's life in particular. The reporters quickly "put a zipper on it" and became serious.

Father McClory was the first resident chaplain and ostensibly the first Catholic priest ever to be paid by the State of Oregon as a prison chaplain. He brought new life to hundreds of prisoners who had lost life's meaning, and he earned their undying gratitude in the process. In addition, he saved other lives by quelling prison riots on more than one occasion. When father was recuperating from surgery in 1966, he received this letter from then-governor, Mark Hatfield:

Father William Joseph McClory, O.P.
Born: November 14, 1891 – Professed: September 18, 1913
Ordained: May 10, 1918 – Died: January 28, 1972

Office of the Governor
State Capitol
Salem 97310
August 17, 1966

Dear Father McClory:

Word has reached me that you have had to undergo surgery recently and I want to send my best wishes for a speedy and complete recovery.

It is never pleasant to be ill but perhaps it gives one a chance for inner reflection seldom possible in the busy lives we lead. We become aware of the wonderful work that is being done by our medical teams and the great strides that have been made in care and treatment.

Take good care and I know that if the good wishes of your many friends can help to speed your recovery, you are well on your way to good health once more.

Sincerely,

[signed]
Mark

According to Father Banfield, "we had no janitor in the 1920s at Holy Rosary," so Father McClory "tended the boiler in the school and hand-fed the furnace in the rectory. He was one tough guy." "One of the best that we had," remarks Father Dominic Hoffman, O.P., and "As tough as nails," says Father Gregory Anderson O.P. – all of them vividly recalled the glory of Father McClory during those trying times.

Father Basil Cole, O.P., a theologian and member of the Western Dominican Preaching Band, who has given many beautiful novenas at Holy Rosary, wrote: *"Father McClory was in some way responsible for my vocation while I was trying to figure out what my vocation was at Mt. Angel Seminary. I used to help him out at the prison as an organist for the choir, while a seminarian (for only three months was I at Mt. Angel). Earlier in his career he was novicemaster for one year. When I celebrated my first Mass, he was the preacher."* Father Cole also confirmed that Father McClory had personally put down several riots at the Oregon State Penitentiary.

Father Banfield also recalled that Father McClory had been a pastor of Blessed Sacrament Parish in Seattle from 1948 to 1951. Father McClory celebrated the 50th anniversary of his ordination to the priesthood at a concelebrated Mass in the Seattle Cathedral on June 5, 1968. Father Banfield described him as "a real hero whose funeral was the best attended for clergy…there were Archbishops present." Father McClory was born in Chicago November 14, 1891, was professed September 18, 1913, and ordained May 10, 1918. He died at Holy Rosary on January 28, 1972 at age 80, on the feast day of St. Thomas Aquinas, having served Our Lord as a Dominican priest for over 53 years. In *Persona Christi*, he "fought the good fight," "finished the race," and "kept the faith."[215] Bless you Father McClory and "until we meet again, may God hold you in the palm of His hand."[216]

"…I formed you, and set you as a covenant of the people, a light for the nations, to open the eyes of the blind, to bring out prisoners from confinement, and from the dungeon, those who live in darkness"
(Isaiah 42: 6-7).

CONTRIBUTIONS IN MEMORY OF FATHER MCCLORY MADE BY ZELLER'S AND ASSUNTA SANTILLI

In a letter to the province dated February 11, 1972, at a time the parish was strapped for cash, Father Arnheim[217] wrote:

The Zeller Funeral director donated across the board for Father McClory's funeral. That's a big help. Mrs. Assunta Santilli's check for $500 was used to start a burse in memory of Father McClory, for the education of Dominican students.

FATHER COLIN VINCENT MCEACHEN, O.P. JOINS HOLY ROSARY STAFF IN 1974

The following history of a great man, in residence at Holy Rosary in 1993, is taken from the June 1990 edition of *Homiletic & Pastoral Review*: [218]

A HEAVYWEIGHT CHAMP IN GOD'S PRIESTHOOD ("MY FAVORITE PRIEST")

Father Colin Vincent McEachen, O.P., Associate Pastor, Holy Rosary Church and Priory, Portland, Oregon is living proof that though many 'good die young,' some also reach advanced age, for this good and holy man celebrated his 85th birthday on May 26, 1990.

Still young at heart, season in and season out, he daily displays his deep and abiding love for Holy Mother the Church and his dedication to the People of God, whom he serves with a degree of courage and strength that can only come to a life which says 'It is no longer I who live, but Christ who lives in me.' (Gal. 2:20).

Father McEachen was born in Charlottetown, Prince Edward Island, Canada on May 26, 1905, the middle of seven children. He attended grammar and middle school in Canada, and then studied at St. Thomas College Prep Seminary in Ross, California, then to Benicia, to begin his studies in philosophy. In 1931, he continued these studies at St. Albert's College in Oakland, California. From there he journeyed to the Dominican theology house in Somerset, Ohio.

Father was ordained a priest at St. Dominic's Church in Washington, D.C. on June 13, 1935 (so he is celebrating 55 years in the priesthood this June [1990]), and there followed a long string of assignments on the West Coast from Los Angeles to Seattle, with two stints in Utah as a Catholic Missionary in Price and Logan in 1941. He was pastor in Benicia, California in 1964, and has been assigned as Associate Pastor to Holy Rosary Church in Portland since 1974.

Father McEachen's preaching and example helped me (and thousands more) survive the onslaught of modernism in the seventies and eighties, when confusion reigned. Upon reflection, perhaps the beating we were taking then seemed more hurtful than the one today, but maybe that was only because the fight was just starting, and we were weak, naive, and unprepared. At that time, it was difficult for me to comprehend what was going on in the Church, as our cherished beliefs were ridiculed. We gradually understood that the enemy, in Pogo's words, was 'us' or, more precisely, modernists who claimed to be a part of the Church but were, in fact, wolves in sheep's clothing. Father's reaffirmation from the pulpit of the Faith of our Fathers more than once brought a lump to my throat. He gave me insight into the cause of the problems, in simple and straightforward sermons at Holy Rosary, one of those few remaining churches in the area

which offer four daily Masses, two in the early morning, one at noon, and one in the late afternoon, to serve working people. They're all well attended.

Many working men like myself, though living in another parish, would participate in the daily noon Mass during lunch break, to partake of that Glorious Mystery and hear Father's insightful sermons, which were always brief, to the point, and concerned with the basics.

He reminded us that the Ten Commandments were still operative, that original sin had not changed, and that we have a Guardian Angel to whom we should pray. He talked about the saint of the day, and how he or she overcame problems and defeats. He constantly reminded us about the efficacy of morning and evening prayer suggesting, for example, that we kick our shoes under the bed at night so that, when we were on our knees in the morning looking for them, it would remind us to start the day on our knees in prayer. He spoke of the devil and how he was intent on devouring us. He reminded us to genuflect in church, and to talk to God in the Tabernacle; not necessarily in formal prayer, for example, but one that could start with 'God, it's me Joe. I'm truly sorry for all I've done, and I need your help.'

In those same decades of the 1970s and 1980s, when many truths of our faith were being watered down, even from some pulpits, Father was exhorting us (as he still does today) to pray for the Pope and for deeper spirituality: by keeping God's Commandments, by frequent attendance at Mass and reception of the sacraments, by constant prayer, especially the Rosary, by studying the lives of the saints, and by daily visiting the Blessed Sacrament which is exposed in the church every afternoon. These eternal verities protected us then, and do now, against modernism, and are necessary for the salvation of our souls. Father has taught this every day with fervor. Those of us who listened learned a lot, and I'll be eternally grateful to this man who, in physical dimensions might be classed as a flyweight, but who in spiritual dimensions is in a class by himself, an undefeated heavyweight champion in God's priesthood.

Father is a voracious reader, and we became more closely associated several years ago. A 'renowned' Protestant and church historian [Martin Marty], in an interview in the local newspaper [Oregonian 5/87], made the startling statement that there existed among Catholics a decline in the belief in hell. My letter-to-the-editor response, which they printed, was that you cannot at one and the same time not believe in hell and still belong to the body of faithful known as the Catholic Church, which does believe in hell; an equivalent of a man saying he was a Rabbi but that he did not believe in the Torah. Father read my letter and called me at home that night to congratulate me for defending my faith. Thereafter, we shared articles from various sources, and he introduced me to HPR,[219] another debt I owe him.

Father Paul Aquinas Duffner, O.P., 1996

About three years ago, he called me to the rectory for a meeting. He said he had two requests. Number one, he wanted me to volunteer to be a CCD teacher. Number two, he wanted me to serve on the St. Vincent de Paul committee, which he chairs. Three years later I'm still teaching CCD, and still serving on Father's St. Vincent de Paul committee, weekly delivering food baskets to the poor, a mission to which he devotes a lot of time.

Despite his age [85], Father walks several miles a day after Mass, and he carries the Sacred Host to the sick and shut-ins. When the weather is particularly nasty, he'll give me a call and we'll make the rounds in my car. He'll bring along dozens of clippings, photo-copied onto several pages, for me to read when he is out of the car. The clippings come from all over the globe. Silence and a sense of the sacred surround us until the last visit is completed. Then he'll break into his famous smile, and tell me his latest joke.

Whenever we depart his final words are "Make a nice day," (instead of "Have" a nice day) and it sets your mind to thinking about what you might do to make a nice day, for everyone you meet.

Father McEachen is truly a man in love with his vocation, with God, with Our Blessed Mother, and the Church, which he serves with honor and fidelity. Perhaps no books will be written about him when he dies, but I am certain our Savior will welcome with open arms into eternal glory his heroic soldier, Father Colin Vincent McEachen, O.P., who has championed Christ's cause for the greater part of this century. [Father McEachen died on 18 July 1993]

FATHER PAUL DUFFNER, O.P. – A SAINTLY PRIEST AND PASTOR

Father Paul Duffner, O.P. took over as pastor at Holy Rosary in 1975 and filled the post for six years. Today, as then, he walks and talks with the serenity of a saint, but it would be a tragic mistake to underestimate either his physical or mental toughness, even as he approaches age 80 as head of the Rosary Confraternity, which is located cater-corner across the street from Holy Rosary Church. He is six feet tall and weighs about 190 pounds, a lot bigger than Saint Paul, his namesake, but no less eager to spread the Good News of Christ all over this planet.

ORIGINS OF RADIO STATION KBVM
(SEE ALSO APPENDIX 8)

Father Paul Duffner's recollection of the formation of KBVM includes the fact that Father Joseph M. Agius, O.P. came up with the idea of having a Dollar-A-Month Club, and it was Father Agius who visited the various parishes and enjoined the pastors to put the Dollar-A-Month Club envelopes in the vestibules of their churches. One day Father Duffner remarked to Elizabeth Hart, who worked in the chancery, that "what we really need is our own Catholic radio station." Elizabeth replied with confidence: "It can be done." Thereafter, Father Duffner, Elizabeth Hart and Russ Niehaus formed the first KBVM board. The Dollar-A-Month Club (begun by Father Agius) eventually accumulated $100,000 which, together with some large bequests and the generosity of most Catholics in the metropolitan area, was used as seed money for the formation of Metro Catholic Broadcasting.[220] KBVM became the first lay-spon-sored Catholic radio station in the United States. The first broadcast took place on December 8, 1989, the feast of the Immaculate Conception from the campus of the University of Portland, on land the Holy Cross Community generously leased to KBVM. The last three of the call letters KBVM stand for "Blessed Virgin Mary."

OPEN REBELLION WITHIN THE CHURCH

Widespread ignorance of Church doctrine, shallow faith, and some malevolence, caused a good number of Catholics to jump onto the Modernist bandwagon in the 1970s. Devout Catholics were fostering prayer and peace while others were declaring warfare on the Church. Modernism had gained so many adherents by the late 1970s, that "open rebellion" was evident. The modernists were no longer whispering their agenda, but flaunting it, and publicly publishing their demands. The Dominicans at Holy Rosary had their hands full, taking a stance behind the Vicar of Christ – that is, backing him – ("Get thee behind me Satan."),[221] and refuting the claims, lies, and false doctrines permeating the parish and the Archdiocese.

FATHER DUFFNER REBUKES LOCAL MODERNISTS'
ATTEMPT TO RECRUIT DOMINICANS AND
THUS HOLY ROSARIANS TO FAVOR A FEMALE PRIESTHOOD

We have said that the Dominican Friars preached the truth about Modernism from the pulpit at Holy Rosary. In addition, they wrote the truth in the Sunday bulletins handed to the parishioners as they left the church after Mass, so that these parishioners could cogitate on these complex matters in the quietude of their homes. Father Paul Duffner, a "voice in the wilderness" of those times, wrote the following article for the Holy Rosary Church bulletin dated December 16, 1979:

In November 1975, Pope Paul VI – in a letter to Archbishop Duggan of Canterbury, declared that the ordination of women to the priesthood was not compatible with Catholic teaching. In October of 1976, the Sacred Congregation for the Doctrine of the Faith issued a decree on the "Ordination of Women" in which the official Catholic position was restated and explained. And Pope John Paul II declared the same teaching in his recent visit to the United States.

Too, the Vatican Council II (which the promoters of the ordination of women like to quote) clearly states that submission of mind and heart should be given to the authentic teaching authority of the Roman Pontiff, even when he is not speaking "ex Cathedra." (Decree on the Church, n. 25). So it should be clear that any Catholic who possesses the gift of faith, should see the will and mind of Christ in the pronouncements of the Holy Father for the whole Church.

Yet, there are some who claim they can be good Catholics, and yet not accept the Holy Father's teaching in this matter, that they can be "responsible dissenters" as they call it. In particular, one member of the Jesuit Order (all Orders have some such dissenters) has been both active and outspoken in his campaign for the ordination of women.

Just recently, however, it appears that the Holy Father has spoken to the Superior General of the Jesuits asking him to see to it that some members of his Order cease publicly opposing this clear teaching that has come from the Magisterium. In keeping with this, Fr. Callaghan (the Jesuit in question) was moved from the Center where he was actively advocating the ordination of women, and was asked that he no longer speak publicly on the matter.

This, apparently, was like throwing a rock into a hornet's nest. Many of those "responsible dissenters" are now openly attacking the central authority of the Church, and its head, the Holy Father.

A letter was received this week – apparently by all priests of the Archdiocese, and others in charge of various groups – inviting them to join the rebellion. The letter read, in part, as follows:

"This is not an isolated case [that is, the silencing of Fr. Callaghan]. It appears to be part of an alarming pattern of recent Vatican activities to bring academic theologians 'into line' through investigations and intimidations.

"Attempts to stifle renewal in communities of women religious are next in line…At issue is our response as a Church to the solemn

teaching of Vatican II against sex discrimination. At issue are fundamental human rights in the Church…the right of responsible dissent…the right to due process in law…

"The time to stop this repression from spreading is NOW, before it eats deeply into all our lives and ministries…We are asking you to write… to the local and national press. The Media are highly significant in this struggle…because they educate a wide range of Catholics to the need for justice in the Church…etc. etc."

[Father Duffner comments]

All of this rebellion is in the name of social justice. True, social justice is a great need today, and is part of the Gospel message, as the recent Vatican Council documents made clear. But those documents make it equally clear that, in the interpretation of the Gospel in these matters, the ultimate responsibility lies with the teaching authority of the Church. This is clear, except in the minds of those who claim the right of "responsible dissent."

It seems we are dealing here not merely with a crisis of obedience, but a crisis of faith. For the basic reason or motive for our submission to the teachings of the Church, is because God has spoken through His Church.

The decree of the Sacred Congregation for the Doctrine of the Faith on this question has stated:

"The Catholic Church has never held the view that priestly or episcopal ordination can be validly conferred on women…The chief reason for calling only males to Orders and a truly priestly ministry was the Church's desire to maintain faithfully the character of priestly ministry as willed by the LORD Jesus Christ and scrupulously handed on by the apostles.

"In the last analysis, it is for the Church to speak through the Magisterium on these matters and to determine which elements of the sacraments are changeable and which are unchangeable.

"We must bear in mind that questions relating to sacramental theology, and especially to the ministerial priesthood, cannot be answered except in the light of revelation. The human sciences cannot give us the answers, for although the knowledge these sciences give is very valuable, they do not apprehend the realities of faith. The latter are supernatural and do not fall within the competence of these sciences."

[Father Duffner continues his comments]

This rebellion can grow. Now is the time to increase your prayers for the unity of the church: Pray for the Holy Father, that he will be able to lead the Church in these troubled times. Pray for those who – in their rebellion – are causing much confusion and division in the Church. Above all, give witness by your daily lives of your full and humble acceptance of all the statements or decrees coming from the Magisterium of the Church.

Father Paul Duffner, O.P.

"…For the strangers came and tried to teach us their ways,
They scorned us just for being what we are,
But they might as well go chasing after moonbeams,
Or light a penny candle from a star…"

From the Irish Ballad
"Galway Bay."

Article in *Catholic Sentinel*[222]
Summarizes Father Duffner's Fifty Years as a
Dominican Priest – His Golden Jubilee

Dominican Father Paul Duffner is unequivocal about his direct call to "preach Christ, and Him crucified."

The words of Christ, "Feed my lambs" and "Feed my sheep," are not quaint verses from Scripture, but commands that animate his life. His aim is to convert to Christ every person on this planet, realizing that he may not do it, but he is willing to die trying.

Priest means "old man" in the original Greek, and Father Duffner is both, having attained the age of 75; but his athletic build (six feet tall, 190 pounds) and agile movements mask this reality, and mirror a man 10 years younger.

Now mature and insightful, he fondly reflects on the athletic prowess of his teenage years, when he was a formidable "three-letter man" (in football, basketball and baseball) in the rural community of Jacksonville, Illinois, where he was born, and where Dominican Sisters, in grades one through 12, saw a priest inside a boy and inculcated in him a love for Christ, his Church, his Blessed Mother, and the manifold riches of the Catholic faith.

On December 16, after the noon Mass, hundreds will gather at the Holy Rosary Church's community center to celebrate his golden jubilee, to honor him and to thank him for his selfless service to them.

The mental and physical strength that he developed during his formative years would be a foundation for him 30 years later as a Dominican priest penetrating the jungles of Central America on horseback, to bring the Good News to the Mayan Indians and all who would listen.

Today he works out of a humble office in the Rosary Center, across the street from Holy Rosary Church at the intersection of Northeast Clackamas and Third in Portland, directing the activities of the Rosary Confraternity.

The Rosary Confraternity is an apostolate that seeks to alert new Catholics (and old ones lost in the confusion of the times) to the efficacy of the Mass, the sacraments and the Rosary as the source of saving grace for sanctity, and even sanity, in a mostly pagan world that rejects if it does not despise traditional Catholic beliefs.

Father Duffner's message is compelling: praying the Rosary is a devotion begun by a fellow Dominican, Alan de Rupe, who in the 15th century reported having a vision that this devotion was revealed to St. Dominic by Our Blessed Mother herself. It is a devotion encouraged by the Church, which celebrates October 7 as a feast day honoring Our Blessed Mother and the Rosary.

Catholics who see this devotion as merely a quest for piety should research the Church-approved apparitions of Fatima; for the warnings contained therein have striking parallels to the prophecies of St. John the Apostle: "prophecies of things that are come to pass in the Church of Christ." Many who have done this research, including Pope John Paul and Father Duffner, are convinced that the message of Fatima is being fulfilled in the present age.

The Rosary Center, which Father Duffner has directed since 1983, has assumed national and even international importance in furthering devotion to the Rosary, dispatching thousands of Rosaries and pamphlets throughout the United States and around the world.

Father Duffner supplies the materials, and a team of 50 volunteers, "the Rosary Makers," assemble 1,200 Rosaries a month in the Portland metropolitan area alone.

Additionally, countless Rosaries, made by dozens of volunteers from all over the United States, are received, packaged and mailed by the Rosary Center staff, which is made up primarily of volunteers.

The staff say that Father Duffner keeps everyone focused on the task at hand and deplores "idle chitchat" and "criticism of others." He takes corrective action promptly.

"Observing his attitude and actions is like reading a spiritual book," says volunteer Norma Monahan, who works 40 hours a week. "I've never heard him complain nor seen him angry. His humility is enormous. No task is too small for him, he picks up, carries boxes and cooks lunches. No task is too lowly." And further, "He's a preacher in the Order of Preachers, and he practices everything he preaches."

Cecelia Hoesly says that, when anyone faces illness or hardship, Father Duffner is quick to remind them: "Don't squander this opportunity for grace. Offer it up!"

Father Duffner writes a monthly newsletter that reaches nearly 38,000 people. It features meditations from the pope, as well as Father Duffner's own observations in a section called "Theology for the Laity," where Scripture and the traditional teaching of the Church are applied to today's problems.

He is also a founding member of the board of directors of Portland's Catholic radio station, KBVM (BVM stands for Blessed Virgin Mary). His work helps support the seminary training of novices and students of the Western Dominican Province, as well as retired Dominican Friars.

He also serves as a consultant and judge for the Roman Catholic Challenge, an annual contest of knowledge for Catholic youth in grades 7-12, held each January at Our Lady of Peace Retreat House in Beaverton. A committee from R.C. Challenge composes the questions and answers (in the format of the TV game show Jeopardy). They send the questions to Father Duffner for editing and for a check that they contain authentic Catholic teaching.

Father Duffner's greatest challenge came in 1967, when he was asked to serve as a missionary in the southernmost state of Mexico near the border of Guatemala – Ocosingo, Chiapas, Mexico, a primitive area, most of which was accessible only by horseback or airplane. He filled this post for eight years.

His mission encompassed an area of approximately 10,000 square miles (about the size of Massachusetts) and was inhabited by 65,000 Mayan Indians. The year was divided into wet and dry seasons.

During the wet season, he brushed up on his Spanish and studied a Mayan Indian dialect of the Tzeltal language and attended to the spiritual needs of the Indians living near his home mission.

In 1975, Father Duffner left Mexico and came to Portland to serve as pastor of Holy Rosary Church, a position he filled for six years. During that period, he built a community center of classrooms, a large banquet hall and a library to accommodate the spiritual, intellectual and social needs of his parishioners.

FATHER DUFFNER LEADS EFFORT TO BUILD PARISH CENTER

As explained in previous chapters relating to the early history of Holy Rosary, the parishioners had always wanted their own parish center to hold large and small meetings, to teach the Catholic Catechism to their kids, and to celebrate their unity as a Catholic community. As pastor, Father Duffner led the struggle

to bring their dreams to fruition. The dedication card contained the following:

The dedication of the new Parish Center will fill a great need in Holy Rosary parish, which has been without a parish hall since the closing of the parish school in 1955. Up to that time the school gym had served as the gathering place for parish activities.

After the school gym was no longer available, several walls were torn down on the first floor of the rectory creating a small hall capable of holding about 50 persons. This has been the only gathering place for the parish for the past 25 years.

The new parish hall, will have a seating capacity of 350 persons. Should it be desirable, the large hall can be divided in two by means of a large electrically controlled partition. At one end of the large hall is a movable stage which can be easily put in place or removed. The hall is also provided with a 12 by 9 foot movie screen which can be lowered or raised electrically, and is equipped with a sound system with 12 loud speakers in the ceiling for a balanced distribution of the speaker's voice, music, etc. The large kitchen will be adequate to serve several hundred persons at one time. As seen in the plan there is also a smaller meeting room sufficient in size for about 75 persons, which can be converted into 3 classrooms by means of sound-proof dividers. At the northwest corner of the building will be the parish library.

We are most grateful to our parishioners and friends who have been most generous in contributing towards equipping the kitchen, and the purchase of chairs and tables, dishes and silverware, and other items needed for the Center.

In gratitude, commencing with the week of the dedication, one Mass will be offered each week for the welfare and intentions of those who have contributed to this cause. These Masses will continue through May 1981.

Also to be remembered in these Masses (and we ask your prayers for them) are some deceased benefactors whose generosity to Holy Rosary is mainly responsible for the construction of the new Parish Center.

The dedication ceremony, led by Archbishop Cornelius M. Power, took place after the 12:10 Mass on Sunday, September 7, 1980. The architect of the 8814 square foot parish center was Richard W. Norman and the general contractor was Brockamp & Jaeger, Inc. The cost came to $425,000.

NOTES TO THE TEXT

208 Most Dominican priests who responded to inquiries about their service at Holy Rosary preferred to describe the community as "Roman Catholic" rather than traditional, conservative, and so forth.

209 The rug can be seen in old photographs of the sanctuary in this book.

210 Modernists knowingly, incorrectly and repeatedly call ours the American Catholic Church, but since there is only one true Catholic Church universally, the terms Catholic Church in America, Catholic Church in Russia, Catholic Church in Cuba, etc. are used, not the American Catholic Church, Russian Catholic Church, Cuban Catholic Church or other designations which are inaccurate and divisive.

211 See Saint Pius X's encyclical *Lamentabili Sane*, dated July 3, 1907, which enumerates, condemns, and proscribes 65 propositions of Modernism.

212 Dated August 24, 1992 on file at the Dominican Priory, Portland, Oregon, referring to his assignment as pastor in 1980.

213 A church bulletin dated May 24, 1987 reported that Father Curtin had died of cancer.

214 Dominican Fathers Joseph Agius, Kieran Healy, William McClory, Barnabas Curtin, Florent Martin and Peter Curran.

215 2 Tim. 4:6-8, 16-18.

216 Last line of *An Irish Blessing*, anonymous.

217 According to Father Basil Cole, O.P., Father Bernard Arnheim, O.P., pastor from 1973 to 1974, "was the first lay brother of the Dominican Order to switch over from that state of life to the priesthood since the fifteenth century."

218 86 Riverside Drive, New York, 10024, pages 62-64 (written by the author of this book).

219 Homeletic & Pastoral Review, 86 Riverside Drive, New York, N.Y. 10024.

220 The name was changed to Catholic Broadcasting Northwest in 1996.

221 Matthew 16:23.

222 Page 19, December 14, 1990, written by the author of this book.

Southern facade of new priory built in 1987.

CHAPTER
14
1981–1990

NEW PRIORY BUILT, GROWTH CONTINUES

To revisit Holy Rosary in different decades is to witness the miraculous intervention of Our Blessed Mother in the affairs of the parish, and the power of this intervention to fascinate permanently. It is impossible to imagine what Holy Rosary Church or even the Catholic Church would be like without the Rosary, the pathway to holiness.

People full of grace know they are wrapped in Mary's mantel when they enter Holy Rosary Church. This desire for motherly love, deeply felt, is on everyone's mind if not on their tongues. They know Mary alone can confer that tender mother-love urgently sought from age to age in sickness and in health, in all seasons, and especially in times of quiet desperation. And so it is not odd at all that one of the great contradictions in Christianity, between Protestants and Catholics, would be the devotion to the Great Mother of the "Sign of Contradiction." Catholic humility honors Mary, whereas Protestant pride, or more accurately ignorance, prefers that Mary be kept in the background. But Catholicism and Mary are one. If Christ entered humanity through a woman and "did not come down on a cloud," then that woman deserves devotion.[223]

Father Gerald Buckley, O.P. Becomes Pastor

On Sunday, August 9, 1981, the Rev. Gerald Albert Buckley, O.P. was installed as pastor, replacing Father Paul Duffner, O.P., who was transferred to Alaska. Like his older brother on the Preaching Band, Father Lawrence Banfield, O.P., Father Buckley possessed a simple desire: to spend his life preaching. His true metier was preaching – not parish administration; therefore, he informed this author, he was sent "kicking and screaming (an exaggeration of course) by Fr. Paul Chrysostom Raftery, the provincial, to Holy Rosary to 'move it along a bit.'"

Father Buckley, O.P.

Father Buckley is a large man with wide blue eyes, an Irish demeanor, and (a mite) gregarious in nature. The Sunday church bulletin dated May 24, 1981 gave this account of Father Buckley's background:

Fr. Gerald A. Buckley, O.P., has been appointed as Pastor of Holy Rosary parish in Portland, – to succeed Fr. Duffner whose second 3-year term as Pastor ends next month. Fr. Buckley, a member of the Dominican Mission Band, conducted the Rosary Novena here in Holy Rosary in October of 1977. Last summer he was one of the professors at the Pontifical Catechetical Course at Our Lady of Peace Retreat House in Beaverton.

Some brief biographical facts of Fr. Buckley: After attending a couple of primary schools in the Los Angeles area where he was born in 1931, he attended Serra High School in San Mateo, Calif., Bellarmine College Prep. in San Jose, and Santa Clara University. He entered the Dominican Novitiate in 1951 and made his seminary studies at St. Albert's College in Oakland, and Albertus Magnus Akademie in Cologne, Germany.

Among his various occupations after ordination: Instructor and Associate Professor in theology at Dominican College, San Rafael, California, and at St. Mary's College, Moraga, California; Newman Chaplain at U. of Oregon, Eugene (1961-62) and at Arizona State, Tempe (1969-73); Diocesan Director of Campus Ministry and member of the Board of Education, Phoenix. He has been a member of the Dominican Mission Band since 1974. He can hear confessions in Italian and German as well as English.

Fr. Buckley will be attending the Provincial Chapter held during July to elect a Provincial Superior for the next 4 years, so he will not be coming to Holy Rosary until around August. Fr. Duffner's term as pastor will be extended until that time.

The plainspoken and irrepressible Father Buckley, never attuned to the tuning fork of political correctness or nuanced speech,

spoke forthrightly without fear or favor on any topic; rare, if ever, was his erudition unequal to a question. Occasionally, to be sure, he could be as irritating as an uneven tooth on a tongue, but it was never a forked tongue. What you saw was what you got from this great and good man! Father Buckley's passion for dispensing reality as he saw it occasionally displeased that small segment whose pieties required lace-curtain language; nevertheless, parishioners respected him. The following quotes come from church bulletin dated April 24, 1983, when Father B. compared his renovation of the interior of the church to his own recent operation:

WELCOME BACK TO OUR CHURCH. Our Babylonian exile is ended, alleluia! Some necessary things have been done – new roof, new ceiling, insulation, new heating system, new lighting system – and some aesthetics as well – appropriate chandeliers, new carpeting, the reexposing of the sanctuary stained-glass window. Of course, whenever you do any renovating work on an old building, it becomes obvious that all kinds of other things should be done as well. But, as for that – later! Something has to be left for the next generation.

The microphones installed in the new ceiling of the church are for recording purposes to avoid the distraction of bringing equipment into the church during Mass. These microphones will not amplify the sound of the choir or organ.

FATHER BUCKLEY sincerely thanks the Parish for your prayers and good wishes on the occasion of his hernia repair (after all if the church is getting it, the pastor too needed some "renovation:" it has been over 50 years! He might be a little slow and listless for a few weeks but he too will eventually get back to normal (O Dear…).

Leonard and Abbie Chase, Dick Dixon, Theresa Alger Thanked

Father Buckley, in the church bulletin dated May 1, 1983, gave:

A WORD OF THANKS to all who gave a hand in preparing the church for our rehabitation last week. We especially want to thank Leonard and Abbie Chase for the beautiful new pamphlet racks in the vestibule, and Dick Nixon for his professional job of covering the kneelers and chairs with red velvet – and, of course, Theresa Alger for her donation of the velvet and her expert interior decoration advice.

Father Buckley's Stewartship Report

Father Buckley's successor, Rev. Edmund K. Ryan, O.P., would not be installed until January 1, 1984. Preparatory to that event, Father Buckley wrote a report, dated 7 October 1983, a retrospection on his stewartship at Holy Rosary, summarizing his thoughts on the linkeage between the past and the future and, with this backdrop, his own ministrations as pastor. Portions of that report considered relevant to our history are quoted below:

In January 1984, I shall resign as pastor of Holy Rosary Parish and superior of the community. My appointment to this two-fold position was effective as of July 30, 1981, so my term would ordinarily expire on July 29, 1984. I have submitted my request to resign to the Provincial and the Council in order, with permission of the former, to return to the province preaching band.

I have taken this step for a number of reasons, even though my attitude toward Holy Rosary is basically positive. Chief among the reasons is that I feel I can be more effective on the preaching band than in my present position, as the band at present cannot meet all the requests for engagements made to it. Furthermore, Holy Rosary is indisputably in need of a new rectory, and in my judgement my designated successor, Edmund Ryan, already in residence as an associate pastor, is more willing to, and could do, a more effective job with such a project than I. Herewith I submit a report of my stewartship. I am doing so at this early date because I anticipate very busy months ahead and should like to take advantage of a blessed lull at this time.

Because the spirit and work of our religious community is governed by the exigencies of the parish, let me begin with a description of the present status of the parish. [a description of parish boundaries follows].

Given the broken-up nature of the neighborhood, it is difficult to determine the exact number of Catholic families within the parish's territorial confines. Due to lack of organization I never took a door-to-door census. My estimate is between 25 and 30 families, and the majority of these are widowed or pensioned residents of Calaroga Terrace. The number of registered families stands around 300.… Estimated Mass attendance on Sundays averages 1100 individuals.

The reason for the discrepancy between the paucity of territorial parishioners and attendants is due to the nature of the parish. Under the 6-year administration of my immediate predecessor, Fr. Duffner, with the wholehearted support of his associates in this matter, the parish came to identify itself as "traditionalist" or "conservative," I myself both inherited this policy and opted to continue it, not only out of my personal inclinations, but also out of a sense of justice to the parishioners, many of whom consider Holy Rosary, with some exaggeration, an "oasis in the desert of madness." At any rate, the parish draws its parishioners (registered and unregistered) from the whole Portland metropolitan area – and beyond. One family, for instance, comes every Sunday from Salem, another from Longview, Wash.

THE PARISH – ACTIVITIES

This policy of Catholic traditionalism involves, as its name would imply, a vigorous commitment to the continuation of traditional devotions and practices. There are six Sunday and four weekday Masses, all well attended. Archbishop Power once advised me to drop a weekday Mass, but since there was such a hue and cry at the prospect, and since I could not determine which one should be dropped, I let the schedule stand, even though it often means (unwarranted, I believe) bination.[224]

The Rosary is publicly recited twice each day. The parish sponsors two solemn novenas a year. Confessions are heard three times daily and for 20 minutes before every Mass. Since we are one of the few places left in Portland that still has confessions, this has become an enormous apostolate, often to the tune of 50 per day. Every month there is a vigil before the Blessed Sacrament from 7 p.m. to 2 a.m. (a workout!). Father DeDomenico conducts a weekly "pilgrimage," principally for teenage youth, where Mass is celebrated in private homes. The parish Holy Name Society meets weekly, and the Metropolitan Holy Name Union monthly, as well as the Marian Movement of Priests. There is an active Legion of Mary, which regularly visits the local hospital and rest homes. We have inaugerated daily choral recitation of morning prayer with a reading from the Fathers, in which a number of the laity (many of them tertiaries) participate.

THE PARISH – EDUCATION

On the educational side the parish runs a weekly CCD program which this semester has enrolled 95 youngsters from kindergarten through grade 8. It is coordinated by a laywoman parishioner and employs (unpaid) male and female parishioners as teachers, together with two Franciscan Sisters from Beaverton. They use the Daughters of St. Paul series as texts. A great deal of emphasis is placed on preparation for confession, First Communion, and Confirmation (which is held every two years). The parish is resisting the prevalent practice in Portland to defer Confirmation to young adulthood. Not surprisingly, a number of the attendant children are pupils in parochial schools.

As mentioned above, Fr. DeDomenico conducts a religious ed program for teenagers and their families. Attendance is moderate but steady. I conduct a weekly class of "Bonehead Catholicism" for Catholic and non-Catholic adults and teenagers. It averages about 20 per semester. Last year I gave a "Bonehead Thomism" course which was remarkably well attended. It was a course that I had prepared previously for another occasion. I should like to have given a scripture course, but alas! had no time to prepare it, and could find no trustworthy volunteers among the laity (a perennial problem at Holy Rosary: they want the priests to do it all). Several attempts to form a young adult apostolate have failed.

THE PARISH – LITURGY

Short homilies are preached at every Mass. A peculiar feature of Holy Rosary is the complete omission of the sign of peace at Mass. I made a half-hearted attempt to introduce this, but was met with the first rumblings of revolt from both inside and outside the community. Since it is not a rubrical requirement, it would seem that the parish community would have its legitimate say here, so I left the matter alone. I did, however, push for what has come to be known as "Buckley's Baby," a high Latin Mass on Sundays. A gracious Providence had sent me a first-class music director. We rebuilt the old organ through the services of the best organ builder in the Northwest, making it one of the best instruments in Portland. We redid the ceiling, getting rid of the old acoustical tiles and replacing them with flat plaster, returning sonal resonance to the church. The high Latin Mass (Novus

Ordo, of course) features congregational Gregorian chant and a superb choir rendering liturgical Masses by such old masters as Palestrina, Byrd, Haydn, and Mozart. The combined adult, boys, "and girls" choir of Holy Rosary has already attained renown in the Portland area.

The Parish – The Staff

The Holy Rosary parish staff comprises, at the time of this writing, four priests, a full-time secretary, a full-time music director, a live-in cook, a live-in overseer of the parish center, a part-time janitor, and employs certain unpaid part-time parishioners on the parish center board, the building financial commission (recently organized by Fr. Ryan), the CCD staff, and the altar society.

The Parish – Finances

The parish has in the past been generously endowed with wills, testimony to the excellent service rendered by former parish priests. It was these wills that made possible the erection of the excellent parish center under Fr. Duffner, as well as my own efforts in rebuilding the organ and remodeling the church interior. Income on our portfolio… also pays the salaries of the employees. Except for a rare occasion, the well of wills has dried up, mainly because Calaroga Terrace (the great source) has changed from a residence of well-to-do retirees to a condominum of hard-pressed middle-class pensioners. Our parishioners are remarkably magnanimous when it comes to special collections, the poor box, and the archdiocesan Stewardship program, but much less so when it comes to weekly plate collections. Our weekly plate intake averages from $1600 (low) to $2100²²⁵ (rare), and since much of this is contributed by eight or ten generous families, the amount vis-a-vis the average parishioner is low. It barely supports the day-by-day running of the parish. It has been suggested to me that people do not rally without a cause, that parishioners do not contribute without a specific debt. I suppose much of this is my fault: I do not seem to have the charisma of the moneymaker, at least on an administrative level. I sincerely hope that my successor, with the debt he will necessarily incur in building, will be able to spur the folks on better than I.

Need for a New Rectory

A new rectory is a crucial necessity. I believe this fact is recognized universally throughout the parish, save among the pockets of eccentric sentimentalists who want nothing to change. The present house is the worst in the province for living conditions; it is eminently inconvenient for smooth parish functioning. It was built in 1894. Next year it will be a nonogenarian. But even over forty years ago Archbishop Howard had advised Fr. Agius, then pastor, "Father, it is so old. Tear it down and build a new one."

What is much worse than simple age, however, is fire danger. There are brethren in this province who refuse to spend a single night here because of fire hazard.

Father Ryan commissioned the construction firm of Brockamp

and Jaeger to do an in-depth study of the house as it is at this moment…

My suggestion is that a new house be built large enough to house a priory. Our location in one of the larger metropolitan areas of our province, which could so easily provide a diversity of apostolates, warrants this. It is also my suggestion that as little of the portfolio as possible be liquidated for this purpose, as a smooth operation of the parish requires its income. Financial drives and bank loans will be necessary.

The Community

The religious community, at present, includes five priests:Frs. McEachen, Ryan, DeDomenico, and myself as a parish man, and Fr. Duffner, who heads the non-parochial apostolate of the Rosary Confraternity in residence. Fr. McEachen is 77 years old. He does a faithful job with Masses and confessions, as sacristan, and as chaplain of Calaroga Terrace (Mass there every Wednesday) and of the St. Vincent de Paul Chapter. He does not answer the telephone or door bell, however, or ordinarily take parlor calls. Even though his health is good, he is not getting any younger.

Fr. Ryan is an associate pastor who is getting familiar with the parish in anticipation of his assuming the pastorate. He is specially oriented to the preliminary building plans. Presently, he is engaged full-time in a 2-month long CPE course at Providence Medical Center.

Fr. DeDomenico does a remarkable job in his own special apostolates, is very popular with the parishioners, is faithful to assigned Masses and confessions, but is a loner and has little to do with the community. He is often out and unavailable to ordinary parish demands.

Fr. Duffner is a good community man and helps out by taking the 7 a.m. weekday Mass, weekday confessions, and Sunday Masses.

> *Respectfully submitted,*
>
> *[signed]*
> *Gerald Albert Buckley, O.P.*
> *October 7, 1983*

The two attachments to Father Buckley's stewartship report showed (1) an investment portfolio worth $135,702, and (2) a two-page inspection report which concluded that the rectory: *"is an old building and has some built-in features because of age and design which are difficult to deal with. Changing of the drainage, electrical wiring, water piping, installation of a heating and ventilation system, and insulation of walls, floors and ceilings, are items which can be very costly. The value of this becomes questionable due to the unknown condition of potential dry rot and structural damage."* Father Buckley, in other correspondence, put it more precisely. He called the rectory "a fire trap;" he urged it be razed and a new one built. That would be Father's Ryan's main mission.

Father Edmund K. Ryan, O.P.,
Named Superior and Pastor at Holy Rosary

The church bulletin of December 11, 1983 announced:

FATHER RYAN PASTOR: Fr. Edmund K. Ryan was named as superior of the Holy Rosary Dominican community yesterday at a meeting of the Western Dominican provincial council, and his name was proposed to Archbishop Power for confirmation as pastor of Holy Rosary Parish. Fr. Ryan, who has been serving as associate pastor for the last few months, succeeds Fr. Buckley in both capacities. Fr. Buckley was reassigned to the province preaching band for mission, novena, and retreat work.

Fr. Ryan, a San Franciscan by birth, studied for the Christian Brothers, but in 1959 transferred to the Dominican Novitiate. After his course of studies at St. Albert's College in Oakland, he was ordained in 1965, and served in apostolates in Los Angeles, San Diego, Thousand Oaks, San Francisco, and Eugene. He also served as prior of Dominican houses in Los Angeles and Thousand Oaks. We welcome him to his new responsibilities.

Fr. Buckley will remain in residence at Holy Rosary until after the first of the year before taking up residence in San Francisco.

And the church bulletin of January 1, 1984 proclaimed:

INSTALLATION OF FATHER EDMUND K. RYAN, O.P.
The new pastor of Holy Rosary will be installed by Fr. John Krall, Vicar of this area, at the 12:30 P.M. Mass on New Years Day. When a new pastor comes to a parish, it is appropriate that the event be marked with prayers and a ritual which expresses the importance of what is taking place. This is a rite of installation and of welcoming. Installation is recognized through the presence of the Vicar as representative of the Archbishop who is pastor of the diocese, the local church, and who now entrusts these two – the new pastor and the people of this parish – to each other. Both of these, the installation and welcoming, are expressed in the rite. The new pastor is presented with the objects which can signify the many dimensions of his ministry in the parish; it is these – scriptures, the oil, the stole and the book of prayers – that bind him and the people of the parish.

The parishioners and Dominican Fathers make a special note of thanks and gratitude to Father Albert Buckley for his leadership of Holy Rosary during the last two and a half years. We wish him safety and success with his work on the Dominican Mission Band.

A reception will be held in the Parish Hall next Sunday (January 8th) following the 12:30 Mass to honor Fr. Buckley and to welcome Fr. Ryan and to which you are invited. Following the reception on the feast of the Epiphany, Fr. Buckley will mount his camel with the other three Kings and head into the sunset.

En route on his camel to other places, Father Buckley could rest assured that his conclusion that "people do not rally without a cause" in the giving of their time and treasure was valid. In this case the parishioners were, in St. Paul's words, "cheerful givers" as well, backing the construction of a new and first-class residence for their beloved Dominican priests. These joyful Holy Rosarian givers gave so abundantly in the fund-raising effort that Father Edmund Ryan exclaimed the funds *"came in so quickly and consistently over the months, that I was running out of institutions in which to bank the funds, since they [the institutions] were only insured up to $100,000. It was a very comforting predicament in which to find oneself, and it did very quickly alleviate the financial hesitations about building."*

Father Ryan, odd as it may seem, gave only a few sermons about financial need. He had planned everything so well including conducting guided tours for the parishioners of the old rectory – a "hovel" which bespoke a million words about how the priests were living. Nothing but generosity could speak after those tours. Father Ryan and the other priests gave their always-beautiful sermons from the pulpit every day and Sunday, and the only mention ever of money was in the context of "thank you." The point also needs to be made that a hush fell whenever Father Ryan spoke, especially when he directed his words to youth or at funeral Masses. He himself admits he could not only "talk the birds out of the trees" but pluck their feathers as well. Had he decided to become a "televangelist," salesman or marketing director, he'd have retired with millions by now.

True, Holy Rosarians love their parish and support it lovingly, but it's our long line of wonderful Dominican priests, with their holiness, learning and straight-forwardness, whether in the privacy of the confessional or on the public pulpit, that evokes moist eyes when we say "God how we love you Dominican Friars, long may your tribe increase."

Father Ryan Institutes Daily Exposition of the
Blessed Sacrament and Benediction

Within a year of his installation as pastor and superior, Father Ryan made plans for the daily exposition of the Blessed Sacrament which, later on, he would exclaim became a spark that ignited great spirituality in the parish. Holy Rosary would be the only parish in the Archdiocese to offer this wonderous gift at that time. In anticipation, Father wrote to Fr. Denis Reilly, O.P., prior at St. Albert's, on 8 January 1985, a letter requesting a loan of one of the beautiful monstrances maintained at the St. Albert's Priory in Oakland, California. He furnished the following receipt for the monstrance he received:

With the approval of Father Denis Reilly and his Council at the House of Studies, a monstrance is loaned from St. Albert's Priory to the Parish of Holy Rosary in Portland. The assessed value of this article by Shreve & Co. of San Francisco is sixteen thousand dollars. It is of silver and commissioned by Fr. Benedict Blank to mark the Centennial of the Dominican Fathers in California (1950).

[signed]

Fr. Edmund K. Ryan, O.P.
Pastor
25 February 1985

COMMUNITY OUTREACH CONTINUES

Holy Rosarians have always expressed their solidarity with the poor and less fortunate, as expressed in this 1985 news release for the Western Dominican Province Newsletter:

The Community [clergy and laity at Holy Rosary] trying to be attentive to the Master General's address to us at St. Mary's College on Peace and Justice has done the following:

(1) Brought a 25-year-old Polish refugee from New York to Oregon. He had been expelled from Poland for writing in defense of Humanae Vitae in the university student papers in Cracow. The parishioners gathered around and supported him during his first months in Oregon and started him off in Clark College. Since that time he has stood on his own and gained a scholastic scholarship and now works part-time for UPS. He comes to say hello to the community about once a month.

(2) In response to a letter of appeal from the Archbishop of Portland, a second collection was taken on one Sunday in response to the hunger and poverty of Ethiopia and the tragedy in that country. The parishioners responding to the challenge of the Gospel, forwarded to the Catholic Relief Society a cheque in the amount of $10,000.00. This was the largest amount collected from any parish in the archdiocese and letters were received both from the archbishop and the director of the relief society in New York in praise of Holy Rosary Parish and reprinted in the bulletin.

(3) The parishioners brought from Madras, India, from the Tamil minority Catholic refugee community, a young man of 21 years for an aortic heart valve replacement. After a month in Providence Medical Center in Portland, the young man is convalescing for a month and a half with the Community at Holy Rosary before going back to his family in India.

HISTORY OF HOLY ROSARY'S NEW PRIORY

Father Ryan possessed an astute insight when it came to fidelity in recording important historical facts concerning the parish. His handiwork is reflected in a memorandum for file – included as Appendix 7 to this book – concerning the building of the new priory.

There are those who swoon over remarkable deeds and those who lampoon them. Some of Father Ryan's brother friars in Oakland, in jest, referred to the new rectory as "Ryan's Taj Mahal by Moonlight,"[226] after the fancy gas stations in California; however, the fact remains that this great house renders silent testimony to Father Ryan's daring endeavor, the love of the people who supported him financially, and the enduring legacy provided to the Western Dominican Province in the Northwest for decades to come.

FORMER PASTORS CELEBRATE COMPLETION OF NEW RECTORY

In 1987, as indicated above, Father Edmund Ryan, O.P. would celebrate the completion of the new priory, a magnificent product of careful planning and execution, by inviting former pastors to come to Portland, as announced in the church bulletin dated February 15:[227]

A TIME OF GRACE: Through these many months of construction I have tried to give you periodic up-dates on the building's progress. Wednesday it all came to its natural conclusion in the ceremony of dedication. Five months ago I sent personal invitations to all the former living pastors and invited them to Portland to partake in this very special day. It was a great joy to all of us to receive these former Dominican pastors back to assist at the private 4:30 p.m. Mass in the fathers' chapel and the evening meal. They were all able to renew old friendships and to spend some time with their present Dominican brethren presently assigned to Holy Rosary.

Former pastors celebrate completion of new priory, 1987:
(left to right) First row: Fathers Arnheim and Agius
Middle: Fathers Ryan and Duffner   Top row: Fathers Cassidy and Buckley

Mural of Our Lady of the Apocalypse, 1989 –
dedicated to Antonio and Maria Fazio – by their children Jack, Tony and Mary Fazio.

THE FORMER LIVING PASTORS ARE:

Father Joseph Agius, O.P	1942 – 1947
	1970 – 1972
Father Felix Cassidy, O.P.	1964 – 1970
Father Bernard Arnheim, O.P.	1972 – 1974
Father Paul Duffner, O.P.	1976 – 1981
Father Gerald A. Buckley, O.P.	1981 – 1984

FATHER RYAN'S TAX REVOLT

Father Ryan authored an internal memo for file, dated October 27, 1987, which speaks volumes in a few words: *The Parish in all previous years has paid a property tax to the City of Portland for the parish residence. Today we received a property tax notice of $8,942.49 and we invited Mr. John Long the tax accessor in for a visit of our facilities. As a result of this visit, the rectory and Parish Center are now and shall be in the future exempt from City of Portland property taxes.*

FAZIO FAMILY COMMISSIONS MURAL FOR FOYER OF NEW PRIORY IN 1989

Parishioner generosity at Holy Rosary produces a melange of products and services. Paul Wolf, owner of a local trucking company, might move a priest's belongings from Alaska to Portland, or dispatch one of his trucks to deliver newspapers to a recycling center, and hand over the profits to the Holy Name Society for their projects. A parishioner who owns a Christmas tree farm yearly provides freshly-cut trees for the manger scene and for the rectory at Christmas time, when baked goods and sweets pour into the rectory from parishioners. Another parishioner, Bob Rengo, buys hundreds of spiritual pamphlets and he keeps the racks in the vestibule of the church filled with them. People buy them and the proceeds go to support the parish.

Siblings Jack, Tony and Mary Fazio commissioned a unique mural for the foyer of the new rectory. Here is the story from a leaflet found in parish files:

OUR LADY OF THE APOCALYPSE
This mural, dedicated to the loving memories of Antonio and Maria Fazio, was designed and executed by the famed Italian ecclesiastical artist, Father Renato Laffranchi of Brescia, Italy. Father Laffranchi visited us in June of this year [1989] following his major exhibit in San Francisco in order to familiarize himself with the lighting characteristics of the Priory foyer and to discuss with the Prior, Fr. Edmund Ryan, the chosen theme and composition of the mural. Work was then continued in Brescia, Italy and the artist returned to Portland to begin his work on April 12, 1989. We are indebted to the fine assistance given him by eight graduate and undergraduate students from Marylhurst College and the Oregon Art Institute.

The mural depicts in a dynamic fashion the age old struggle between good and evil, pivoting itself on the Person of the Savior. Evil is depicted with the personification of the seven deadly sins of: (from top, clockwise) Pride, Lust, Anger, Gluttony, Sloth, Envy and (middle) Avarice. To the far right is a theological reflection of the Incarnational and Virgin Birth through the power of the Holy Spirit. The Marian theme is carried forward as Mary, the Mother of the Savior, continues to give assent to the Messianic role of Her Son even in the tumult of the Apocalyptic struggle. The Savior, although wounded by the ferocity of the Beast throughout time, is nonetheless victorious, bathing, as He does, the Church – The City of Zion – with his salvific Blood. Throughout, the ministers of Christ's church, depicted by St. Dominic, the founder of the Dominican Order, pray for God's grace to perservere and to one day be numbered among the Elect.

We dedicate this Marian mural on this seventh day of May, in this month of Mary, 1989. We thank the artist, Fr. Laffranchi for leading us in prayer by the sharing of his talents with us.

POPE JOHN PAUL'S MARIAN YEAR
SPARKS REVIVAL OF DEVOTION TO THE ROSARY

In his annunciation of a Marian Year lasting fourteen months, from Pentecost to the Feast of the Assumption (June 7, 1987 – August 15, 1988), Pope John Paul II, specifically indicated, in his encyclical *Redemptoris Mater*, that it would be "*a preparation for the third millennium of Christianity.*"[228] John Paul's announcement sparked an explosion of interest in the Rosary and, like metal shavings quickly drawn to a magnet, Oregonian and southern Washingtonian Catholics converged on Holy Rosary Church to contemplate the past, bring it to the present, and look forward to the future in a prayerful place where they were sure Our Blessed Mother was present.

PARISHIONERS SPEARHEAD DRIVE TO HAVE VISITATION OF THE
INTERNATIONAL PILGRIM VIRGIN STATUE THROUGHOUT OREGON

One of the highlights of this decade, and certainly that of the Marian Year at Holy Rosary, centered on the visitation of Fatima's Pilgrim Virgin Statue. An historical account of that wondrous venture written by Father Gabriel M. Weber, O.S.M.,[229] dated November 21, 1986,[230] identified the innovative David Schaaf of Reedsport, Oregon as the sparkplug behind that project three years earlier. David, unfortunately, could not arouse sufficient interest and support; whereupon, he invited the Archdiocesan Rosary Committe to sponsor the visit. Father Weber, whose devotion to Our Mother knows no bounds, would be the spiritual director of the project. Holy Rosary parishioners George Stubblefield and Norma Monahan assumed the roles of Chairman and Secretary-Treasurer, respectively. David Schaff joined other committee members (mostly from Holy Rosary) which included:

Peggy Brandes	Activities Coordinator
John White	Publicity
Mrs. Ivan Manning	Contests
Mrs. Raymond Thomas	Publicity
Don Jessup	Informational Materials
Marcel Hurliman	Transportation
Rev. Paul Duffner, O.P.	Rosary Confraternity Director
Nita Willis	Archdiocesan Rosary Committee Director
Mrs. Frank Hamel	Scapular Makers Director
Nicholas M. Mariana Sr.	President, Metro Catholic Broadcasting

Mary, in her July 1917 message, stated: "*God wishes to establish in the world devotion to my Immaculate Heart. If you do what I tell you, many souls will be saved, there will be peace. The war* [i.e. World War I] *will end, but if men do not cease offending God, another and more terrible war will break out during the pontificate of Pius XI.*[231] *When you see a night lit up by an unknown light, know that it is the sign God gives you that He is about to punish the world for its crimes by means*

of war, hunger, and persecution of the Church and the Holy Father."

God fulfilled these prophecies to the letter: (1) World War I ended in November 1917, (2) a great light, inexplicable to astronomers, lit up the night sky in 1938 and, (3) the German Army marched into Austria three months later, introducing the planet to World War II – and, yes, during the pontificate of Pope Pius XI. Pope Pius XII's episcopal concecration took place on March 12, 1939. World War II ended with 50,000,000 dead and "countless millions maimed, mentally and physically crippled, homeless and hungry."[232] These three prophecies, enunciated out of the mouths of three small children, confirmed the truth emanating from Mary's "*Peace Plan from Heaven.*" But informed people in their pride ignored the plan. The others needed to be told.

In May 1947, post-World War II Catholics from all over the world, mindful of the accuracy of those prophesies, descended on Mary's shrine at Fatima in Portugal. These pilgrims, aware of the fulfillment of these prophesies, had been humbled by them. They had experienced the reality of the myriad changes wrought by the war in their own lives and in the lives of everyone they knew. Trepidation ensued, but a true love of neighbor and a conviction that this monumental message to the world from Our Blessed Mother ought to be shared, led thousands of Catholics on a pilgrimage to Fatima, Portugal nearly two years after World War II's hostilities ended. At this shrine, they would concentrate their minds on the crowning of the *Our Lady of Fatima* statue and perhaps discover other truths worthy of widespread dissemination. This is what Louis Kaczmarek wrote in his book *The Wonders She Performs*:[233]

Mary's servant Jose Thedium, the Michaelangelo of Portugal, completed his carving of Our Lady of Fatima. In May, 1947, in the presence of thousands, the Pilgrim Virgin Statue was crowned at the Fatima Shrine. The image of the Queen of Heaven was borne by her faithful subjects from city to city, from church to church. Grace exploded; cures occurred; white doves miraculously appeared. Crowds were everywhere. Pope Pius XII exclaimed: 'We can scarcely believe our eyes as we see the wonders she performs.'"

Sister Lucia, the sole survivor of the three children who actually saw the Fatima apparitions, directed Thedium's work. The 39-inch-tall, white statue was carved out of wood. Plans were laid to bring this statue to every continent on earth, so convinced were the True Believers in Mary that it would be a vehicle of grace for the entire world. Later, in union with Pope Pius XII, they could scarcely believe their eyes at the "wonders she performs."

Even though it happened nearly 50 years ago, most adults are well aware of the atomic bombing of Japan's Hiroshima, on August 6, 1945, and Nagasaki on August 9. Japan surrendered on August 15th, which effectively ended World War II.[234] It was the first and only use of "the bomb," which literally incinerated everything within a radius of several miles, killing an estimated 80,000 to 200,000 people. When the pilgrim statue was introduced at Hiroshima, the Japanese people told the statue's escorts that *"in the midst of all this destruction, one building [stood] alone in the eight-block perimeter of the blast. The rosary had been prayed in that building every day!"* [235]

The monumental task of planning, organizing, controlling and leading the effort to display the Pilgrim Virgin Statue statue at 42 churches and 19 schools and rest homes in Oregon fell primarily on the shoulders of parishioners George Stubblefield and Norma Monahan, ably assisted by other members of the committee, and all were equal to the task. A summary report[236] made by Father Gabriel M. Weber, O.S.M. noted:

Existing Rosary and Scapular makers groups held classes to teach others to make rosaries and scapulars and we set a goal of 5,000 rosaries and 10,000 scapulars. As time went on we could see that many more would be needed and they were provided.

Coordinators were appointed in every parish by their pastors A poster and essay contest was conducted for high school and grade school students with cash prizes being awarded the winners…

A welcoming ceremony was held at noon on Labor Day, September 1st, 1986, at the National Sanctuary of the Sorrowful Mother in Portland. An outdoor Mass was held there at the Grotto with 1500 people in attendance…

The highlight of the month was a Rosary Rally for World Peace at the University of Portland Chiles Center [September 13] with an attendance of over 3,000. Archbishop Power presided and 30 priests concelebrated.

May 17, 1987 First Communicants

BOYS

Joshua Baeckel	Richard Poulin
Damian Barron	Aaron Pratt
Daniel Ellis	William Rubeck
John Patrick Jacks	Kenny Selam
Jason Kempster	Craig Spiering
George Pongracz	

GIRLS

Anne Marie Barron	Lisa Hefflinger
Brande Castello	Jennifer Juby
Teresa Castillo	Cathlin McDonnell
Aimee Cysewski	Christina Murray
Rachel Endres	Sarra Murray
Tehya Golik	Felicia Perez
Joelle Glennon	Bridgett Pongracz
Shannon Harvey	Rebekah Sims
Bridget Hanson	

Holy Rosary Becomes A Priory Again

The provincial council of the Western Dominican Province met on the afternoon of 14 June 1988 and approved a petition submitted by Father Ryan and the fathers at Holy Rosary to raise the status of the community to a priory. On the heels of this approval the community elected Father Ryan as prior. The provincial, Father John C. Flannery, O.P. approved of Father Ryan's election as prior on 12 July 1988.

The Parish Library
BY ANNE FRIEDHOFF

Actually, the present[237] library came into being when Father Paul Duffner was pastor and the Parish Center was built in 1981. A notice appeared in the bulletin for volunteers interested in working with books. The first meeting was in March 1981. Father Duffner asked Sister Mary Thomas, SSMO, from Saint Mary's of the Valley Convent, a trained librarian, to advise him and the staff on the many procedures necessary to establish a library, and to instruct the many volunteers who came to the first meeting. The small room was filled with women eager to proceed. The bare and beautiful new shelves soon blossomed with books and quickly outnumbered the volunteers, who were slowly reduced to a few regulars. Sister's time was limited to one summer and she did a marvelous job teaching all of the volunteers the Dewey System of cataloging, typing, filing, shelving, and repairing of books. We shall be eternally grateful to Sister Mary Thomas and to the Sisters of Saint Mary of Oregon for their generosity on our behalf, and at a time when we needed them most.

All the volunteers had their favorite jobs to do. Eva Smith and Hazel Quirk liked to do the printing on the books. Betty Sousa brought bakery goodies to go with the coffee, which was always hot, and performed a variety of chores. Virginia Stormes was very good at typing and most of the cards in the catalog file are her work. Other typists who helped were Prudence Ford, Norma Monahan and, currently, Blanche Breiling. Charles Awad, God rest his soul, was the Assistant Librarian from the beginning, with Anne Friedhoff taking over leadership responsibility from Sister Mary Thomas upon her departure. Charlie was the jack-of-all-trades who typed cards, made signs, fixed shelves, and gave input on the many decisions which had to be made. Father Duffner, in addition to providing dynamic leadership, wielded a hammer and, among other things, put up the curtain rods and curtains that softened the light from the upper windows. He also provided the electric heaters for the chilly days and gave encouragement in all areas. Father McEachen was always a strong supporter of the library, every Sunday reminding the congregation to visit the library after Mass and take home a book on the lives of the saints or some other suitable reading material to increase their spirituality.

A library is an orderly arrangement of books. Ours was now full of books and the volunteers were trained and willing to work. The volunteers learned by doing – and undoing. They found out that "close enough" is not the way to shelve a book. Charlie's sense of humor kept them laughing. One book tickled his fancy and each time the book "Kisimusi" came to hand we would rock with laughter. It became a byword. Charlie scrounged for furniture and would liberate for the library whatever was loose in the hall. The first picture hung in the library was that of Pope John Paul II and Charlie observed the interesting fact that one of his cufflinks was unbuttoned, a saintly man so perfect in so many ways, but with imperfections nontheless. They laughed a lot while working with Charlie. When Charlie was named Holy Name Man of the Year they kept his rosary on display in the library (but he had a duplicate for daily use).

In the spring of 1982 the library was ready for business. No special opening ceremony, just Charlie's sign saying "OPEN." The volunteers agreed among themselves to work two days a week, Sunday and Monday. For a while Norma Wetzel had the library open on Fridays as well, but availability exceeded demand and the library ended up with the two-day schedule. Gradually, the parishioners routinely visited the library before or after Mass on Sunday, as they do to this day. On Mondays, with fewer interruptions, Anne and Jack Friedhoff process the paperwork.

We started out with dozens of books, which soon grew to a few hundred, and then to a thousand. Now we have over 4,000 volumes, and the reputation as one of the best (if not *the* best) church library in Portland. The books come from many sources. Some of library's angels are known, while others wish to remain anonymous. Jim Ross has been a book donor from the beginning. Mt. Angel's Father Athanasius and the University of Portland's Father Brown have donated many reference works. Editions have been received from the estates of Bishop Leipzig, Father Feucht, Kit Bogran, and Velma Clyde. Dominican Fathers McEachen, Buckley, and Ryan have donated special volumes, and the Karpiet collection added many more valuable volumes to the treasury. The Dominican Third Order books add a precious dimension under the subject heading Dominicana.

It was not long before audio and video religious tapes began arriving and, when they accumulated over 400 of them, Laszlo Lantos came to the rescue with his carpentry skills and made special shelving for their storage.

The work has progressed but the regular in-house volunteers are now down to two: Anne and John Friedhoff. However, Blanche Breiling still helps out with the typing, working out of her home and, once a month, Helena Sells comes down from Longview, Washington to help out. The work is under control, but the job is never done.

On Sunday and Monday mornings the library, an oasis of peace and tranquillity, awaits its visitors. The few good pictures the library rescued from the old rectory before it was razed, now adorn its walls. The small radio on low volume is tuned to classical music, and the books stand ready to tell their stories about God and his heroes and heroines. Coffee is no longer available, but candy treats await the children.

The goal of our library is to spread the Good News of Salvation, to enrich lives by introducing people to God and His Church in a special way, through the media of books, tapes, films, compact discs, and any new communications technology appropriate for the advancement of our goal. After all, a parish library is a precious resource that provides both doctrinal guidance and devotional information. It offers enrichment and spiritual nourishment, and is a valuable resource center for adult education instructors and students, CCD teachers and pupils, workshop participants, and all parishioners intent on studying their faith. The Priory has continually recognized and supported the library's goals and the parishioners have constantly expressed appreciation for the work being done there. At this point in time, we have high hopes for the future as we celebrate our Centenary.

Father Gregory Anderson, O.P.

A highly respected and beloved Dominican at Holy Rosary, Father Anderson joined the parish staff in May 1987, as announced in the Sunday bulletin dated 7 May:

We are very pleased to welcome Father Anderson to Holy Rosary as a member of the parish staff. Father was ordained in 1947 as a member of our province and has had a varied career on the west coast in leadership positions ranging from missionary work in Utah to pastorships in Reno, Los Angeles, and Berkeley. He comes to us after spending three years with the Christian Brothers in Napa, California. Father will be with us for a few days to complete his unpacking and then be back on board July 28th to begin his parish work with us. I ask that you give a kind welcome to Father Anderson. [Fr. Ryan].

Father Anderson's spiritual odyssey from young manhood to being a major force for good in the affairs of Holy Rosary is an invigorating narrative worthy of reflection. An article headlined *The good we do takes on a life of its own*, which appeared in the August 31, 1990 edition of the *Catholic Sentinel*[238] relates the primary facts:

This is a true story! Once upon a time, a boy named Gregory had a call to faith. He discussed it with his mother, who loved him dearly. She sensed that Gregory was somehow special and that he would grow in grace and wisdom, given the proper guidance.

They were living in Los Angeles at the time. Gregory had never been baptized but his mother belonged to a Protestant Church. In their view, that church did not plumb the depths of their spirituality. Something was missing. This loving mother could think of only one person she had ever met whose life seemed to be worthy of emulation: a Catholic girl in Texas, a girl whose name she could not even recall.

She reasoned that if the Catholic Church produced such fine people, then Gregory should investigate Catholicism. She told Gregory to talk to a priest, and he did. Gregory took instruction and joined the Catholic Church. Two years later, Gregory entered the Dominican Order. In 1947, he was ordained a priest, and last June he celebrated 43 years in the priesthood. He is Dominican Father Gregory Anderson of Holy Rosary Church in Portland. [A "first" occurred when Father Anderson later brought not only his mother but his grandmother as well into the Church].

And now the story behind the story! Catholics not versed in their faith do not understand why, after that "final and fearful passage" into eternity we face first Particular Judgement and then, at the end of the world, General Judgement. The just lot we receive at Particular Judgement is not altered at General Judgement; however, it is the teaching of the Church that at General Judgement "every sin and good deed of every human being will be manifested to all." But not when we die; because, even though we die, what we have done lives on in the lives of others. In Shakespeare's Julius Caesar we read: "The evil that men do lives after them, the good is oft interred with their bones."

But the good we do is not interred with our bones; it takes on a life of its own after we are gone. In fact, through geometric progression, our own lives may affect the lives of thousands, even millions, of people. So it is our life's entirety that will be judged at the General Judgement, after all human acts have been terminated.

Think of how inspiring was the life of that Catholic girl who once lived in Texas, a girl whose name could not be recalled, and the profound effect she has had on so many lives through the life of Father Anderson.

This same mystery of salvation is occurring at this very moment in each of our lives. Yet many do not understand, much less take advantage of, this magnificent opportunity to work through God for the glory of his name and our own salvation. We must spread this good news.

The hidden designs of God must be unearthed, proclaimed, and glorified. We must respond to this minute by minute challenge within our own spheres of influence, not by what the world would consider "great deeds," but by simple everyday acts of adoration of God and love for our neighbor which, foremost, is our own earthly family – keep it free from discord, so that the lives of its members might radiate love outside the family. Christ came to earth so that we might (1) have an image of the Blessed Trinity, and (2) understand how human beings are supposed to act (by His example).

We'll all be there on Judgement Day. Our actions this day and every day will show whether we believe this truth of our faith.

Father Anderson spoke with a deep, booming voice and great presence. As the old saw goes, even the choir boys listened as he spoke. He gave inspiring sermons and actively engaged in his many religious pursuits. The following article, which appeared on the front page of the parish's Holy Name News [239] dated June 1, 1990 gives an accurate summation of Father's tenure at Holy Rosary:

FOND FAREWELL FATHER GREGORY ANDERSON, O.P.

Words do not come easy in expressing the loss we all feel over the impending departure of our chaplain and foremost supporter, Father Gregory Anderson, O.P. Father's life is a witness of love and, during his three years here at Holy Rosary, thanks in large part to his leadership, the membership in our Society doubled; a treasured milestone in these troubled times. Our greatest gift for his departure would be to keep the momentum going, to ensure that his labors have not been in vain, a task also demanded by conscience if we are sincere in our pledge to spread devotion to the Holy Name of Jesus. (Just think: it was Father's namesake, Pope Gregory, who commanded the Dominican preacher, now Blessed John of Vercelli, to found our Society in the 13th Century.)

Father became a convert to the Church in 1939. He joined the Dominican Order in 1941 and was ordained in 1947. His first assignment was associate pastor at St. Dominic's Church in San Francisco. His illustrious labor in the Lord's vineyard includes: associate pastor of four parishes and pastor of five, director of the Newman Center at the University of California at Riverside, Master of Students (in charge of formation of Dominican students for the priesthood) at St. Albert's College in Oakland, California where he also taught preaching and pastoral theology. His last assignment before coming to Portland was chaplain to the Christian Brothers in Napa, California. He returns to St. Dominic's in San Francisco in September to be associate director of the St. Jude Shrine.

Holy Rosary parishioners have been genuinely moved by the great solemnity with which Father Anderson offers the Eucharistic Sacrifice, and by the clarity of this thought in preaching the word of God, so there is a great sense of loss associated with his departure from our parish in general, as well as from the Society, which he has served with fidelity. This loss will also be felt by his catechumens, by all to whom he has administered the sacraments, by the sick he visits in nearby hospitals, and by Catholics from all over Oregon and southern Washington who attended his retreats at Our Lady of Peace Retreat House in Beaverton.

In this contemplation on Father's departure from our parish, which we love and cherish, one and all are urged to recall the many times Father, in his sermons, urged us to be "joyful Christians," ever mindful of Christ's constant presence in our midst; our Savior who, by proffering the rewards of eternal happiness in heaven, helps us to disallow the vicissitudes of life from unduly intruding upon our earthly happiness.

We thank you, Father, for continually reminding us of this profound message. We thank you, too, for your selfless service to us. We thank God for sending you to us to help us keep our faith alive. In the certainty that our loss is St. Dominic's gain (but, thank God, its all in the family), we wish you Godspeed, Father, and we render our sincere gratitude to you for giving us your best when it was needed the most! God bless you Father Anderson!

Father Ryan Joins the Navy as Chaplain

Father Ryan mailed the following letter, dated 5 December 1990, to all Holy Rosarians registered in the parish:

With the reception of this Christmas card you will please receive my warmest wishes for a Blessed Christmas 1990.

God, the Church and the United States Navy are calling me from Holy Rosary to other duties. On the nineteenth of this month I begin my eighth year as pastor. Although my term of office runs until the beginning of July, I am convinced that the present extreme need the Navy has for Catholic Chaplains warrants this transition in my life.

It is terribly important for me to share with you the very public and expressed happiness that has been mine during these years in Portland and most especially at Holy Rosary. Together really, we have fashioned something of great and lasting beauty. I speak not so much of the buildings but of a Catholic Spirit and the living out of our common faith. In this place we have never had to compromise our Catholicism, nor its legitimate expression. This has been a daily joy for me and I just want to say that up front.

It comes as a great surprise to me that some 38% of our Navy is Catholic. A Navy, I might add, that needs Priests to minister to the Sacramental needs of these men and women. I am answering this call to service both to Church and to Country not from self-service but rather self-sacrifice, because that is what it costs me to leave you all and this sacred place.

There are ... e is sure that God Himself is ... s one of those times for me. I a... efore the altar of Holy Rosar... igh honor to lead you to the ...

You must ac... rand time to be entering the ... Country. I will hope to bring the rest of what and who I am to this service.

In the meantime you have my thanks from the bottom of my heart for all the kindnesses and courtesies extended to me throughout these many years.

Pray for me please, that God bless me in this new and challenging endeavor.

Entry date: mid January

   In Him

   [signed]
   Fr. Ryan, O.P.

Notes to the Text

223 Though we do not "worship" Mary, we worship only God.
224 Permission given to a priest to celebrate more than one Mass on a single day.
225 In 1994 it rose to between $8,000 and $9,000 per week, expressing the gratitude of those those who love Masses and sermons surrounded by sanctity.
226 According to Rev. Charles Hess, O.P., archivist for the Western Dominican Province.
227 Parishioners were also given tours of the new rectory so they could see what their money had bought.
228 *Our Sunday Visitor's Catholic Encyclopedia*, Publishing Division, Huntington, IN, pg 622.
229 A Servite priest serving at the Grotto in Portland.
230 On file in the archives of Holy Rosary Church.
231 The prophecy was made during the pontificate of Pope Benedict (Sep. 3, 1914-Jan. 22, 1922.), four years before the election of Pius XI.

232 Page 17, The Wonders She Performs, by Louis Kaczmarek, Trinity Communications, 9380 C1 Forrest Lane, Manassas, Virginia 22110, 1986.
233 Page 19, ibid.
234 Japan surrendered August 15, 1945.
235 Page 39 from *The Wonders She Performs*.
236 On file in the archives of Holy Rosary Church, Portland.
237 Actually the parish had a "Dominican Lending Library" from its earliest years. Books, were allowed to be checked-out from the rectory.
238 On page 5 and written by this author.
239 Written and published by this author.

The Portland Fire Bureau responded in force to the fire which engulfed the church November 9, 1993. Photo by Paul Delgado, Catholic Sentinel.

CHAPTER

15

1991-1994

CHURCH RESTORED, RESURRECTS FROM FIRE

The appointment of Father Anthony M. Patalano, O.P. to the post of pastor and prior. God had gifted this street-wise, twenty-second pastor and FBI man (i.e. Full-Blooded Italian) with an abundance of intellectual and physical gifts. He would need all of them to rise above and control the oncoming calamities hovering beyond the distant horizon.

A fellow friar of many years described "Father Anthony" accurately as "God-loving, compassionate, hard-working, playful, beauty-loving, combustible and simple-souled." The parishioners took to him at once but, with characteristic vigilance, they would remain objectively "wise as serpents and harmless as doves" toward their new leader. All of the property deeds belonged to the Dominicans but it was also the parishioners' property as well. They built up, supported and loved this parish and they would not tolerate a repeat of the "innovative" liturgical and architectural changes that they felt made a mockery of Catholic worship and drove them from their former parishes. This parish is their last stop on an earthly journey to eternity and they are solidly opposed to radical change. In their opinion, priors, pastors and priests come and go while they remain, convinced that their dignified solidarity with the pope and the magisterium requires no explanation. Father Anthony was senstive to their dignity. He took his cue from individual parishioner comments concerning "change." He proceeded with caution but, characteristically, he also focused on the grandiose goals now forming in the recesses of his fertile imagination. Gradually, he meshed his own ideas with those of the parishioners and together they worked wonders.

Father Anthony was born on 31 July 1944, the feast day of St. Ignatius of Loyola, to first generation Americans Gaetano Vincenzo Patalano and Lucia Maria DiMeglio, both of whose parents immigrated to the United States from the lovely island of Ischia, next to the Isle of Capri in the Bay of Naples. The Sisters of the Immaculate Heart of Mary taught him in grades K-12, in Los Angeles. They provided not only an excellent education but, moreover, a deep and abiding love for God and His Church. Two weeks after graduation from high school he entered the novitiate of the Brothers of Holy Cross who decided, after three years, that he was not called to remain with them. Knowing he was eligible for the draft during the Vietnam War, he enlisted in the United States Navy, where he spent four years, rose to the rank of Second Class Petty Officer, and finally served aboard the USS Pictor, whose home port was in Alameda, California. This supply ship carried mostly food but also fuel and ammunition to the Western Pacific war zone eleven times.

ammunition to the Western Pacific war zone eleven times.

About a year before his discharge from the Navy, while his ship was dry-docked for repairs in San Francisco, a more mature Petty Officer Patalano contacted the friars at Saint Dominic's Church in that city, and was subsequently accepted as a Cooperator Brother candidate. After discharge from the Navy, he was clothed with the habit on 1 October 1970, made his first profession a year later, and his solemn profession on 2 October 1974. After completing his initial studies he taught religion at Daniel Murphy College Preparatory in Los Angeles and Mater Dei High School in Santa Ana, California. In 1983, he began studying for Holy Orders and was sent to Holy Family Cathedral in Anchorage, Alaska where he experienced parish ministry for a year and received the minor ministries of acolyte and lector. Thereafter, he completed a two-year course of study at the Dominican School of Philosophy and Theology at the Graduate Theological Union in Berkeley, California. He was ordained a deacon in 1985 and a priest on 30 May 1986. He was again assigned to Holy Family Cathedral in Anchorage and remained there until his election/appointment as pastor and prior at Holy Rosary in 1991.

CHOIR DIRECTOR DEAN APPLEGATE HIRED
The Sunday bulletin of December 8, 1991 contained this message from Father Patalano, O.P.:

Holy Rosary takes great pride in thinking of itself as traditional. Yet, to any stranger who visits our parish, there is one aspect of Catholic practice that is blatantly absent – and that is sacred music and singing.

I have decided to hire the services of Dean Applegate and asked him to form a small schola. They will sing at the 11:00 a.m. Sunday Mass for the parish. The 9:30 a.m. and 12:30 p.m. Masses will have congregational singing. The 8:00 a.m. and the two 5:30 p.m. Masses will not have any singing.

I realize for some, music and singing are a bother which lengthen the Mass. If this be the case, then those conclusions (which are in the minority) give cause for regret.

I know for a fact that in the nine months I have been here, there has been a considerable "groundswell" for more liturgical music and singing. For me to deprive this parish of the beautiful and rich treasury of the Church's sacred music would be a crime.

After an appropriate period of time I will assess the entire music program. Until then, if any parishioners have any comments please address them to me.

FIRST COMMUNICANTS ON MAY 17, 1992

Joseph Bartholomew	Rachael Barron
Thomas Freiling	Madeleine Brink

Andrew Grewell   Chantle Chambliss

Father Anthony M. Patalano, O.P.

James Lexow	Mary Kate Fredrickson
Anthony Navarra	Lauren Hickok
Nathan Perkins	Elizabeth Illias
Daniel Shuell	Joyce Ilias
Peter Van de Couvering	Inga Ommodt
Brandon Zikowski	Ashley Perry
Mary Frances Poulin	

ALTAR SERVERS

Damien Barron	Ryan Perkins
John Paul Bartholomew	Richard Poulin
Michael Hefflinger	

ORGANIST:
Cynthia Rampone

VIOLINIST:
Christopher Young

CELEBRANT:
Fr. Anthony Patalano, O.P., Pastor

HYMNS:
On this day O beautiful Mother
Sweet Sacrament
Lord, I am not worthy
Let hymns of grief to joy succeed

NEW TABERNACLE FOR HOLY ROSARY
In the church bulletin of June 19, 1994 Father Patalano described the new tabernacle he had commissioned for Holy Rosary, its inspi-

ration being the church of San Giorgio Maggiore in Venice, Italy:

"The new tabernacle, which is Palladian in design, is constructed of white Carrara marble with variegated dusty rose and gray marble columns. There are four splendid solid bronze doors covering the two separate, specially designed compartments. The top campartment will contain a monstrance of adoration of the Sacrament; whereas, the bottom will contain the Reserved Sacrament for Holy Communion."

HOLY ROSARY – ITS HUMBLE PARTS

As soon as one wills to do good, genuine joy enters every fiber of one's body, there to remain until an opposite course is chosen; and the sum total of Holy Rosary's heroic spirituality consists of humble parts, all willing to do good: societies, sodalities, and even single efforts which, collectively, make the parish work like a well-oiled machine. And ninety-nine percent of the work is done by volunteers, backed by a few paid staff members. An example of individual, voluntary effort is Ted Deiss, for several decades the owner of a large nursery in the Portland area and who, now in his 80s, tends the flowers and shrubs surrounding the church and parking lot, adding an extra touch of beauty with his seasonal plantings. Nobody asked Ted to be a volunteer gardener. It's just something he does well, a gift from God, so he toils for the greater glory of God to partly repay God and Mary for the many blessings he's had in his life.

ST. VINCENT DE PAUL SOCIETY MEMBERS DELIVER FOOD TO THE POOR

Led by George Blatner, the following parishioners maintain a food warehouse and deliver food and other groceries as well as furniture and other household needs to the poor in our parish area: Ham Bullard, Pat Adams, Peter and Tess Schechtel, Norma Monahan, Jim Altenhofen, Joe Foye, Coran Bourdeau, and Larry Williams.

GOD'S HOUSEKEEPERS AT HOLY ROSARY

One cannot enter Holy Rosary Church without being transformed by its simple beauty and serenity, an ambiance akin to an oasis in the desert, with the added immanence of God's presence. One knows that this is a holy place. The sanctuary lamp is lighted,

New Tabernacle

and Christ's message radiates from the Tabernacle: *"I am the bread of life. He that cometh to me shall not hunger; and he that believeth on me shall never thirst."* All is right with the world during these visits with Christ, "and the joy we share as we tarry there, no other has ever known." We feel sorrow for non-believers and fallen-away Catholics (some very close to us), and pray they may one day come to see the Way, the Truth, and the Life.

Daily and innumerable heartfelt prayers to God, to his Blessed Mother, and to our angels and saints are what make this House of God a haven of rest, yet hard physical labor, performed generously by many, provides us with what former pastor Edmund Ryan, O.P., referred to as "frosting on the cake" – the beauty and cleanliness of the church.

Sitting quietly alone in the pew, one observes how it all comes together so beautifully, this exquisite blending of the natural and the supernatural. Cleanliness being next to Godliness, the floors are clean, the statues dusted, sacred altar cloths cleaned and pressed, the candles trimmed, the brass polished, and the flowers appropriately placed and beautifully arranged. Though those heartfelt prayers summon the presence of angels, one asks "Who bends to the other tasks?" Do little leprechauns descend at night to bring us this little bit of heaven?"

"No," comes the straightforward and reasonable response from Eileen Landregan, President of the Altar Society, "it's Mr. Old Dutch Cleanser chasing dirt." Mrs. Landregan is modest about, yet proud of, the results achieved by the dedicated women of the Society, whose members include: Jeanne Ford, Toni Kucrea, Julie Amato, Elizabeth and Maryetta Foley, Anita Rappe, Pamela Jacks, Bobbie Harrah, Rose Brogna, Deanna Cross, Cecilia Cable, Margaret Powell, Marjori Mottau, and Dolly Ballentine. These are our secret benefactors. And they come from as far away as Vancouver and Gladstone to donate considerable time and energy to beautify God's House; and we relish the results. As we sit alone in church and contemplate God's many blessings, let us say a quiet prayer for His housekeepers, past, present, and to come.

GOD'S ACCOUNTANTS AT HOLY ROSARY

Harmonizing the practical needs of the parish with its spiritual mission the following parishioners, who have been successful in the business world, take time out of their busy lives to serve as a parish finance committee, and it is to them we owe a debt of gratitude for the solvent situation in which Holy Rosary finds itself at this Centenary's end:

Bob Franz
Bob Rengo
Joe Wetzel
Paul Wolf
Randy Young

GOD'S ADORERS AT HOLY ROSARY

Father Edmund Ryan, O.P., our pastor/prior from 1984 to 1990, God bless him, once remarked that a great resurgence of spirituality enveloped the parish when he reinstituted Adoration of the Blessed Sacrament. We are all indebted to him and the following parishioners who pray before the Blessed Sacrament throughout the week: Kathleen Lynch, Joan Delaney, Eileen Landregan, Bonnie Johnson, Bertelle Barrett, Joe Weber, Darlyne Yocum, Raymond Delaney, Joe Wetzel, Jo Banz, Josephine Jaeger, Kelly LeClaire, Florence McEachern, Helen Stein, Bonnie Manion, Margaret Powell, Carol Hamel, Rita MacDonald, Pauline Wagner, Delores Judge, Dolly Ballantyne, Adele Fergus, Jeanne Ford, Don Jessup, Anita Rappe, Thelma Stubblefield, Velma Abrahamson, Bernadine Gent, Peggy Brandes, Linda LaGrand, Jean Cassidy, Ignatius and Teresa Custer, Becky Lewis, Mary Burns, Virgil and Rosemary Billingsley, Dayle and Ann Blauvelt, Jack Basic, Ham and Bernice Bullard, Norma Monahan, Pam Jacks, Maryetta and Elizabeth Foley, Norma Grierson, Margaret Magnan, Ted and Helen Deiss, Mary Parmantier, Marie McCurdy, Betty Wolf, Eva Smith, Helen Spengler, Marcella Parriott, Margaret Dundon, Evans McLean, Nellie Allen, Frances James, Virginia Storm, Kathleen Donovan, Dorothy O'Donnell, Margaret McManus, Madeline Nosbush, Emma Hambright, Irene Lamme, Nancy Jacks, Phyllis Weber, Beth Bailey, Louise Neuschwander, Michele Neth, Julie Amato, Lillian Olsen, Pete and Tess Schechtel, Jo Sullivan, Mr. and Mrs. Joe Ozura, Kathy Thomas and Audrey Hyatt.

Adoration of the Blessed Sacrament

LATEST HOLY ROSARY CCD PROGRAM HAD ITS ROOTS IN THE LEGION OF MARY

The seeds of faith have been sown in the classrooms at Holy Rosary Church from the beginning by priests, nuns and lay men and women concerned with the souls of our children, so that these youngsters might meditate on God's infinite perfection and, possessed of Church teaching, robustly "know, love and serve God in this world and be happy with Him forever in heaven." After the grade school closed in 1955, small sessions were held in private homes and in the rectory. In the words of Margaret Powell, the present program:

began not long after Father Duffner became pastor, when he took on the task of spiritual director of the Legion of Mary. Somehow I found myself joining, along with Ann Blauvelt, Theresa Lorentz, Marie Kluge, Asunta Santelli and Mary Fazio. Father needed a parish census and, through the census, found a need for a religious education program for youth.

We began by having weekday night classes in the parish rectory – for high schoolers who were attending public schools. Jerry Brady, Ken Jacks, Dan Doran, Gary Williams, and Kathy and Jim Bobzien were the beginning teachers. News of the program soon spread via Sunday bulletin notices and by word of mouth, attracting parents with young children. In short time we started holding Saturday morning classes, taught by Mary Walsh, Estelle Fitzgerald, Angie Hefflinger, Kathy Blauvelt, Ann Blauvelt (helper), Terri Mersereau and Matt Powell.

Under the direction of Father Duffner, who supervised the use of proper books and materials faithful to the teaching authority of the Church, the program grew to the point where we were using every corner of the rectory as well as the choir loft in the church for class space.

When the erection of the parish center, also under the direction of Father Duffner, was completed in 1980 (and I think the parish center ought to be named Duffner Hall), the program continued to grow in numbers – students as well as teachers.

This year, 1995, marks the 17th year Mary Walsh has prepared the children to receive their First Holy Communion. Other teachers now included: Cecelia Hoesly, Taylor Kendall (11 years), Gary Sims, Joe Foye, Bob Powell, Becky Lewis, Jane Hoesly, Debra Connell, Sue Jensen, Gary Williams, Gerry Parmantier and Sister John Morris, OSF, of the Franciscan Missionary Sisters of Our Lady of Sorrows in Beaverton. Marie McLean and Jim Ott are tutors. Father Bartholomew de la Torre, O.P. teaches the 11th and 12th grades and conducts semi-annual retreats for students preparing for the Sacrament of Confirmation. When Father Ryan began building the new rectory and the parish center was needed for storage space, Our Lady of Sorrows provided classroom space so our program could continue without interruption. When the new rectory was completed we returned to the parish center, and the program grew to its current size of about 200 students.

From 1978 to 1989, Margaret Powell took on the arduous task of Director of Religious Education. Jane Hoesly assumed that role in 1989 and has continued as Director ever since.

THE DOMINICAN LAITY AT HOLY ROSARY
(SEE APPENDIX 3 FOR LIST OF VOCATIONS 1894 – 1994)

We are grateful to Father Paul Duffner, O.P. for the following account of the Holy Rosary Chapter of the Dominican Laity, as recorded in a newsletter, *Third Order Thoughts*, for January 1980:

To My Friends in St. Dominic,

Thanks for the untiring efforts of Lucille Beatty and Betsy Darby, we have a number of details relating to the history of the Holy Rosary Chapter to send to Fr. Zammit, who is working on a history of the Third Order in the Western Province. Unfortunately, minutes of the meetings prior to the 1940s have been lost. Nevertheless I thought it might be interesting to list a few items that many of our newer members would not be aware of. Did you know, for example:

– that the presence of Dominican Tertiaries in Holy Rosary Church goes back almost to the very beginning. The Church was dedicated Jan. 28, 1894, and the first Tertiaries (Geo. Manning & Rose Manning) were received in 1896. Not yet a Chapter, but a beginning.

– that our Third Order Library is not a new project. One was begun back in 1940, and was flourishing in the mid 1940s. At that time it was open 3 days a week and Sat. p.m. In those days book borrowing from the library was not "free." A small fee was paid for each book borrowed, with a fine for overdue books. Hmmmm! Not a bad idea. (This library is now a part of the parish library).

– that in 1930 the Third Order held a social on the lawn (what lawn?) in back of the Church. Ice cream and hotdogs were served.

That was before the days of Fr. Norton – who converted the rectory garden north of the church into the present parking lot. In those days the present Lourdes shrine at the side of the church was located on the corner of Halsey and Third streets.

– that occasional donations were sent to Fr. Hofstee, our Dominican Father working since World War II with the lepers in the Philippines, and to the Dominican Mission in Chiapas Mission, and saved S&H Green stamps and sold Rosaries for the same cause – all this apparently before the beginning of our yearly collection for the Dominican seminarians.

– that members of our Chapter were instrumental in establishing the Radio Rosary broadcasts.

– that the minutes of 1955 speak of the Annual Silver Tea together with an organ concert by Fr. O'Brien, one of the priests of our province. The proceeds went to the Radio Rosary and the Dominican library.

– that at meetings in those days questions were placed in a box – which were to be answered at the following meeting, in the newsletter. (How about reestablishing that practice?)

– that in 1969 our Chapter sent a letter (signed by members) to NASA counter-attacking the atheistic protests against the astronauts reading from the Scriptures on Christmas of 1968.

– that on the occasion of St. Catherine of Siena being declared a Doctor of the Church in 1970, our Chapter invited members of the Seattle Chapter to celebrate the occasion by a joint meeting of the two chapters in Portland. A good number came, and accommodations for the Seattle Tertiaries were provided by our own members.

– that a member of our Chapter, Elsie Montgomery, wrote and had published a life of St. Dominic. She spent much time in Europe searching the libraries for information used in her book. It was translated into French and German, and steps were taken to get movie rights on it. Miss Montgomery died in 1958.

– that a member of our Chapter, Vivian Snodgrass (professed 1939) entered the Dominican Sisters of Mission San Jose, Calif. in 1946 – as Sr. Edwina, O.P.

– that Francesca Gabriel was chosen Catholic Woman of Achievement of the Archdiocese by Archbishop Howard in 1971.

– that our President, Alvin Batiste, was appointed by the Governor of Oregon to the State Board of Higher Education in 1978.

There are many other items that should be mentioned, but space

THE PROPHETIC VOICE OF THE CHURCH

History's central event is the Incarnation from which, in logical progression, the Catholic Church came about, inviting adults to be witnesses to the truth, to see the world through the eyes of faith, to discover the world's rational consistency, and to avoid sin and thus its effects; namely, murder and violence, hedonism and lust for the material, confused and broken families, and aimless and promiscuous youth. Some statistics:

[THE CHURCH TEACHES THAT: CONTRACEPTION LEADS TO ABORTION]

	1972[242]	1990
Abortions in the U.S	583,760	1,429,577
Number of abortions (per 1,000 live births)	180	344

[THE CHURCH TEACHES THAT CONTRACEPTION RUINS FAMILIES]

	1960	1990
Divorce rates (per 1,000 of pop.)	26%	49%
Children born to unwed mothers	5%	28%
Children under age 3 living with one parent	37%	28%
Children under 18 living with one parent	10%	25%

does not allow. We will have to wait until Fr. Zammit presents us with a History of the Third Order in the whole Western Province. Say a little prayer that St. Dominic and St. Catherine of Siena will aid him to produce a work that will make us appreciate more our membership in the Family of St. Dominic.

Sincerely in St. Dominic

[signed]
Fr. P. A. Duffner, O.P.

HOLY ROSARY IN THE CONTEXT OF THE CHURCH IN AMERICA AT CENTENARY'S END

Only a naive optimist would not know that the Catholic Church in America is in shambles, and that it appears destined to suffer that disintegration at least until the end of the millennium. Whenever such discombobulation occurs in any age, the world loses its bearings, because the Church is the Teaching Authority of Christ Himself, an authority subverted by the many voices of false Catholicism. When these voices convince the world that the Church is wrong, that contraception, abortion, homosexuality, divorce and euthanasia are permissible, then the compass designed to steer the world on a correct course points in the wrong direction and utter chaos and anarchy become manifest. This bodes ill for all of humanity (and for the Church as well because She will surely suffer the destructive consequences). Yet, we are reminded by St. Thomas Aquinas that *"The wise man brings order out of [presumed]chaos."* By this St. Thomas teaches that our vision should see the mind of God working at all times, and grasp not merely the microcosmic but the cosmic significance of what is occurring. We know the Church will prevail. And we also know that we, too, shall also prevail if we follow Her teachings.

RESULTANT CRIME AND CORRUPTION

Meanwhile, the crime and corruption in American society at this period in our history led Pope John Paul II to declare (absent empty optimism) in 1993 during a visit to the United States, that America was in danger of losing its "soul." The Pope's message contained a call for devout and resolute Catholics to plant the seeds of true renewal. He provided the New Catholic Catechism, as the primary source for re-teaching the authentic message of the Church and the Second Vatican Council with regard to doctrine, the sacraments, morals, and prayer life. This Catechism in the hands of learned Catholics should be sufficient to overcome the false teachings of the modernist cults currently plaguing the Church. In 1993, Pope John Paul II also issued his great encyclical "Veritatis Splendor" (The Splendor of Truth) designed to be a moral compass not only for Catholics but for countries and whole continents awash in sin as the result of untruths taught and proclaimed in every sphere of political, social, cultural, and scientific thought.

HOLY ROSARY AND ITS SURROUNDING OREGON CULTURE
(FOUNDER OF OREGON WAS A CATHOLIC)

It is little wonder that Holy Rosarians perceive their parish as an oasis in the desert. Oregon, historically, has been a predominantly pagan state whose citizens, in December, celebrate the winter solstice but offer scant recognition to the birth of Christ; an ironic twist considering the fact that Catholic John McLoughlin who, in the early 1800s, came as a representative of the Hudson's Bay Company and built Fort Vancouver (in Washington, across Columbia River from Portland), was considered the Founder of Oregon. McLoughlin's generosity and good works would fill a large volume. He built Fort Vancouver, which "became the capital of a tremendous 'kingdom' that included Washington, Oregon, California, Idaho, Nevada, Utah, Colorado, Wyoming, part of Montana, and a stretch through Canada to the Yukon." His business acumen and humanitarian accomplishments are legendary. After his death, McLoughlin's portrait "hung over the speaker's desk in the Oregon senate with the inscription 'Founder of Oregon.'"[243]

**POPULATION AMONG THE 50 STATES
WHO ATTEND CHURCH REGULARLY?**

A study reported in the July 18, 1992 edition of The Oregonian (page C12) on church attendance in the United States:

STATE	RANK	PERCENTAGE WHO ATTENDED
Utah	1	79.8
Washington	47	33.1
Oregon	49	32.2
Nevada	50	32.1

On the positive side, Catholic Church membership in Oregon outnumbers the largest sect three to one, and by itself exceeds the total of the three largest Christian denominations.

DENOMINATION	CHURCHES	MEMBERS	ADHERENTS
Catholic	199	*NA	279,650
Latter-day Saints	228	NA	89,601
Evangelical Lutheran	118	36,116	48,958
Assemblies of God	216	23,788	47,035
United Methodist	177	33,607	42,209

*not available
Source: Glenmary Research Center

A BAFFLING PARADOX

So the paganism extant in the general population is a baffling paradox for Christians, for whom a reverence for nature nurtures the spirituality of their innermost thoughts, proceeding from the fertile earth to the elegant unity of our cosmos. They immediately perceive God's munificence in Oregon's snow-capped mountains, immense forests, fish-filled lakes, rivers, and streams, lush valleys, verdant pastures, flower-filled meadows, fruit-filled orchards, and abundantly rich soil which generously surrenders, in season, food sufficient to feed the populations of several states. (In 1993 its orchards produced well over 50% of all the apples in the U.S.). Perplexed Catholics, observing these treasures ask incredulously: "How can one possibly be a pagan in such a land? We come to know God through the things He created. This truly is God's country! Why don't all of us fall down on our knees and thank Him for all of his gifts?" They immediately recognize this excruciating irony and are at a loss to decipher the puzzle which is the pagan mind.

Such notions of spirituality do not seem to engage the interest of two-thirds of the population in Oregon, estimated at 3,000,000 in 1993. While these pagans love the outdoors and are most at peace in the mountains or by the seashore, they seem not to wonder why such places secure such peace of mind and soul, whereas Christian discernment realizes that the therapeutic properties of those places comes from the mind of their Maker, who created this quasi-paradise so that the pinnacle of his creation might be one with Him and thus experience the inner peace that enraptures the soul when one is surrounded by nothing but the product of His goodness and beauty.

Unbelievers, unwilling to wrestle with this question of why, claim such thinking is an absurd leap in logic. Perhaps we Christians reasonably make this metaphor of goodness and beauty and juxtapose it with unbelievers as a gentle reminder to ourselves of the comparison between the Garden of Eden and our first parents, who did not appreciate that Garden for what it was and forsook it for sin, a grim lesson which Catholics of mature discernment take seriously.

FATHER EMMERICH VOGT, O.P. ASSOCIATE PASTOR AT HOLY ROSARY FROM 1991-1995

"Father Emmerich" was a superb preacher, teacher, philosopher and theologian. He was born on January 7, 1948 in New Britain, Connecticut, the second child of Justus and Mary Vogt. His older brother died of cancer at age 26. Father attended public schools and then Central State Connecticut University for two years. He entered the Norbertines in 1968 and then

Fr. Emmerich Vogt O.P. offers a priestly blessing.

switched to the Dominicans in 1970 after studying at St. Albert's Priory in Oakland, CA.

He received a B.A. in philosophy from St. Alberts, a M. Div. from the Dominican School of Philosophy and Theology and an M.A. in theology from the Graduate Theological Union. He also did graduate studies toward a Ph.D. at the University of California at Berkley.

He was ordained in 1978 and taught at Marist High School in Eugene, OR and Daniel Murphy High School in Los Angeles and Holy Rosary College in Fremont, CA. He also taught Hebrew at the Graduate Theological Union at Berkley, CA.

He has given retreats and seminars to Mother Teresa's Sisters for the past 17 years. It was a sad day in 1995 when he transferred from Holy Rosary to the Western Dominican Preaching Band.

FATHER EMMERICH IN AN INSPIRING SERMON[244] DECLARES THIS CHASM BETWEEN BELIEF AND UNBELIEF A UNIQUE OPPORTUNITY FOR CATHOLICS – THE SOUL OF SOCIETY

While it is true that Catholics in Oregon live in a largely pagan culture and suffer from it, their situation should not be perceived in the negative sense as a problem, but rather in the positive sense as an opportunity (to which Latter-day Saints' evangelizing in the state testifies). Father Emmerich proclaimed this insight in a beautiful sermon, in the fall of 1993; that Catholics ought to grasp the moment, that this large population of unbelievers in Oregon constitutes a fertile missionary field for all Catholics, who ought to go without fear into the depths of men's minds and hearts. "If they do not learn the Good News from you, who will they learn it from?" "You possess the Good News and are obliged to share it daily, at work, in your civic organizations, in your everyday contacts, by your every word and deed." Powerful words from a powerful man!

> "Be doers of the word and not hearers only, deluding yourselves." (James I:22)

ANTI-CATHOLIC BIGOTRY CONTINUES IN 1993 AND 1994 OREGON

In April and May of 1993, huge billboards portraying the Catholic Church as the "beast" in the Book of Revelation, and our holy and learned Pope John Paul II, as the antichrist, began appearing in Medford, Salem, and Portland. Photographs of these billboards, along with reportorial coverage appeared in The Oregonian[245] as well as the Catholic Sentinel.[246] The Oregonian piece reported that the billboards were "paid for by Printed Page Ministry, a splinter group of the Seventh-day Adventist Church, based in Troy, Mont." a "loose-knit organization with ties to Laymen for Religious Liberty. That is a Florida-based ultra-conservative sect led by David Mould, a 43-year-old Jamaican."

The story also related that "Jay Prall, director of communications for the Oregon Conference of the Seventh-day Adventists, disavowed any association with the group" which "did not represent the church's teachings nor did he have any control over their actions." This same Oregonian article contained the following paragraphs:

Rick Breckenridge, assistant director of Printed Page Ministry in Troy, acknowledged that the billboards were part of a national campaign to discredit the Catholic Church and denounce the pope as the leader of a worldwide conspiracy of evil.

Breckenridge attributed such historical events as the Civil War, the assassination of Abraham Lincoln and the collapse of the Soviet Union to a Catholic conspiracy. He said that the Seventh-day Adventist Church had become "too ecumenical" and had strayed from its original mission.

"We are not trying to get people to join our denomination to come up here," said Breckenridge from his Montana headquarters. "We are simply trying to agitate minds and to awaken the Protestant nation."

We see in all of this the ultimate paradox: people claiming to be disciples of Christ attacking His Church in His name.

CATHOLICISM'S LOST OPPORTUNITY IN AMERICA

Catholics know that the forces of the anti-Christ can do nothing but self-destruct in the end, when the true Springtime of the New Church will come about. This Springtime could have begun in the 1960s had Catholics remained faithful to the Magisterium. As country after country succumbed to "sexual liberation" with all of its self-

In 1992, Father Antoninus Wall, O.P. came to Holy Rosary from the provincial house to make video-taped interviews with parishioners. He is shown here interviewing teenagers Rose Parmantier (left) and Sarah Sims.

destructive behavior, those lay Catholics who were raising large families were sure, one day, because of their increasing numbers alone, to be huge voting blocs and meaningful participants in the "sanctification of the world" as mentioned by Pope John Paul II in his 1983 address to secular institutes:[247]

You must consider yourselves part of the world, committed to the sanctification of the world, with full acceptance of its rights, its claims upon you, claims inseparable from the autonomy of the world, of its values, of its laws.

This is not to say that Catholics ought to become some sort of monolithic political force. Such a role would be alien to them; in fact, most Catholics eschew politics entirely. Nevertheless, practically speaking, Catholics ought to realize that they deserve what they and their offspring get from the local, county, state and federal governments, whose laws not only severely impact their lives, but have the opposite effect of sanctification in their culture.

And so it is true, lay men and women in the United States could have elected Catholic and Christian candidates for public office, ensuring thereby non-passage of laws in contradiction of natural law and Catholic teaching. Instead, the faithful elected and re-elected unfaithful "Catholic" politicians like Senator Edward Kennedy of Massachusetts, Senator Daniel Patrick Moynihan of New York, Senator Joseph Biden of Delaware, and House Speaker Tip O'Neill of Massachusetts, all of whom ignored Church teaching and voted to legalize and subsidize unrestricted abortion. Catholic couples also forsook Church teaching and practiced contraception and abortion, killing their unborn and thereby contributing to the future shortage of priests. These Catholics lost an exquisite opportunity to help build a new nation based on beauty, truth, and goodness.

> *"To every thing there is a season, and a time to every purpose under heaven. A time to be born, and a time to die; a time to plant, and a time to pluck up that which is planted. A time to kill, and a time to heal; a time to break down and a time to build up."* (Ecc. 3:1)

HOLY ROSARY CHURCH RESTORED (NOT DESECRATED) IN 1993

The restoration of Holy Rosary would begin in earnest under Father Patalano in the early part of 1993, following a year of planning and consultation with all of the parishioners, who met with father on several occasions during 1992 inside the church (the Blessed Sacrament having been removed from the tabernacle). The doubtful among the parishioners, who were aware of the desecration of hundreds if not thousands of Catholic churches in the United States were wary of change, and would not countenance such changes at Holy Rosary. Father Patalano, himself steeped in the history of Holy Rosary, would not let them down. Father envisioned not a reconstruction (a term now syn-

onymous with "destruction" and modernism in our churches) but true *restoration*, which would return the church to its original interior design, albeit with a few unavoidable changes. The major tasks agreed upon in this consensus decision-making included:

Returning the Tabernacle to the center of the sanctuary (from the side altar) and placing it on an altar behind the altar of sacrifice (how gladdened were the hearts of the parishioners at this prospect!).

Refurbishing the marble altar of sacrifice (brought here to Holy Rosary in 1927 from St. Dominic's Church in San Francisco by Father Pope – see Chapter 8).

Replacing the glass windows above the sanctuary with stained-glass windows depicting St. Dominic (left), the Blessed Trinity (center), and St. Catherine of Siena (right).

Replacing remaining glass windows in the church with stained-glass windows depicting the mysteries of the Rosary (how marvelous!).

Rearranging the altar rails to provide easier access to the sanctuary during baptisms, weddings, etc. (all the while maintaining the original altar rails so that parishioners may kneel when receiving the Blessed Sacrament).

Moving the Shrine of Our Lady of the Holy Rosary from the left side altar to a refurbished niche on the south wall. The statue of St. Martin dePorres would receive a private, smaller niche on the

New niche on north wall.

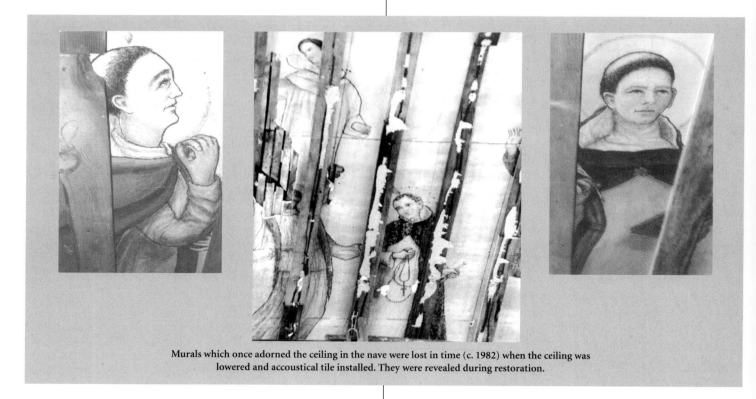

Murals which once adorned the ceiling in the nave were lost in time (c. 1982) when the ceiling was lowered and accoustical tile installed. They were revealed during restoration.

north wall next to the side entrance to the church. A statue of the Sacred Heart of Jesus would now occupy the left side altar.

Moving the ranks of intention candles to either side of the Our Lady of the Holy Rosary niche and installing heavier exhaust fans to extract the candle smoke from the nave (this smoke had continually blackened the interior walls at the old location).

A statue of St. Joseph with Child would occupy the right side altar, which had been occupied by the old Tabernacle. Remodeling and enlarging of the crying room.

HOW MUCH IS RESTORATION OF CHURCH GOING TO COST?

In a teasing moment at the close of the last planning meeting with parishioners, on 2 May 1992, Father Patalano queried: "Now that we have discussed what we want to do, What have we not discussed?" Silence ensued, then one of the parishioners said: "How much all of this is going to cost." Father Patalano stood there smiling: "Yes." Seconds passed as the silence became deafening and everyone's eyes focused on Father's face. "And I'm happy to announce that, due to your generosity, I have been setting aside funds for many months and have saved enough money to pay for *all* of the restoration without holding a fund drive." The parishioners responded with astonishment, grateful smiles and rousing applause.

CHURCH FIRE ON NOVEMBER 9, 1993 HINDERS RESTORATION

Fire, a highly valued servant but also a cruel task master, engulfed Holy Rosary in 1993. Personal charisma, bravery and

intelligent decision-making are the hallmarks of the leadership required when a destructive force like this attacks an enterprise. And when this frightful fire almost consumed Holy Rosary Church on November 9, 1993, the requisite leadership was manifested in the person of Father Patalano. Though he must have been emotionally distraught to the extreme by the fire that ruined seven months of renovation, in which he had been intimately involved, he outwardly appeared confident and cheerful; but most parishioners present suspected that these outward appearances masked a surfeit of sadness.

Father Patalano confirmed their insight during the following Sunday's sermon. He related that, during the fire, he received a message that Archbishop William Levada had telephoned him to express his condolences and concern. Father was "down" and did not wish to immediately return the call and exhibit his emotional state, but he rose to the occasion. Before he became connected to the archbishop on the phone, Father looked out his living room window with a heavy heart and spied a large group of young school children, standing on the sidewalk across from the rectory with their teachers. The children were waving to the firemen, obviously elated over the splendid show the fire and firefighters were putting on for them on this otherwise dreary morning. Seeing their shining, happy faces, Father mused over this telling contradiction (his sadness vs. their happiness over the same event) which made him question the boundaries of his spirituality. His insightful recognition of this absurdity became pivotal in altering his emotional state; for he possessed sanctifying grace, which delivered him out of the doldrums of despair on that eventful morning.

Photo by Paul Delgado, Catholic Sentinel.

The Portland Fire Bureau responded in force to the fire which engulfed
the church November 9, 1993. God aided by these heroic men
and women saved the church. Photo by Bob Ellis, The Oregonian.

Photo by Denise Hogan, Catholic Sentinel.

Photo by Paul Delgado, Catholic Sentinel.

I'll nod and smile at passerby
And not give in to thoughts that cry.
I'll smell the flowers as they bloom
Within, without my living room.
I'll watch the children near the gate
And let their freedom compensate.[248]

HOW THE FIRE BEGAN

The construction workers employed by the local firm of Brockamp
& Jaeger, and other firms which had contracted to renovate the
church, reported for work as usual at 7:00 a.m. on Tuesday,
November 9, 1993. By this date, approximately 95% of the
restoration had been completed. Unfortunately, the workers had
stored most of their paints, varnishes, etc. in the recently-renovated
crying room. The storage of so many flammables, both liquid and

solid, in such a confined space resulted in a great concentration
of vapors. The flashpoint? A spark, presumably[249] from the wiring
being worked on by Roger Aday,[250] age 54, who was installing an
electrical outlet in the crying room, caused an instantaneous
combustion and conflagration. Chemicals surrounding Aday, as
well as the clothing he was wearing, caught fire. Aday suffered
second degree burns on his legs. His coworkers covered him with
dropcloths to extinguish the flames, and an ambulance took him
to the burn unit at nearby Emanuel Hospital and Health Center.
Miraculously, he was the only one seriously injured.[251]

PARISHIONERS RICHARD CLOUD AND
RICHARD UNGER ON THE SCENE

Parishioners Richard Cloud and Richard Unger, who were chatting
in the foyer of the priory at the time, heard Aday's loud scream.

They rushed through the door of the sacristy to the sanctuary and saw the blaze in the crying room, which is located at the rear of the church from the sanctuary. Cloud immediately rounded up three fire extinguishers, which he passed to Aday's coworkers to put out the fire. Unger ran to the priory office and dialed 911, the police and fire emergency number. Cloud said the fire extinguishers first seemed to put out the fire but, all of a sudden, the crying room re-ignited into an inferno, and fire shot up into the air shaft in the southwest corner of the crying room into the choir loft, forcing Cloud and all the workers to make a hasty retreat from the church.

The flames also spread throughout the choir loft, engulfing the organ,[252] melting its lead and tin pipes, leaving it a mute and molten mess. The organ, built by Kilgen Organ Company of St. Louis, had been installed in the 1920s.[253] The November 13, 1993 issue of The Oregonian, reporting on this organ, stated: "It originally contained five ranks, or sets of pipe and one tone but was enlarged by 15 ranks a decade ago by Richard L. Bond Pipe Organs of Portland."[254]

The fire also shot through the crawl space above the nave, setting the ceiling and the roof ablaze. Mushrooming clouds of black smoke sat over the surrounding sky as a second, then third, then fourth alarm was sounded. A total of "more than 100 firefighters, 12 engines, eight trucks and other emergency vehicles" converged on the church. The firefighters got the fire under control about an hour after it had started, according to news reports, but the firefighters remained on the roof all day removing charred roofing material, scorched boards, and insulation. When the firefighters were finished, the construction crew covered the roof with tarps to protect the interior of the church from rain, which was expected at any hour.

During the fire, smoke entered the priory through the air and electrical vents in the ceiling above the foyer. Richard Unger quickly covered these vents, but the smoke had already permeated the priory, and it remained a miracle that the priory too did not catch fire. Considering the number of people involved, it was also miraculous that only one member of the Fire Bureau was injured: a firefighter injured his hand.

The interior of the church which, on that morning, had been immaculate with new floor boards, walls, and wainscoting – put in place over a six-month period beginning in April 1993 – was now a disaster area, with burnt debris, puddles of water, and smoke stains everywhere. The fire stopped the clock, on the wall of the choir loft, at 7:49 a.m.

Fortunately for all, the newly purchased stained-glass windows over the sanctuary remained undamaged, and the new windows which were destined to surround the nave had not yet been installed, otherwise they too could have been melted in the intense heat. Even so, the total losses were estimated at between $750,000 to $850,000.

Of course the parishioners were saddened, some devastated, but Father Patalano patiently put things in perspective in the following Sunday's sermon and in the church bulletin. The following reflections, quoted from the 11/14/93 church bulletin, were proof positive again, if needed, that tenacious Dominican spirituality was still alive and well at Holy Rosary. Wrote Father Patalano:

I could not have chosen a better day for a disaster than Tuesday, 9 November, the Feast of the Dedication of the Roman Basilica, Saint John Lateran. After the fire, Father Emmerich [Vogt] and I, with heavy hearts and spirits, celebrated the noon Mass. All the prayers and Scripture readings for this feast poignantly reminded us, and those present, what it truly means to be a Church. To quote the first reading from Saint Peter: "You too are living stones, built as an edifice of spirit, into a holy priesthood, offering spiritual sacrifices acceptable to God through Jesus Christ... . The stone is of value for you who have faith. For those without faith, it is rather 'A stone which the builders rejected that became a cornerstone.'"

Put simply, what Saint Peter is telling us is what the Second Vatican Council decreed, that we are the People of God. We are the Church. Though we can, and do, become attached to beautiful and inspiring buildings and works of art, what is important are the "living stones" built upon the cornerstone which is Jesus Christ.

My dear good and patient people of Holy Rosary, we have suffered and sustained quite a loss. But, thank God and His Holy Mother, our church has been saved and it will be fully and perfectly restored. Though we may not be able to commence the celebration of our centenary as planned, WE WILL celebrate it.

It is estimated that we will be back in the church in April or May. Our return depends on the findings of the structural engineers who will fully assess our building. Please pray for Mr. Roger Aday, the electrician, who was burned. He is doing very well and should be out of the hospital the early part of this week.

Again, I ask for your prayers and patience, especially for all the inconvenience regarding the Adult Education and CCD programs, and the various requests for use of the Parish Center.

Finally, a parishioner related an adage, "When you build (in our case restore) a church, the devil pitches a tent across the street." That may be. But let me relate to you what a young, exhausted fireman told me when the fire was put out. "Father, on the way to work this morning I was saying the Rosary which is broadcast on the radio [Catholic Metro Broadcasting]. I know the radio Rosary

Elizabeth Ann Jacks and Erik Sten Olson were the first couple united
in marriage in the renovated church, on May 28, 1994.
Pastor and Prior Anthony Patalano, O.P. was the celebrant.

*got its start from this very church. This church, which I thought
was going to be lost, was saved by Someone above Who was watching."* The devil may pitch his tent across the street, but Our God
lives in the heavens and His gentle mercy rained down from
heaven Tuesday morning, 9 November, on the Feast of the Mother
of All Churches, Saint John Lateran.

May God and His Holy Mother Mary love you.

This was not the first fire at Holy Rosary. Nancy Guinn of
Investigations for the Portland Fire Bureau kindly researched
their records in November 1993 and reported that the Bureau
had previously responded to fires at Holy Rosary in 1963, 1974,
and 1982. Details of the two earlier fires were not contained in
the records, but the May 23, 1982 fire was the result of a cigarette
being discarded into a wastepaper basket on the second floor of
the priory, resulting in a $750 loss to the building and $100 loss
to the contents of the room. No other information was available
in the Fire Bureau files; however, Father Gerald A. Buckley, O.P.,
pastor at the time, remembered the 1982 incident and wrote, in
his inimitable fashion:

*"Fr. [Peter] Miles, my late classmate, was with us but a short time…
One Sunday morning he tossed a still-lighted cigarette into a
wastepaper basket and caught his room on fire. Luckily it shorted
out the intercom system and my call bell persisted in ringing,
which brought me to the scene. The Portland Fire Dept. was there
within minutes and managed to save the old firetrap."[255]*

*Let nothing disturb you,
Nothing affright you,
All things pass, God is unchanging.
Patience obtains all:
Whoever has God
Needs nothing else,
God alone suffices.*
— Teresa of Avila

FIRST MARRIAGE CEREMONY IN OUR RESTORED CHURCH

Parishioner Elizabeth Ann Jacks, who graduated from Holy Rosary's
CCD program, was united in marriage at Holy Rosary to Erik
Sten Olson, on May 28, 1994. Erik, now a Navy Seal, went to Lake
Oswego High School. Elizabeth is the daughter of Nancy Jacks
and the late Kenneth Ray Jacks of Vancouver, Washington. Father
Patalano, our Prior/Pastor, officiated at the wedding. The wonderful
Jacks family is well known, loved, and respected in the parish. In
1989, Nancy, on behalf of the family, donated the two beautiful
marble holy water fonts that we use today at the main entrance to
the church – in memory of her deceased husband Kenneth. The
family asks that when people bless themselves they remember the
soul of Kenneth and all the holy souls in purgatory. The other seven
Jacks children are: Anne Michele, Pamela Marie, Kenneth William,
Mary Theresa, Catherine Louise, Margaret Rose, and John Patrick.

HOLY WATER FONTS – REAL WORKS OF ART [257]

Eugene Bertolli, who is listed in *Who's Who in American Art* and
in *Who's Who in the World*, made the fonts. He obtained the
Beige-Rose Classico Rosa marble from Italy. Eugene and his wife,
Jean Tamburine Bertolli, a personal friend of Nancy Jacks and a
sculptor and artist in her own right, designed the fonts. Nancy

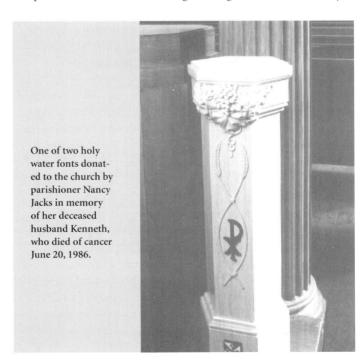

One of two holy
water fonts donat-
ed to the church by
parishioner Nancy
Jacks in memory
of her deceased
husband Kenneth,
who died of cancer
June 20, 1986.

commissioned the work in December 1989. Nancy explains: *If one looks at the fonts, one notices the use of grapes, leaves, and wheat. Jean works for the Church and uses quite a bit of symbolism. This is her way of catechizing people. Also, because this is a Dominican parish, it was decided by Father Ryan,*[258] *who granted permission to install the fonts in the church, that it would be appropriate for the Dominican coat of arms to be included in the design.*

MOST REV. FRANCIS LEIPZIG, D.D. ARCHDIOCESAN HISTORIAN

The saintly Bishop of Baker, Francis Leipzig, now deceased, retired in 1971. Living in Portland afterwards and quite advanced in age, he became the archdiocesan historian par excellence. Historians owe him a great debt of gratitude, for he brought to life reams of documents that had been gathering dust, and ensured that all sorts of minutiae (which might have been consigned to the scrap heap of history by unseasoned observers) made it into the archdiocesan archives. His painstaking scholarship and that of the writers of the Catholic Sentinel, who provided most of the facts, are the key. Bishop Leipzig was a special friend of Holy Rosary, where he was a member of the Holy Name Society, and where he frequently celebrated Mass and received the sacraments, especially when he resided in retirement across the street at Calaroga Terrace. He celebrated the 25th anniversary of his consecration as a bishop in September 1975 at Holy Rosary, in the presence of Archbishop Howard and Archbishop Dwyer, who delivered the homily.

I am likewise indebted to Bishop Leipzig's talented and faithful secretary, Dorothy M. Hanley, to whom Leipzig paid wages out of his own pocket to help him gather and type innumerable pages of historical data. Dorothy is currently in retirement at Calaroga Terrace. We thank her for giving us an interview and, while in the employ of Bishop Leipzig, for completing the arduous task of typing thousands of excerpts from newspapers, books, and sometimes mere conversations, focusing on individual parishes. Dorothy collated them, thus allowing future historians like this writer to retrieve rather quickly historical information about Holy Rosary without laboriously reading a hundred years of newspapers. We also owe a debt of gratitude to Archdiocesan Archivist Mary Grant who maintains all those records and exhumed and photocopied for us hundreds of documents used in the preparation of this book.

FAITHFULNESS TO THE TRUTH OF HISTORY

Faithfulness to the truth of history involves far more than a research, however patient and scrupulous, into special facts. Such facts may be detailed with the most minute exactness, and yet the narrative, taken as a whole, may be unmeaning or untrue. The narrator must seek to imbue himself with the life and spirit of the time. He must study events in their bearings near and remote; in the character, habits, and manners of those who took part in them. He must himself be, as it were, a sharer or a spectator of the action he describes. Francis Parkman (1823–1893).

I have here recorded, meaningfully and truthfully I hope, deeds which took place during 100 years of time, all the while recognizing that God Himself is outside of time – and our own lives are intended to transcend the very limits of time. God's goodness in this aspect of time is evident in the parish we have today as this centenary comes to a close. Our parish is a miracle in this almost spiritually-arid land of Oregon, and the spirituality that abounds within the parish makes no small contribution to this miracle. Insightful parishioners, especially that saintly segment who attend daily Mass – and they number in the hundreds – recognize the sad Catholic situation in this country, and they pray with fervency that a flowering of sanctity may one day engulf the Church in the United States. They would agree with Francois Mauriac's insightful commentary on the priesthood,[240] because it is so apropos for the parish we have in 1994:

> *"People say there is a scarcity of priests. In truth, what an adorable mystery it is that there are still any priests. They no longer have any human advantage. Celibacy, solitude, hatred very often, derision and, above all, the indifference of a world in which there seems no longer room for them – such is the portion they have chosen. People would laugh at their virtue if they believed in it, but they do not. A thousand voices accuse those who fall. As for the others, the greater number, no one is surprised to see them toiling without any sort of recognition, without appreciable salary, bending over the bodies of the dying or ambling about the parish schoolyards."*

Such priests, with their great Dominican spirituality, have been a tradition at Holy Rosary throughout these 100 years, assuredly fulfilling Archbishop Gross's greatest expectations, as well as Christ's injunction to feed His lambs and sheep. On the topic of fewer priests, Holy Rosary parishioners (in agreement with devout Catholics everywhere) would prefer two priests of deep spirituality and doctrinal soundness over 10 with an indifferent presence,[241] for the parishioners actually experience and perceive the presence of the Holy Spirit where spirituality abounds, bringing with it as it does peace of mind, heart, and soul; continually reminding us of our true identity, who we really are, what our goals in life should be, and what we should be doing with our lives to attain those goals.

These same parishioners also realize that the overall effect is doubly beneficial in that their own spirituality and generosity impacts the lives of the priests dedicated to serve them, as well as stray Catholics and non-Catholics who enter the hallowed halls of Holy Rosary Church for the first time and later leave with a sense of the sacred not experienced in many years.

This balance of spirituality and generosity on both sides has as its fulcrum the Universal Shepherd, the Vicar of Christ, who today suffers more from the slings and arrows of outrageous

"Catholics" than he does from the traditional enemies of Catholicism outside the Church. Thus, the parishioners' and priests' prayers for the Pope are heartfelt, and when the Peter's Pence collection is taken, Holy Rosary parishioners' generosity is second to none in the archdiocese. In a recent collection, for example, they contributed 10% of the total archdiocesan collection, yet Holy Rosary is but one of 129 parishes in the archdiocese. Holy Rosarians have also participated with generosity in the annual "Pennies for the Poor" campaign conducted by the Down Town Chapel on Burnside Street. A solicitation article in the December 11, 1994 church bulletin stated that "Last year [1993], Holy Rosary led the city parishes in this campaign, which helps the city's homeless." Additionally, in 1992, they gave generously to the archdiocesan priests' retirement campaign, which established a fund to built a new retirement center for the priests of the archdiocese in Beaverton on the grounds owned by the Sisters of St. Mary of Oregon.

This spirit of generosity is not a recent phenomenon, but has a long history. For example, a report in the archdiocesan archives for the Easter Collection of 1921 (for seminary students and the purchase of a seminary site) showed Holy Rosary parishioners gave $209 (a princely sum in those days) and ranked sixth among all of the parishes in the state, outdone only by much larger parishes such as Cathedral, The Madeleine, Immaculate Heart, and the Salem, Oregon City, and Albany parishes. This is, admittedly, a bit of braggadocio, but it is considered justifiable for the purpose of setting the "cheerful giver" record straight, as well as making youngsters who read this book in later years aware of the generosity of those who preceded them, a generosity they ought to emulate in gratitude for the parish they have.

A TREASURE OF PROMISES KEPT

A thing of beauty is a joy forever, said the wise man. The silver thread linking all of us to Holy Rosary's astonishingly rich and moving record is fidelity's courage and spirituality, manifest in its priests, nuns and laity. The story of their grace under pressure cannot be captured in mere words. The generosity Divine Providence has bestowed on this parish will become fully visible only in Heaven, for Holy Rosary Church is more than a story of this parish, its priests, its religious, and its laity – past and present.

It is a miracle. This house of God, combined with these living stones, aided by our Lord, who promised to be with us all the days of our lives, is truly an earthly treasure. All treasures must be shared in order to be defined as treasures in the truest sense (as the Blessed Virgin quickly shared the Greatest Treasure of all when She said "Thy will be done."); therefore, as we publish this book, we offer praise and thanksgiving in humble gratitude, to the living and the dead, but especially to the Blessed Trinity and Mary, Queen of the Most Holy Rosary, at the close of this centenary. We pray for fidelity within ourselves, and within those who follow – to carry on this tradition – and say, at the end of this one hundred years, with one voice: Thanks for these memories, and for this treasure of promises kept.

We have reached the endpoint of this first century of Holy Rosary's existence. But it is no more a point of arrival than it is a point of departure as we face the coming decades, now just below the horizon.

ABOUT OUR OBLIGATIONS FOR THE FUTURE?

Only from history will you learn to place value on those goods from which habit and unchallenged possession so easily deprive our gratitude; priceless, precious goods, upon which the blood of the best and most noble clings, goods which had to be won by the great effort of so many generations! And who among you, in whom a bright spirit is wedded to a feeling heart, could bear this high obligation in mind, without a silent wish being aroused in him to pay that debt to coming generations, which he can no longer discharge to those past? A noble desire must light in us to also make a contribution out of our means to this rich bequest of truth, morality, and freedom which we received from the world past, and which we must surrender once more, richly enlarged, to the world to come; and, in this eternal chain which winds itself through all human generations, to make firm our ephemeral existence. However different the destinies may be which await you in society, all of you can contribute something to this.

Friedrich Schiller[259]

Home Schooling Support Group teaches boys and girls about the liturgy, sacred vessels and vestments, etc.

From left to right:
Patty Defilippis, unknown, Rose Gebken, Anna Freiling, Katie Milton, Mary Helen Owen, Cecilia Freiling, Eve Owen and Maria Glavin

Father Lawrence E. Banfield, O.P. on the front lines of protest against abortion, Portland, OR c.1991

First Holy Communion June 5, 1994

(left to right):
Front row:
Paul Ryan, Mark Turina, Jonathon Hickel, Joseph Poulin, Joseph Reilly, Aleksandor Nagy-Deak, and Christopher DeNicola.

Second row:
Mary Helen Owen, Katie Hoesly, Victoria Austin, Margaret Bailey, Anna Joshu, Jessica North, Jackie Koch and Elizabeth Raetz.

Back row:
Emily Endres, Elizabeth Rose Wade, Father Edmund K. Ryan, O.P. (celebrant), Rose Gebken, Christopher Webb, Father Anthony Patalano, O.P. (Pastor and Prior), Aaryn Lexow, Eyle Moore, Esther Sims and Lisa Huibregste. Missing from photo: Matthew Gibson.

First Holy Communion May 16, 1993

(left to right):
First row:
Nathaniel Carlson, Joseph James, Christopher Toffler, Derek Foss, Nathaniel Alles, Andrew Joshu, and Paul Clowes.

Second row:
Karina Wehrman, Catherine Hiekel, Kristina Ford, Martha Bailey, Erin Fleenor and Allison Vasquez.

Third row:
Rosemary Tyson, Rose Marie Weinhart, Kathleen Rooney, Elizabeth Laskowski, Nicole Kluthe, Katherine Milton and Joanna Hefflinger.

Top row:
Jeannie Roura, Lucinda McVicker, Natalie Leathers, Father Anthony Patalano, O.P. (celebrant) and Rebecca James.

Bishop Francis Leipzig, after he retired as Bishop of Baker, Oregon took up residence at Calaroga Terrace and became a daily communicant and member of the Holy Rosary Holy Name Society. He celebrated the 25th anniversary of his consecration as a bishop, at Holy Rosary, in September 1975.

From left to right: Rev. John E. Larkin, Rev. Joseph M. Agius, O.P., Rev. Charles T. Grant, Right Rev. Anselm Galvin, OSB, Most Rev. Thomas J. Connolly, Bishop of Baker, Mr. Richard Hedlund, Most Rev. Edward Daniel Howard, retired Archbishop of Portland, Most Rev. Leipzig, Most Rev. Robert J. Dwyer, Archbishop of Portland, Rev. Paul A. Duffner, O.P., Pastor of Holy Rosary, Rev. Msgr. Edmund G. Van der Zanden, Rev. Joseph M. McMahon, Right Rev. Bernard McVeigh, OCSO and Rev. Thomas Brockhaus.

NOTES TO THE TEXT

240 From his book *Holy Thursday – an intimate remembrance*, Sophia Institute Press, Box 5284, Manchester, NH 03108, 1992.

241 One priest who read this prior to publication commented that you would find fewer than five (out of 130) in the entire Province who might be considered "indifferent."

242 Taken from page 211, the *Universal Almanac*, 1994, by John W. Wright, Universal Press Syndicate Company, 4900 Main Street, Kansas City, Missouri 64112.

243 Page 158, *Our American Catholic Heritage*, Albert J. Nevins, M.M., Our Sunday Visitor, Inc., Huntington, Ind. 46750, 1972.

244 It must be said that all of Father Vogt's sermons are inspiring.

245 Page D1, May 22, 1993.

246 May 14 & 28, 1993 editions.

247 The Code of Canon Law (canon 710) describes the secular institute as: "an institute of consecrated life in which the Christian faithful living in the world strive for the perfection of charity and work for the sanctification of the world especially from within."

248 From the poem *Recovery* by Roxie Lusk Smith, page 34 of *Threads of Gold*, Salesian Missions, 2 Lefevre Land, New Rochelle, N.Y. 10801.

249 The origin would never be known with certitude; speculation would have to suffice.

250 The November 12, 1993 *Catholic Sentinel* reported on page 1 that Aday was employed by Atlas Electrical of Milwaukie, Oregon.

251 On page B5 of the 11/15/93 *Oregonian*, Reporter Erin Hoover Schraw wrote: "He [Aday] remains in serious condition in the burn unit at Emanuel Hospital & Health Center, but is up and walking, reported a nursing supervisor."

252 Choir Director Dean Applegate and Richard Bond had rebuilt this organ as a labor of love according to Father Gerald A. Buckley (in a letter dated August 24, 1992 sent to this author – on file at Holy Rosary).

253 The *Catholic Sentinel* of February 2, 1928 reported: "A donation of a new organ for the Church has been announced. The Church has been requested that the name of the donor be withheld." Mr. Edward J. VanCoelen, age 91, a former parishioner, in 1993 said this was the third organ at Holy Rosary.

254 Reporter Judy McDermott related most of this information reporting on an interview with Cynthia Rampone, the church organist, in the November 13, 1993 edition of *The Oregonian*.

255 Letter to Joseph F. Foye from Father Buckley, dated August 24, 1992, on file in the archives at Holy Rosary Parish.

256 Ken died of cancer on June 20, 1986.

257 The font has its origin in the mezuza on the doorposts of Orthodox Jewish homes. When occupants enter the home they touch it to remind themselves to act in accordance with God's laws while within the home; and, on leaving, touch it again to remind them to act that way in their dealings with others. (Deut. 6:4-9)

258 The Very Reverend Edmund Kenneth Ryan, O.P., pastor/prior from 1983-1991.

259 Taken from page 3, *Fidelio – Journal of Poetry, Science, and Statecraft*, Fall 1993, Schiller Institute, Inc., P.O. Box 20244, Washington, D.C. 20041-0244.

HOLY ROSARY CELEBRATES ITS JUBILEE YEAR
THE CHURCH IS FINALLY DEDICATED

"Ye shall hallow the fiftieth year, and proclaim liberty throughout all the land unto all the inhabitants thereof: it shall be a jubilee unto you." (Leviticus 25:10)

Holy Rosary's priests and parishioners celebrated the centennial with prayers, pilgrimages, a barbecue and a formal dinner. Because the church was still under restoration from the fire, its dedication could not take place until 1996, exactly 102 years after it had been opened and blessed by Archbishop Gross.

FATHER BART RELATES THE EVENTS SURROUNDING
PARISHIONERS' PILGRIMAGE TO THE LANDS OF ST. DOMINIC

Rev. Bartholomew de la Torre, O.P., a highly respected priest and a man of great learning, served as associate pastor at Holy Rosary from 1992 to 1995. Father Bart was born January 29, 1940, in Los Angeles, California of Mexican parents. After three years of college he entered the Order of Preachers (AKA the Dominicans after their founder St. Dominic). Once in the Order, he earned his bachelor's degree, majoring in Thomistic Philosophy. This was followed by an M.A. in Thomistic Philosophy, an M. Div. and a second M.A. in Thomistic Philosophy, all from the Dominican School of Philosophy and Theology, which is a founding member of the Graduate Theological Union in Berkeley, California.

Ordained a priest on June 16, 1967, he then spent a year as a hospital chaplain in Houston, Texas, where he received his Licentiate in Medieval Studies from the Pontifical Institute of Medieval Studies in Toronto, Canada. Thereafter he received a Ph.D. in medieval studies from the University of Toronto, majoring in the history of theology and minoring both in the history of philosophy and in Latin paleography, the science of deciphering ancient shorthand, reading ancient writing and editing medieval manuscripts.

dedication of Holy Rosary
urch – January 28 1996

Upon receiving his doctorate, Father Bart was for a year associate pastor in Benicia, slightly north of Oakland, California. Father next spent a year as part of the Leonine Commission in Grottaferrata, Italy, preparing medieval manuscripts of the writings of his fellow Dominican priest, St. Thomas Aquinas, for publication. This was followed by eight years at the same task as a staff member both of the Leonine Commission and of the Catholic University of America in Washington, D.C. In 1989, he was made associate pastor at St. Dominic's Church in Los Angeles and served there until his assignment to Holy Rosary in 1992.

During his three happy decades of priestly life, Father has given retreats, taught religion in primary and secondary schools, and conducted adult education seminars on the teachings of St. Thomas Aquinas. He left Holy Rosary on September 5, 1995 to serve as chaplain at Thomas Aquinas College in Santa Paula, California.

The following letter Father Bart wrote to this author on October 30, 1994 sums up the pilgrimages parishioners participated in celebrating the Centenary.

Dear Joe,

In August I accepted the offer of an all-expense-paid pilgrimage to Venezuela. You may wonder how Venezuela can rank as an object of pilgrimages. On December 8, 1982, the Solemnity of the Immaculate Conception, people started to report visions of the Blessed Mother in the town of Betania (Spanish for Bethany, near Caracas) – these have continued ever since on feast days of Our Lady. The people went to the local bishop for guidance. He followed the procedures given to him by the Vatican, conducting an exhaustive investigation of many years' duration, interviewing over 700 witnesses. He concluded that the evidence was overwhelming and conclusive, that the apparitions were authentic, and he gave permission for daily Mass to be celebrated there.

Ten years later, on December 8, 1992, at Communion time, the large Mass Host was broken as usual by the priest and he consumed half of it. He was about to break the second half and put the pieces in with the small Hosts to be distributed to the people when he noticed that the second half was bleeding; so he saved it. The local bishop had the top medical lab in the country analyze the bleeding half and the lab reported it was definitely human blood. So the bishop put the Host with the now dried blood into a monstrance for adoration by the faithful.

A group that had heard about Betania (and the Eucharistic Body of Christ that had bled) needed a priest to accompany them, so they offered me a free trip. First, I investigated the matter and became satisfied it was all genuine. I also learned that the young people especially see Our Lady. So I invited the teens of the parish

Father Bartholomew de la Torre, O.P.

and four came along, two girls and two boys – plus a teenage girl from another parish. She and the two boys were the ones that saw Our Blessed Mother quite clearly – and just a few feet away – for quite a while. The girl was a fallen-away Catholic, but is now not only practicing her faith but also evangelizing her fellow public high school students. The two boys are not the type that easily believe in such things, but they were clearly stunned by what they saw, and I am continuing to affirm that momentum in the faith which Our Lady herself gave to them. A large contingent of Venezuelan pilgrims present also saw Our Lady.

Our group totaled 57 people and, of that number, 38 of us, including myself, saw various heavenly phenomena of a supernatural character. Additionally, two of our group experienced important healings: a deaf lady who had used hearing aids for years got her full hearing back and no longer needs those aids, and she is still radiant over this miracle; and a man who was in a wheelchair because of nerve deterioration and muscle atrophy, both conditions well-documented over a period of 10 years by his doctors, began walking – and his nerves and muscles grew back. When we returned home his doctors in the Portland area confirmed his. The doctors were amazed because the man had an advanced case of an incurable degenerative disease, and further because his blood tests showed that the destructive protein is still in his system but not producing its negative effects; quite the contrary, its negative effects have all been reversed.

In October [1994] I was off again on an all-expense-paid trip, this time for a 20-day pilgrimage as part of Holy Rosary's first centenary celebration. We six Dominican priests (four from Holy Rosary), and 36 lay people, 35 of whom were parishioners, visited the Lands of St. Dominic who, in 1216, founded our Order of Preachers, informally referred to as the Dominican Order. We went to Spain, France and Italy, sites where St. Dominican was born, worked, died and is buried. Our first stop, on October 4, was a Madrid monastery of Dominican Cloistered Sisters where we celebrated Mass in the Chapel containing Dominic's baptismal font. This font formerly reposed in Dominic's birthplace, Caleruega, Spain, where he was baptized. In the 1600s the font was taken to Spain's capital, Madrid, so that all the kings of Spain could be baptized in it – and all have, except the present king, who was born in exile in Greece during the Franco regime. But this king's children have all been baptized in St. Dominic's font, so the next king or queen will be one who was baptized in it. Fittingly, our pilgrimage began at the font where St. Dominic's sanctity and his spiritual journey through life also began.

We next traveled (in a comfortable modern bus) to Caleruega, St. Dominic's birthplace, a village populated by 16 cloistered Dominican sisters, nine Dominican priests, three teaching Dominican sisters and 80 lay villagers. It is situated off the beaten path in the area of old Castile dominated by agriculture and the raising of sheep, some 100 miles northeast of Madrid. The people are devoted to St. Dominic and to his mother, Bl. Jane of Aza, whom they refer to as St. Jane of Aza. The population remains small because the young move away to the bigger cities, a migratory practice that has diminished the pool of vocations; nevertheless, there are currently six priests in the Order who were born in this small hamlet.

When St. Dominic was canonized in 1233, a miraculous spring arose in the bedroom of his birth; a crypt of the basilica was built over it. Water from this crypt reposes in the baptismal fonts of all of the churches in the province (Burgos) and is identified as having been instrumental in bringing fertility to sterile couples – a great irony, because Dominic fought against the heresies of the Albigensians, who taught that getting married and having children was bad. I returned to Portland with four bottles of this miraculous water and have shared it with infertile friends and acquaintances, some of whom later had children.

We also visited the nearby tomb and monastery of Santo Domingo

de Silos (St. Dominic of Silos), which the resident monks made famous by recording and marketing their choral Gregorian chants. When Jane of Aza was pregnant with Dominic, she went to this tomb of St. Dominic of Silos, prayed for a healthy son and promised to name the boy Dominic were her prayers answered.

We next visited the beautiful and hoary 10th century cathedral in the neighboring village of Osma de Burgos, where St. Dominic spent many years as a diocesan priest prior to founding the Order of Preachers.

Caleruega, Sto. Domingo de Silos and Osma de Burgos are tiny specs in a vast, lonely, flat and fertile landscape. During our visit, the days were sunny and blue and the nights purple – punctured by many sparkling stars – altogether a perfect place for a spiritual retreat and contemplative quietude. Over the centuries, it must have produced many prayerful and saintly people like St. Dominic, his brother Bl. Mannes and his mother, Bl. Jane, wonderful people whose stories never made it into history books. We were all saddened to so soon depart such heavenly tranquillity but the bustle of Lourdes was beckoning.

We arrived there on October 6, the vigil of the Feast of the Rosary and the occasion of the French National Rosary Pilgrimage organized yearly for nearly one hundred years by the Dominican Friars (we planned our itinerary to participate). Some 40,000 Frenchmen and thousands of other nationalities participated as well. That night and the next we prayed the Rosary in an impressive candle-light procession. The next morning, on the Feast of the Rosary, we celebrated Mass at the outside Grotto where Our Lady appeared to Bernadette Soubirous and told her, "I am the Immaculate Conception," leaving the child, who had never heard those words before, confused; and it was precisely her confusion, and ignorance of the meaning of those words, which ultimately convinced her local pastor of her truthfulness when she repeated those words and gave the pastor a first-hand account of that wondrous event.

When I was 14, I was cured from 11 years of asthma by making a nine-day novena to Our Lady of Lourdes and Saint Bernadette, each day consuming a little water from the spring which welled up at the spot where the Blessed Virgin appeared. So this, my first visit to Lourdes, became for me a trip of thanksgiving 40 years after that cure.

A rather remarkable phenomenon occurred after I and many other pilgrims bathed in the cold spring water at Lourdes; when we got out of the spring and donned our clothing we were completely dry, without benefit of towels. Everyone experiences this constant miracle, which happens to be ultimately practical. Thousands of towels would be required for the bathers to dry themselves, limiting the number of pilgrims who would be able to wash in these waters every day. As you know the waters have effected many cures, but I'm not aware of any cures among our group.

Continuing our journey, we passed some days in southern France – at Toulouse, Fanjeaux, Prouilhe, Montreal and Carcassone – where St. Dominic spent many years preaching to the Albigensian heretics, also known as Catharists. Carcassone is one of the few medieval cities in Europe which has its surrounding wall intact. One is reminded of Old Quebec City, but the buildings inside Carcassone are 300 years older. They are very charming. Our hotel was within the walls and the two nights I spent there I felt magically transported to a distant past – like Mark Twain's Connecticut Yankee in King Arthur's Court.

I celebrated Mass at the Cathedral of St. Sernin (French for Saturninus) in Toulouse. I have a deceased uncle named Saturnino and a young cousin Saturnina, so I was grateful for the opportunity to pray for them in this cathedral – the most beautiful of Romanesque church structures – where St. Saturninus is buried.

We then went to the town of St. Maximin where in a Dominican church are kept the mortal remains of St. Mary Magdalene who, after our Lady, is the patroness of the Order of Preachers. I was moved to pray devoutly at the tomb of this great saint who had spent time with Jesus himself, as recorded in the pages of the New Testament.

We went on to the Italian Riviera, where we met with Italian relatives of three members of our group and thence to Bologna, where we were privileged to celebrate a sung Mass in honor of St. Dominic at his tomb. From there we traveled to Florence, where many Dominicans exercised their ministry, including: Blessed Fra Angelico, with his heavenly paintings; Savonarola, burnt at the stake by a few outsiders but loved by the Florentines to this day (his four-year rule marked the only period no one was executed in the Florentine republic – a record brought to a close by his own execution); St. Antoninus, after whom the Czech composer Antonin Dvorak and U.S. Supreme Court Justice Antonin Scalia were named. St. Antoninus' incorrupt body lies under the altar where we celebrated Mass in the Dominican church of San Marco. We also celebrated Mass nearby at the home of St. Catherine of Siena.

From Florence we drove to Assisi, where St. Francis and St. Dominic met, and we said Mass in the crypt of the great Basilica of St. Francis, right at his tomb. I remembered especially the eternal happiness of my recently deceased aunt Frances. Then we went to the Church of St. Claire and to her tomb. There I prayed for my departed Aunt Clara, who was my mom's older sister and the wife of my aforementioned Uncle Saturnino, and for those on my mom's side of the family.

From Assisi we boarded the bus for Rome where, at his Wednesday public audience in St. Peter's Square, the Pope came within a few feet of our group. He spoke, in a dozen languages, on the need of devotion within the home, and on the need for families to promote vocations to the priesthood and sisterhood. He asked young people to pray the Rosary to discern their vocations.

Members of Holy Rosary's Dominican Laity at Madrid, Spain, on "Lands of Dominic" Tour (October 1994)
1st row: Lori Lorenzo, Mary Lorenzo, Mary Walsh.
2nd row: Frances James, Theresa Lorentz, Dick Cloud, Cecelia Hoesly, Mary VanBuren and Mary Vaetz.
3rd row: Mary Fazio, Rosemary Young, Pat Jordan and Randy Young.

In all the sacred places of our pilgrimage, I prayed for you and all those dear to both you and me, but I did so especially in front of the main altar of St. Peter's Basilica where are kept the mortal remains of St. Peter, because he is the Rock upon which our faith and Church have been built by Jesus Himself.

In Rome, I also had time to search out and visit for the first time the tombs of two special saints, Monica and Robert. At Monica's tomb I offered prayers for my own dear sister Monica and her boys, and for all mothers who worry about the eternal salvation of their children. It was through the 18 years of prayers and tears of St. Monica that her son was converted and became the great St. Augustine. Consequently, the Christian faithful hold Monica dear as the patron saint of mothers with worrisome children. At this holy spot I also offered a prayer of thanksgiving on behalf of all mothers of my acquaintance who are blessed with practicing Catholic children.

At St. Robert's tomb my thoughts and prayers turned to so many relatives, including my deceased paternal grandfather, and friends named after this great saint. Finding the tomb involved some difficulty as I reached it by walking through some winding, narrow streets near the Pantheon in Rome. There at his tomb, I prayed for my grandfather, my uncle, and all my cousins and friends named Robert.

Archbishop Thomas Cajetan Kelly, O.P. (Archbishop of Louisville, Kentucky) and Deacon Brother Xavier Lavagetto– Dedication of Holy Rosary
January 28, 1996

Finally, on Sunday morning, October 23, we flew from Rome to New York and Seattle, landing in Portland 20 hours later, a tired but happy crew with many bright memories and encouragements to be better Christians. All the wonderful and holy sights and activities we had engaged in for the previous 20 intense days, through three countries, amounted to a real retreat on the road, and after all my trips to bury dear relatives, followed by a beautiful wedding and intense pilgrimages, I am emotionally worn out.

Thank you, Joe, for your mailing of your letter published in Fidelity. Congratulations on being so pro-active regarding the Faith and the unborn and our parishioner Bill Witt [who was running for Congress – and lost – on a pro-life platform].

Yours sincerely,

(signed)
Fr. Bart, O.P.

CHURCH IS FINALLY DEDICATED
JANUARY 28, 1996

The church was blessed by Archbishop Gross on January 28, 1894. It was not "dedicated" as reported by the press – because it was considered a temporary structure at the time. And it could not be dedicated on the 100th anniversary because of the fire. So, on January 28, 1996 Archbishop Thomas Cajeton Kelly, O.P., Archbishop of Louisville, Kentucky performed the ceremony for a happy throng of about 300 Holy Rosarians. See Appendix 9 for a copy of the entire dedication booklet.

A QUICK GLIMPSE INTO THE GRANDEUR OF THE NEXT CENTURY AT HOLY ROSARY

His juggernaut of expansion and improvement would tax the time, treasure, and talent of even the most ardent parishioners in the years 1997-1999, as their tireless pastor, Rev. Anthony G. Cordeiro, O.P., guided them toward their rendezvous with the Millennium. See Appendix 10.

STAINED GLASS WINDOWS
HOLY ROSARY
Artist: Robert Hill, Hill Associates, Snoqualmie, Washington
Photos by Mark Barnes

Our Lady, Patroness of the Dominican Order.
(This window is over the front entrance to the church.)

Sanctuary Tryptic (with Crucifix): Top middle small window, depicting God the Father with God the Holy Spirit. Left large window, Saint Dominic. Right large window, St. Catherine of Siena.

Choir loft (South West). Left large window, St. Thomas Aquinas. Right Large window, St. Pius V.

Choir loft (North West). Left large window, St. Louis Marie Grignon de Montfort. Right large window, Blessed Alan de la Roche.

The Annunciation. *(1st Joyful Mystery).*

The Visitation. *(2nd Joyful Mystery).*

The Nativity. *(3rd Joyful Mystery).*

The Presentation in the Temple. *(4th Joyful Mystery).*

The Finding of Jesus in the Temple. *(5th Joyful Mystery)*

Left, The Agony in the Garden. *(1st Sorrowful Mystery)*
Right, The Scourging at the Pillar. *(2nd Sorrowful Mystery)*

Left, The Crowning with Thorns. *(3rd Sorrowful Mystery)*
Right, Jesus Meets His Mother. *(4th Sorrowful Mystery)*

Left, The Crucifixion. *(5th Sorrowful Mystery)*
Right, The Resurrection. *(1st Glorious Mystery)*

Left, The Ascension. *(2nd Glorious Mystery)*
Right, The Descent of the Holy Spirit. *(3rd Glorious Mystery)*

(Left) The Assumption. (4th Glorious Mystery)
(Right) The Coronation. (5th Glorious Mystery)

Coat of arms of Pope John Paul II (North West).

Coat of arms of the Dominican Order (South East).

Coat of arms of Pope Leo XIII (North East).

Coat of arms of the Province of the Most Holy Name of Jesus.
(aka Western Dominican Province) (South West).

APPENDICES

VERITAS

APPENDIX 1

JMJ

Portland:
Sept. 28th 1885

V. Rev. F. S. Vilarasa:
Sup. Prov.   O.P.

V. Rev. Dear Father:

On arriving some months ago, in Portland, I found a large number of Catholic Germans. Nothing has ever been done for them and consequently, many are cold and neglectful of their religion; and many have almost completely lost the faith. I have had several meetings of the Catholic Germans, and they manifest a most excellent spirit. We have purchased a large piece of ground situated most favorably – and we have all the money to pay for it. My desire is to place this much needed work for the Germans in the hands of one of the religious orders: and I would feel highly gratified if the zealous sons of St. Dominic will accept of this position in Portland. **You may perhaps be surprised that I do not introduce the Rev. Redemptorist Fathers for this work, since I myself am a Redemptorist. My reason is that Portland is my place of residence and were I to introduce the Redemptorists here, it might cause unpleasant consequences. I will probably at some other time offer my confreres – a foundation in some part of my diocese distant from Portland.** (emphasis added). If your reverence can accept of the foundation which I now offer, I would be much pleased if you can send on a German Father immediately. For he can gather in our Germans in the large and handsome basement of our Cathedral and hold the regular Sunday Services for the Germans there – thus forming the German congregation; begin to bring back the many stray ones; and go to the work of erecting a modest church on the property which we have already secured and on which there is no debt. I hope that the Order of St. Dominic which has been so highly favored by the Sacred Mother of God will come and by their labors spread in my diocese the great love and devotion to the Queen of Heaven and Earth.

Yours Most Truly
in Christ Jesus –

+W.H. Gross, C.S.S.R.
Archbp. el. Oregon

APPENDIX 2

DOMINICAN PRIESTS AND BROTHERS WHO SERVED AT HOLY ROSARY CHURCH AND PRIORY, PORTLAND, OREGON

*Prior/Rector/Pastor (w/assistants/associates)   **Missionaries   ***In residence.

1894	*Very Rev. James Benedict McGovern, Fathers Aerden and Riley.
1895	*Father J. B. McGovern, Father Thomas L. Breen, Father O'Connor, Father Rourke.
1896	*Father Patrick Fitzsimons, Thomas L. Breen, J.B. O'Connor, E.C. Warren, H.S. Shaw.
1897	*Father Patrick Fitzsimons, Thomas L. Breen, Newell, E.C. Warren, H.S. Shaw.
1898	*Thomas L. Breen, Newell, Warren, H. S. Shaw
1899	*Thomas L. Breen, Newell, Warren, H. S. Shaw
1900	*Very Rev. Thomas J. Henry, Father O'Brien, Warren, H. S. Shaw
1901	*Very Rev. Thomas J. Henry, Father O'Brien, Warren, H. S. Shaw
1902	*Very Rev. Thomas J. Henry, Father O'Brien, Warren, H. S. Shaw
1903	*Very Rev. Albert .Sadoc Lawler, O'Brien, Warren, H. S. Shaw
1904	*Very Rev. Albert .Sadoc Lawler, H. S. Shaw, O'Brien, Lamb
1908	*Very Rev. Albert .Sadoc Lawler, H. S. Shaw, O'Brien, Lamb, Hunt.
1909	*Very Rev. Albert Sadoc Lawler, H. S. Shaw, O'Brien, Lamb, Schmidt, Laurence.
1910	*Very Rev. Albert Sadoc Lawler, H. S.Shaw, O'Brien, Lamb, Schmidt, Lewis
1911	*Very Rev. Albert Sadoc Lawler, H. S.Shaw, O'Brien, Lamb, Schmidt, Corcoran
1912	*Very Rev. Henry Humbert Kelly, O'Brien, Skelly, Lamb, Sturla
1913	*Very Rev. Henry Humbert Kelly, O'Brien, Skelly, Lamb, Sturla
1914	*Very Rev. Henry Humbert Kelly, O'Brien, Lawler, Clancy, Clyne and Sturla
1915	*Very Rev. Edwin Stanislaus Olsen, Lawler, Riley, Lamarre, Lewis, Chamberlain
1916	*Very Rev. Edwin Stanislaus Olsen, A.S. Lawler, Alphonsus Riley, A. Lamarre, A.S. Chamberlain, R.A. Lewis.
1917	*Very Rev. Edwin Stanislaus Olsen, A.S. Lawler, Alphonsus Riley, A. Lamarre, A.S. Chamberlain, R.A. Lewis.
1918	*Very Rev. Edwin .Stanislaus Olsen, A.S. Lawler, Alphonsus Riley, A. Lamarre, A.S. Chamberlain, R.A. Lewis.
1919	*Very Rev. Edwin Stanislaus Olsen, A.S. Lawler, Alphonsus Riley, Skelly, E.B. Kenny, R.A. Lewis
1920	*Very Rev. Edwin Stanislaus Olsen, Peter A. Riley, A. S. Lawler, A.M. Skelly, Joseph R. Cocoran, E.B. Kenny.
1921	*Very Rev. Edwin Stanislaus Olsen, Peter A. Riley, A. S. Lawler, A.M. Skelly, Joseph R. Corcoran, E. B. Kenny
1922	*Very Rev. Edwin Stanislaus Olsen, Peter A. Riley, A. S. Lawler, A.M. Skelly, Joseph R. Corcoran, E. B. Kenny
1923	*Very Rev. Arthur Townley, Peter A. Riley, A.S. Lawler, A.M. Skelly, Joseph R. Corcoran, E. B. Kenny
1924	*Very Rev. Arthur Townley, Peter A. Riley, A.M. Skelly, E. B. Kenny.
1925	*Very Rev. Arthur Townley, E. S. Olsen, A.M. Skelly, A.S. Chamberlain, A.A. Healy, T.S. Connelly.
1926	*Very Rev. F.A. Pope, L.A. Nasselli, A.M. Skelly.
1927	*Very Rev. F.A. Pope, L.A. Nasseli, A.M. Skelly
1928	*Very Rev. F.A. Pope, A. Riley, R.C. Kane, J.A. McKeon, M.S. Bohan, D. Mueller.
1929	*Very Rev. F.A. Pope, R. C. Kane, J.A. McKeon, Wm. McClory, W.S. McDermott, E.G. McMullan
1930	*Very Rev. F.A. Pope, R. C. Kane, J.A. McKeon, Wm. McClory, W.S. McDermott, E.G. McMullan
1931	*Very Rev. W.S. McDermott, J.A. McKeon, William McClory, J.W. Ryan, E.S. Olsen.
1932	*Very Rev. T.S. Connelly, R.L. Lindsay, F.B. Clyne, Aquinas McDonnell, P.M. Purcell, E. S. Olsen.
1933	*Very Rev. T.S. Connelly, Leo T. Halloran, F. B. Clyne, Aquinas McDonnell, P.M. Purcell, E.S. Olsen. Brother John Barry.
1934	*Very Rev. T.S. Connelly, F.B. Clyne, J.A. McKeon, A.L. Hofste, A.S.Chamberlain. Brother John Barry.
1935	*Very Rev. T.S. Connelly, G.M. Knauff, J.A. McKeon, Leo T. Halloran. Brothers John Barry and Martin Allen.
1936	*Rev. Edward G. McMullan, L. Robert Lindsay, William Feehan. Brothers John Barry and Martin Allen.
1937	*Rev. Edward G. McMullan, V.H. Palmer, L. Robert Lindsay, William Feehan.
1938	*Rev. Edward G. McMullan, L. Robert Lindsay, William Feehan.
1939	*Rev. Edward G. McMullan, L. Robert Lindsay, William S. McDermott.
1940	*Rev. Edward G. McMullan, L. Robert Lindsay, William S. McDermott, John W. Ryan.
1941	*Rev. Edward G. McMullan, L. Robert Lindsay, William S. McDermott, John W. Ryan.

1942	*Rev. Edward G. McMullan, J.W. McClory, William McDermott, John W. Ryan.
1943	*Rev. Joseph M. Agius, J.W. McClory, William S. McDermott.
1944	*Rev. Joseph M. Agius, Daniel J. Wolf, Lawrence E. Banfield, William S. McDermott.
1945	*Rev. Joseph M. Agius, Patrick B. Condon, Thomas A. Feucht, William S. McDermott, James L. Mitchell, Lawrence Banfield.
1946	*Rev. Joseph M. Agius, Patrick B. Condon, Thomas A. Feucht, James L. Mitchell, Lawrence E. Banfield.
1947	*Rev. Joseph M. Agius, Joseph P. Sanguinitti, Thomas A. Feucht, William McClory, Lawrence E. Banfield.
1948	*Rev. Thomas S. Connelly, Patrick M. Purcell, Thomas A. Feucht, **William McClory, Lawrence E. Banfield, Patrick R. Sullivan. ***John A. Myhan.
1949	*Rev. Thomas A. Feucht, Patrick R. Sullivan, Dominic Hoffman, **Patrick Purcell, and ***John A. Myhan
1950	*Rev. Thomas A. Feucht, A.A. Healy, L. P. Cross, and ***John A. Myhan.
1951	*Rev. Thomas A. Feucht, A.A. Healy, M. M. Donnelly and ***John A. Myhan.
1952	*Rev. Thomas A. Feucht, A.A. Healy, M. M. Donnelly and ***John A. Myhan and Joseph P. Sanguinetti.
1953	*Rev. Thomas A. Feucht, A.A. Healy,. M. M. Donnelly. ***John A. Myhan and Joseph P. Sanguinetti.
1954	*Rev. Thomas A. Feucht, A.A. Healy,. M. M. Donnelly. ***John A. Myhan and Joseph P. Sanguinetti.
1955	*Rev. Thomas A. Feucht, A.A. Healy,. M. M. Donnelly. ***B. F. O'Brien and Joseph P. Sanguinetti.
1956	*Rev. Thomas A. Feucht, A.A. Healy,. J. S. Jenner. ***B. F. O'Brien and Joseph P. Sanguinetti.
1957	*Rev. Thomas A. Feucht, A.A. Healy,. P. B. Condon. **Joseph Sanguinetti.
1958	*Rev. Thomas A. Feucht, A.A. Healy. **L. Banfield.
1959	*Rev. William A. Norton, Francis U. Bates. **L. Banfield.
1960	*Rev. William A. Norton, Gabriel Knauff, Damien Girard. **L. Banfield.
1961	*Rev. William A. Norton, Gabriel Knauff, William Curtin. **L. Banfield. ***Martin Donnelly.
1962	*Rev. William A. Norton, Gabriel Knauff, William Curtin. **L. Banfield. ***John A. Myhan.
1963	*Rev. William A. Norton, Cyril E. Burns, William Curtin. ***John Fearon
1964	*Rev. William A. Norton, Cyril E. Burns, William Curtin.
1965	*Rev. Francis F. Cassidy, William B. Curtin, Jerome Schmitt.
1966	*Rev. Francis F. Cassidy, Jerome Schmitt. ***Joseph Agius, Kiernan Healy, John M. Giannini.
1967	*Rev. Francis F. Cassidy, Florent Martin Gutierrez. *** Kiernan Healy, John M. Giannini.
1968	*Rev. Francis F. Cassidy, Florent Martin Gutierrez. *** Kiernan Healy, John M. Giannini. Joseph Agius.
1969	*Rev. Francis F. Cassidy, Florent Martin Gutierrez. *** Kiernan Healy, Frank B. Wilks, Joseph Agius.
1970	*Rev. Francis F. Cassidy, Florent Martin Gutierrez *** Kiernan Healy, William Curtin, Joseph Agius.
1971	*Rev. Joseph M. Agius, Florent G. Martin Gutierrez. *** Kiernan Healy, William Curtin, William McClory.
1972	*Rev. Joseph M. Agius, Florent G. Martin Gutierrez. *** Kiernan Healy, William Curtin, William McClory.
1973	*Rev. Bernard Arnheim, Florent G. Martin Gutierrez. *** Kiernan Healy, William Curtin, Joseph M. Agius
1974	*Rev. Bernard Arnheim, Albert G. Pinheiro. *** Gordon Harvey, William Curtin, Joseph M. Agius.
1975	*Rev. T.A. Feucht, C.V. McEachen. ***Gordon Harvey, Joseph Agius.
1976	*Rev. P. A. Duffner, C.V. McEachen, D. F. Hoffman. ***Joseph Agius and T.A. Feucht.
1977	*Rev. P. A. Duffner, C.V. McEachen, D. F. Hoffman. ***Joseph Agius and T.A. Feucht.
1978	*Rev. P. A. Duffner, C.V. McEachen, D. F. Hoffman. ***Joseph Agius and T.A. Feucht.
1979	*Rev. P. A. Duffner, C.V. McEachen, D. F. Hoffman. ***Joseph Agius and T.A. Feucht.
1980	*Rev. Gerald Buckley, C.V. McEachen, D. F. Hoffman. ***Joseph Agius and T.A. Feucht.
1981	*Rev. Gerald Buckely, C.V. McEachen, D. F. Hoffman. ***Joseph Agius
1982	*Rev. Gerald Buckley, C.V. McEachen, Dominic de Domenico. ***Joseph Agius, Peter Miles.
1983	*Rev. Gerald Buckley, C.V. McEachen, Dominic de Domenico, Paul Duffner, ***Joseph Agius.
1984	*Rev. Edmund K. Ryan, C.V. McEachen, Dominic de Domenico, ***Paul Duffner.
1985	*Rev. Edmund K. Ryan, C.V. McEachen, Dominic de Domenico, Paul Duffner. *** Vincent A. Serpa.
1986	*Rev. Edmund K. Ryan, C.V. McEachen, Dominic de Domenico, Paul Duffner. *** Robert A. Davis.
1987	*Rev. Edmund K. Ryan, C.V. McEachen, Dominic de Domenico, Paul Duffner. *** Robert A. Davis, William Kent Burtner.
1988	*Rev. Edmund K. Ryan, C.V. McEachen, Dominic de Domenico, Paul Duffner. *** Gregory Anderson, William Kent Burtner.

1989	*Very Rev. Edmund K. Ryan, C.V. McEachen, Dominic de Domenico, Paul Duffner. *** Gregory Anderson, William Kent Burtner, Dominic Hoffman.
1990	*Very Rev. Edmund K. Ryan, C.V. McEachen, Leo Tubbs, Paul Duffner. ***Gregory Anderson, William Kent Burtner, Dominic Hoffman.
1991	*Very Rev. Anthony Patalano, Emmerich Vogt, Paul Duffner. ***C.V. McEachen, Dominic Hoffman
1992	*Very Rev. Anthony Patalano, Emmerich Vogt, Paul Duffner. ***C.V. McEachen, Dominic Hoffman
1993	*Very Rev. Anthony Patalano, Emmerich Vogt, Bartholomew de la Torre, Paul Duffner, ***C. V. McEachen, Dominic Hoffman.
1994	*Very Rev. Anthony Patalano, Emmerich Vogt, Bartholomew de la Torre, Gerald A. Buckley, Paul Duffner, ***Dominic Hoffman.

Taken from Catholic Directories of the Archdiocese on file in the library at the University of Portland, and kindly furnished by Catherine Unger, who advised there were no entries for Holy Rosary in the editions of the directories published up to 1916. Some corrections were made using authoritative sources. Names of assigned priests for the years 1894-1916 were obtained from a listing in a booklet celebrating Holy Rosary's Silver Jubilee. See Appendix 5 for the names of Dominican nuns who served at Holy Rosary School.

APPENDIX 3

VOCATIONS TO THE THIRD ORDER OF DOMINICANS HOLY ROSARY CHAPTER, PORTLAND, OREGON PROVINCE OF THE HOLY NAME

deceased as of 1 July 1995 (Note skip in sequence from 5 to 7)

Name	Reception	Profession		Name	Reception	Profession
			*45.	Sr. Mary Lynch	12/15/05	no entry
			*46.	Sr. Mary Damian Concannon	5/20/06	8/7/07
*1. George A. Manning	12/8/1895	2/2/1896	*47.	Sr. Mary Elizabeth Whipple	5/20/06	no entry
*2. Rose Louise Manning	12/8/1895	2/2/1896	*48.	Sr. Ann. Maria Alb. Campbell	10/24/06	2/8/08
*3. Catherine Taylor	1898 (sic)	2/6/1898	*49.	Sr. Frances Collins	2/7/07	1909 (sic)
*4. Catherine Correy	2/15/1899	2/28/1900	*50.	Sr. Mary Joseph Kenwick	8/17/07	10/11/08
*5. Rose Ryan	2/6/1898	no entry	*51.	Br. Joseph Smith	2/8/08	10/3/09
*7. Margaret O'Neill	6/4/1899	8/15/1900	*52.	Sr. Agnes Smith	2/8/08	10/3/09
*8. Mary Damian O'Dea	2/2/1901	2/2/1902	*53.	Sr. Catherine Ramsdell	5/10/08	no entry
*9. Flora Sharkey	8/23/01	no entry	*54.	Br. Lawrence Ramsdell	5/10/08	no entry
*10. Sr. Paul Metzler	9/13/01	9/15/02	*55.	Bernice Gorzelauzcick	7/22/08	no entry
*11. Sr. Albert Oblasser	11/10/01	5/10/03	*56.	Hannah McGlinchey	9/22/08	9/24/08
*12. Sr. Aloysius Stoltz	ll/10/01	12/7/02	*57.	Anna Hughes	10/11/08	no entry
*13. (fnu) Powers	12/8/95	12/8/96	*58.	Rev. Charles McAleer	11/8/08	no entry
*14. Mary Shelland	2/9/02	3/7/03	*59.	Catherine Vicich	1/11/09	2/13/10
*15. L. L. Smith	3/25/02	no entry	*60.	Mary Dunn	6/13/09	1910 (sic)
*16. Sr. Francis Wolf	6/8/02	8/10/03	*61.	Sarah Maria Sullivan	6/13/09	12/11/10
*17. Sr. Thomas Wynne	6/8/02	7/17/03	*62.	Timothy A. Sullivan	6/13/09	12/11/10
*18. Sr. Mary McLaughlin	10/6/02	10/4/03	*63.	Sr. Maria Alphonsa L. Ryan	7/10/09	11/13/10
*19. Sr. Veronica Healy	5/1/03	no entry	*64.	Sr. Mary Heufert	10/10/09	no entry
*20. Br. Damian Courtney	5/10/03	5/22/04	*65.	Sr. Bertrand McNamara	10/10/09	9/10/12
*21. Sr. Mary Dominic Welter	8/1/03	no entry	*66.	Sr. Rita McGrath	10/10/09	7/3/19
*22. Br. Dominic Mary O'Connor	8/4/03	8/14/04	*67.	Sr. Agnes Dolores McNamara	12/12/09	12/12/09
*23. Br. John James Buchanan	9/13/03	no entry	*68.	Elizabeth Christie	2/13/10	1911 (sic)
*24. Sr. Mary E. Walsh	10/11/03	10/11/04	*69.	Catherine Bedy	4/10/10	4/10/11
*25. Sr. Mary Francis Manning	no entry	4/9/05	*70.	Maria Anna Brousaur	11/22/10	no entry
*26. Br. Dominic Eder	no entry	12/11/04	*71.	Rev. L.A. Brosseau	12/15/12	no entry
*27. Sr. Rose Goram	11/8/03	5/2/05	*72.	Sr. Maria Ann Huguencon	1/8/11	no entry
*28. Sr. Mary Margaret Franks	11/8/03	5/2/05	*73.	Sr. Catherine Anna Gayron	3/18/11	10/30/11
*29. Sr. Bridget Damian Neeson	no entry	1/8/05	*74.	Sr. Maria Sienna Sypneski	3/24/11	no entry
*30. Sr. Mary Burrows	1/23/04	no entry	*75.	Sr. Maria Catherine Lehnfield	3/10/11	5/12/12
*31. Sr. Mary Margaret Leonard	2/13/04	12/10/05	*76.	Sr. Anna Maria Cordano	12/10/11	12/8/12
*32. Sr. Mary Elizabeth Brady	4/10/04	5/9/05	*77.	Sr. Maria Theresa Schneider	5/12/12	12/14/13
*33. Elizabeth O'Malley	6/3/04	10/14/12	*78.	Br. Donimic Henry Manning	10/13/12	10/19/13
*34. Mary Campbell	5/10/04	no entry	*79.	Sr. Agnes Mary Stryker	10/13/12	12/13/13
*35. Gertrude Klebina	7/10/04	8/15/05	*80.	Sr. Agnes Healy	11/12/12	1913 (sic)
*36. Anna Klebina	7/10/04	8/15/05	*81.	Sr. Mary Agnes Dunphy	11/9/13	no entry
*37. Sr. Elizabeth Burns	12/11/04	12/10/05	*82.	Mary Joseph Nally	3/8/14	no entry
*38. Sr. Mary Magdalene Curtin	2/12/05	no entry	*83.	Sr. Frances Teresa Saul	4/12/14	no entry
*39. Sr. Mary Mosier	2/12/05	no entry	*84.	Sr. Mary Anna Pacque	5/10/14	no entry
*40. Sr. Mary Joseph Fox	3/12/05	8/4/06	*85.	Sr. Louise Maria Lougel	10/11/14	9/12/15
*41. Sr. Mary Gertrude Lenzen	5/14/05	no entry	*86.	Sr. Mary Manion	11/8/14	no entry
*42. Sr. Mary Dominic Roth	10/8/05	no entry	*87.	Sr. Rose Cogan	3/19/15	4/9/16
*43. Sr. Mary O'Connor	12/8/05	12/26/07	*88.	Sr. Mary Veronica Galvin	3/11/15	no entry
*44. Sr. Joseph Butler	12/15/05	8/11/07	*89.	Sr. Ambrose Cushing	6/13/15	no entry

*90. Sr. Mary Ann Hughes	9/12/15	no entry
*91. Sr. Catherine Henrietta Williams		
	11/14/15	no entry
*92. Sr. Catherine Mary Maul	8/13/16	10/17/17
*93. Sr. Mary Assissi Hennessy	10/8/16	no entry
*94. Sr. Mary Agnes Shannon	10/8/16	10/2/21
*95. Sr. Faith Joan de Aza Boillot	8/19/17	no entry
*96. Sr. Mary Collins	11/11/17	no entry
*97. Sr. Mary Coyle	11/11/17	3/28/19
*98. Michael G. Munley	12/7/17	no entry
*99. Sr. Josephine Mary Hartmann	1/13/18	1/12/19
*100. Sr. Mary Florence Sullivan	2/20/18	4/30/19
*101. Sr. Mary La Vette	6/30/18	no entry
*102. Sr. Joan Albert Maginnis	12/30/18	no entry
*103. Sr. Ann Kennedy	3/28/19	2/26/20
*104. Br. Francis Edmund O'Regan	3/29/19	no entry
*105. Sr. Mary Catherine Atkinson	4/22/19	no entry
*106. Sr. Victoria Mary Atkinson	4/22/19	no entry
*107. Sr. Mary Catherine Ginty	5/2/19	no entry
*108. Sr. Mary A.E. Buckley	5/9/19	3/9/30
*109. Rev. J. Dominic Cunningham	5/18/19	no entry
*110. Sr. Mary Rita McGrath	7/3/19	see 66
*111. Sr. Margaret Hartman	11/7/19	4/14/20
*112. Sr. Maria Joanna Tracy	5/29/20	3/9/30
*113. Sr. Maria Magdalena Maloney	5/29/20	no entry
*114. Sr. Mary Boccarich	12/12/20	no entry
*115. Rev. Thomas Joseph Cantwell	1921 (sic)	1921 (sic)
116. Sr. Mary Mercedes Ryan	3/13/21	3/13/21
*117. Sr. Mary Agnes Nolan	no entry	10/2/21
118. Rev. Francis Swift	11/3/21	3/13/21
119. Sr. Broun (sic)	1/1/22	7/4/22
*120. Mary Maher	1927 (sic)	no entry
*121. Elizabeth Maher	1927 (sic)	no entry
*122. Sara Sheehy	1927 (sic)	3/9/30
*123. Anna Mayer	1927 (sic)	3/9/30
*124. Mary McCaffery	1927 (sic)	3/9/30
125. Brigid Ehlinger	1927 (sic)	no entry
*126. Elizabeth Fretland	6/4/27	3/9/30
127. Rose Mangin	9/27/29	no entry
*128. Mary Vanderbeck	9/27/29	1/1/31
*129. Catherine Gette	10/6/29	10/12/30
Number 130 not used		
*131. Sr. Catherine Rose Meagher	12/14/30	no entry
132. Rev. Caspar Salz	10/12/31	10/12/31
133. Elize Hopetzke	12/13/31	no entry
134. Lillian Watson	12/13/31	" "
*135. Aloysius Gambee	12/13/31	" "
*136. Mary Gambee	12/13/31	" "
*137. Rev. Thomas Tobin	3/25/32	" "
*138. Elizabeth Cocoran	12/10/34	1935 (sic)
*139. A. Duggan	12/10/34	1935 (sic)
*140. Mary Cushman	12/10/34	1935 (sic)

*141. Mary Walsh	3/8/36	6/39 (sic)
*142. Minnie Studly	6/14/36	12/20/38
*143. Mary Aloysia Techtman	6/14/36	4/16/44
*144. Lillian Hughes	1/17/37	12/20/38
*145. Margaret O'Keefe	11/30/37	11/30/37
*146. Elizabeth O'Keefe	11/30/37	11/30/37
(entries 145 and 146 with special permission from Provincial)		
*147. Emma Hoerner	2/20/38	5/20/39
*148. Mary Niedermeyer	2/20/38	5/20/39
*149. Margaret McParland	2/20/38	5/20/39
*150. Mary Noreen Miller	11/27/38	12/17/39
151. Elizabeth O'Brien	9/8/39	9/8/39
(entry 151 received and professed in Butte, Montana)		
*152. Rose Keherli	11/25/38	12/17/39
*153. Nell Sherry	11/20/38	4/21/40
*154. Alice Leahy	11/20/38	12/17/39
*155. Margaret Conway	12/18/38	10/18/42
*156. Helen Conway	12/18/38	12/18/38
*157. Caroline Kirkendall	3/19/39	4/21/40
*158. Bertha Murphy	3/19/39	4/21/40
*159. Mary Tatom	3/19/39	4/20/40
*160. Margaret Sarsfield	10/22/39	1/1/40
161. Mary Frances Callahan	10/22/39	1/1/40
162. Kathleen Lynch	10/22/39	4/20/41
*163. Gussie Pember	10/22/39	12/15/40
*164. James Nelson	11/26/39	1/19/41
*165. Walter James	11/26/39	no entry
*166. Anna Keenan	12/17/39	12/15/40
*167. Catherine Faber	12/17/39	no entry
*168. Pauline Diggerdorfer	12/17/39	4/20/41
*169. Nellie McDevitt	12/17/39	12/15/40
*170. Mary Francisca Sherbert	12/17/39	12/15/40
171. Dora Engerman	12/17/39	no entry
*172. Theresa Allen	12/17/39	no entry
*173. Anna Papineau	12/17/39	no entry
*174. Cecilia Gaws	12/17/39	5/30/42
*175. Mary Woodrum	12/17/39	12/15/40
*176. Blanche Boisnert	no entry	12/17/39
*177. Margaret Campbell	4/21/40	4/20/41
178. Agnes Murphy	4/21/40	4/20/41
*179. Louise King	4/21/40	4/20/41
180. Anna Maloney	4/21/40	10/18/42
*181. Bertha English	4/21/40	4/20/41
*182. J. Kemp	4/21/40	4/20/41
*183. Francisca Yuscat	4/21/40	4/20/41
*184. Mary Manning	4/21/40	4/20/41
*185. Mary Gilbaugh	4/21/40	4/20/41
186. Margaret Fleming	4/21/40	4/20/41
187. Vivian Snodgrass	11/20/38	12/17/39
*188. Mary Farrell	6/20/40	6/20/40
(entry 188: Permission of Fr. Blank to profess in one day due to illness)		

189. Vivian Bolton	9/15/40	10/17/43		237. Mrs. Anna West	4/15/45	4/28/46
*190. Genevieve Drapeau	9/15/40	10/17/43		*238. Mrs. C.E. Royer	4/15/45	4/28/46
*191. Catherine Heim	9/15/40	10/19/41		*239. Miss Vina Sadler	4/15/45	4/28/46
*192. Minnie Heizsiefer	9/15/40	4/19/42		*240. Miss Agnes Dowd	4/15/45	4/28/46
193. Caroline MacDonald	9/15/40	no entry		241. Miss Alice Baadte	4/15/45	4/28/46
*194. Josephine Meagher	9/15/40	10/19/41		*242. Mrs. Ida Nibler	10/21/45	no entry
*195. John Francis Meagher	9/15/40	no entry		*243. Mrs. Florence Masat	10/21/45	no entry
*196. Anna Maurer	9/15/40	4/19/42		*244. Mrs. Agnes Capperal	10/21/45	10/20/46
*197. Appollonia Willing	9/15/40	4/19/42		245. Mrs. Amelia Shasky	10/21/45	10/20/46
198. Bessie Muchlfeit	9/15/40	no entry		246. Mrs. Ima Meyer	10/21/45	10/20/46
*199. Mary Frances Gobbi	4/20/41	4/19/42		247. Miss June Tessie	4/46 (sic)	4/20/47
*200. Elizabeth Dresser	10/19/41	4/19/42		*248. Miss Dolores Reynolds	4/46 (sic)	4/20/47
*201. Florence Noyes	10/19/41	10/18/42		*(Re: entry 248. "1st black 3rd Order person.")*		
*202. Marie Kluge	10/19/41	no entry		249. Miss Margaret Mary Collins	4/46 (sic)	no entry
(Re: entry 202. "Transferred to Servites)				*250. Mrs. Mary Lillis	4/46 (sic)	no entry
*203. Anna Sharkey	10/19/41	10/18/42		*251. Mrs. Ellen Anderson	4/46 (sic)	4/20/47
204. Mary Alderson	10/19/41	10/18/42		252. Mr. J. W. Weick	10/20/46	10/14/47
*205. Jessie McMahon	10/19/41	no entry		*253. Mrs. M. Lyons	10/20/46	10/17/48
206. Elizabeth Gilsdorf	10/19/41	no entry		*254. Miss Marie Brezzolaire	4/20/47	4/18/48
207. Mrs. George Fety	10/19/41	10/17/43		*255. Mrs. Mary Brown	4/20/47	4/18/48
*208. Mary Agnes Arnold	5/18/41	4/19/42		256. Mrs. Ann Theresa Van	4/20/47	no entry
209. Mary Casey (Connolly)	5/18/41	4/19/42		*257. Miss Hannah Linehan	4/18/48	5/15/49
210. Thomas Hamilton	1/4/42	2/25/42		*258. Mrs. Monica Renner	4/18/48	5/15/49
(Re: entry 210. Seminarian. Deacon St. Edw. Sem.)				259. Miss Carrie Scott	4/18/48	no entry
*211. Mary Agnes Corcoran (died 3/7/42)				*260. Mrs. (sic) Steinbock	4/18/48	5/15/49
	2/25/42	2/25/42		261. Runa Guisti	5/15/49	10/16/49
*212. Agnes Schmitz	3/15/42	4/18/43		*262. Mary Jane Curtin	10/17/48	8/49 (sic)
213. Mildred Dewar	3/15/42	no entry		263. Anastasia Stetson	10/17/48	10/15/50
214. Martha Quinn	3/15/42	no entry		264. Miss Mary D'Ambrosia	5/15/49	10/15/50
*215. Eva Caldwell	8/24/42	4/18/48		265. Miss Mary Mastrandrew	5/15/49	4/16/50
*216. Mrs. Cecilia Gratton	10/18/42	10/17/43		266. Lena Graves	5/15/49	4/16/50
*217. Mrs. Margaret Mann	10/18/42	10/17/43		267. Mary McCoy	10/16/49	10/15/50
218. Mrs. Marjorie Mertz	10/18/42	10/17/43		*268. Mrs. Ellis Brady	10/16/49	4/15/51
*219. Mrs. Elizabeth Lindgren	10/18/42	10/17/43		*269. Katherine Pletka	4/16/50	4/15/51
*220. Jane S. Yettick	4/18/43	4/16/44		*270. Rose West	4/16/50	4/15/51
*221. Miss Pauline Gobbi	4/18/43	10/15/44		271. Mrs. William Griffiths	4/16/50	11/18/56
*222. Mrs. Elizabeth Ryan	4/18/43	4/16/44		*272. Gertrude Schafer	4/16/50	4/15/51
223. Mr. Matilda Ringo	6/28/43	1944 (sic)		*273. Joann Kempster	4/16/50	4/15/51
224. Miss Margurite Lawrence	8/27/43	no entry		*274. Margaret Blier	4/16/50	4/15/51
*225. Mark A. Sweeney	3/2/41	3/2/41		*275. Mary Conklin	4/16/50	4/15/51
(Re: entry 225. Special permission from Fr. Blank, Provincial)				276. Catherine Proudfast	4/16/50	4/15/51
*226. Rev. Gerald Linahen	1/18/44	5/23/46		*277. H.B. Kempster	6/50 (sic)	3/18/51
*227. Mrs. Lucy Sharrar	10/17/43	4/15/45		*278. Mrs. J. B. Conklin	4/16/50	3/18/51
*228. Mrs. Louella Chamberlain	10/17/43	no entry		*279. Ann Kirby	4/16/50	no entry
229. Miss Cora McCarty	10/17/43	10/15/44		*280. Fred (Ferdinand) Gross	10/16/49	10/15/50
*230. Mrs. Lucille St. Marie	4/16/44	5/15/45		281. David Haggerty	2/4/51	4/20/52
*231. Mrs. Lillian Scott	4/16/44	4/15/45		282. Mrs. Frieda Haggerty	2/4/51	4/20/52
*232. Mrs. Mary P. West	4/16/44	4/15/45		283. John Graham	2/4/51	no entry
*233. Miss Anna Skelly	4/16/44	4/15/45		284. Mrs. Lawrence Graham	2/4/51	no entry
*234. Mrs. Anna Coyle	10/15/44	4/28/46		*285. Jean Kies	3/18/51	4/20/52
*235. Mrs. B. Mullins	10/15/44	10/21/45		*286. Fred Kennedy	11/18/51	10/19/52
236. Miss Estelle Bogner	4/15/45	4/28/46		*287. Harry Earley	7/11/49	2/7/51

#	Name	Date 1	Date 2
*288.	Marian Campbell	4/16/50	4/15/51
*289.	Rosalia Donovan	4/16/50	5/20/51
*290.	Margaret Callen	4/15/51	10/18/53
*291.	Sally Kulze	4/15/51	4/20/52
*292.	Margaret Gerhards	4/15/51	4/20/52
*293.	Virginia Pigeon	11/18/51	4/20/52
294.	Ida Steinkellner	11/18/51	10/19/52
*295.	Lucile Krueger	11/18/51	10/19/52
296.	Mary Harris	11/18/51	10/19/52
297.	Elizabeth Hilbert	11/18/51	4/19/53
*298.	Georgia May	11/18/51	10/19/52
*299.	Mrs. George Donnerberg	11/18/51	10/19/52
300.	Francesca Gabrielle	11/18/51	10/19/52
*301.	Mrs. Ellen Molohan	11/18/51	10/19/52
*302.	Anna M. Haley	11/18/51	10/19/52
*303.	Mrs. Corinne Markowski	11/18/51	10/19/52
304.	Irene Bonley	11/18/51	no entry
305.	Josephine Layman	11/18/51	no entry
*306.	Catherine Lynes	4/20/52	10/19/52
*307.	Blanche Fritz	11/18/51	10/19/52
308.	Mabel Rick	11/18/51	no entry
309.	Ellen Russell	received privately	10/19/52
*310.	H. J. Bowen	11/18/51	10/19/52
*311.	Alvin Harris	11/18/51	10/19/52
*312.	Mrs. Joseph Schmitz	4/20/52	10/19/52
*313.	Mrs. Nina Lemma	4/20/52	10/19/52
314.	Fred Crews	3/52 (sic)	3/52 (sic)
*315.	Mrs. Anna McClernan	4/20/52	10/19/52
316.	Ellen Rehkopf	7/16/52	10/18/53
*317.	Mary C. Kavanaugh	10/19/52	4/19/53
318.	Lou Stears	10/19/52	no entry
319.	Mercedes Niivanon Haupert	10/19/52	5/16/54
320.	Mrs. Rita Hess	10/19/52	no entry
321.	Jane Merrick	10/19/52	10/18/53
322.	Margaret Mary Johnston	10/19/52	no entry
323.	Robert Gersten	10/19/52	no entry
*324.	Philip P. Pfeufer	10/19/52	10/18/53
*325.	Dr. Hugo Miller	10/19/52	10/18/53
*326.	William J. Whelan	4/19/53	5/16/54
*327.	C. E. McLean	4/19/53	5/16/54
328.	Mrs. Gladys Whelan	4/19/53	5/16/54
329.	Mrs. Frances Lee	4/19/53	5/16/54
*330.	Mrs. Florence Clark	4/19/53	10/17/54
331.	Emma Varner	no entry	10/18/53
332.	Barbara Hart	10/18/53	10/17/54
333.	Mrs. Faith Sweeney	10/18/53	no entry
334.	Anna Douthit	10/18/53	10/17/54
335.	Miss Phyl Callan	10/18/53	4/15/56
336.	Miss Rhoda Pettengill	11/7/53	no entry
*337.	Mrs. Mary Esh	5/16/54	10/16/55
*338.	Rodney J. Brown	10/17/54	10/16/55
339.	Leona M. Jenck	10/17/54	10/16/55
340.	Maria McLaughlin	12/25/54	no entry
341.	Larry Johnson	12/25/54	no entry
342.	Beth Johnson	12/25/54	no entry
343.	Margaret Myles	10/16/55	10/20/57
*344.	Estelle Davis	10/16/55	11/18/56
*345.	Altha McLean	10/16/55	11/18/56
*346.	Olive E. Brown	10/16/55	" "
*347.	Mrs. O. E. Reilly	10/16/55	" "
348.	Rev. Louis G. Rodakowski	11/26/55	6/27/57
*349.	Esther E. Ferguson	11/26/55	6/27/57
350.	Mrs. Florence Quigley	4/15/56	no entry
351.	Miss Elizabeth Johnson	5/15/56	10/20/57
352.	Miss Dorothy Gilliland	4/18/56	no entry
353.	Mary Rei	11/18/56	dropped out
354.	Miss Rose Salway	10/20/57	11/23/76
*355.	Agnes C. Mahoney	10/19/58	10/18/59
*356.	Mrs. Maude L. Beauchamp	10/19/58	10/18/59
357.	Mrs. Rosemary Gallinger	10/19/58	10/18/59
	(Re: 357. Transferred to Carmelite Order 10-1-73)		
*358.	Miss Vera Wharton	10/19/58	10/18/59
359.	Alvin R. Batiste	10/19/58	4/24/60
*360.	Margaret E. Mills	4/19/59	11/27/60
361.	Ann Thompson	4/19/59	4/24/60
*362.	Elizabeth McKinnon	4/19/59	4/24/60
*363.	Elizabeth Hearn	4/19/59	4/24/60
364.	May Walsh	4/19/59	4/24/60
365.	Martha J. Reis	4/19/59	no entry
*366.	Thelma Sandstrom	5/2/59	11/27/60
*367.	Mrs. Amy White	10/18/59	11/27/60
368.	Miss Lydia Strnad	10/18/59	11/27/60
*369.	Mrs. Assunta Santilli	10/18/59	11/27/60
370.	Jane Crosby	10/18/59	no entry
371.	Angela Hearn	10/18/59	no entry
*372.	Dominic Brown	no entry	10/18/59
373.	Michael Dillon	3/15/59	3/15/59
*374.	Mrs. Ruth Gunvordahl	4/24/60	no entry
*375.	Mrs. Anna M. Ferguson	4/24/60	5/28/61
376.	Irene A. Dawson	4/24/60	no entry
*377.	Miss Barbara Lisoski	4/29/60	no entry
378.	Mrs. Eileen Huddleson	4/24/60	no entry
*379.	Mrs. Emma Chartrey	10/13/60	no entry
*380.	Mary Evelyn Munly	11/17/60	no entry
*381.	Malcolm McLean	11/27/60	11/26/61
*382.	John Kelly	11/27/60	11/26/61
*383.	John W. Kelly	11/27/60	11/26/61
*384.	Mrs. Josephine Lammers-Valliere	11/27/60	11/26/61
*385.	Mrs. Grace McDonough	11/27/60	11/26/61
386.	Mrs. Mary Smith	11/27/60	11/26/61
387.	Mrs. Vivian Blair	11/27/60	no entry
*388.	Mrs. Ella Daskalos	11/27/60	10/28/62
389.	Mrs. Mary Peterkin	11/27/60	11/26/61

*390. Mrs. Anne Yager	11/27/60	10/28/62	
391. Mrs. Marian McGuire	11/27/60	10/28/62	
*392. Mrs. Mary Rose Leeb	11/27/60	11/26/61	
393. Miss. Eileen Biecke	11/27/60	11/26/61	
394. Mrs. Katherine Oreskovich	11/27/60	11/26/61	
*395. Frances Charistman	5/28/61	10/28/62	
396. Elizabeth Sousa	5/28/61	10/28/62	
397. Kathryn F. Quinn	10/28/62	10/27/63	
*398. Eileen M. Fitzpatrick	10/28/62	10/27/63	
399. Mrs. Helen Louise McDaniel	10/28/62	10/27/63	
400. Janet Garrett	10/27/63	dropped out	
401. Diana Gail Diekman	10/27/63	no entry	
*402. Mary Ann Kresnak	7/19/63	10/25/64	
403. Mrs. Alice Marshall	3/12/61	3/11/62	
404. Mrs. Mary Agnes Harpole	5/24/64	10/24/65	
405. Edith Roland	5/24/64	5/23/65	
*406. Miss Vera Rayho	no entry	10/27/63	
*407. Mrs. Julia Holland	10/24/65	10/23/66	
*408. Mrs. Mary Buras	4/24/66	4/29/67	
409. Mrs. Teresa Niedermeyer	4/24/66	4/27/67	
*410. Mary Anne Voeller	4/24/66	10/22/67	
411. Albert Mickel	4/24/66	4/27/67	
*412. Anne Seifert	4/24/66	4/27/67	
413. Mrs. Barbara Feist	2/27/66 professed privately		
*414. James Morris	9/1/66	9/1/66	
415. Mae Walsh	10/23/66	10/22/67	
416. Leo Greiner	10/23/66	10/22/67	
*417. Mrs. Leo Greiner	10/23/66	10/22/67	
*418. Andrew Murray	10/23/66	10/22/67	
419. Mrs. Mary C. Connolly	4/24/67	10/22/67	
*420. Mrs. Anna Schriek	10/22/67	10/27/68	
421. Dennis Sizemore	10/22/67	10/27/68	
422. Mr. Robert Nolan	10/22/67	dropped out	
423. Louise Parker	10/21/67	10/21/67	
*424. Mary Lobb	5/28/68	10/27/68	
425. Irma Swartz	10/22/67	5/28/68	
*426. Margaret Freeman Meehan	10/27/68	10/26/69	
*427. Mrs. Mary Loprenzi	10/27/68	10/26/69	
*428. Mrs. M. Stolen	10/26/69	10/25/70	
429. Mrs. A Chase	10/26/69	10/25/70	
430. Mrs. Rozetta Zorich	10/26/69	10/25/70	
*431. Marie Mullen	10/25/70	4/23/72	
*(none) Mrs. A. Santilli – vow of chastity		6/26/66	
(none) Helen Louise Daniels – vow of chastity		6/26/66	
432. Mrs. Frances Schierer (Pastorino)			
	10/25/70	10/22/72	
433. Mrs. Clara Johnson	10/22/72	10/28/73	
*434. Mrs. Julia Lower	4/24/73	12/22/74	
*435. Mary Fitzpatrick (trf fr Hartford, Conn.)			
	4/12/65	10/9/66	
*436a Al Parent	2/22/75 (received privately)		
*436b Minnie Parent	2/22/75 (received privately)		

436c Mrs. Kathleen Porter	6/26/49	1950	
437. Mrs. Lucille Beattie	10/26/75	11/23/77	
438. Jerome O'Neill	10/26/75	no entry	
439. Mrs. Pat O'Neill	10/26/75	no entry	
440. Mrs. Pat Bingham	10/26/75	4/24/79	
441. Elizabeth (Betsy) Darby	5/24/76	4/24/77	
*442. Mrs. Nita Willis	5/24/76	4/24/77	
443. Mrs. Eloola C. O'Neil	11/21/76	no entry	
*444. Mrs. Ethel M. Garreson	2/26/50	10/14/51	
445. Mrs. Carol Braugh	no entry	no entry	
446. James E. Wilson Jr.	4/24/77	4/23/78	
447. Mrs. Carol Tyler	4/24/77	4/23/78	
448. Jerry Van Loo (Jeremy Salquenetti)			
	10/30/77	10/22/78	
449. Essie MacDaniels	4/23/78	10/25/81	
450. Robbie Wesley	4/23/78	10/28/79	
451. Gloria Hicks (Carter)	4/23/78	10/28/79	
*452. Samuel A. Jackson Sr.	4/23/78	4/22/79	
453. Harry Watson	4/23/78	dropped out	
454. Mrs. Frances Sheridan	4/23/78	4/22/79	
*455. Mrs. Cecilia Siberz	4/23/78	4/22/79	
456. Mrs. Frances Frison	4/23/78	10/28/79	
457. Linda Nickerson	10/22/78	dropped out	
*458. Rosario Moran	10/22/78	4/27/80	
*459. Betty Ahern	10/22/78	no entry	
460. Mary A. Fazio	4/22/79	4/27/80	
461. Margaret Powell	5/27/79	4/27/80	
462. Ann Blauvelt	5/27/79	4/27/80	
463. Lori Navarra	10/28/79	dropped out	
464. Terri Mercereau	10/28/79	10/26/80	
465. Janice Smith Nibler	10/28/79`	4/5/81	
466. Catherine Hampton Cole	4/27/80	4/5/81	
467. Julia Amato	10/26/80	10/25/81	
468. Mary Ardreg	10/26/80	10/25/81	
*469. Charles Awad	4/5/81	4/25/82	
470. Joanne Moore	4/5/81	4/25/82	
*471. Laura Patnaude	4/5/81	4/25/82	
472. Kathy Richards	4/5/81	4/25/82	
*473. Eva Smith	10/25/81	10/23/83	
474. Jane Smith	10/25/81		
	(transferred to Passionist)		
475. David Havlicik	4/25/82	10/24/82	
476. Theresa Lorentz	10/24/82	10/23/83	
477. Jose C. Castillo	4/24/83		
	Trf. to New Hope, Ky.		
478. Bertha Castillo	4/24/83		
	Trf. to New Hope, Ky.		
479. Anne Marie Castillo	4/24/83		
	Trf. to New Hope, Ky.		
480. Mary Van Buren	4/24/83	4/15/84	
481. Henry Endres	4/24/83	4/15/84	
482. Julie Endres	4/24/83	4/15/84	

483.	Teresa Waits	4/24/83	4/15/84
484.	Mary Walsh	4/24/83	4/15/84
485.	Martha Williams	4/24/83	4/15/84
486.	Gary Williams	4/24/83	4/15/84
487.	Judy Bartholomew	4/24/83	dropped out
488.	Walt Bartholomew	4/24/83	dropped out
489.	Jerome K. Byrd	4/24/83	4/15/84
490.	Helen M. Dwyer	4/24/83	10/21/84
491.	Geraldine Mitchell	4/24/83	4/21/85
492.	Thelma M. Stubblefield	4/24/83	4/15/85
493.	George Stubblefield	4/24/83	4/15/84
494.	Cecilia Hoesly	4/24/83	4/15/84
495.	Rosemary Young	4/24/83	4/15/84
496.	Daniel Shuell	4/24/83	4/15/84
497.	Marcie Shuell	4/24/83	4/15/84
498.	Therese Lee	4/24/83	4/15/84
499.	Randy Young	5/22/83	4/15/84
500.	Janette Jackson	5/22/83	4/15/84
501.	Betty Martin	5/22/83	4/15/84
502.	Mary Murphy	4/25/82	5/22/83
503.	Jean Schindler (Rec'd privately)	4/6/83	dropped out
504.	Joyce Timberman	10/23/83	10/21/84
505.	Leonard (Bing) Chase	10/23/83	4/21/85
506.	Oliver LaPlante	10/23/83	10/21/84
507.	Phillip Winchester	10/23/83	dropped out
508.	Frances James	4/15/84	4/21/85
509.	Garry S. Sims	10/21/84	10/13/85
510.	Nancy Sims	10/21/84	10/13/85
511.	Eugene A. Vandecoevering	10/21/84	10/13/85
512.	Maria Vandecoevering	10/21/84	10/13/85
513.	Gerald Joseph Parmantier	10/21/84	10/13/85
514.	Mary Jane Parmantier	10/21/84	10/13/85
515.	Michael Freiling	10/21/84	10/13/85
516.	Elizabeth Freiling	10/21/84	10/13/85
517.	Pauline Jensen	10/21/84	10/13/85
518.	Sharon K. Beveridge	10/21/84	dropped out
519.	Thomas DiNova	10/21/84	dropped out
520.	Mary Gretsch	10/21/84	10/13/85
521.	Anne Gretsch	10/21/84	10/13/85
522.	Joseph Whalen Jr.	10/21/84	10/13/85
523.	Raymond Delaney	10/21/84	4/20/86
524.	Inez Green	10/21/84	dropped out
525.	Christopher Laboe	10/21/84	dropped out
526.	Richard Cloud	4/21/85	4/20/86
527.	John Fazio	4/21/85	4/20/86
528.	(not issued yet)		
529.	Becky Lewis	April '87	4/24/88
*530.	Omar Mackenberg	April '87	deceased
531.	Jane Hoesly	4/24/88	4/22/90
532.	Robert Golik	April '88	4/23/89
533.	Annette Wostl	April '88	4/22/90
534.	Edna McGouoran	April '88	no entry
535.	James Ross	April '88	dropped out
536.	John Austin	April '88	4/22/90
537.	Alice Golik	4/22/90	4/29/91
538.	Suzie King	4/22/90	4/29/91
539.	John Wostl	4/22/90	4/29/91
540.	Susan Walsh	4/29/91	4/29/92
541.	David Walsh	4/29/91	4/29/92
542.	Victoria Kangiser	4/29/91	4/29/92
543.	Frances Hoesly	4/29/91	4/29/92
544.	Joyce Schile	4/29/91	4/29/92
545.	Dorothy Krikstanas	4/16/50	4/15/51
546.	Charlotte Krikstanas	4/16/50	4/15/51
547.	Adelino Lorenzo	4/29/92	4/29/94
548.	Mary Lorenzo	4/29/92	4/29/94
549.	Sandra Miller	4/29/92	4/29/93
550.	Antoinette Kucera	4/29/92	4/29/93
551.	Ken Kucera	4/29/92	4/29/93
552.	Alexander Adebawa	4/29/94	no entry
553.	Ann Hach	4/29/94	no entry
554.	Maxine Buse	4/29/94	no entry
555.	Daniel Arneson	4/21/94	no entry
556.	Mary Beth Egan	4/29/94	no entry

APPENDIX 4

HOLY ROSARY   HOLY NAME SOCIETY 1894-1995

Adams, Bruce
Adams, Pat
Adams, Donald
Adelman, Stephen
Agius, Joseph Fr. OP
Amaya, Greg
Anderson, Greg. Fr. OP
Andreas, Mark
Archer, Robert
Arthur King
Austin, John
Awad, Charles
Bailey, Don
Baker, Michael
Baker, Robert
Bann, James
Banzer, Thomas
Barrett, Ed
Bartholomew, Bert
Baurer, Herman
Bax, Eugene
Bechtold, Harold
Beede, Robert
Bernard, Fr.
Blatner, George
Bleything, Harold
Bobzien, James
Bobzien, O. J.
Bogren, Frank
Bourdeau, Coran
Brackenbrough, Steve
Brady, Neal
Brandes, Jack
Brennan, John
Brink, Jim
Bross, Stephen
Brosterhous, Stan
Buckley, Gerald Fr
Bucheit, Roy
Buczkowski, Mark
Bullard, H. B.
Bunch, John
Byrne, J.
Byrnes, Don
Cable, Robert
Callaghan, Arthur D.
Campbell, Richard
Carley, Harry Jr.

Carpenter, Michael
Caven, Daniel
Chaney, Donald T.
Chase, Leonard
Cichoke, Anthony
Cieslak, Paul R
Collins, D. W.
Collins, J.
Conover, Dana
Conrat, Robert
Conte, Pat
Conway, James
Cooper, Jim
Creegan, Matthew
D'Arcy, F.
Darby, J. J.
Davis, Vincent
Dawson, James
Day, Warren
Dean, Frank
Deiss, Ted
DeLafontaine, J. P.
Delaney, John
Delaney, Raymond
Dennis, Don
DeSemple, Dave
Detweiler, Scott
DiNovo, Thomas
Doll, Vines
Donnerberg, Fred
Donnerberg, George
Donnerberg, Joe
Donnerberg, Vincent
Donovan, Martin
Doran, Dan
Dowd, Thomas
Dresser, B. J.
Dufault, Leroy
Duffner, Paul Fr. OP
Eaglin, George
Eilers, F. J.
Eixenberger, Frank
Ellis, John
Engerman, Robert
Farrell, Thomas
Fazio, Anthony
Fazio, David
Fazio, John

Fehland, George
Feucht, Thomas Fr. OP
Fitzgerald, M. E.
Fleskes, J. F.
Flynn, Thomas
Foye, Joseph
Friedhoff, Jack
Galbrish, Lou
Gallagher, Joseph
Gebken, Matthew
Goodyear, John
Graf, V.
Granato, William
Grant, Fred
Graves, William
Gray, Henry
Green, Dan
Green, Ronald
Gregory, Ray
Greenfield, V. Steven
Guanero, Ray
Guiher, John
Hamel, Frank
Hannigan, Francis
Harold, Fred
Harper, Bob
Harrington, Michael
Harris, Jim
Harris, Rocky
Hass, Ken
Hartman, George J.
Havlicek, David
Healy, James
Healy, Patrick Fr. OP
Hefflinger, Jerry
Hemmerling, Harold
Henry, Matt
Henry, Ralph
Hethcote, Don
Hickok, Steven G. *BPA*
Higgins, Peter
Higgins, Tracy
Hite, Marion J.
Hoff, Frank
Hoff, Harvey
Hoerner, Fred
Hogan, Charles
Huibregtse, Randy

Hughes, Chester
Hughes, J.B.
Hughes, Thomas V.
Hughs, Thomas
Ingram, Michael S.
James, Larry G.
Johnson, Angus
Johnson, Darold
Johnson, Michael
Johnson, T. B.
Jones, Prince
Kalvelage, W. J.
Kehoe, J. W.
Keith, David
Kelly, Henry Fr. OP
Kelly, Joel
Kempster, Brian
Kempster, Kevin
Kent, Milton
Kindred, Jack
Kindred, Thomas A.
King, A. J.
King, Guy
Klein, Randy
Kluthe, Clem
Kluthe, Jason
Kluthe, Loran
Knauff, Gabriel Fr. OP
Koch, Joe
Koppes, Ed
Laidlaw, Lansing
Lalic, Jose
Larkin, J. C.
Larkin, J.D.
Lassell, Don
Lavin, John J.
Lazenby, Dennis M.
Leipzig, Francis, Bishop
Leonard, Ed
Lewis, Bud
Littlejohn, Elmer
Locati, Norman
Loftus, Peter
Logan, William
Lorenzo, A. R. "Lorie"
Lorimer, Wilfred L
Ludowese, B.
Machowski, T.

Madden, Ed D.
Maderos, Herb
Madigan, Matthew
Maginnis, C.P.
Maginnis, Cyril
Maginnis, John
Mahoney, T. F.
Manning, Henry
Martin, Florent Fr. OP
Martinez, Dave
McAllen, Dan
McAllen, E. H.
McAllen, Mark
McCabe, Stephen Fr OP
McCaffery, Norman
McCaffrey, Walter
McCawley, Elton
McClory, Wm. Fr. OP
McCormick, Joseph
McDermott, W.S. Fr OP
McDonald, P. J.
McDonnell, Brian
McDonnell, Chris
McDonnell, E.M.
McDowell, Charles
McDowell, Francis
McEachern, Donald
McGinnis, C. P.
McGrath, E.A.
McKay, Albert
McLean, Evans
McMahan, Frank
McVicker, Brendan
McVicker, Brian
Meehan, James
Mendoza, Rudy
Meyers, Paul
Miler, James
Miller, James
Miller, Jeff
Milton, Fred
Moreau, Phil
Moreschi, Bruno
Morris, David A.
Mottau, Conrad
Mulvehill, Dan
Munly, Michael G.
Murphy, C.

Murphy, John
Murphy, J. R.
Murray, Andrew
Murray, Neal V.
Newby, Cliff
Niedermeyer, B. E.
Niedermeyer, A.
Niedermeyer, Cyril A.
Niedermeyer, Fred J.
Niedermeyer, Joseph F.
Niedermeyer, Joseph Jr.
Neppach, Carl J.
Nolan, Bob
Nolan, Michael J.
Nolan, William
Norton, William Fr. OP
O'Hara, J. P.
O'Hare, Peter
O'Keefe, J. J.
Olsen, Don
Onyima, Ken
O'Reilly, M.E.
Orso-Manzonetta, B.
Ozura, Joseph
Palmer, Michael
Paque, John J.
Park, Daniel A.
Parmantier, Gerry
Pashley, Dick
Perkins, David
Perkins, Nathan
Perkins, Ryan
Perry, Fred
Perry, Thomas
Perussi, Matei
Popenoe, H. L.
Prentice, Barry
Raetz, Nathaniel
Raetz, Randolph
Raffaele, Richard
Ramsdell, Norman
Rardin, David
Rardin, Joseph
Rardin, Lee
Reil, David
Reil, Dennis
Reilly, Owen
Rekart, John

Rengo, Robert
Renner, Nick
Reynolds, Brian C.
Richard, John E.
Rolison, Joe
Rondeau, Fred P.
Rothschild, Warner
Roura, Oscar Manuel
Rousseau, Rob
Rowley, Richard
Royer, Brian
Royer, Craig
Royer, Justin
Russell, James
Ryan, Edmond Fr. OP
Safranek, Stephen
Schade, Fred
Schantin, Don
Schechtel, Peter
Schmitz, Joseph Jr.
Schmitz, Joseph Sr.
Schneide Alex
Scott, Joseph
Sharkey, Jack
Sharkey, John J.
Sharkey, W. J.
Sharkey, W. T.
Sheahan, John
Sheahan, William
Sheehan, John R.
Sheehy, Robert
Sheetz, David
Silva, Michael
Sims, Gary S.
Singleman, Edward
Sinnott, J. Frank
Skayhan, Richard J.
Socinsky, Leo J.
Sohm, Frederick
Sophy, James
Stafford, Sam
Stearn, Henry
Stewart, Trent
Stirling, Charles
Stubblefield, George
Sullivan, Harvey E.
Sullivan, Larry
Sullivan, Tim

Sweeney, A.
Sweeney, Frank
Sweeney, Mark
Sweeney, M. J.
Terheyden, Frank J.
Terheyden, J. J.
Toffler, Christopher
Toffler, William
Tomassi, Tim
Touhey, Thomas
Trausch, Terry
Unger, Richard
VanCoelen, Henry
Van Smoorenburg, B.
Velguth, A. F.
Velguth, George M.
Verbiest, Christopher
Virnig, Urban
Vogt, Emmerich Fr. OP
Walsh, Ed
Watt, Don
Weinhart, Bob
Weinhart, Dominic
Weinhart, Erich
Weinhart, Stephen
Welch, John
Westrup, Leo
Whalen, Joseph
White, M.C.
Wieck, Paul
Wieck, Tim
Wilhelm, Christopher J.
Williams, Larry
Williams, Victor
Williams, W. N.
Wilson, James
Wilson, Xavier
Winneman, B. H.
Witt, Austin
Witt, Bill
Witt, Eric
Wolf, Paul
Wurzer, Conrad
Yager, Jacob
Zimmerman, Marion

The writer expresses undying gratitude to Michael Palmer for perusing reams of documents to recover some of these names.

APPENDIX 5

DOMINICAN SISTERS WHO SERVED AT HOLY ROSARY SCHOOL, GRADUATION CLASSES AND LIST OF VOCATIONS TO RELIGIOUS LIFE

Religious Name	Surname	Religious Name	Surname	Religious Name	Surname
Sister Agnes Mary	Dembrowski	Sister Cornelia	Leitner	Sister Kathleen	Corbett
Sister Ancilla	Althaus	Sister Cyrilla	Poschmann	Sister Lioba	Doehman
Sister Angela (Eileen)	Molahan	Sister Dolores	Stopper	Sister Marcella	Ashton
Sister Angela Marie	Boedigheimer	Sister Dominic	Engelhard	Sister Modesta	Bauer
Sister Anthony	Rusting	Sister Emilia	Techtman	Sister Paul Marie	Batiloro
Sister Bernard	Cline	Sister Emygdia	Joras	Sister Peregrina	Henglberger
Sister Bernice	Sherlock	Sister Exilda	Meunier	Sister Raphael	McCarthy
Sister Brendan	Bonney	Sister Genevieve	Duffy	Sister Rosalia	Monaghan
Sister Callista	Stopper	Sister Geraldine	Kelly	Sister Rose	Weir
Sister Carola	Dietl	Sister Gonzaga	Loftus	Sister Rufina	Doran
Sister Catherine	Dentlinger	Sister Honorata	McEntee	Sister Sophia	Kettlewell
Sister Celeste	Gardner	Sister Jerome	Delsman	Sister Valeria	Cummings
Sister Celestine	Stiebritz	Sister Julia	Perez		

With the kind aid of Kathleen Lavin, Florence McEachern, Barbara Reidy, Jim Bobzien, and the March 5, 1944 edition of the then "Parish Digest," we compiled this list of names of the graduates of Holy Rosary School by year, noting that although the school opened in 1912, the first graduates did not complete their studies until 1915. We regret any spelling errors or absence of names, and beg your indulgence for any mistakes, those being due to typographical errors, the author's stupidity, absent records, or faulty memories, but certainly not due to malice. Many of these students are presently on our parish rolls; and some have gone to their eternal reward, God rest their souls.

GRADUATION CLASSES AT HOLY ROSARY SCHOOL

1915: Lauren Murphy, Mildred Galvin, Marie O'Day, Marguerite Logus, Lenore Callaghan, Helen Andre, Mabel Sullivan, Genevieve Foster, and Marjorie Foster.

1916: Ambrose Murphy, Laurence Ryan, Anna Meagher, Evelyn Kissel, Eleanora Young, Mabel McDonough, Marie Rutto, Mary McMahon, Grace McDonald, Margaret Mims, and Florence Pugsley.

1917: Leo Murphy, James Lavin, Jules Andre, Joseph Hartman, Bernard Albers, Mark Morrison, Carlotta O'Connor, Beatrice White, Anna Marie McCormick, Marie Stryker, Ruth Barry, and Edna Schweitzer, Ambrose Larkins, Alex McEachern and Ted McGrath.

1918: George Eilers, Leo White, Leo de la Fontaine, Richard Maher, Leo Delaney, Clemence Eilers, Ellen Lavin, Gertrude Carter, Florence Hellendorn, Lucile Stryker, Margaret McDowell, Mary Clare Larkins, Helen Sisk, Helen Mullen, and Lucille Veatch.

1919: Harry McDowell, Fred Hoerner, Valentine Young, Joseph Niedermeyer, James Veatch, Alfred Albers, Norman Burk, Delores Murphy, Lucille Hellendorn, Margaret O'Day, Doris Carter, Frances Galvin, Leonore Tutto, Mercedes Larkins, Margaret Neary, Marie Fassbender, Nora Price, Katherine McGrath, Frankie Edgar, and Ernestine Hamilton.

1920: Ferdinand Sharkey, Vincent O'Connor, Ronald McDonald, Walter Grant, James Bracy, Thomas Duggan, Marie Duggan Dorothy Sisk, Marion Neer, Agnes O'Sullivan, Dorothy McMahon, Madeline Brown, Mary McEachern, Frances Hartman, and Thelma Rutto.

1921: Leroy Duggan, Clarence Carter, Ernst Albers, Oswald Byrne, Raymond Murphy, Jack Gaus, Alice McGrath, Mary Lou Moser, Thelma Burk, Grace Isley, Dorothy McDowell, Eleanor Bracy, Marie Niedermeyer, Helen Kirkendall, and Dorothy de Grandpre, Bill Gagnon, and Stan Brosterhous.

1922: William Gagnon, Joseph McCormick, Charles Vasey, Joseph Lavin, William McCue, Ruth Gaus, Eleanor Farrell, Helen Grant, Anna Barta, Alma Hoerner, Mary Phillips, Helen Murphy, Sophie Gobbi, Josephine Veatch, Dorothy Veatch, Florence Kennedy, Donald McEachern, Loretta McCormick, Herbert Crampton, and Joseph Quirk.

1923: Frances McDowell, Jack Farrell, Malcolm O'Connor, Harold Beyer, Tom Geoghegan, John Nelson, Francesca de Grandpre, Henrietta Fassbender, Helen Farrell, Mary Gobbi, Frances Healy, Georgia Karafotas, Bibiana Maher, Clare McGrath, Thelma McCreary, Eileen O'Day, Catherine O'Farrell, Elizabeth Price, Marie Rassier, and Hazel Foster.

1924: Paul Gagnon, Herbert Hamilton, Bill Lynott, Walter Illk, Edward Crowe, John Eilers, Don Geoghegan, Lawrence McCann, Marie Murphy, Marie Healy, Frances Stam, Helen Carr, Ione McCreary, Annie Duggan, Marjorie Merrick, Cecelia Hartman, Evelyn McCann, and Helen Phinney.

1925: Adrian Breckon, Francis Conner, George Hoerner, James Carr, James McDevitt, Alexander Will, Dan Mullen, Claude O'Connor, Broderick O'Farrell, Lawrence Sisk, Joseph Rollins, Kathleen Faber, Pauline Gobbi, Nancy Healy, Clare Hartman, Margaret Kelly, Agnes Larkins, Bernadette la Chapelle, Kathleen Lavin, Dorothy McGrath, Dorothy Scherfen, Mary Frances Walsh, and Laura Phillips.

1926: Edward Conner, Luke Murphy, George O'Farrell, James McGinnis, William Langen, Kathleen Fisch, Elizabeth Hicks, Alice Illk, Carlotta Kennedy, Florence McEachern, John Mullen, and Anna Krebs.

1927: Samuel Conchuratt, Theodore Karafotis, Thomas Larkins, Melvin Swanson, Eva Gobbi, Elizabeth Collins, Lucille Brewster, Anna Leonard, Dorothy Gaus, Helen Matschiner, Mary McDowell, Margaret O'Connor, and Lucille O'Day, Harry Guerra, and Vetta Courtney.

1928: Philip Gambee, Thomas Kelly, Howard McGrath, Paul McGrath, Edward Wilson, Paul McGinnis, Michael Plecas, William Quirk, Charles Burns, William Veatch, Gertrude Doyle, Barbara Fraights, Elisabeth McEachern, Ernestine Phinney, Melba Mc Coy, Helen Daskalos, Theresa Kennedy, and Kathleen Conner.

1929: Anthony Faber, Robert Healy, Vincent Byrne, John Conchuratt, Edward Kelly, Edward Scherfen, William Dixon, Bernard Tobkin, Donald Wilson, John Schmitt, John Tennant, Lillian Darby, Christina Daskalos, Ermith Phinney, Mary Plecas, Elizabeth Silva, Ruth Sandow, and Bill Staudemeier.

1930: Basil Byrne, James Courtney, George DeCamp, George Gould, Fred Eilers, Edward Hoerner, Alfred Illk, Bernard Leonard, Regan McCoy, Joseph Staudenmaier, George Swanson, Ambrose Tobkin, Geraldine Brifey, Kathleen Darby, Madeline Conner, Frances DeCamp, Virginia Eivers, Margalee Holmes, Eileen Langman, Irene Morrell, Anna Plecas, Mary Reilly, and Florence Tobkin, Dorothy English, and Madeleine Conner.

1931: Robert Coyne, John Dixon, Joseph Mayer, Kenneth Warburton, Mary Canich, Bernard Courtney, Ruth Hartman, Eileen Kelly, and Mary Swanson.

1932: Roland Jackson, John McCarthy, William Phinney, Leo Tobkin, Jean Eivers, Mary Fox, Margaret Leonard, Patricia McCarthy, Doris Staudenmaier, Elizabeth Strauss.

1933: John Daskalos, William Daskalos, John Elich, April Niedermeyer, Joseph Illk, Marie Fahey, Marjorie Walsh, Maxine Barrett and Margaret Lindsay.

1934: Peter Guerra, George Hornby, Harold Scott, Paul Tobkin, William Walsh, Donald Warndahl, Dorothy Browning, and Mary Hensel.

1935: Harold Challis, Francis Forner, Norman Moshberger, Helen Atre, Amanda Canich, Marion Ligatich, Constance Martin, and Margaret Tobkin.

1936: James Barrett, Jerome Barta, Dante Guarnero, Ralph Guerra, Ray Hunt, Helen Churich, Olga Elich, Margaret Harold, and Marjorie Silva.

1937: Frank Churich, James Fleskas, Edward Illk, John Oreskovitch, Mike Pezel, William Randall, Edward Tobkin, Joseph Yuscat, Marie Metzenberg, Georgia Rickett.

1938: Eugene Arnold, Milton Lennon, George Randall, Albert Schneider, Irene Barrett, Josephine Elich, Mary Guerra, and Frances Smith.

1939: Nick Elich, Jack Fleskes, Owen Lennon, Frances Barta, Sophie Ann Bell, Norma Challis, Ann Canick, Katherine Frane, Patricia Harris, Margaret Lorimer, Ruth Sandow, and Jean Wiseman.

1940: Charles Allen, Vincent Arnold, James Frahler, Joe Ligatich, James West, Mildred Fleskes, Catherine Grahams, Marilyn Hayhie, Jane Harold, Patricia Hunt, Patricia Knight, Madonna Knight, Barbara Lorimer, Mary Malitis, Louise Metzenberg, Mary Oreskovitch, Katie Pezel, and Mary Tyler.

1941: James Bobzien, James Coyle, Jack Erskine, Wallace MacRitchie, John Matschiner, Vincent Peterson, Frank Shafer, Donald Walsh, Lou Bell, Natalie Cox, Marjorie Dewey, Catherine Jackson, Joan Janek, Lillian Ligatich, and Rose Pezel.

1942: Dwaine Dumas, Kenneth Seal, Barbara Barrett, Dolores Bobzien, Lois Hill, Angela Lorimer, and Jean Morehouse.

1943: Richard Bender, Roy Briggs, James Demas, Catherine Conratt, Dolores Lennon, Marjorie Roberts, Mary Renner, Nadyne Routtu, and Jacqulin Youngman.

1944: Matthew Ligatich, James Creegan, Lyle Fleskes, Dolores Lennon, Jo Ann Harkins, Richard Ehr, Dick Guarnero, Don Adkison, and Bob Adkison.

1945: John Bobzien, Frank Deitz, Gerry Flannigan, Jerry Mills, Joseph Smidtz, Thomas (Toby) Renner, and Robert Bender.

1946: Sue Adkison, Mary Mills, Anthony Ligatich.

1947: Paul Adkison, Richard Brosterhouse, Danny Craven, Oliver Renner, and Richard Brosterhous.

1948: Leon Bobzien, Frank Schmitz, Robert Howard, Timothy Sweeney, Don Karavanich, Rosalee Gurtina, Elizabeth Holliman Donald Karovonich, Joe Oreskovitch, Kenneth Westrupp, Mary Helen Pupil, Gail Guillory, Marilyn Guillory Catherine Carley and, Louise Fleskes.

1949: Gene Brosterhous.

1952: Robert Bleything, Barbara Britt, Freddia Brooks, Sonjia Brooks, Darryl Christman, Joseph Clark, Nancy Connolly, Louis Day, Harley Frisby, Kenneth Hoff, Susan Hyde, Andrew Johnson, Elharsel Lewis, Patricia Macabeo, Mary Ann Mulvey, Kaye McDonald, Stephen Pongracz, and Caroline Pupil.

1953: Andrea Coleman, Dennis Connor, David Connor, Arleen DeBenedetti, Carrolyn Evitt, Suzanne Fugere, Charles Harris, Laura Isaacs, Peter Jackson, Kathryn Moisan, Michael Pigeon, James Rardin, John Reid, Jack Tuggle, and James Winczewski.

1954: Walter Brooks, June Chipman, Charonne Dennhardt, Judith DePass, Curtis Fugere, Alan Kempton, Pearl Nielson, Nancy Serean, Robert Tuggle, Gail Walker, Edward Woodward, and Brian Yustin.

1955: Andrew Davis, Judith DeBenedetti, Norman Jean Douglas, Mary Eley, Delores Fugere, James Gieler, Donald Rardin, Ramona Walker and Russell Whitney.

*"In those years of innocent childhood, I began to feel in my heart
two different inclinations which Holy Week helped me to realize.
All the enchantments of the world were uniting against the child
who wished to enter into agony with Christ.
I was still indignant towards the disciples who could not watch for
one hour with Jesus and then, looking around, I was amused watching the aimless
flutter of a butterfly driven into the chapel by the wind."*

... Francois Mauriac

From his book "Holy Thursday – an intimate remembrance,"
Sophia Institute Press, Box 5284, Manchester, NH 03108, 1992.

INESTIMABLE GIFT OF VOCATIONS

Catholic grammar schools and churches are beautiful marriages which produce vocations essential for the perpetuation and spiritual growth of Catholic communities. In this instance we recognize with gratitude, and pay tribute to, the legacy of the Dominican Fathers, Brothers, and Sisters who served at Holy Rosary School and Church during the 43 years the school existed, and who, by their good example and guidance, helped lead the following 33 students into religious life:

Sr. Mary Rosaria Neppach, RSM
Sr. Rosarita (Marie) Duggan, O.P.
Sr. Mary Constance Larkins, O.P.
Sr. Catherine Grams, SNJM
Sr. Mary Patrick English, O.P
Sr. Margaret Lorimer, S.A.
Sr. Reginald (Alice) McGuire
Sr. Patricia McKenzie, SNJM
*Sr. Agnetta McNulty, SSMO
Sr. Amata (Marian) Morris, O.P.
Sr. Mervina O'Connor, SNJM
Sr. Mary Charles (Mary) Reilly. O.P.
Sr. Elizabeth Niedermeyer, SNJM
Sr. Mary Louis (Barbara) Seal, O.P.
Sr. Laurentia (Mary) Sharkey, O.P.
Sr. Dolores (Elsie) Stopper, O.P.
Sr. Rose Augusta (Frances) Smith, SSMO
Sr. Mary Catherine (Mabel) Connor, RGS

Fr. Robert Anderson, OSI
Fr. Patrick Dooley
Fr. E. A. McDonald, O.P.
Fr. John Laidlaw
Fr. Thomas A. Hamilton
Fr. Aquinas McDonnell, O.P
Fr. Kevin Meagher, O.P.
Fr. Stephen McEachern, OP
Fr. Richard Meagher, S.J.
* Fr. Edmund McNulty, S.J.
Fr. William Dooley

*Brother and sister

Compiled from various sources, Recollections from Father C.V. McEachen, O.P., Parish Bulletin dated March 19, 1944, and List provided by Sister Evangela, O.P., archivist for Dominican Sisters, Mission San Jose, California, May 5, 1992.

APPENDIX 6

HOLY ROSARY'S GOLDEN JUBILEE CELEBRATED IN MAY 1944
JUBILEE BOOKLET PUBLISHED

[The parish published a four-page booklet announcing that the actual celebration would take place not in January, but in May, Mary's month, on Sunday, the 21st, 1944. The subsequent celebrations superbly dramatized the noble character of what had occurred during these five decades. The opening page addressed the subject]:

Devoted service over a considerable period of time has the effect of bestowing upon the persons and institutions thus engaged something of the nobility of the cause to which they have dedicated themselves. It is fitting that upon occasion this nobility be accorded special and joyous recognition.

For Holy Rosary Parish, clothed in the dignity of fifty years of service in the cause of dispensing God's grace to souls, we have woven a crown of golden memories, as week by week we related the fruitful labors of her clergy, Sisters and faithful.

To this diadem we add the precious jewels of our solemn and sacred functions. The first of these was the return of Father C.V. Lamb, who ministered to the flock of our parish in the second decade of its existence. Father Lamb inaugurated the Jubilee Year by offering the Solemn Mass and preaching the sermon, on Sunday, January 30, just two days after the fiftieth anniversary date. (The church was dedicated and opened for services under the title of Queen of the Most Holy Rosary by the Most Reverend Archbishop Gross on January 28, 1894.)

Since the beginning, Our Blessed Mother has figured largely in the history of Holy Rosary Parish. So the principle celebrations were postponed to Mary's month, in order that the solemnities of our Jubilee Year might find greater favor in her eyes.

The month opened with the combined First Communion of the children and the General Communion of the faithful, Sunday, May 7. That same evening Mary was crowned Queen of the Parish, and the Fathers and parishioners solemnly and publicly consecrated themselves to her Immaculate Heart.

This, on May 12, 13, 14, was followed by a Triduum of Thanksgiving to God through Mary for the countless blessings showered on our parish. Besides the Solemn Mass of thanksgiving (May 14), Masses were offered for those now living (May 12) and for those who have departed this life (May 13). On the afternoon of the 14th, the Fathers, Sisters, people and children formed a Living Rosary outdoors, and offered its recitation as a Mother's Day gift to Mary, their Blessed Mother.

Today, May 21, His Grace, the Most Reverend Archbishop Edward D. Howard, presides as we place the final jewel in Holy Rosary's golden crown. Our Jubilarians form a group to honor before the Altar. During the Solemn Mass celebrated in his presence by the Very Reverend Benedict M. Blank, Prior Provincial of the Holy Name Province, our Chief Shepherd speaks to us in grateful accents of the wondrous works which God's grace has wrought in the souls He has touched through the parish.

Under God, it is to Mary that Holy Rosary Parish owes the greatest debt of gratitude in this year of its glory. Still, we cannot forget that many hands have helped throughout the years to mould that parish history which is our pride and joy today. So to our Archbishop, our fellow priests of the archdiocese, to our old timers and countless friends we extend our heartfelt and prayerful thanks.

The Dominican Fathers

[The fourth and fifth pages of the Golden Jubilee Celebration booklet contained the schedule of the Low and Solemn High Masses]:

SUNDAY, MAY 21, 10:00 a.m. – Low Mass
Holy Rosary Senior Choir will sing the following:

1. Choir – "Hail Queen of Heaven.....................Traditional Melody
2. Solo – "On This Day, O Beautiful Mother...............Lambilotte
Patricia Hunt
3. Solo – "Aspirations of Communion"..........Holy Name Hymnal
Cyril Niedermeyer
4. "O God of Love"...............................Holy Name Hymnal
5. "Queen of the Holy Rosary"..........................Traditional Melody

Organist – Mrs. J. H. Yager
Directress – Miss Anna Marie McCormick

*   *   *

Holy Rosary's Jubilarians

Mrs. Mary Baccarich
Mrs. Carlotta O'Connor
Miss Katherine Dowd
Mrs. May Schoenfeldt
Mr. Harry J. Hayes
Mr. William Sheahan
Mrs. Harry J. Hayes
Mrs. Sarah Sheehy
Mr. Frank McMahan
Mrs. Robert Thompson
Miss Elizabeth McMahan
Mrs. Margaret Tracy
Mrs. Benjamin Neer
Mrs. Agnes Winneman

———————————

Sunday, May 21, 11:15 a.m.

Golden Jubilee Solemn High Mass
in the presence of

His Excellency, The Most Reverend Edward D. Howard, D.D.
Archbishop of Portland in Oregon

Chaplains of Honor to His Excellency:
Reverend George J. Campbell
Reverend John R. Laidlaw

Celebrant – The Very Rev. Benedict M. Blank, O.P.
Prior Provincial of the Holy Name Province

Deacon – The Very Rev. Thomas C. Connelly, O.P.
Pastor of Blessed Sacrament Church, Seattle, Wash.

Sub-Deacon – The Rev. C. V. Lamb, O.P.
Chaplain of the Dominican Sisters, Everett, Wash.

Preacher – His Excellency,
The Most Reverend Edward D. Howard, D.D.

Musical Program for
Holy Rosary's Golden Jubilee Solemn High Mass
May 21, 1944, 11:15 a.m.

Procession – "Ecce Sacerdos"....................................Stadler
Introit – "Exaudi, Domine"............................Proper of the Mass
Holy Rosary Junior Choir
The Mass – "Missa Quarta"...................................Beltjens
Graduale – "Alleluia, alleluia"............................Proper of the Mass
Chorus – "Salve Mater"...................................Gregorian

Sermon –
The Most Reverend Archbishop Edward D. Howard, D.D.
Credo..Tone I
Offertory - "Ascendit Deus"...............................Proper of the Mass
Chorus "Ave Maria".......................................Cesar Franck
Sanctus...Choir
Augus Dei...Choir
Communion – "Pater, cum essem"......................Proper of the Mass
Closing Hymn – "Holy God, We Praise Thy Name".......Traditional
Choir and Congregation
Recessional – "Jubilate Deo"...................................Mozart

——————————————

GOLDEN JUBILEE SOLEMN BENEDICTION

Given by the Dominican Fathers
Sunday Afternoon, May 21st, 4:00 p.m.

MUSICAL PROGRAM

1. Organ Prelude..A. Hesse
2. Choir: "Sacris Soleminiis"....................................Mohr
3. Solo: "Ave Virgo Virginum".......................................J. M. Garin
Irene C. Barrett
4. Choir: "Ave Maria"...Arcadelt
5. Hymn: "Cor Jesu"..Schultes
Dolores Bobzien   Jacquline Youngman
Mary Renner   Virginia Kudrna
6. Choir: "O Salutaris Hostia"
"Tantum Ergo"
7. "Praise Ye The Father".......................................Gounod
Choir and Congregation
8. Organ Postlude...Gounod

GOLDEN JUBILEE RECEPTION
Holy Rosary Parish Hall
Sunday Afternoon, May 21st, 4:30 - 8:00 p.m.

MUSICAL PROGRAM
1. Immaculata Academy Glee Club and String Ensemble
2. Songs by Members of the Parish

THE GOLDEN JUBILEE DINNER

[The Who's Who of Holy Rosary in those days participated in all areas, and the contribution of so many parish members is an impressive reminder of what solid community resolve can accomplish. Preparations for the Golden Jubilee dinner and reception resembled a military operation in its organizational thoroughness (no doubt attributable, at least in part, to Anna Mayer whose Austrian upbringing demanded a great deal of order in all undertakings)].

A) GOLDEN JUBILEE DINNER

1) Cooking	*Menu*
Mrs. Anna Mayer (Cook)	Cocktail
Miss Grace Sweeney	Salad
Mrs. Lawrence Dumas	Rolls
Mrs. Annie Foster	Roast Beef
Mrs. M.K. Brooks	Baked Ham
Miss Margaret Agius	Wax Beans
2) Serving	Asparagus
Miss Mary Slaird (Chairman)	Olives-Pickles-Celery
Miss Rose Brogna	Ice Cream & Cake
Miss Estelle Bogner	Coffee & Wine
Mrs. Harry Koeper	
Mrs. W.K. Volkers	*Note:*
Mrs. Edward Stoffel	*1) The above ladies will*
Miss Florence McEachern	*cook the dinner.*
Miss Margaret O'Connor	*2) They will tend to*
Miss Mary Frawley	*purchasing the menu."*
3) Decorating & Setting of Tables	*3) They will not have to*
Mrs. R. Guarnero (Chairman)	*worry at all about dishes,*
Mrs. Ed. Barrett	*silverware, or the decorat-*
Miss Ellen Lavin	*ing of the tables.*
Mrs. Maurice Pigeon	*4) Dinner will be served as*
Miss Kathleen Lavin	*soon as possible after Mass.*
Miss May Lavin	*5) They will eat with*
	waitresses, after the dinner.

B) GOLDEN JUBILEE RECEPTION
(4:30 - 8:00 p.m., Parish Hall)

1) The Preparation of Refreshments	
Mrs. Zeno Tobkin)	Jean Wiseman
Miss Emma Zara) Co-Chairmen	Angela Lorimer
Mrs. Wilfred Lorimer	Margaret Lorimer
Mrs. Katherine Neidenthal	Mary Fitzpatrick
Miss Mary Gobbi	Mary Renner
Mrs. A.V. Arnold	Dolores Bobzien
Miss Helen Zara	Frances Gardiner
Miss Anna Zara	Jacqualine Youngman
Miss Dorothy Zara	Dolores Tobkin
Mrs. A.J. Dooney	Patricia Hunt
Mrs. James Davenport	Dolores Lennon
Miss Alice Illk	Catherine Grams
Mrs. Fred Rutto	Mary Ann Grams
Mrs. J.H. Yager	Mary Ellen Gaffney
4) Decoration of the Hall	Ann Louise Gaffney
Mrs. Joseph Schmitz)	Irene Barrett
Mrs. Roy Briggs) Co-Chairman	Barbara Barrett
Mrs. Stanley Brosterhous	Patricia Mulfeit
Mrs. W. Tickle	*7) Pouring the Coffee*
Mrs. Mayme H. Cushman	Miss Francis Dowd (Chairman)
Mrs. W.K. Graves	*4:30 - 5:40*
Mrs. Margaret Ehr	Mrs. E.A. McGrath
Miss Barbara Brown	Mrs. Joseph Niedermeyer
Miss Clarence Fisher	Mrs. J.R. Murphy
Mrs. Fred Fritz	Miss Helen McRaith
Mrs. A.M. Jorgenson	*5:40 - 6:50*
6) Cutting the Jubilee Cake	Miss Elizabeth Corcoran
Mrs. E.P. Murphy (Chairman)	Miss Abigail McRaith
Mrs. P. Lavin	Mrs. H. Hellendorn
Mrs. W.C. Kavanaugh	Mrs. Fred Hoerner
Mrs. Margaret Madden	*6:50 - 8:00*
Mrs. Matt Madigan	Mrs. Fred Eilers
2) Arrangements of Refreshments	Mrs. Ann Sharkey
Mrs. James Davenport)	Mrs. May McCaffery
Miss Pauline Gobbi) Co-Chairmen	Miss Marguerite Sheehy
Mrs. L. Gattuccio	
Mrs. Jack Kindred	*The Entertainment*
Mrs. Charlotte Kinkella	Miss Anna Marie McCormick
3) Coffee	
Mr. Wilfred Lorimer	*C) The Golden Jubilarians*
5) Serving the Refreshments	Fr. Stanislaus McDermott
Miss Agnes Dowd (Chairman)	(Chairman)
Jane Harold	
Helen Church	*D) Ushers for Solemn High*
Mary Orescovich	*Mass and Benediction*
	Mr. Matt Creegan (Chairman)
	Mr. Thomas Weick
	Mr. Joseph Schmitz
	Mr. Matt Madigan

APPENDIX 7

HOW OUR HOUSE IN PORTLAND CAME TO BE

This is written on the Feast of the Assumption, 1987, since, on numerous occasions I have been encouraged by the Brethren to set down the chronology of events by which, in this year of grace, the Province erected a new residence in the City of Portland, Oregon.

Unknown to me, in 1983, while I was assisting with the Newman-University ministry at St. Thomas More in Eugene, Oregon, Father Albert Buckley decided that it would be best for him to serve but one term as pastor at Holy Rosary in Portland, so he could return to his first love, the itinerancy of the Mission Band of Preachers. While this idea was being developed, I was approached to go as Rector to Holy Family Cathedral in Anchorage, Alaska, and I was preparing for that assignment.

When Fr. Buckley heard of this, as he was at the time a member of the Provincial Council, he called me in Eugene and said that, in his opinion, it would be better for me to come to Portland and rebuild the old rectory. This would assure our continued presence in Portland, to say nothing of the Dominicans then being able to live and work there in safety, removed from the ever-present danger of fire from the then 100-year-old rectory.

To understand the process and the enthusiasm it engendered, I think it should be said that I have always loved a good project - and the more details which are involved, the better.

With this in mind, the thought of rebuilding was a project par excellence, and I began in earnest even before leaving my assignment in Eugene. Once I was named pastor, the first order of business was to make a visit to Portland and get a feel for the place and then, early on, select an architect, which was no mean feat.

The architectural process went like this: I had met, somewhat by accident, a Mr. Thomas Moreland, an architect from Eugene, while visiting some parishioners named Mr. and Mrs. Joseph Gonyea, lumber people from the area. The University of Oregon in Eugene had a nationally-known architectural school and some of the professors of that school regularly came to our liturgy at St. Thomas More, and so I inquired from them about the reputation of Tom Moreland.

In short, it was their assessment to a man that if he would take on the project, we could not find ourselves in better hands. Then came the convincing part, with me trying to coach him into our corner. His only serious concern, having worked on occasion with other religious groups, was that finances would eventually so constrict us that the end product would not be worthy of his name.

Although that might have been a problem for him elsewhere and with other folks, I assured him that was not my - or our - intention, and with that, he accepted the challenge.

At this time in our history, Holy Rosary Parish was quite solvent, but it was in no way fiscally prepared to even think of rebuilding. That, coupled with design phases, would require some three years and would take me through my first term of office.

All of this was going on in the early months of 1983, and in July of that year I moved from Eugene to Portland to work with the community and Fr. Buckley for some six months before taking office as pastor. This was ample time for me to work with the architect on initial design phases.

I should say something about the design phase for the rectory at Holy Rosary. I have had the good fortune of living in a goodly number of our houses throughout the Province, and that experience greatly assisted me in knowing what works for community life and what does not. It was my thinking that this was a critical area of concern, and with the right planning we could have something to pass on, which would strengthen community life and about which we could be proud in our association with Portland.

My first concern for the house was that it must be silent; that is, as quiet as it was humanly possible to make it. The old house had no insulation whatsoever, and it was like living inside a tunnel. It was so noisy that not only did no one come to live in Portland, they would only stay overnight as a very last resort.

My other concern was lighting: what light there was outside, I wanted brought indoors. Then began the laborious process of defining our living needs in terms of space, movement, privacy, accessibility and function. This, joined with materials for duration, took up a year's time of effort and meetings with architects. We went through four major options, constantly refining according to the criteria mentioned above, and finally arrived at what we now have.

There was, however, one major exception to all of this. Originally I had planned for six rooms and a guest room, but when it finally came before the Provincial Council for approval to proceed with construction in September of 1984, the Council wanted eight full rooms so that at some future date the house could be a full Priory. That decision meant that the entire north face of the building had to be redesigned to allow natural light to flow to the downstairs rooms. The Council also determined that all of the exterior windows of the house were to be double-paned, thermal windows. It was at the Council meeting, as well, that I mentioned it was my intention to have all the water piping in copper, which was completely insulated, and silver soldered as opposed to lead soldering.

Even before I had arrived on the Portland property, Fr. Buckley had mentioned to the parishioners that it would fall to the new pastor to build a new Dominican residence, so it came as no surprise to them when I began organizing a Building Fund Campaign only a few months after taking office. We cleaned up the old house and had an open house one Sunday, inviting all in for a tour following each of the Sunday Masses. Since, through the decades, the place had been cloistered, the people were aghast to see how the priests were living, and from that moment on all of the finances that were eventually necessary began to flow in on a regular basis.

A few months later, south on Union Avenue [Martin Luther King Boulevard] there was an enormous fire in a building called the Ice House, which years before was a production plant for ice blocks. The walls of this building were insulated with sawdust by the ton and, as a result, the fire burned there for a month. The Fire Department marshals then began to comb the area for other likely fire targets, and one day showed up with the news that we were to rebuild or vacate because it was their intention to condemn the rectory as a fire danger - built, as it was, before the existence of any fire codes.

With the parish lawyer, Mr. Tomas Ryan, we met twice at the downtown Fire Marshal's office, and convinced them it was our firm intention to rebuild. They consented to give us an 18-month reprieve before starting condemnation proceedings on the old rectory. This was all the parishioners needed to hear. The financial resources came in so quickly and consistently over the months that I was running out of institutions in which to bank the funds, since they were only insured up to $100,000.00. It was a very comforting predicament in which to find oneself, and it did very quickly alleviate the financial hesitations about building!

It was precisely for this reason, and in response to the generosity of the faithful, that I had the plaque made which hangs to the left of the secretarial area in the new rectory. We needed to give public credit to all the participants and do it a way which was permanent. For that reason, the plaque is embedded into the wall with braces wrapped around a steel girder: quite permanent.

The choice of a construction company was very straightforward. The firm of Brockamp and Jaeger had, seven years previously, put up the Parish Center. It was very well done and since this firm had a sterling reputation in the Portland area, I did not even put the construction out to bid. In this case, and in hindsight, this was the correct decision. You will be pleased to read that during construction and before the concrete (which covers the entire basement area) was poured, I laid plastic packets of Our Lady of the Holy Rosary, into the extreme corners, north, south, east and west.

The entire construction project took some nine months, and we moved in, bits and pieces at a time, in January 1987. During the construction time, Father Robert Davis and I lived at 6355 N.E. 8th Avenue, and Father Dominic DeDomenico joined us for the last three months in a borrowed trailer which we parked in the driveway. The nine months of the building were documented in photographs, in two volumes, and so marked, which are in the house library. Fathers Duffner and McEachen lived during the building period in the Confraternity Building, contiguous to the front of the church.

All during our first month in the new residence, we geared up for our dedication day of February 10, 1987, when we set aside the later afternoon and evening for a Dominican gathering of the community and all the living former pastors: Fathers Agius, Cassidy, Arnheim, Duffner and Buckley. A formal portrait of that event was taken in the recreation room prior to supper, and a copy sent to the Province archives, as well as to all participants.

Perhaps the next thing I should mention is the window in the house chapel. This was a gift of Mrs. Rosemary Lee, a parishioner, who, as a child, grew up in Salt Lake City when Father (later Archbishop) Robert Dwyer was a curate. They were friends all of their lives and, in time, she married and moved to Portland, where Bishop Dwyer became the local Ordinary.

Mrs. Lee wanted the window in the loving memory of Archbishop Dwyer, and the design I put together goes thusly: we are the ribbons coming together in work, ministry and friendship - touching in various stages of our lives and growing deeper as we descend, signified by the deepening of the color. There is always the rough individual doing his thing apart from the rest, but all experience the tension points of our lives - and of life in general - as marked by the strikes of black around and through the ribbons. In a nutshell, this depiction represents our life in and with each other.

As for the crucifix and tabernacle in the house chapel, these, too, were Archbishop Dwyer's and were for many years in his private chapel. He designed them in the early 1950s and they were made in Bruges, Belgium, in 1953. When he retired and left Portland, he entrusted them to the cloistered Sisters of the Precious Blood. When these Sisters moved from their large monastery into smaller quarters, the superior contacted me to see if we might make good use of them, since she did not want them to just go into storage. When Mr. Tom Moreland and I went to see them, he was so taken by the artistry of the enamel on bronze that his words were, "We will build a room around them."

This brief summary of events would not be complete without explicit mention of the untiring dedication of Mr. George Kirkham, C.P.A., who, during the entire time of fundraising and construction, served as parish secretary. During these days, perhaps this was the only parish in the country to have a certified public accountant as parish secretary! He was the difference to us between light and darkness and helped make all financial decisions easier with his gentlemanly character.

The above is a brief story of how the rectory-priory of Holy Rosary came to be built in Portland, Oregon. It is often said that Dominicans are so caught up in the present and its varying demands that we forget the past, and that we are thus rather cavalier about our history. It was the prompting of various of the brethren which caused me to put down these memories of planning and building for the future, which were put into permanent form by Brother Norbert Fihn in Antioch, California, in the latter months of the year 1987.

[SIGNED]   (Rev.) Edmund K. Ryan, O.P.
                Pastor

APPENDIX 8

A PERPETUAL TRUST FUND FOR OUR LADY

The following is quoted from an undated leaflet found in the archives of the Western Dominican Province, Oakland, California:

Radio Rosary Perpetual Trust Fund

On behalf of the Radio Rosary Committee we are pleased to state that Bishop Leipzig has graciously consented to write an historical account of our Radio Rosary Program in Metropolitan Portland. Bishop Leipzig, together with Archbishops Power, Howard and Dwyer, has always been a dedicated supporter of the Radio Rosary. We wish to express our prayerful gratitude to them and to all who have worked for and contributed to the Rosary broadcasts.

Joe Santilli, Chairman
Fr. Joseph M. Agius, O.P. Spiritual Director

THE RADIO ROSARY PROGRAM

by

MOST REVEREND FRANCIS P. LEIPZIG, D.D.
Former Bishop of Baker

The history of the generosity of friends to keep the daily Radio Rosary broadcasts from Holy Rosary Church, Portland, is legendary. Only one parish in the United States, Rochester, New York, has been longer on the air than we have been here in Portland.

Commencing September 23, 1951, the Rosary has been recited over the Radio every night until August 1977. Presently the Rosary goes over Station KWJJ (1080 KHz), Monday through Friday, beginning at 9:30 p.m.

The encouragement of the supporters of the daily Radio Rosary has been most admirable. The financial contributions of the sponsors, such as parishes, organizations and individuals, is to be highly lauded. Special thanks is due to the Radio Rosary Committee, which works under the auspices of the Portland Metropolitan Holy Name Union. This Committee has been most faithful all down the years in arranging schedules and personnel needed to set up the equipment each evening of the Rosary broadcasts.

Just think of the thousands of shut-ins and faithful, even some non-Catholics, who have the privilege and joy of joining in their homes in this splendid tribute to Our Blessed Mother. Letters received tell how happy they are to have the Rosary on the air, and they hope that it will always come to them over the radio.

In the beginning, and for the past twenty-six years, the Radio Rosary Committee, with the financial support from parishes, organizations and individuals was able to meet the cost of the Rosary broadcasts, which for that period of time was $145,386.89.

Up until the new contract with KWJJ (July 13, 1976), the nightly broadcast cost fifteen dollars, then twenty dollars. Now the nightly broadcast cost, due in part to inflation, has risen to $60.00-plus dollars. This seems to be a high price to pay for fifteen minutes on the air, but when we realize that this is fifteen minutes of prayer for peace in our world, the price does not seem so high. Only Heaven knows how much good the Radio Rosary is doing for peace in our times and for all who play a part in keeping it on the air.

The present financial problem faced by the Radio Rosary Committee is the difficulty involved in raising the $60.00 dollars for each broadcast, which amounts to $300 per week; $15,600 for 52 weeks. With your help the Committee can solve this financial problem.

At the suggestion of a number of people, the Radio Rosary Committee has printed a Radio Rosary envelope which, in brief, tells how you can help by making a Special Gift or an offering by the month or by the year. The latter way might be called offerings from "The Dollar-a-Month-Club." The Committee is hopeful that Pastors will give their permission to place this Radio Rosary envelope on tables at the exits of their Church. One Pastor has already given such permission.

As already noted, the Rosary broadcasts have been financed by sponsoring groups and by voluntary donations. Another means of support is "The Radio Rosary Perpetual Trust Fund, Inc." This Perpetual Fund was started in November of 1975. As of May 13, 1979 it has reached the sum of $46,030.64. Of this amount, $45,137.50 has been invested. Only the interest goes to help pay the Radio Rosary daily expenses. In the first weeks of this Perpetual Fund, donations ranged from one dollar to two thousand dollars. Since then, contributions received have been from one dollar to one thousand dollars. Some people have contributed to this Fund, in lieu of flowers, in memory of a deceased relative or friend. Others have remembered the Fund in their wills.

Banking on the continued support of the above-mentioned sources the Radio Rosary Committee is confident that the Rosary broadcasts for world peace and for the intentions of all who contribute to this worthy cause will be on the air for many, many years to come.

[Note: It was this fund which provided seed money for the start of KBVM in 1989.]

QUEEN OF THE MOST HOLY ROSARY CHURCH PORTLAND, OREGON

"OLD HOLY ROSARY CHURCH"

HOLY ROSARY'S ONE HUNDRED YEARS
by Joseph Foye

Time is a necessary ingredient in all growth, maturity always an ongoing process. The great storehouse of faith we have in this parish today, refined in the fire of tradition (that is, reason and revelation) for 2,000 years, is a creation of God and a miracle in our midst, made possible in no small part by devout Catholic workers, religious and lay; all of them God's people on their earthly pilgrimages from diverse countries and cultures, whose self-denial and daily cross-bearing have left us this enduring legacy. The earliest census, taken in November 1906, showed 88 Catholic families in the area. We now number over 900 families, from southern Washington to southern Oregon.

Early Beginnings

Most Reverend William H. Gross, C.Ss.R., the third Archbishop of Portland, was devoted to Our Blessed Mother, and he wanted to share this devotion with his flock. He was convinced that the Sons of St. Dominic, because of their devotion to the Queen of the Most Holy Rosary (the official name of our church), would, by God's grace, "introduce this Blessed, this channel of all grace, into their homes." In 1892, the Dominicans accepted the archbishop's offer to spread devotion to the Rosary, and the Very Reverend John Pius Murphy, O.P., then Vicar General of the Dominican Province, arrived in Portland to build this church. The original building site was situated between NE 10th and 11th Avenues and between NE Multnomah and Wasco Streets.

Roll 'em, Roll 'em, Roll 'em

Commercial interests did not want the church at that site for reasons too lengthy to describe in this brief survey. So Father Murphy and the original designer and contractor, Lionel D. Dean, moved the partially-completed church and rectory onto logs. Horses pulled them ten blocks west to our present location. Scribbled notations in the archives show that the cost of building the church was $22,300 and the (former) rectory $911. The first superior was the Reverend James Benedict McGovern, O.P.

Originally a Missionary Church

At that time, our church was considered a conventual church (in the order a monastery) and not a parish church. And since plans called for the church to become a school once a new church was built, it was not *dedicated* but *blessed* on January 28, 1894, by Archbishop Gross. So one hundred and two years later we *dedicate* our church.

Dominicans Start New Schools

In 1908 we became a full-fledged parish at the request of Archbishop Gross' successor, the Most Reverend Alexander Christie, D.D. We opened an elementary school, run by the Dominican Sister of Mission San Jose, with 43 pupils. Situated on the block now occupied by the Roadway Inn and the Golden Dragon Restaurant, it graduated hundreds of students between 1912-1955. We also purchased and operated Christian Brothers College, located at Grand Avenue and Clackamas Street from 1922-1927, renaming it Aquinas School. Tepid support forced its closure. The rapid commercialization of the surrounding area, accompanied by the departure of most of the parish families, compelled us to close Holy Rosary School in 1955.

Radio Rosary

A few prayerful women initiated the first Radio Rosary broadcast on Portland station KPOJ in 1950. With the aid of the Archdiocesan Holy Name Union (organized at Holy Rosary in 1917), regular broadcasts of the Rosary were made from this church. By 1976, we would be the second church in the U.S. to have broadcast the Rosary for 25 years—over 228,725 people prayed with us. In 1989 the priests and people of Holy Rosary took the lead in establishing radio station KBVM (for Blessed Virgin Mary), the first lay-sponsored Catholic radio station in the U.S. We still provide crucial support for that station.

New Parish Center and Priory Built

In 1980, Holy Rosary's "cheerful givers" built our parish center, during the tenure (1975-1983) of Fr. Paul Duffner, O.P., who had earlier founded the Western Dominicans' Rosary Confraternity in California, which was moved to Portland in 1975 and is now located across the street from the church on the southwest corner of N. Third and Clackamas. In 1987, then-Pastor Edmund Fr. K. Ryan, O.P. gave the parishioners a tour of the old rectory, built 93 years earlier for $911. They agreed that it was "a hovel," unsafe against fire as well as burglars. So they razed it and built the present house in 1987.

Restoration of the Church

When Father Anthony M. Patalano, O.P. took the reins of the parish in 1991, he observed that the church was sorely in need of restoration. The parishioners agreed. Father timed the construction to coincide with the centenary celebration in 1994. Restoration included, among other changes, the following: returning the Tabernacle to the center of the sanctuary; refurbishing the marble altar of sacrifice; replacing glass windows with stained-glass windows depicting the Blessed Trinity, Dominican saints, and the mysteries of the Rosary; providing a special shrine for the statue of Our Lady of the Rosary on the south wall; and expansion of the crying room. On November 9, 1993, when the restoration was about 90 percent complete, a disastrous fire engulfed the church. It was caused by a spark that ignited vapors from the paints and varnishes stored in the crying room. Miraculously, only one workman was injured, suffering second-degree burns on his legs. Earlier that morning the church had been immaculate with new floor boards, walls and wainscoting. Now it was covered with burnt debris, puddles of water, and smoke stains everywhere. Damage was estimated at $750,000 to $850,000. Thank God we survived to carry on His work.

Dedication

Holy Rosary's priests and parishioners have always maintained the practices of those who preceded them with daily praying of the Rosary, Rosary processions, and a sacred liturgy designed to "make the faithful realize the presence of the living Christ." We, as beneficiaries of that tradition and as the living stones of this church, must be animated by daily spiritual renewal. Believing in our Lord's words and relying on God's help, we must pledge ourselves faithfully to pass on intact to future generations this treasure—Queen of the Most Holy Rosary Church—that we dedicate today.

Pastors
Queen of the Most Holy Rosary Church

1. The Reverend Benedict James McGovern, O.P., 1894-1895

2. The Reverend Thomas Aquinas Patrick Fitzsimons, O.P., 1895-1896

3. The Reverend Lawrence Thomas Breen, O.P., 1896-1899

4. The Reverend Paul Thomas Henry, O.P., 1899-1903

5. The Very Reverend Albert Sadoc Patrick Lawler, O.P., 1903-1912

6. The Very Reverend Humbert Henry Kelly, O.P., 1912-1915

7. The Very Reverend Stanislaus Edward Olsen, O.P., 1915-1922

8. The Very Reverend Arthur Ignatius Townley, O.P., 1922-1925

9. The Very Reverend Andrew Francis Pope, O.P., 1925-1930

10. The Very Reverend Stanislaus William McDermott, O.P., 1930-1931

11. The Very Reverend Stephen Thomas Connolly, O.P., 1931-1935 & 1947-1948

12. The Very Reverend Gabriel Mary Aloysius Knauff, O.P., 1935-1936

13. The Reverend Gerard Edward McMullen, O.P., 1936-1942

14. The Reverend Joseph Mary Agius, O.P., 1942-1947 & 1970-1972

15. The Reverend Thomas Aquinas Bernard Feucht, O.P., 1948-1958 & 1974-1975

16. The Reverend William Aquinas Norton, O.P., 1958-1964

17. The Reverend Felix Francis Cassidy, O.P., 1964-1970

18. The Reverend Bernard Charles Arnheim, O.P., 1972-1974

19. The Reverend Aquinas Paul Duffner, O.P., 1975-1981

20. The Reverend Albert Gerald Buckley, O.P., 1981-1983

21. The Very Reverend Edmund Kenneth Ryan, O.P., 1983-1991

22. The Very Reverend Anthony Maria Dominic Patalano, O.P., 1991-Present

The title *Very Reverend* is given to those friars, who in addition to being pastor, were priors (religious superior) of the Dominican community.

January 28, 1996

Dear People of Holy Rosary,

On this most happy and historic day, I extend to you my heartfelt congratulations on the occasion of the dedication of our beloved and venerable church.

Let us never forget that the purpose of this building is to provide us with a sacred environment for the worship of the Triune God. This worship is accomplished each time when you, the People of God, along with your priests, gather to celebrate the Eucharist. May God in His Providence allow this church to stand many more years, so that together as a parish under the guidance of the Order of Preachers, we may continue to do what we do best. That is to praise, to bless, to preach that Jesus is Lord and that Mary, under title of Queen of the Most Holy Rosary, is His Mother.

Thank you for allowing me to restore and renovate this historic building. I especially wish to thank the contractors, architects, artisans and craftsmen who through their wonderful skills and expertise have made this church so beautiful. Without your faith, patience and financial support nothing would have been accomplished.

With every good wish and prayer, I am

Sincerely yours,

fr. Anthony-M. Patalano
Prior and Pastor

SOLEMN MASS OF DEDICATION

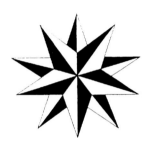

MOST REVEREND THOMAS CAJETAN KELLY, O.P.

ARCHIBISHOP OF LOUISVILLE, KENTUCKY

PRESIDING

RITE OF DEDICATION

INTROIT   *Terribilis est*   Plainsong, Mode II

H OW AWESOME IS THIS PLACE: it is the house of God and the gate of heaven, and it shall be called the court of God. *Ps.* How lovely are thy tabernacles, O Lord of hosts! My soul longeth and fainteth for the courts of the Lord.

When the entrance rite is completed, the bishop blesses water with which to sprinkle the people as a sign of repentance and as a reminder of their baptism. As the bishop sprinkles the people with holy water the following antiphon is sung:

Vidi aquam   Plainsong, Mode VIII

I SAW WATER coming forth from the temple on the right side, alleluia. And all those to whom this water came were saved and shall say alleluia. *Vs.* Give thanks to the Lord, for he is good. His mercy endureth forever.

After the sprinkling the bishop returns to the chair and, when the singing is finished, standing with hands joined, says:

M AY GOD, THE FATHER OF MERCIES, dwell in this house of prayer. May the grace of the Holy Spirit cleanse us, for we are the temple of his presence. Amen.

GLORIA   *Mass in D Major, Opus 86*   Antonin Dvorak (1841-1904)

All may be seated during the singing of the Gloria. When the hymn is finished the bishop, with hands extended, says:

L ORD, FILL THIS PLACE WITH YOUR PRESENCE and extend your hand to all those who call upon you. May your word here proclaimed and your sacramens here celebrated strengthen the hearts of all the faithful. We ask this through our Lord Jesus Christ, you Son, who lives and reigns with you and the Holy Spirit, one God, forever and ever. Amen.

❖ LITURGY OF THE WORD ❖

READING I   Revelation 8:3-4

GRADUAL   *Locus iste*   Anton Bruckner (1824-1896)

READING II   Hebrews 12:18-19, 22-24

ALLELUIA   *Domine, dilexi*   Plainsong, Mode II

O LORD, I LOVE THE BEAUTY OF YOUR HOUSE and your tabernacle where you glory resides, alleluia.

HOMILY   Most Reverend Thomas Cajetan Kelly, O.P.

CREDO is said

A Treasure Of Promises Kept

LITANY OF THE SAINTS

Cantor: Kyrie, eleison.
All: Kyrie, eleison.
Cantor: Christe, eleison.
All: Christe, eleison.
Cantor: Kyrie, eleison.
All: Kyrie, eleison.

Cantor: Christe, audi nos.
All: Christe, audi nos.

Cantor: Pater de cælis, Deus, miserere nobis.
All: Pater de cælis, Deus, miserere nobis.
Cantor: Fili Redemptor mundi, Deus, miserere nobis.
All: Fili Redemptor mundi, Deus, miserere nobis.
Cantor: Spiritus sancte, Deus, miserere nobis.
All: Spiritus sancte, Deus, miserere nobis.
Cantor: Sancta Trinitas, unus Deus, miserere nobis
All: Sancta Trinitas, unus Deus, miserere nobis.

Omnes sancti beatorum spiritum ordines — orate…
Sancte Joannes Baptista — ora pro nobis
Sancte Joseph — ora…
Omnes sancti Patriarchæ et Prophetæ — orate…

Sancte Petre — ora…
Sancte Paule
Sancte Andrea
Sancte Jacobe
Sancte Joannes
Sancte Thoma
Sancte Jacobe
Sancte Philippe
Sancte Bartholomæe
Sancte Matthæe
Sancte Simon
Sancte Thaddæe
Sancte Sancte Matthia
Sancte Barnaba
Sancte Marce
Sancte Luca
Omnes sancti Discipuli Domini — orate…
Omnes sancti Innocentes — orate…
Sancte Stephane — ora…
Sancte Clemens
Sancte Corneli
Sancte Cypriane
Sancte Laurenti
Sancte Vincenti
Sancte Dionysi cum sociis tuis
Sancte Mauriti cum sociis tuis
Sancte Januari cum sociis tuis
Sancti Fabiane et Sabastiane — orate…
Sancti Cosma et Damiane — orate…
Sancte Thoma Cantuariensis — ora…
Sancte Petre Martyre
Sancte Joannes cum sociis tuis
Sancte Ignatie Delgado cum sociis tuis
Sancte Laurenti Ruiz
Omnes sancti Martyres — orate…
Sancte Silvester — ora…
Sancte Gregori
Sancte Pie Quinte
Sancte Ambrosi
Sancte Augustine

Sancte Hieronyme
Sancte Hilari
Sancte Martine
Sancte Nicolaë
Sancte Antonine
Sancte Alberte
Sancte Pater Dominice
Sancte Pater Dominice
Sancte Thoma Aquinatis
Sancte Vincenti Ferrari
Sancte Hyacinthe
Sancte Raymunde
Sancte Ludovice Bertrande
Sancte Martine de Porres
Sancte Joannes Massias
Sancte Antoni
Sancte Benedicte
Sancte Bernarde
Sancte Francisce
Sancte Ludovice de Montfort
Beate Henrice Susonis
Beate Reginalde
Beate Jordane Saxonie
Beate Joannis de Fiesole
Beate Jacobe a Voragine
Beate Mannis
Beate Ceslæ de Polonia
Beate Raymunde a Capua
Beate Batholomæe Longo
Beate Jacobe ab Ulma
Beate Pier-Georgi Frassati

Beate Joannes de Salerno
Beate Joannes Dominice
Beate Joannes de Vercelli
Beate Henrice
Beate Fra Angelico
Beate Raimunde
Beate Jacobe de Ulma
Sancte Thoma
Sancte Vincenti
Sancte Hyacinthe
Sancte Raymunde
Sancte Ludovice
Omnes sancti Confessores, — orate…
Sancta Anna — ora…
Sancta Maria Magdalena
Sancta Martha
Sancta Felicitas
Sancta Perpetua
Sancta Agatha
Sancta Lucia
Sancta Agnes
Sancta Cæcilia
Sancta Catharina
Sancta Margarita
Sancta Ursula dum sodalibus tuis
Sancta Catharina Senensis
Sancta Rosa
Sancta Agnes de Monte Politiano
Sancta Catharina de Ricciis
Sancta Margarita ab Hungaria
Beata Imelda
Beata Joanna de Aza

Beata Margarita de Castello
Beata Diana et Cæcilia
Omnes sanctæ Virgines et Viduæ   orate...
Omnes sancti
Cantor   Propitius esto.
Choir: Parce nobis, Domine.
Cantor: Propitius esto.
Choir: Exaudi nos, Domine.

Cantor: A damnatione perpetua,
Choir: libera nos, Domine.

A subitanea et improvia morte   libera...
Ab imminentibus peccatorum nostrorum periculis
Ab infestationibus dæmonum
Ab omni immunditia mentis et corporis
Ab ira, et odio, et omni mala voluntate
A cæcitate cordis
A fulgure, et tempestate
A peste, fame, et bello
A flagello terræmotus
Ab omni malo
Per mysterium sanctæ Incarnationis tuæ
Per Passionem, et Crucem tuam
Per gloriosam Resurrectionem tuam
Per admirabilem Ascensionem tuam
Per gratiam Sancti Spiritus Paracliti
In die judici

Cantor: Peccatores
All: Te rogamus, audi nos.

Ut pacem nobis dones,   te rogamus...
Ut misericordia, et pietas tua nos custodiat
Ut Ecclesiam tuam sanctam regere et
    conservare digneris
Ut Domnum Apostolicum, et omnes gradus Ecclesiæ in
    sancta religione conservare digneris

Up Episcopos et Prælatos nostros, et cunctas
    Congregationes illis comissas in tuo sancto servitio
    conservare digneris
Ut inimcos sanctæ Ecclesiæ humilare digneris
Ut regibus et principubus nostris pacem, et varam
    concordiam, atque victoriam donare digneris
Ut cunctum populum christianum preetioso Sanguine tuo
    redemptum conservare digneris
Ut omnes errantes ad unitatem Ecclesiæ revocare, et
infideles
    universos ad Evangelii lumen perducere digneris
Ut omnibus benefactoribus nostris sempiterna bona
    retribuas
Ut animas nostras et parentum nostrorum ab æterna
    damnatione erpipias
Ut fructus terræ dare, et conservare digneris
Ut oculos misericordiæ tuæsuper nos reducere digneris
Ut obsequium servitutis nostræ rationabile facias
Ut mentes nostras ad cælestia desideria erigas
Ut miserias pauperum et captivorum intueri et relevare
    digneris
Ut civitatem istam, et omnem populum ejus protegere, et
    conservare digneris
Ut omnes fideles navigantes et itinerantes as protum salutis
    perducere digneris
Ut regularibus disciplinis nos instruere digneris
Ut omnibus fidelibus defunctus requiem æternam dones
Ut nos exaudire digneris
Fili Dei

Cantor: Agnus Dei, qui tollis peccata mundi
All: Parce nobis, Domine
Cantor: Agnus Dei, qui tollis peccata mundi
All: Exaudi nos, Domine.
Cantor: Agnus Dei, qui tollis peccata mundi.
All: Miserere nobis.

DEPOSITING OF THE RELICS

As the bishop places relics of the saints beneath the altar, the following antiphon is sung with Psalm 15:

℟ Saints of God, you have been en-throned at the foot of God's al- tar;

pray for   us   to the   Lord Christ Je- sus.

Lᴏʀᴅ, ᴡʜᴏ ᴍᴀʏ ᴅᴡᴇʟʟ in your tabernacle?
who may abide upon your hill?

Whoever leads a blameless life and does what is right,
who speaks the truth from his heart.

There is no guile upon his tongue; he does no evil to his friend;
he does not heap contempt upon his neighbor.

In his sight the wicked is rejected,
but he honors those who fear the Lord.

He has sworn to do no wrong
and does not take back his word.

He does not give his money in hope of gain,
nor does he take a bribe against the innocent.

Whoever does the things
shall never be overthrown.

ANOINTING OF THE ALTAR AND THE WALLS

The bishop goes to the altar with the deacons and other ministers, one of whom carries the chrism. The bishop proceeds to anoint the altar and the walls of the church. Meanwhile the following antiphon is sung with Psalm 84:

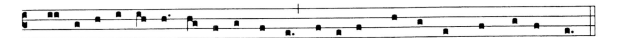

℟ Ho-ly is the tem-ple of the Lord of hosts; it is God's hand-i-work, his dwell-ing place.

How DEAR TO ME is your dwelling, O Lord of hosts!
My soul has a desire and longing for the courts of the Lord;
my heart and my flesh rejoice in the living God.

The sparrow has found her a house and the swallow a nest where she may lay her young;
by the side of your altar, O Lord of hosts, my King and my God.

Happy are they who dwell in your house!
they will always be praising you.

Happy are the people whose strength is in you!
whose hearts are set on the pilgrim's way.

Those who go through the desolate valley will find it a place of springs,
for the early rains have covered it will pools of water.

They will climb from height to height,
and the Gods of gods will reveal himself in Zion.

Lord God of hosts, hear my prayer;
hearken, O God of Jacob. .

Behold our defender, O God;
and look upon the face of your Anointed.

For one day in your courts is better than a thousand in my own room,
and to stand at the threshold of the house of my God than to dwell in the tents of the wicked.

For the Lord God is both sun and shield;
he will give grace and glory.

No good thing will the Lord withhold
from those who walk with integrity.

O Lord of hosts,
happy are they who put their trust in you!

INCENSING OF THE ALTAR AND THE CHURCH

After the rite of anointing, the brazier is placed on the altar for burning incense. The bishop puts incense into some censers and incenses the altar; he returns to the chair, is incensed, and then sits. Ministers, walking through the church, incense the people and the walls. Meanwhile the following antiphon is sung with Psalm 138:

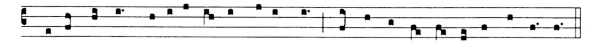

℟. An an-gel stood by the al-tar of the tem-ple, hold-ing in his hand a gold-en cen-ser.

I WILL GIVE THANKS to you, O Lord, with my whole heart;
before the gods I will sing your praise.

I will bow down toward your holy temple and praise your Name,
because of your love and faithfulness.

For you have glorified your Name
and your word above all things.

When I called, you answered me;
you increased my strength within me.

All the kings of the earth will praise you, O Lord,
when they have heard the words of your mouth.

They will sing of the ways of the Lord,
that great is the glory of the Lord.

Though the Lord be high, he cares for the lowly;
he perceives the haughty from afar.

Though I walk in the midst of trouble, you keep me safe;
you stretch forth your hand against the fury of my enemies; your right hand shall save me.

The Lord will make good his purpose for me;
O Lord, your love endures forever; do not abandon the works of your hands.

LIGHTING OF THE ALTAR AND THE CHURCH

The deacon goes to the altar and lights the candles for the celebration of the Eucharist. Then the festive lighting takes place; all the candles, including those at the places where the anointings were made, and the other lamps are lit as a sign of rejoicing. Meanwhile the following antiphon is sung with the Canticle of Tobias:

℞. Your light will come, Je - ru - sa - lem; the glo - ry of the Lord will dawn

Blessed be the God who lives forever,
for his kingdom is unending.

Exalt him before every living being,
for he is the Lord our God, our Father and God forever.

Bless the Lord of righteousness,
and exalt the King of all the ages.

Let all people speak of his majesty,
and sing his praises in Jerusalem.

A radiant light will shine over all the earth;
many nations shall come to you from afar.

Drawn to you by the name of the Lord God,
bearing in their hands their tribute for the King of heaven.

Happy are those who love,
and happy are those who rejoice in your peace.

For they shall rejoice in you
as they behold all your joy forever.

My spirit blesses the Lord, the great King;
Jerusalem shall be rebuilt as his city forever.

The gates of Jerusalem shall be built with sapphire and emerald,
and all your walls with precious stones.

The towers of Jerusalem shall be guilt with gold,
and their battlements with purest gold.

The streets of Jerusalem shall be paved with rubies and jewels of Ophir.
The gates of Jerusalem shall sing hymns of gladness, and all her houses cry out,

"Alleluia! Blessed be God who has raised you up!
May he be blessed for all ages." For in you they shall praise his holy name forever.

❖ LITURGY OF THE EUCHARIST ❖

OFFERTORY *Ave verum corpus* Colin Mawby (b. 1936)

HAIL, TRUE BODY, born of the Virgin Mary, who has truly suffered, was sacrificed on
the cross for mortals, whose side was pierced, whence flowed water and blood. Be for
us a foretaste of heaven during our final examining. O clement, O sweet Jesus, Son of
Mary.

PREFACE from Dedication of a Church

SANCTUS *Missa de Angelis* *Liber Cantualis,* p. 43

EUCHARISTIC PRAYER I

❖ COMMUNION RITE ❖

OUR FATHER Schola and congregation together, sung in English

AGNUS DEI *Mass in D Major, Opus 86* Antonin Dvorak

COMMUNION *Domus mea* Plainsong, Mode V

MY HOUSE shall be called the house of prayer, says the Lord. Everyone who knocks
therein receives, and he who seeks, finds. And to him who knocks, the door shall be
opened.

Behold, O God our defender Herbert Howells (1892-1983)

BEHOLD, O GOD OUR DEFENDER, and look upon the face of Thine Anointed.
For one day in thy courts is better than a thousand.

Behold, the tabernacle William H. Harris (1883-1973)

BEHOLD, THE TABERNACLE of God is with men, and the Spirit of God dwelleth
within you. For the temple of God is holy, which temple ye are, for the love of whom
ye do this day celebrate the joys of the temple with a season of festivity. Alleluia.

EPISCOPAL BLESSING

DISMISSAL

Christ is Made the Sure Foundation

WESTMINSTER ABBEY 87.87.87

Henry Purcell (1659-1695)

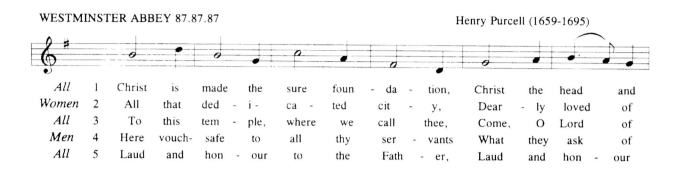

All	1	Christ	is	made	the	sure	foun -	da -	tion,	Christ	the head	and
Women	2	All	that	ded - i -	ca -	ted	cit -	y,	Dear -	ly	loved	of
All	3	To	this	tem - ple,	where	we	call	thee,	Come,	O	Lord	of
Men	4	Here	vouch- safe	to	all	thy	ser -	vants	What	they	ask	of
All	5	Laud	and	hon - our	to	the	Fath -	er,	Laud	and	hon -	our

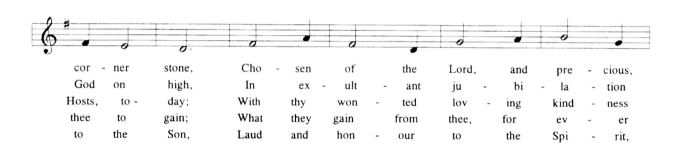

cor -	ner	stone,	Cho -	sen	of	the	Lord,	and	pre -	cious,
God	on	high,	In	ex - ult	- ant	ju -	bi -	la -	tion	
Hosts,	to -	day;	With	thy	won -	ted	lov -	ing	kind -	ness
thee	to	gain;	What	they	gain	from	thee,	for	ev -	er
to	the	Son,	Laud	and	hon -	our	to	the	Spi -	rit,

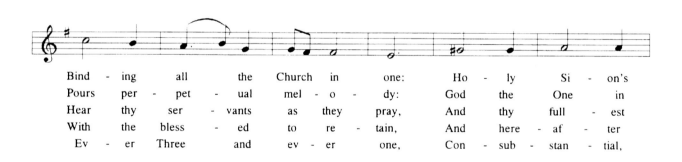

Bind -	ing	all	the	Church	in	one:	Ho -	ly	Si - on's
Pours	per - pet	- ual	mel -	o -	dy:	God	the	One	in
Hear	thy	ser -	vants	as	they	pray,	And	thy	full - est
With	the	bless -	ed	to	re -	tain,	And	here -	af - ter
Ev -	er	Three	and	ev -	er	one,	Con -	sub -	stan - tial,

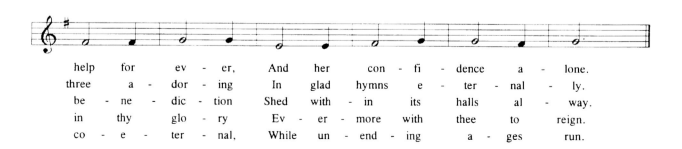

help	for	ev -	er,	And	her	con - fi -	dence	a -	lone.
three	a -	dor -	ing	In	glad	hymns	e -	ter - nal -	ly.
be -	ne -	dic -	tion	Shed	with -	in	its	halls	al - way.
in	thy	glo -	ry	Ev -	er -	more	with	thee	to reign.
co -	e -	ter -	nal,	While	un -	end -	ing	a -	ges run.

Latin, 7th c.
tr. John Mason Neale (1818-1866)

Participating Ministers

PRESIDER
Most Rev. Thomas Cajetan Kelly, O.P.

IN ATTENDANCE
Most Reverend Cornelius Power

CONCELEBRANTS
Very Reverend Reginald Martin, O.P.
Very Reverend Anthony Patalano, O.P.
Rev. Paul Duffner, O.P.
Rev. Dominic Hoffman, O.P.
Rev. Lawrence Banfield, O.P.
Rev. Christopher Moschini, O.P.
Rev. Felix Cassidy, O.P.
Rev. Albert Buckley, O.P.
Rev. Paul Raftery, O.P.

DEACONS
Br. Dominic Briese, O.P.
Br. Xavier Lavagetto, O.P.

ACOLYTES
Br. Carl Schlichte, O.P.
Christopher Laboe
Thomas Freiling
Christopher Toffler
Joseph Lee

MUSICIANS
Cantores in Ecclesia
directed by Dean Applegate

James O'Donnell
Master of the Music
Westminster Cathedral
London

APPENDIX 10

A BRIEF GLIMPSE INTO THE SECOND CENTENARY

Father Anthony Cordeiro, O.P.

"A Time to Build…A Time to Grow" & "Complete the Dream."

A visitor to Holy Rosary would find a church alive and well and bustling with activity in June 1999, when this history of the church was first sent to the publisher for printing. Two years prior, in June 1997, Father Anthony Patalano, O.P., transferred from Holy Rosary to become pastor at St. Dominicís in Los Angeles and Father Anthony Cordeiro, O.P. took over the helm.

In addition to taking on the challenge of a pastoral assignment, Fr. Cordeiro inherited the monumental task of raising funds for the erection of a new 14000 square foot education building. Prior to his departure, Fr. Patalano started the building campaign, with the theme "A Time to Build—A Time to Grow", by surveying the congregation and securing parishioner consensus for the project. He hired professional fund raiser Ed Lemma, who interviewed dozens of key parishioners to determine the financial commitment they were willing to make. With that as his starting point, Fr. Cordeiro expanded the project by securing commitments from key parishioners to serve as his executive committee to drive the fund raising and planning activities. He then proceeded to orchestrate a campaign that gradually spread out 360 degrees to reach everyone in the parish.

Fr. Cordeiro's first two years at Holy Rosary consisted of more than just the challenge of a large building project. Though a priest for over 30 years, he had little or no pastoral experience and was unacquainted with the parishioners. In addition, he continued to serve as treasurer of the Western Dominican Province and chairman of its finance commission, positions he had held for several years. The stress of managing the financial affairs of the province, mastering the art of pastoral care, getting to know and gaining the trust of 1,000 parish families would be more than most men could handle. Not so for Fr. Cordeiro, for he possessed the mental acumen and physical stamina to successfully meet these challenges including the challenge of convincing those 1,000 parish families to contribute a fortune for the new building project.

By late summer 1998, Father Cordeiro had secured the needed $2.4 million in pledges, and a groundbreaking ceremony, with Archbishop John Vlazny officiating and dozens of clergy and laity in attendance, took place on 8 August, the feast day of St. Dominic. Construction was scheduled to begin in April 1999.

MAN PROPOSES, PROVIDENCE DISPOSES

The goal of building the 14,000 square foot education building was now within reach. The funds had been raised and the parish congratulated itself on a job well done. Then came the astounding news that the 28,000 square foot Upjohn building, occupying the entire block south of the church, was to be put up for sale—for $2.4 million. This meant we could acquire a whole block of new land and a building with twice the planned square footage for the same $2.4 million price tag. Might this confluence of chance be an indication that God wanted Holy Rosary to retake this block, which had been a part of the original two-for-one swap in 1894 (see Chapter 4) and sold in the late 1940s? With the concurrence of the executive committee, Father Cordeiro moved quickly and had the property appraised. It proved to be a sound investment, so he bought the property. But remodeling of the Upjohn building to suit our specific needs, that of both Education and Parish Center, would cost an additional $850,000 and require another fund raiser. Thus began a new campaign with the slogan "Complete the Dream". As this addendum to the 100-year history went to press, 45% of this new goal had been met, with only 18% of the pledge cards returned. If past history and tradition are credible yardsticks by which to predict future events, Holy Rosarians will be savoring God's blessing of a new Education and Parish Center throughout the second centenary of Holy Rosary Parish.

CAMPAIGN EXECUTIVE COMMITTEE
Back row (L to R): Ed Lemma, James Glavin, Mary Lorenzo, Darline Locati, Norm Locati, Michael Palmer, Robert Harper, Joseph Foye, Linda Hickok, and Joseph Wetzel. **Front row (L to R):** George Stubblefield, Marlene Toffler, Dr. Bill Toffler, Randy Young, Rosemary Young, A.R. "Lorie" Lorenzo. **Not pictured:** Robert Franz, Terri Mersereau, Peggy McLean, Paul Wolf and Betty Wolf. **Joe Wetzel and Paul Wolf chaired the first campaign; Bill Toffler and Randy Young the second campaign.**

NEW PARISH CENTER & EDUCATION BUILDING